PLAYWRIGHTS
BEFORE THE FALL

DRAMA IN EASTERN EUROPE IN
TIMES OF REVOLUTION

PLAYWRIGHTS
BEFORE THE FALL

DRAMA IN EASTERN EUROPE IN
TIMES OF REVOLUTION

Martin E. Segal Theatre Center Publications
New York

PLAYWRIGHTS BEFORE THE FALL

DRAMA IN EASTERN EUROPE IN TIMES OF REVOLUTION

Portrait
Sławomir Mrożek

Military Secret
Dušan Jovanović

Chicken Head
György Spiró

Sorrow, Sorrow, Fear, the Pit, and the Rope
Karel Steigerwald

Horses at the Window
Matei Vişniec

Edited by Daniel Gerould
with a preface by Dragan Klaić

Martin E. Segal Theatre Center Publications
New York

Professionals and amateurs are hereby warned that this material, being fully protected under the Copyright Laws of the United States of America and all other countries of the Berne and Universal Copyright Conventions, is subject to a royalty. All rights including, but not limited to, professional, amateur, recording, motion picture, recitation, lecturing, public reading, radio and television broadcasting, and the rights of translation into foreign languages are expressly reserved. Inquiries concerning production rights should be addressed in advance, before rehearsals begin, to the following: *Portrait*, Diogenes, Gesine Lübben, lub@diogenes.ch; *Military Secret*, AA media ius, lado.hribar@siol.net; *Chicken Head*, Marton Agency, info@martonagency.com; *Sorrow, Sorrow, Fear, the Pit, and the Rope*, Aura-Pont Agency, Jitka Sloupova, Literary Manager, jitka.sloupova@aura-pont.cz; *Horses at the Window*, Société des Auteurs et Compositeurs Dramatiques, info-sacd@sacd.fr.

Library of Congress Cataloging-in-Publication Data

Playwrights before the fall : Eastern European drama in times of revolution.
    p. cm.
ISBN 978-0-9790570-8-3
1. East European drama--20th century--Translations into English. I. Mrożek, Sławomir. *Portret*. English. II. Spiró, György, 1946- *Csirkefej*. English. III. Jovanović, Dušan, 1939- *Vojaška skrivnost*. English. IV. Vișniec, Matei. *Caii la fereastră*. English. V. Steigerwald, Karel, 1945- *Hoře, hoře, strach, oprátka a jáma*. English. VI. Martin E. Segal Theatre Center.
PN849.E92P63 2009
    808.82'00947--dc21

                    2009033011

This book is published by the Martin E. Segal Theatre Center in collaboration with the New York Public Library for the Performing Arts *Performing Revolution in Central and Eastern Europe* festival; Czech Center, New York; Hungarian Cultural Center, New York; Polish Cultural Institute, New York; Romanian Cultural Institute, New York; Consulate General of Slovenia, New York.

Copyright 2009 by Martin E. Segal Theatre Center

Daniel Gerould, Director of Publications
Frank Hentschker, Executive Director
Jan Stenzel, Director of Administration

Copyediting and typography by Margaret Araneo

Table of Contents

FOREWORD

This volume is the contribution of the Martin E. Segal Theatre Center to Performing Revolution in Central and Eastern Europe, a performing arts festival marking the twentieth anniversary of the fall of communism in Central and Eastern Europe, presented by The New York Public Library for the Performing Arts. It explores the role of the writer in registering the changes that would remake society. *Playwrights Before the Fall: Drama in Eastern Europe in Times of Revolution* is a multi-author anthology of Eastern European plays from the 1980s dealing with the fall of communism. It is the first such collection of drama to appear in English.

In the communist satellite countries of Eastern Europe, the 1980s was a period of deepening stagnation, mounting tension, and increasingly overt opposition to the oppressive regimes, culminating in the triumph of the Polish Solidarity movement, the opening of the Hungarian border with Austria, the Czech Velvet Revolution, the fall of the Berlin wall, and the violent end of the Ceauşescus in Romania. As the communist regimes crumbled, popular action in the streets seemed more dramatic than anything happening on stage in the theatres. But dramatists too played their part in the revolutions that overturned communism.

In compiling the anthology, I have chosen key playwrights writing before the fall from Poland, Slovenia, Hungary, Czechoslovakia, and Romania, who are able to show the moral and psychological dimensions of the transformations taking place in society during these years of transition. Their plays reveal the absurdities of an inflexible system based on belief in an abstract ideology that sacrifices the individual to dogma. These authors bear witness to the ravages of communism and to the traumas of its disintegration. They lend voices to the frightened and the manipulated whose lives were stunted by entropic regimes.

The five playwrights of the 1980s in the anthology respond in strikingly different ways to the impending fall of communism in the Soviet Bloc. What they share is the experience of living and writing under totalitarian rule in their native countries (even if they go into exile), and their recognition that these deteriorating regimes are on the verge of collapse. Their contrasting approaches can in part be explained by the generation to which each belongs and by their different relations to the history of communism in their countries.

The eldest of the group, born in pre-war Poland, Mrożek creates a historical fable about Stalinism and its seductions, as he himself experienced them, in order to probe the sources of Eastern European totalitarianism. Jovanović, born on the eve of WWII, portrays the dissolution of Yugoslavia through the microcosm of the life of an institution carrying out a utopian experiment about interspecies communication that unravels into a cacophonous dystopia. A child of the failed revolution of 1956 against the

Soviets, the Hungarian Spiró puts a *fait divers* under the microscope and sees the germs of spreading infection, prefigured in a putrid "slice of life" about the down-and-out of Budapest, foreshadowing the foul-mouthed neo-naturalistic plays about discarded human lives that flourished in the new post-communist theatre of Eastern Europe in the 1990s. Coming of age at the time of the Warsaw pact invasion of his homeland that drove many of his elder playwriting colleagues into exile, the Czech Steigerwald—through the use of multiple time perspectives and shifting character identities—follows the whirlwinds of revolution backward and forward in dizzying jumps from the 1930s in Russia up to the still unfolding Velvet Revolution. Born almost a full generation after Mrożek and in flight from an ossified regime, the Romanian poet-playwright Vişniec through metaphor and image exposes the linguistic traps used to perpetuate endless conflict within families and among nations, renewing the avant-garde tradition of the absurd manifest in earlier anti-war diatribes from Central Europe, such as Frigyes Karinthy's *Long War*, Karl Kraus's *Last Days of Mankind*, and Miroslav Krleža's *Finale*.

Dragan Klaić, who witnessed and reported on many of the major theatrical events of the period as they occurred, in his preface provides a broad taxonomy of drama and theatre under communism and then places the five playwrights within the contexts of the 1980s. Separate introductions by experts provide background information and interpretive guides for each of the plays. The order of the plays in the volume is both thematic and generational, designed to create an unfolding commentary on the approaching fall of communism in Eastern Europe.

Daniel Gerould
New York, 2009

PREFACE

RETRIEVED FROM OBLIVION

It would be quite difficult to sketch the life and career of a typical playwright in Central and Eastern Europe during communism, in other words before 1989. That could mean embarking on a huge oral history project, interviewing playwrights, but also theatre directors, dramaturgs, actors, and critics; seeking out some of the former censors and party apparatchiks; reading old reviews, diaries, and ideological articles of party hacks. The end result would in all probability be a composite picture of many contradictions, of mutually incompatible accents and features, an intersubjective mythology in which most authors involved would refuse to recognize themselves, insisting on the particulars of their own biographies.

Despite the many contradictions such an investigation would yield, some common elements of the professional and cultural-political context in which playwrights under communism operated from the early 1960s to 1989 could be drawn. All communist countries sustained a developed theatre infrastructure of dozens of repertory companies with a permanent artistic ensemble and a steady administrative and technical staff. Such companies existed even in smaller places of fifty to one-hundred-thousand inhabitants and were generously subsidized by the public authorities. Actors enjoyed unlimited contracts, but moved occasionally from one company to another, from smaller towns to larger cities, and moonlighted for film, television, and radio. Theatre directors were employed by the repertory companies or worked as freelancers. Authors were mainly freelancers, but some enjoyed a comfortable employment in a cultural institution that allowed them much free time for writing. They could get away to mountain cottages, seaside villas, and spas maintained by their artistic associations, to seek inspiration in nature and write in tranquility.

Plays were sometimes commissioned by theatres or acquired through open competitions. Once a play was approved and premiered, its success could easily generate several subsequent professional productions in other repertory companies in the same country. Publication of a play in magazines and books was quite common, and translations into other languages could lead to productions in some of the fraternal communist countries. Rep companies were expected to submit their season plans to the authorities for advance approval and to match classics with the contemporary plays by native and foreign authors, especially from the other communist countries. A privileged place was reserved for Soviet authors.

But to get the first professional production of a new play was not easy even for well-established authors since theatres were subject to formal and informal censorship along governmental and party lines, and every new play was exposed to a considerable ideological scrutiny, first as a text and then again at the dress rehearsal. At this time censors could impose alternatives and cuts, or even forbid the premiere. In some instances the repressive mechanism of censorship was activated only after the premiere, prompted by audience reactions that were deemed unsuitable or dangerous.

To have a text smuggled to the other side of the Iron Curtain for translation and production abroad before it was authorized for staging at home could be considered by the authorities as a treacherous act, punishable by blacklisting the author—that is, banning the publication and staging of his or her works, at least for a while. The system nourished self-censorship on the part of authors and theatre directors and demanded from them considerable diplomatic skills to negotiate with the authorities about small details, to cajole and appease them by gestures of innocence and loyalty. There was a great deal of insecurity about what might prompt censorial interventions that were often perceived as irrational and unpredictable. At certain points, the censors of some countries, regions, and cities seemed to be more permissive and lenient than others, but then at other times those same censors appeared severe and vindictive.

Against this background, serious playwrights under communism could be divided into roughly three groups: exiles, dissidents, and boundary pushers. The rest were mere entertainers and opportunists, hacks and scribblers whose work should be of little concern today as it was little appreciated during the communist era. Exiles were very few in number. Those that left the country to go to the West and enjoy the freedom it offered lost opportunities for staging their plays at home. They were practically banned from cultural production and commentary and erased from official cultural memory. Mrożek, was an exception, being well established and much produced internationally and at home, while living in France and Germany.

Dissidents living in their own countries as blacklisted persons— banished from the public life, and exposed to additional pressures if their work was staged and published abroad—were even harder to find. Václav Havel had his own ways to smuggle his plays abroad for rapid translation and multiple staging, but he had to pay the price for his disobedience. When he was not in jail, he attempted in vain to stage small-scale performances in his own apartment in Prague with the blacklisted actress Vlasta Chramostová, but even the four or five friends who courageously dared to join him as tentative audience members were habitually arrested and harassed by the secret police. The Hungarian playwright István Eörsi, who was blacklisted in the 1980s when his plays were banned at home but staged in Germany, found work as a translator and dramaturg in the Kaposvár theatre, but Budapest theatre companies were off limit to him.

The ability to push boundaries was the defining mark of the remaining playwrights of quality who, with more or less ingenuity and perseverance, attempted to move the limits of what was possible and permissible by finding disguised ways of indicating the unsettling truths behind the official ideological smoke screen. They did not engage in open public debates and polemics, for they all claimed that they were only seeking to improve on the inherent qualities of the communist system. In practice, they developed, together with the theatre directors and actors, an aesthetic of allusion, insinuation, and innuendo, a coded language of critique and resistance, a tacit alliance with an appreciative and understanding public. This made playwriting inevitably metaphorical and symbolic; with dramatic action removed to historical, pseudo-historical, or abstract settings; with characters that invoked in shorthand a contemporary typology of political opportunism and obedience, abusive and ignorant power, or intellectual dissidence and martyrdom.

While public life was dominated by predictable ideological discourse filled with wooden language overloaded with clichés and phraseology—newspapers and magazines expressing a limited gamut of facts and views—the stage appeared as a privileged public forum, an ersatz civil society, if only for two to three charged hours each evening before dissolving after the final curtain and the last tumultuous applause. In this way theatre served as a compensation for banned public disputes and confrontations, as a critical medium in which some precious values could be re-examined and reaffirmed and the humiliating, repressive features of reality exposed and denounced.

This precarious constellation made playwrights much appreciated even if they engaged in minimalist, oblique, and convoluted critique. Theatre repertories, however, tended to be chosen by theatre directors and their dramaturgs, who preferred to play things safe by staging classics, using their literary repute and high cultural status as a shield against political interference. To stage new plays by contemporary authors was to risk censorial intervention and retribution. Euripides, Shakespeare, and Schiller could, of course, be deployed in the stratagems of allusion and disguised critique, but as classics they stood stronger against the authorities than a contemporary author and his or her new play. Therefore, contemporary drama took a minor position in the repertory since it meant more hassle and increased scrutiny.

It would be wrong, however, to conceive of cultural production under communism in a static manner, as one frozen, monochromatic constellation, identical in every country, with the same scrutiny applied to every theatre company for decades. As an ideology, political regime, and cultural system, communism dominated Central and Eastern Europe from the end of WWII to 1989 when it collapsed, seemingly all at once, in the course of a few months. But throughout these decades, cultural-political circumstances changed in every country, shifting between severity and permissiveness, producing temporary zones of greater or lesser tolerance, empowering sometimes the open-minded, sometimes the dogmatic ideological arbiters of cultural life who acted as artistic benefactors or paranoid crusaders. Theatre repertories and playwrights' careers reflected these shifts. Critical, dissident, subversive drama was everywhere a small minority in the total theatre output, dominated otherwise by appeasement, opportunism, escapist entertainment, and allegiance to official interpretations of reality.

Pushing the boundaries of the possible and permissible was a common and widespread goal of many theatre artists, not so much in a socio-political sense but in an aesthetic one, as an affirmation of creative freedom and a quest for innovation, beyond the muddled notions of Socialist Realism. Since the 1960s, failing to yield any convincing theatre, Socialist Realism was gradually discarded by playwrights in artistic practice (if not in the official artistic discourse). And yet, most of the theatrical productions emerged in an illusionist key, overloaded by psychology, vacillating between versions of naturalism and realism, with satire tamed by comedy and irony balanced by sentimentality. Playwrights and their directors had to keep in mind the pervasive moralism of the communist authorities and to reckon with the official optimism of a doctrine that left little space for genuine tragic emotions.

Socialist Realism was in its stage practice often closer to socialist romanticism (dramatic or comic) and embraced more often simplistic melodrama, as the most successful Soviet plays amply illustrate. *Oedipus Rex*, *King Lear*, and *Hamlet* had enough cultural capital to stand on their own, even with the addition of some delicate political implications that could be read as contemporary allusions, but Musset's *Lorenzaccio* was risky if not impossible to stage. Beckett's *Waiting for Godot*, for instance, was difficult for communist censors of several countries to swallow, not so much for its absurdist dramaturgy and the enigmatic figure of Godot, but primarily because of its intransigent, unredeemable pessimism. For many authors behind the Iron Curtain, Beckett was at the same time an unexpected mentor and ally, as opposed to Brecht who was despite his impeccable East Berlin credentials resented for his didacticism and twisted dialectics.

When Gorbachov introduced *glasnost* and *perestroika* in the mid 1980s, his reformist zeal found allies among some playwrights in the USSR, such as Mikhail Shatrov, whose plays about Bolshevik rivalries and betrayals and about the Chernobyl disaster quickly found their way to the Soviet stage and inspired more critical writing and staging throughout communist Europe. Heiner Müller, whose reputation was rapidly growing in the West with numerous productions of his plays, was in East Berlin neither a dissident nor a canonical author, but a puzzling figure, much envied for his iconoclastic talent and even more for his unique unfettered access to West Berlin beyond the Wall. Despite his elusive, fragmentary dramaturgy, he was moving from the margins and periods of disgrace to a position of authority at the center of the DDR theatre.

But Gorbachov's reforms unsettled many Eastern and Central European apparatchiks, and their resistance to change kept Havel an isolated dissident in Prague and made Mrożek, Kohout, Głowacki, and several other playwrights remain as exiles in the West. At the same time, censorial standards became more lenient, and classic and contemporary Western plays, unacceptable a year or two ago, could be staged in the communist countries. The zeal of theatre people to make up for many theatre seasons of imposed fasting by a potlatch of foreign plays now reached absurd proportions: seventeen Tennessee Williams plays were running in the same season in Moscow theatres, riding on the wave of rediscovered individualism and private emotions penetrating the public arena. This breakthrough in the make-up of the repertory and the collapse of the habitual quotas came inevitably at the expense of contemporary native authors whose plays were instantly driven out by the foreign titles that responded to the enormous curiosity of the public.

Accelerating social and political changes had a disorienting impact on many playwrights. Their courageous critique would in no time appear as a timid flirtation with sensitive issues. The issues themselves would be marginalized by the overwhelming interest in themes previously kept off of the stage because of ideological taboos. With the collapse of communism in the turbulence of 1989–1990, theatre lost most of the public attention to the spectacular theatricality of street demonstrations, television debates, and documentary revelations of revisionist history, to the political forums of the newly founded civic movements and political parties, to the outbursts of freedom in the authentic collective life. Theatre became a minor diversion compared to the destruction of the Berlin Wall and many symbolic walls and took a backseat to coups in Bucharest, Tirana, and Moscow; riots and clashes; celebrations; proclamations of the new order; and the pulling down of communist monuments. The whole pantheon of communist heroes was dismissed and relegated to the proverbial graveyard of history, or rather to the junkyard of scrap metal and broken marble.

In due time theatre recovered and regained some of its public, but it was itself changed by the systemic shift in politics, the economy, society, and cultural systems. Censorship was quickly eliminated. The newly formed political parties for a while played a hard-nosed game as to who would control the theatre boards and who would nominate the general managers. They quickly learned, however, that the real influence of the public and the real slush money lie in the media. Consequently they lost interest in the theatre. Left to their own devices, many theatre companies and venues sought to entertain and amuse. Even subsidized theatre jumped on the bandwagon of commercialism, claiming as an excuse reduced subsidies. Foreign plays became more numerous; the moonlighting of actors in film, television, and commercial gigs more common; musicals and revues started altering the prevailing taste, and imported industrial culture began to set new standards.

Playwrights who survived communism found themselves marginalized, even superfluous; the plays that they kept in their desk drawers for better times turned out to be obsolete and it became difficult to interest theatre managers in the new dramatic work. In the so-called post-communist transition, the repertory of the previous epoch was quickly discarded and in the new one, native playwrights could claim only an occasional slot on the small stage or in a studio production. Those who craved attention, fame, and money, moved to television. Some younger dramaturgs emigrated to the advertising agencies, their familiarity with Heiner Müller and non-linear dramaturgy giving them a competitive advantage over their colleagues of more conventional training in marketing. Young theatre directors initially jumped at the opportunity to stage Jarry, Vitrac, Pinter, and Müller, but then decided that they could best establish their credentials by staging plays by canonical writers, such as Shakespeare, Ibsen, and Chekhov. The pressures of the box office, however, forced them eventually to agree to adapt new popular novels for the stage and to write film scripts that would have strong name recognition. The generation of authors that was skillful at manipulating censors proved quite inept at achieving success in the market economy and in the growing culture of leisure and entertainment that has annexed theatre companies and venues.

Toward the end of 1990s a new generation of playwrights appeared in Central and Eastern Europe, who were outspoken about the vagaries of transition and sensitive to the emerging cultural gaps and to the socio-economic stratification of post-communist societies. They took gibes at the distorting impact of consumerism and critiqued the corruption and arrogance of the newly enriched tycoons. Some of those authors reached international success thanks to festivals, tours, and the Internet, such as the brothers Presniakov from Moscow, Biljana Srbljanović from Belgrade, and Saviana Stanescu from Bucharest.

In the meantime, theatre in Central and Eastern Europe has changed considerably; repertory companies still dominate, but dramatic theatre is losing ground to other sorts of performance that tends to be driven more by music, dance, movement, visual arts, and new media. Such work is produced by a growing number of autonomous groups that choose to reduce the importance of language in order to facilitate international touring, whether the goal is primarily entertainment or experimentation. The intellectual and ethical concentration of dramatic theatre prominent under communism, despite all the imposed restraints, has waned in the newly established democratic societies, in confrontation not with the suspicious censor but with the indifferent, impatient consumer.

The plays selected for this anthology come from the last years of communism in Europe, and yet they do not anticipate the radical uprooting that was soon to ensue. Instead they expose the accumulated contradictions and defects of a tired and increasingly dysfunctional system, revealing the worn-out credibility and spent emancipatory promises of an ideology reduced to rhetoric and the crude mechanisms of power. They are very divergent thematically, in the dramaturgical models chosen, and in the degree of explicitness/allusiveness with which they refer to the context of communism as an ideology, political system, way of life, and corpus of values.

How the plays withstand the wear and tear of historic change is another matter. Let us assume, however, that a mere reading of the plays cannot do full justice to their implicit values. Their publication in this anthology has more than just historical meaning. What these plays are worth today, perhaps more as performance material than as literature, can be ascertained only by attempting to stage them, both in the much-altered European theatre cultures in which they originally emerged, as well as in some radically different theatre contexts—North America for instance, where there is no "surplus of history," so characteristic of Central and Eastern Europe, and where the collective memory of communism is indirect, vague, and oblique.

Sławomir Mrożek's *Portrait* (*Portret*, 1987) offers a prolonged perspective on an act of denunciation, committed in the remote years of Stalinism, creating a debilitating sense of protracted guilt. Rehabilitation of the victims of Stalinist repression comes with much delay, in an arbitrary, superficial fashion, with no space for the remorse of the accomplices and no sorting out of their responsibilities. Mrożek tames his essentially moralistic vision with an absurdist rendering of the victim and the former stooge, of the auxiliary characters and their mutual relationships. He stresses the vagueness of circumstances, the elusiveness of remembrance, the mechanical nature of communication. The genre he has chosen vacillates between farce and the grotesque. The complex nature of Stalinism is reduced to a seductive personality cult, an iconic power image that dominates, subjugates, and persecutes, a portrait of the great helmsman that overshadows individual and collective existence.

In this way Mrożek distances himself from the shifts and twists of slow and gradual de-Stalinization in his native Poland. He in fact avoids any specifics that would tie his play to the repeated Polish anti-Stalinists upheavals (1956, 1968, 1970) or to the clashes of the Solidarity movement with the authorities since 1980 or especially to the military rule that was imposed in December 1981. Away from Poland's perils and humiliations of the time, Mrożek avoids any historical or sociological prism and focuses instead on the remorse of the stooge that becomes his central emotion, his intellectual obsession, and makes him consume all his energy and time in the futile search for repentance and pardon that no one is willing to give him because he has been utterly marginalized. His anguish attracts no attention, being socially superfluous. The victim of the main character's denunciation seems to be able to think of his own years in jail with good-humored resignation and to pick up the threads of his life with relief and relish after being freed. The betrayer remains the ultimate and definite martyr long after the crippling system fades away—a lonely keeper of memories that no one needs.

Karel Steigerwald in *Sorrow, Sorrow, Fear, the Rope, and the Pit* (*Hoře, hoře, strach, oprátka a jáma*, 1989) discards a chronological sequence in order to render a chaotic image of communism as revolution, upheaval, and permanent menace. The play was conceived of and for the most part written before the sudden outburst of the Velvet Revolution in Prague in November 1989, but it was finished only in early 1990 after the fall of communism. It does not invoke the drabness and predictability of "normalization" that marked the rule of Gustáv Husák and his pro-Soviet loyalists after the crash of the Prague Spring in 1968. Even though there is very little that anchors the play in the Czech circumstances at the end of the Cold War, the wide strokes of the author do convey an idea of communism as a world process and an international force, propelled by an odd energy mix of idealism and arbitrary violence. Steigerwald must have known that his play stood no chance of being staged at home while he was writing it. By the time the completed play could be directed by Jan Grossman at the Divadlo na zábradlí in Prague, the collapse of the Husák regime and the rapid shift to democracy and liberalism made *Sorrow* immediately seem obsolete. With all collective energies mobilized to shape a new post-communist reality, any interest in retrospection quickly disappeared from the Czech stage for quite a while.

Even twenty years later, a production of Steigerwald's play in all probability would have difficulties affirming its convulsive aesthetic against the ideological simplifications and political opportunisms of the current Czech Republic, which has drawn a curtain of indifference and collective amnesia over the entire shared experience of communism. Against the ironic, melancholy, and almost realist traditions of Czech dramaturgy of the 1970s and 1980s, with its common melodramatic and tragicomic accents, Steigerwald's play is unique for its tempestuous course and rich imaginary, and yet one must wonder who would have dared then and who would dare now to stage it in Prague or elsewhere.

After 2000 in Slovakia some plays recalled the turbulent histories through a biographical focus on Jozef Tiso, the prime minister of the short-lived Slovak "independent" state installed by the Nazis, and on Gustáv Husák, the Slovak communist and Soviet loyalist ruler of Czechoslovakia from the crushing of the Prague Spring in 1968 to the Velvet Revolution in 1989. Czech playwriting in contrast stayed by and large away from any ideological or historical revisionism. Enormous amounts of material, released from the former Soviet and Komintern archives in the 1990s and a library of new historical studies, would probably endorse Steigerwald's intuitive vision of the communist hurricane but would also nuance the picture with its petty-minded sweeping bureaucracy, tired ideological jargon, and sheer drabness of everyday life. I must admit I would be rather curious to see how his play would work today as a grotesque, furious puppet theatre performance, or as a high-tech staging, with numerous video screens, conveying documentary evidence of the turbulent epoch of communism, juxtaposed with the live action of actors.

Horses at the Window (*Caii la fereastrâ*, 1987) by Matei Vişniec could be read as another exilic echo of the inability of the individual to control his or her own destiny under the assaults of big history and especially in Ceauşescu's Romania. Abstract in its rendering of place and time, remote and parabolic in its tripartite structure, with the repetitive destruction of a family relationship through war and its accompanying rhetoric, Vişniec's play brings much fatalism and a sense of drama that takes place far away from the scenes staged and removed from his small-scale domestic milieu. While death on the battlefield, remote and futile, breaks apart the relationships of mother and son, daughter and father, wife and husband, it is repeatedly announced and rationalized by a suave, enigmatic intruder, a diplomatic messenger of the absent and remote powers that be.

One could look at Vişniec's play as a historic or pseudo-historic allegory, signaling that the author probably thought in 1987 that Ceauşescu's rule had no expiration date. Ceauşescu thought that himself, even while his comrade rulers were toppled in Berlin, Sofia, and Prague during the short weeks of October–November 1989. Possibly Vişniec was seeing his fellow Romanians as people condemned to eternal martyrdom because his play reiterates the mechanics of death and loss in the futile grinding of history, in the weight of a super-patriotic rhetoric used to justify the status-quo. In all three segments, the simple word home refers to a place that is cold, shabby, stern, and deprived of intimacy. The big outside world, barely revealed, is even worse—destructive, wild, and condemned to repeated massacres. Since the play avoids any direct reference to Romanian reality, the author postulates the lot of these ordinary people who die for abstract matters of a higher order as part of a *condition humaine* rather than as a consequence of the ruling ideology and political machinery at work.

But those features probably facilitated the reception of *Horses at the Window* outside Romania, especially in the outpouring of sympathy for and solidarity with Romanians that came after the bloody palace coup/rebellion/ revolution that liquidated Ceauşescu and ended communism in Romania during Christmas 1989. The parabolic features of Vişniec's play made the misery of Romania more universal and accessible for foreign readers and spectators, who were most likely little informed about the everyday life under the great Conducator. The minutia of daily misery, repression, and surveillance in Romania during 1980s has been unraveled only in some recent Romanian feature films that received much international acclaim. In post-Ceauşescu Romania contemporary domestic plays have been largely ignored by theatre managers, who prefer to pander to audiences with commercial Western entertainment, and by Romanian stage directors, who stubbornly stick to the European classics. A slowly renewed interest in contemporary Romanian drama, stubbornly advocated by a few dramaturgs and critics, is again linked to the reappearance of Vişniec's plays as an integral part of the theatre repertory in the recent years.

Hungarian literary scholar and playwright György Spiró calls his *Chicken Head* (*Csirkefej*, 1985) a "tragedy," even though "social reportage in dramatic form" would be a more fitting label. Situated in the inner courtyard of a shabby apartment house on the poorer outskirts of Budapest, the dramatic action makes no tragic evolution from hubristic ignorance to delayed insight and merited suffering but remains entrenched in a circle of violence, poverty, and hopelessness. Shocking from the very beginning with its emblematic gesture of futile cruelty against an animal, it reiterates this brutishness in the outer-city slang of its characters—an incoherent, disjointed mumbling, overloaded with profanities and curses. This adolescent slang asserts its own authenticity and the veracity of the circumstances and indicates social marginalization, but more importantly, it rudely tears apart any ideological banner that the Hungarian authorities of the time could seek to wave as proof of social progress and emancipation in the "merriest barrack of the socialist camp," as Kádár's Hungary was once called.

Spiró must be credited for doing away with, in one brash gesture, the platitudes of "goulash communism," the widespread vision of Hungary in the 1980s as a restricted but essentially comfortable and complacent petit-bourgeois order. Instead, he shows the violence and despair of losers at the edge of the metropolis, unscathed by ideology, and forgotten by politics, but at the same time barren in their vulnerability and impatience. Even figures associated with authority—cops on their tiresome beat and a woman official from the city council—are not rendered as any better.

After many years I can still hear the shrieks of Hilda Gobi, in the memorable production of the Budapest Katona József Theatre, playing an inconsolable old woman, mourning her savagely killed cat, then turning angry and vituperative. Today with economic privatization practically completed in Hungary, after the surge and crash of the real estate market and reckless gentrification of shabbier Budapest neighborhoods, *Chicken Head* deserves a new reading and a new staging, one that addresses the present-day losers of globalization, the lumpen proles of the post-communist transition. Spiró was merciless in his portrayal of the offended and humiliated strata of the communist society, discarding the sugary tales of harmony and solidarity in a supposedly classless society. A staging today would inevitably lash out at the tales of a capitalist bonanza, recasting the original characters as the bag ladies, homeless drunks, and hopeless street vendors of trinkets that one sees on the streets of Budapest nowadays.

And finally there is the strange case of Dušan Jovanović's *Military Secret* (*Vojaška skrivnost*, 1983), one of the paradoxical moments of the idiosyncratic self-management socialism in former Yugoslavia. Unlike other communist countries, Yugoslavia did not have a formal censorship system but had occasional public and secret political interventions to eliminate undesirable or irritating theatre productions. As Spiró had done in *Imposter* (*Imposztor*, 1984), Jovanović played with the metatheatrical device of a play-within-a-play to expose the spectacle of power and the duplicity of political loyalty, breaking political taboos with his *Liberation of Skopje (Osloboditev*

Skopja, 1977) and *Karamazovs* (*Karamazovi*, 1980) and earning him as an author and theatre director the reputation of a political iconoclast among artists.

In *Military Secret* the Slovenian playwright takes us to a scientific institute, where the researchers are stuck in their attempts to discover the secrets of animal speech and allow the various animal species to talk to one another. A military officer takes over the project from the doubt-ridden and manipulative scientists to ensure that the experiment continues. Clearly, the zoological allegory served to reveal the flaws in the Yugoslav venture after Tito, and the utopian resonances of the Yugoslav socialist experiment in brotherhood and unity could be played off against its authoritarian risks. In one of those ironic twists of theatre history, Jovanović's play premiered in 1983 at the Split Summer Festival, staged at the Yugoslav Navy base Lora. The production was greeted with enthusiasm by the military top brass, who read the military intervention in the play as a patriotic gesture, revealing their reluctance to acknowledge the ambiguities implicit in the takeover of the experiment.

Eight years later, during the disintegration of Yugoslavia as the result of a protracted armed conflict, Lora became the site of war crimes against those same Navy officers, who were tortured by Croatian independence fighters. The crime became an emblematic test case for latter day judicial proceedings that dragged on for years and made Lora's name ominous. Today it seems that a utopian energy has moved from Split to Brussels, and Jovanović's zoological allegory could come in handy in probing the present contradictions of European integration—an elite project of substantial accomplishments, now seemingly mired in the resistance and suspicion of disgruntled European citizens and imperiled by the demagoguery of populist politicians, as amply demonstrated by the most recent elections for the European Parliament in June 2009.

These plays by Mrożek, Steigerwald, Vişniec, Spiró, and Jovanović echo bygone times and convey the systemic difficulties and risks of theatre as a social and cultural institution in the minefields of the Cold War epoch. They also await resolute and imaginative theatre directors who will test them outside of their original context of communism and endow them with new meaning, despite the present ideological vacuum that has resulted from the recent crash of neo-liberal capitalism, once celebrated as a triumphant force after 1989. The five plays presented here are just the first of many plays from the last communist decade that deserve new critical scrutiny rather than oblivion.

Dragan Klaić
Amsterdam, 2009

PORTRAIT

Sławomir Mrożek

SŁAWOMIR MROŻEK
Photo courtesy of Sławomir Mrożek

MROŻEK AND HIS *PORTRAIT*

Daniel Gerould

Quickly recognized in the West as one of the truly distinctive voices of Cold War era theatre, Sławomir Mrożek came to occupy a very special position in the Soviet Bloc after he left Poland in the early 1960s. He is, as far as I know, the only major Eastern European writer to emigrate, live in the West, adopt foreign citizenship, and yet be allowed by a communist regime to publish in both the state-run and émigré press and to have his plays successfully performed at home and abroad, although certain works were sometimes banned at sensitive moments.

During his self-exile Mrożek maintained a critical stance toward the regime, but because he was never identified with any dissident movement, the communist authorities learned to tolerate him. The playwright left Poland not for political reasons, but rather to establish his own individual identity and pursue his career as a writer independent of the state and its cultural apparatus. A loner and outsider, Mrożek felt the need to maintain his distance from the sources of power. Once he had established secure footing somewhere, he moved on and began anew.

Mrożek left Poland in 1963 on a tourist visa for Italy, where he stayed for five years until moving to Paris. When the Polish army took part in the Soviet-led Warsaw Pact invasion of Czechoslovakia in 1968, the outraged playwright published a sarcastic letter of protest in *Le Monde*, *The International Herald Tribune*, and the émigré Polish journal *Kultura*. After the Polish authorities ordered his immediate return home, Mrożek asked for political asylum in France, and all publication and performance of his work in Poland came under a total ban. In 1971 Mrożek resigned from the Polish Writers' Union.

However, the banning of his plays left a conspicuous gap in the Polish theatrical repertory detrimental to the international cultural prestige so important to the regime. Because both the Polish communist authorities and the Polish theatre needed Mrożek as their star playwright, the ban was lifted in 1973 when his new plays started to appear in the influential drama monthly *Dialog* and in theatres throughout Poland. In 1975 *Emigrés*, about a pair of exiles, one political, the other economic, was widely performed to great acclaim in Poland and abroad.

The Polish authorities now let it be known that the playwright would be welcomed back home if he chose to return. In 1978 Mrożek obtained French citizenship, but also requested readmission to the Polish Writers' Union and visited Poland, privately and without fanfare. The Polish premieres of *The Ambassador* and *On Foot*, both sharply critical of the regime and its domination by the Soviet Union, took place during the rise of Solidarity.

After the military coup and imposition of martial law in December 1981, Mrożek wrote an open letter to *Le Monde* and the *International Herald Tribune* protesting Jaruzelski's dictatorship and ridiculing the spurious rationalizations used to justify it. The playwright also refused to allow publication of his work in the Polish press or the showing of his plays on Polish television, because of the complicity of these media in parroting the regime's propaganda. Polish theatres, however, continued to perform his plays, although *The Ambassador*, *Vatzlav*, and *Alpha* were at this point prohibited by the censor. Despite his attacks against the regime's attempted suppression of the workers' rebellion, Mrożek never joined the Solidarity movement, doubting that a writer should be directly involved in politics.

By the later 1980s it was evident that the stagnant totalitarian regime was disintegrating from within, although no one could have predicted its imminent fall. Written in 1987, during the waning days of communism as the banned Solidarity movement gained strength, *Portrait*, Janus-faced, looks in two directions—back to the onset of tyranny in Stalinism and forward to the time of reckoning soon to come in the post-communist era when old scores would be settled and blame assigned for the debacle. The play is both retrospective and prophetic. (The censorship, already in disarray, passed the play, with restrictions on mentioning the Party in the songs cited in the text.)

In going back to the Stalinist roots of People's Poland, Mrożek was returning to his own youth and formative years. One of Mrożek's most personal and autobiographical works, *Portrait* deals with Mrożek's own Stalinist past, his skeleton in the closet. Fond of simple, concrete one-word titles of multiple resonance, Mrożek, a cartoonist skilled at drawing caricatures, makes *Portrait* a depiction of the smiling Soviet dictator, but also a picture of himself and his own generation that was crippled by fanaticism in the cause of utopian abstractions

Nine years old when the Nazis invaded Poland, Mrożek was a member of the lost generation of those too young to fight, but whose lives were scarred by war, German occupation, and imposition of Soviet-style communism in 1949 that crushed any hopes for a free Poland. Yet contrary to customary thinking about the repressive nature of totalitarian regimes, Stalinism gave Mrożek and other talented members of his generation (Andrzej Wajda, Zbigniew Cybulski, Jerzy Grotowski, Roman Polanski) an unexpected opportunity to start careers in the arts and gain access to privileged positions in the new society. From a lower-middle-class family, Mrożek lacked any prospects for the future when at twenty he discovered Marxist-Leninist ideology and the rewards it could offer a child of the common people. His youthful infatuation with Stalinism was, as the playwright later explained, a form of rebellion against his conservative rural background that enabled him to embark on a meteoric career as a journalist .

Writing in 1983, Mrożek, explained, "I fell in love with Joseph Stalin almost overnight, with the intensity which equaled my former hatred of myself. It took the practical form of getting a job, first as a reporter, and then a columnist . . . I expressed my love in that paper, at first ardently, then gradually cooling off. My love lasted about three years." The playwright concludes, "I am neither a historian nor a literary critic. I am an aging gentleman who feels the need to settle accounts. I cannot do it unless I settle accounts with everything that once shaped me and almost did so decisively. Some of those affairs of mine are not exclusively mine, but also those of many people like me. That is why I do not keep them to myself."

Thus Mrożek wrote *Portrait* to settle accounts with his own youthful embrace of communism and to assess the human costs of its liquidation. The legacy of Stalin's poisoned heritage is everywhere apparent in the ruined lives of the dictator's acolytes and of his enemies. Neither victimizers nor victims can free themselves from his spell.

In his early plays Mrożek developed a parable form of drama that explored the mechanisms of power and its inexorable laws. After *Emigrés* the playwright moved increasingly toward a direct confrontation with twentieth-century Polish history, without, however, abandoning his preference for the metaphorical and mythic, often in parodic form. Reluctant to deal with a Polish reality that he no longer was a part of, Mrożek now wrote a series of overtly political plays that transform fact into fiction. *On Foot* (1980) is a concrete historical drama at the end of WWII that explores Poland's drift toward totalitarianism and also a fable about the human condition in times of chaos and social disintegration. *Alpha* (1984) moves ahead to contemporary Polish history, presenting Lech Wałęsa and Solidarity in a fictionalized guise. The hero is identified simply as the leader of a popular uprising crushed by a military coup.

The last of Mrożek's political plays, *Portrait* (1987), set for the most part in 1964, examines the consequences of Stalinism. It takes place in real time and space, although these dimensions often seem remembered rather than actual. The play deals concretely with Poland and its history, evoking the atmosphere of the period through the use of songs, slogans, and popular culture of the time.

It is not hard to follow the general plot lines of *Portrait*, although many of the details and sequences are not fully articulated and the significance of the whole remains ambiguous. It is the story of two schoolmates, Bartodziej and Anatol, a symbiotic pair of contrasting characters—a dramatic configuration that enables Mrożek to peer deeply into the duality of personality. Mrożek liked to develop pairs of characters of contrasting yet complementary temperaments who together comprise a single whole, but who, when split in two, constitute a divided psyche, individual, or nation. Bartodziej and Anatol are such antithetical doubles who can be seen as opposing halves of the same character. They have been interpreted as twin images of Mrożek who, in a case of extreme schizophrenia, denounces himself.

In the new landscape of communist Poland, Bartodziej becomes a fanatical believer in Stalin and a security agent who in 1949 denounces his anti-regime friend for dangerous anti-state terrorism. Anatol is condemned to death, then has his sentence commuted to life imprisonment. None of these political events is shown; we learn of them only through their repercussions as experienced by Bartodziej.

After the exposure of Stalin's crimes in 1956, the repentant Bartodziej—now a psychotic wreck—retires to the provinces and is haunted by Anatol's ghost, called forth by his guilty conscience. Once Anatol is amnestied and fully rehabilitated in 1964, Bartodziej seeks him out, convinced that he must be punished for the crime of betraying his friend if moral order is to be restored to the world.

Bartodziej accordingly discloses that he was the one who denounced Anatol, sure that this will call forth retribution—but the flesh-and-blood Anatol refuses to sentence his executioner. The betrayer continues to pursue abstractions, hoping to impose ideological meaning on reality, while the martyred Anatol wants only to live well as compensation for the years lost in jail.

When Bartodziej invokes the spirit of Stalin, Anatol is swept up in a ritual that parodies the invocation of the spirits of the ancestors in *Forefathers' Eve*, Mickiewicz's great romantic drama. In an unexpected reversal, Anatol is rendered mute and paralyzed by a stroke. It is not the victimizer, but the victim who is punished—for the second time.

In the third act, the self-centered Bartodziej, again withdrawn into his shell, is compelled by his wife to behave like a human being (even if he is not one) and care for his helpless victim, who, deserted by his young lover, has become a zombie. Nothing but a puppet himself, Bartodziej pushes the crippled Anatol around in a wheelchair and reads him "The Spirit of History," a poem by Czesław Miłosz, the exiled poet whose works were banned in the 1960s.

Strangely imbalanced and awkward in structure by the standards of Mrożek's earlier abstract fables, *Portrait* unfolds less as a logical plot than as a recurring series of remembered images and musical sound motifs evoked from a buried fund of remembrance, nostalgia, yearning, and fearful apprehension about past and future. Mixing historical circumstances with myth and ritual, the play is obsessive in its grappling with guilt and punishment, wasted lives, blind ideological dedication, human isolation, and need to heal.

Critical opinion on *Portrait* has been divided. The prevailing view is that it is a flawed but major work because of its powerful emotional impact and the important themes that it develops: betrayal, guilt and punishment, fatality, and the spirit of history.

Portrait is a play with an ambivalent moral. The lesson, contained in the final act, might seem to be that we must replace abstract ideology by a simple trust in everyday realia, the fundamental routines and rituals of daily existence. "Life doesn't ask about abstractions and ideals. Life is made up of concrete things," Anatol declares. But Bartodziej's attempts to overcome guilt and lessen the pain of their wrecked lives produces no healing. Victim and victimizer are inseparably linked as the denouncer becomes the nurse of the betrayed.

A play about calling up the dead and exorcising ghosts, *Portrait* is an epitaph for communist Poland and its human casualties, an attempted reckoning with the past, and an assessment of the immense damage done by almost half a century of communism. As an obituary in advance for communism two years before it died, *Portrait* challenges the rationalizations used to justify submission to historical necessity and protests against history itself as a modern tragic fatality.

The final words heard in the play are the street peddler's traditional cry, "Pots to mend," coming from offstage. But Bartodziej and Anatol are beyond mending, as is their world. Unable to reach any settlement with the past, they can create no future, but remain caught in an entropic closed circle. There are still gaping holes in their psyches and in the life of the nation.

The three major premieres of *Portrait* were: December 1987, Teatr Polski, Warsaw, directed by Kazimierz Dejmek; January 1988, Teatr Stary, Cracow, directed by Jerzy Jarocki; and October 1988, Moscow Art Theatre, directed by Valentin Kozmenko-Delinde.

PORTRAIT

Sławomir Mrożek

Translated by Jacek Laskowski

CHARACTERS

(in order of appearance)

BARTODZIEJ—approaching 40 years of age

OCTAVIA—age 43

ANATOL—approaching 40 years of age

PSYCHIATRIST—a woman age 30

ANNABELLE—age 20

The quotations come from Czesław Miłosz's poems: "The Spirit of History" and "The Plain."

ACT ONE

SCENE 1

MAN'S VOICE IN THE DARK: I loved you. Both my present and my future were in you and I could not forgive my past that you were not in it. Even if at that time my past was brief. I was young when you came into my life. Yes, but not a mere child. Not an infant who opens his eyes for the very first time and sees you right away. The childhood I had without you was like a sin that could not be redeemed.

Yes, I know, I wasn't the only one who loved you. Was I jealous? You were loved by so many it was impossible to be jealous. How can one be jealous of the whole world? Yes, I wanted to fight the entire world. Not to win you: to win the whole world for you. I wanted to lay the world at your feet. It seemed natural to me that others should love you. Anyone who didn't love you, who was capable of not loving you, was a monster, an inhuman creature unworthy of human consideration. People like that I could have . . . I could have . . . You know who I'm talking about.

My strength came from you. Before I met you, I was nothing. Nothing to others, nothing to myself. My love for you gave me strength. With you by my side I felt strong, wise, and beautiful. Almost beautiful. Does that make you smile?

How well I know your smile. An ordinary smile, it seemed, and yet so mysterious. The smile of a being watched by others but looking at no one; yet without even looking at me, a being who sees only me. Or did I imagine it? Am I still only imagining it? What wouldn't I give to find out for sure. And even now, when we're alone at last, when you are only with me, and there's only me with you—you listen, but do you hear me when I speak to you? No one can listen like you, no one understands me like you do, and yet . . . Is there not a part of you, some area within you from which I'm excluded? A thought which is distant from me, a feeling not meant for me. Is it just a thought, just a feeling, or is it something else, something I can't describe? Is everything slipping away from me, or is it just a part of something else? Maybe it's simply my imagination, a fever, the hallucinations of a poor madman. Are you listening to me?

I do so want some certainty. Who are you? Just an illusion of mine or the truest of truths. Am I only imagining that you are here with me, that you really exist, you and only you, that the rest is just illusion? I'm confused and lost. How inadequate I was for you, how weak I am without you, how confused have all my paths become. You're smiling.

Don't deny it, I can sense it, your smile is with me wherever I am, I don't have to be with you for that smile, that damned smile of yours, to be with me! Say something to me . . . (*Pause.*) And stop smiling! (*Pause.*) No, don't stop. Forgive me, I didn't mean . . . No, not damned—beloved, desired. It's not the smile that follows me, it's I who chase after the smile, always . . . I chase after it and want to catch up with it hoping that one day I'll succeed. Your beloved, sweet smile . . . My salvation and my destruction.

Pause.

Are you angry with me? No, of course not. That would be too great a joy for me, it would mean you'd noticed me. Do you notice me? Do you know that I exist, do you notice that? The confessions and questions are mine, but yours is the silence. Well? I'm listening. (*Pause.*) Ah, yes. Of course. Nothing. Just silence.

Pause.

You're right. I don't know what's happening to me. I'm sorry. But then you know why I'm so . . . You understand . . . You understand everything. (*Pause.*) Stop that! Say something! I want to talk to you, that's why I've come here, after all these years . . . Somehow we've got to explain it all to each other once and for all. It's high time we did! I can't go on like this any longer. Understand? I can't! And once and for all stop that smile of yours—look at me, look at me!

Lights full on. The speaker, BARTODZIEJ, *is wearing a gabardine coat, and he's holding a suitcase in one hand and an umbrella in the other. He is standing with his back to the audience, and he is speaking to a portrait which is hung high up, facing the audience. It's a portrait of Joseph Stalin. Simultaneously, the sound of fanfares and choirs is heard. Blackout.*

SCENE 2

BARTODZIEJ *and* OCTAVIA *are sitting close to the front of the stage, facing the audience, quite a distance from each other. They both have a small lamp next to them.* OCTAVIA *is reading an illustrated magazine. The atmosphere is that of a peaceful, marital evening.*

BARTODZIEJ: Rabbits.

OCTAVIA: What?

BARTODZIEJ: We'll breed rabbits. You've got to do something in life. It seems to me that rabbits would be the most suitable. They have the capacity to cheer one up. Often a man will be sitting exhausted, or depressed, life's treating him badly, he's tortured by memories in other words, he is not in good heart. He looks and sees a rabbit. Which is jumping about and wagging its tail. That makes a man happier right away. (*Pause.*) I know what you're going to say: a rabbit's tail is small so a rabbit cannot wag its tail. That's what they say, that's how the case is presented, and that's what's been generally accepted. But as far as I'm concerned, it does wag its tail, regardless of public opinion. I know the claim that the phenomenon of a rabbit wagging its tail is only an illusion probably stemming from the mobility of the rest of the body. A rabbit wags, so to speak, the whole of its body and so, according to the scientists, also wags its tail in a manner of speaking. But only our experiences, which is as much as to say our inner lives, matter. I do believe there's something banging.

OCTAVIA: The neighbor's window.

BARTODZIEJ: There it goes again.

OCTAVIA: They left it open.

BARTODZIEJ: Rabbits are kept in cages, two in each cage is best. Their number increases sharply, however, if the units at our disposal are of different sexes. Therefore it is not long before the problem ceases to be one of individual importance and becomes a social problem. We are faced by society and its structures. I think my throat's hurting.

OCTAVIA: Let's see.

BARTODZIEJ *stands up, leans over toward* OCTAVIA, *opens his mouth.* OCTAVIA *looks at his throat.*

OCTAVIA: I can't see anything.

BARTODZIEJ: Are you sure?

OCTAVIA: Your throat's quite clear and your tongue's normal.

BARTODZIEJ: I had angina.

OCTAVIA: Seven years ago.

BARTODZIEJ: As long ago as that?

BARTODZIEJ *returns to his place.*

BARTODZIEJ: Rabbits don't have political parties. In that respect a comparison with human societies is inappropriate and observations made in that field are not applicable to human societies. Nevertheless one must not draw premature conclusions. For one must not rule out that with continued development and more detailed research, rabbit society will not turn out to be as highly organized as human society. Indeed, all my efforts will be directed toward this research. And if I discover that politics play the same role in the life of rabbits as they play in that of human beings, I shall wipe them out immediately, make myself a rabbit-skin coat, and start breeding cockroaches. How long have I been talking about these rabbits?

OCTAVIA: Five years.

BARTODZIEJ: That's right. Five years. But that doesn't mean one shouldn't have specific plans for the future. Mind you, they've flown by . . . Think I can smell something.

OCTAVIA: What?

BARTODZIEJ: Something burning. There's something burning, isn't there?

OCTAVIA: Where?

BARTODZIEJ: In the loft, I think.

OCTAVIA: Go and have a look, then.

BARTODZIEJ: I can't. Don't you remember how I fell down the stairs?

OCTAVIA: Six years ago.

BARTODZIEJ: I still fell.

OCTAVIA: Don't go, then.

BARTODZIEJ: But what if it is burning? When did it burn last?

OCTAVIA: Five years ago.

BARTODZIEJ: Exactly. As long ago as that . . . It's flown by . . . It's curious how the longer something lasts, the quicker it goes by. But to go back to the rabbits.

Rabbits must be treated gently. At least they must be in the first phase. In later phases, too. If one notices that the affective vibrations one is sending out in the direction of the rabbits are getting weaker then one must use an amplifier. You do that to protect them from shock, which is particularly painful for small creatures. One has to accustom them slowly and gradually to the falling-off of our affection toward them. An over-sudden disillusionment could be a shock they may not survive. That's what every beginning breeder ought to remember. Where are my socks?

OCTAVIA: Which ones?

BARTODZIEJ: The woolen, check ones.

OCTAVIA: I washed them and put them in the wardrobe.

BARTODZIEJ: I found them in the hall. (*Pause.*) On the floor in the hall.

OCTAVIA: You must have thrown them there.

BARTODZIEJ: They'd been worn. (*Pause.*) I said: they'd been worn.

OCTAVIA: You wear socks, so they've been worn.

BARTODZIEJ: I did not wear them.

OCTAVIA: Neither did I.

BARTODZIEJ: Are you trying to tell me that there are ghosts walking about in my socks? (*Pause.*) If we're not breeding rabbits today, it means we'll not be breeding rabbits tomorrow. That's why everyone who does not consider himself to be a breeder, or is even proud of not being one, should show maximum restraint. We should only regard the balance of our life to be final when all the sums have been done. That is not an observation from which only breeders in the strictest sense of the word might benefit. It is intended for a more general audience, though it does include breeders. (*Pause.*) Did you use my shaving brush?

OCTAVIA: What would I use your shaving brush for?

BARTODZIEJ: To shave.

OCTAVIA: Well, really!

BARTODZIEJ: Today someone used my shaving brush to shave. Before I did.

OCTAVIA: Who?

BARTODZIEJ: Maybe I did. Maybe I absentmindedly shaved myself twice. I doubt it, though.

OCTAVIA: I don't. (*Pause.*)

BARTODZIEJ: What's for dinner tomorrow?

OCTAVIA: Macaroni.

BARTODZIEJ: Is that all?

OCTAVIA: You've always liked it.

BARTODZIEJ: True, but it's a little frugal . . .

OCTAVIA: Why? Did you want to invite someone?

BARTODZIEJ: Who knows? Who knows . . . ?

SCENE 3

BARTODZIEJ, ANATOL, PSYCHIATRIST *in a psychiatrist's consulting room. A metallic, clinical desk, cupboard, three chairs and a couch—everything clinical and metallic. The* PSYCHIATRIST, *an attractive thirty-year-old woman is behind the desk, and* BARTODZIEJ *and* ANATOL *are sitting in front of her.*

PSYCHIATRIST: Excuse me, but I don't understand. Which of you gentlemen is the patient?

BARTODZIEJ *and* ANATOL (*together*): He is!

PSYCHIATRIST: In that case I must ask you to wait your turn. One of you gentlemen will have to wait outside.

BARTODZIEJ: You heard what the doctor said. You're to go outside and I'll speak to the doctor. (*Pause.*) He doesn't want to go.

PSYCHIATRIST: Please decide who's first between you.

ANATOL: You go. And I'll talk.

BARTODZIEJ: He's stubborn.

ANATOL: I'm not stubborn.

BARTODZIEJ (*to* PYSCHIATRIST): You can see how stubborn he is, can't you?

PSYCHIATRIST: I'd like each of you gentlemen to speak for yourselves, please.

BARTODZIEJ: He can't speak for himself.

ANATOL: I can.

BARTODZIEJ: There you go. He's stubbornly insists on speaking, but he doesn't know what he's saying.

ANATOL: I do.

BARTODZIEJ: You don't. You haven't a clue.

ANATOL: I have!

BARTODZIEJ: You can see, can't you, doctor?

ANATOL: Don't believe him, doctor. He keeps imagining that I don't exist.

BARTODZIEJ: You do exist, but not the way you think you do.

PSYCHIATRIST: How long have you gentlemen known each other?

BARTODZIEJ: I used to go to school with him, but he didn't go to school with me.

PSYCHIATRIST: That's very interesting. (*To* ANATOL.) Is that true?

ANATOL: In part.

PSYCHIATRIST: Very, very interesting. So you're friends, are you?

ANATOL: He doesn't like me.

BARTODZIEJ: That's not the point!

ANATOL: But he can't manage without me.

BARTODZIEJ: That depends.

PSYCHIATRIST (*to* ANATOL): What about you?

ANATOL: Like him? If you only knew . . .

PSYCHIATRIST: But can you manage without him?

BARTODZIEJ: Ho-ho-ho!

PSYCHIATRIST (*to* BARTODZIEJ): Please stop interrupting. (*To* ANATOL.) Do you feel a kind of dependence on your friend?

ANATOL: He's no friend. He's a pig.

PSYCHIATRIST: Your acquaintance, then. Do you?

ANATOL: I don't feel. I have to.

BARTODZIEJ: Of course he has to.

PSYCHIATRIST: I've changed my mind. You'll both stay here. Use group therapy.

BARTODZIEJ: I'm not a group. I'm here independently.

ANATOL: So am I.

BARTODZIEJ: No, you're not. You're here with me.

PSYCHIATRIST: I get the impression that you are very close to each other.

ANATOL: I can't deny that.

PSYCHIATRIST: There's a very tight and mutual psychological dependency at work here.

BARTODZIEJ: That's how it's turned out, but . . .

PSYCHIATRIST: Even a physical dependency.

ANATOL: Only to some extent.

BARTODZIEJ: And not a mutual one, either. Not at all.

PSYCHIATRIST: Do you gentlemen . . . live together?

BARTODZIEJ: What do you mean by that?

PSYCHIATRIST: As a doctor I must know everything.

BARTODZIEJ (*to* ANATOL): She thinks we're . . .

ANATOL: That we are . . . ?

BARTODZIEJ: Yes. You and me.

ANATOL: Well, I never!

PSYCHIATRIST: There's no need to be embarrassed. It's a classic case of a guilt complex resulting from the influence of the Judeo-Christian culture. But there's no need for that, no need at all. Psychiatry doesn't have these prejudices.

BARTODZIEJ: No, doctor. We are not living together.

PSYCHIATRIST: What, really?

BARTODZIEJ: Well, I should know, shouldn't I? (*To* ANATOL.) Perhaps you . . . ?

ANATOL: Out of the question.

BARTODZIEJ (*to* PSYCHIATRIST): See? Out of the question.

PSYCHIATRIST: Maybe subconsciously, then.

BARTODZIEJ (*to* ANATOL): What do you think? Maybe subconsciously you're . . . ?

ANATOL: Not me. What about you?

BARTODZIEJ (*to* PYSCHIATRIST): No, doctor. Not even subconsciously.

PSYCHIATRIST: Nevertheless, the mere fact that you both deny it would suggest . . . A typical repression of the subconscious.

BARTODZIEJ: Unfortunately, the answer's no.

PSYCHIATRIST: Unfortunately? Did you say "unfortunately"?

BARTODZIEJ: I did.

PSYCHIATRIST: So there is a tendency there after all?

BARTODZIEJ: I said "unfortunately" because if it was just that everything would be quite straightforward. We wouldn't have come here.

PSYCHIATRIST: Then what's it all about?

BARTODZIEJ: The fact is that he . . .

ANATOL: Not me, you!

BARTODZIEJ: Me?

ANATOL: Yes, you!

BARTODZIEJ: No!

PSYCHIATRIST: Please calm down! I must ascertain all the facts in an orderly fashion and from the very beginning. Please tell me what the problem is. (*To* BARTODZIEJ.) You first.

BARTODZIEJ: Do you want me to take my clothes off?

PSYCHIATRIST: No. Just loosen your collar.

BARTODZIEJ *lies down on the couch.* PSYCHIATRIST *moves a chair close to the couch and sits next to* BARTODZIEJ *with a notebook in her hand.* ANATOL *takes another chair and places it next to* BARTODZIEJ *and the* PSYCHIATRIST.

PSYCHIATRIST: No! You sit there!

ANATOL *moves the chair to where the* PSYCHIATRIST *is indicating, far from the couch. He sits down.*

PSYCHIATRIST: Go ahead. I'm listening.

BARTODZIEJ: Well, it was like this. To begin with, everything went well. He set fire to my house.

PSYCHIATRIST (*writing*): Your house.

BARTODZIEJ: Twice. Once in the cellar, and once in the loft.

PSYCHIATRIST (*writing*): . . . cellar . . . Just a minute. Who set fire to it?

BARTODZIEJ: He did.

PSYCHIATRIST: What do you mean—set fire to it?

BARTODZIEJ: What I say. Strictly speaking, he tried to set fire to it. He failed, but I don't hold that against him. It's not the fire that's important, it's the principle. His intentions were good.

PSYCHIATRIST: Just a minute, please.

PSYCHIATRIST *gets up, goes to the desk, finds a pill, swallows it, drinks it down with some water from a jug, returns to her place.*

PSYCHIATRIST: Please go on.

BARTODZIEJ: It was only later he started to be spiteful.

PSYCHIATRIST: Really? What did he do?

BARTODZIEJ: Nothing.

PSYCHIATRIST: Nothing?

BARTODZIEJ: Made banging noises, or stole my socks, that's all. Piffling little things. And he's still doing nothing. Just to spite me.

PSYCHIATRIST: You'd rather he'd set fire to your house?

BARTODZIEJ: That's what he's for.

PSYCHIATRIST (*to* ANATOL): Is it true you set fire to his house?

ANATOL: Yes.

PSYCHIATRIST: And is it also true that you've stopped setting fire to his house?

ANATOL: Yes.

PSYCHIATRIST: Why?

ANATOL: Because I don't care anymore.

PSYCHIATRIST: Why did you do it in the first place?

BARTODZIEJ: There's no point asking him. He won't explain anything.

PSYCHIATRIST: Why not?

BARTODZIEJ: Because he's a ghost.

PSYCHIATRIST: Just a minute, please.

PSYCHIATRIST *gets up and walks toward the exit door.* ANATOL *stands up and bars her way.* PSYCHIATRIST *turns and comes back to her chair.* ANATOL *sits down.*

PSYCHIATRIST: I'm very pleased that you gentlemen came to see me. This is an extraordinarily interesting case. Really. Very.

BARTODZIEJ: You think we're crazy, don't you?

PSYCHIATRIST: Of course not! What I meant was that this case is very interesting from a scientific point of view. It's a most instructive experience. (*To* ANATOL.) So you're a ghost, are you?

ANATOL: In a manner of speaking.

PSYCHIATRIST: I see. (*To* BARTODZIEJ.) And what about you?

BARTODZIEJ: Not me. I'm perfectly normal.

PSYCHIATRIST: Of course you are, of course you are. You are perfectly normal. And what's your connection with this gentleman?

BARTODZIEJ: He appears. To me.

PSYCHIATRIST: Since when?

BARTODZIEJ: Since about two years ago.

PSYCHIATRIST: Let's go back to the arson. Did you catch him red-handed?

BARTODZIEJ: What do you mean?

PSYCHIATRIST: Did you see him set fire to your house? Was he visible when the fire was burning?

BARTODZIEJ: No, he wasn't.

PSYCHIATRIST: So how do you know it was he who set the fire?

BARTODZIEJ: Who else?

PSYCHIATRIST: Perhaps you did it yourself.

BARTODZIEJ: I'm not a madman—I'm not likely to set fire to my own house. Besides, he's admitted it.

PSYCHIATRIST: Apart from the arson, were there any other acts of aggression?

BARTODZIEJ: He tried to suffocate me.

PSYCHIATRIST: Often?

BARTODZIEJ: Nearly every night. Once he very nearly succeeded in strangling me—I couldn't breathe for a week.

PSYCHIATRIST: An asthmatic attack. What else?

BARTODZIEJ: He's pushed me down the stairs.

PSYCHIATRIST: Classic. And did you break anything?

BARTODZIEJ: Only once. My leg, I think.

PSYCHIATRIST: Excellent. Did you see him then? Strangling you, or pushing you? During the act of suffocation, or during the act of throwing you down the stairs, was he visible to you?

BARTODZIEJ: No, he wasn't. He strangled and pushed me in absentia.

PSYCHIATRIST: Very good. When was this?

BARTODZIEJ: A long time ago.

PSYCHIATRIST: How long?

BARTODZIEJ: It started about nine years ago. Maybe ten . . .

PSYCHIATRIST: And when did it stop?

BARTODZIEJ: It's difficult to say exactly when.

PSYCHIATRIST: Why is it difficult?

BARTODZIEJ: Because to start with it happened nearly every day, nearly every night, and then it happened less and less frequently until it stopped altogether.

PSYCHIATRIST: So when was the last time you were asphyxiated, or pushed down the stairs?

BARTODZIEJ: I can't remember.

PSYCHIATRIST: Approximately.

BARTODZIEJ: Must be about seven years ago now.

PSYCHIATRIST: And it was only afterwards that you started seeing him?

BARTODZIEJ: Yes. But not right away.

PSYCHIATRIST: When was the first time you saw him?

BARTODZIEJ: Like I see him now, you mean?

PSYCHIATRIST: Yes.

BARTODZIEJ: Well, only when he came to dinner, really.

PSYCHIATRIST: Dinner. I see. And how did that happen?

BARTODZIEJ: I invited him.

PSYCHIATRIST: Of course you did. But what happened exactly?

BARTODZIEJ: I told my wife we ought to invite someone and I invited him.

PSYCHIATRIST: So you're married?

BARTODZIEJ: Yes.

PSYCHIATRIST: Since when?

BARTODZIEJ: Since 1953.

PSYCHIATRIST: And did your wife see him, too?

BARTODZIEJ: Of course not. She doesn't even know I invited him.

PSYCHIATRIST: But you said . . .

BARTODZIEJ: Only generally speaking. She listens to everything I tell her, but I don't tell her everything.

PSYCHIATRIST: I see. And could I talk to her?

BARTODZIEJ: No.

PSYCHIATRIST: Why not?

BARTODZIEJ: Because she'll only think I'm a madman. She worries about me enough as it is.

PSYCHIATRIST: To go back to this dinner. What did you have?

BARTODZIEJ: Macaroni.

PSYCHIATRIST: And was the dinner a success?

BARTODZIEJ: It was not. He was supposed to come at eight, and he didn't arrive till midnight. My wife had gone to bed and I was waiting for him. He dragged himself in wearing my dressing gown and my slippers. He crawled in, yawned, sat down on the sofa, and asked if there was a late-night program on television. And that was it.

PSYCHIATRIST: But he did come?

BARTODZIEJ: Yes. But he was late.

PSYCHIATRIST: And he spoke?

BARTODZIEJ: Yes, but what did he say!?

PSYCHIATRIST: Let's re-cap. First he committed acts of aggression against you during which he was invisible. Then the acts of aggression stopped, but you started to see him. Is that right?

BARTODZIEJ: Yes.

PSYCHIATRIST: In other words you experienced these attacks of asphyxiation and feelings of panic at the head of the stairs less and less frequently until they stopped altogether. But then you started to have hallucinations, neuro-optical phenomena combined with acoustic delusions. Between the disappearance of the asthmatic attacks and feelings of panic and the appearance of the hallucinations, there was a break, or, in other words, a transitional phase.

BARTODZIEJ: That's what it looks like.

PSYCHIATRIST: The first phase started nine, or maybe ten, years ago and lasted some two years. The second, or transitional, stage started seven years ago and lasted the longest, that is to say, about five years. During the second stage you did not experience any particular indispositions other than a slight persecution mania, moderate aural delusions, a tiny motorial disorder, a certain disturbance of time-space coordination, and an imperceptible weakening of memory. Only in the third stage did hallucinations and powerful aural delusions begin. And this third stage has continued to this day.

BARTODZIEJ: That's absolutely right.

PSYCHIATRIST: Not quite. There's something I don't understand. But before we go into that . . . How would you describe your relations since the time of that—let's call it—dinner?

BARTODZIEJ: Unrelieved tedium.

PSYCHIATRIST: You don't feel any attacks of panic any more?

BARTODZIEJ: None at all! He's even stopped banging. He just drifts about the house, even in the daytime, and does nothing. There's no entertainment to be had from him, just minor worries. He behaves like an ordinary lodger, except he doesn't pay any rent. Now he's taken to shaving with my razor and wearing my socks. He sits between us at mealtimes, and he spends whole evenings reading the paper when my wife's knitting and I'm occupied with my hobby.

PSYCHIATRIST: And what is your hobby?

BARTODZIEJ: I like looking out of the window.

PSYCHIATRIST: But you can't see anything out of the window in the evenings.

BARTODZIEJ: That's why I like it. But what's most irritating is that he never folds the paper back the way he found it, but is always throwing it down any old way. Then I have to arrange the pages in numerical order. And generally speaking he's slovenly and careless. He scratches himself in front of people. He yawns . . . Nothing amuses him and he's not interested in anything. You have no idea how boring he is, doctor.

PSYCHIATRIST: Do you have any conversations with him?

BARTODZIEJ: Only now and again these days.

PSYCHIATRIST: What about?

BARTODZIEJ: The weather, mostly.

PSYCHIATRIST: That's what I can't understand. If there's been an intensification of hallucinations, why has there been a deterioration of the internal monologue?

BARTODZIEJ: Because we've discussed everything and now there's nothing left to talk about.

PSYCHIATRIST: But in the normal development of this illness, the opposite should be true.

BARTODZIEJ: But it's not me who's ill, it's him.

PSYCHIATRIST: Is he?

BARTODZIEJ: I'm just bored. That's not an illness. But he's suffering from profound apathy and that's why I've brought him to you, doctor. I thought maybe a psychiatrist could help.

PSYCHIATRIST: This is the first time I've come across a case like this.

BARTODZIEJ: What? You've never seen a case of apathy before?

PSYCHIATRIST: Up to a certain point everything is clear. As a result of some circumstances, which we still have to explain, there's been a strong projection of your problem which I still don't know about. This projection has turned into a fixation, or an obsession. You see and hear someone who, in reality, does not exist, but your mental processes have taken on his shape. Your case is difficult, but not incurable. (*To* ANATOL.) We'll try to make you disappear.

BARTODZIEJ: But I don't want him to disappear. I just want him to behave like . . . like . . .

PSYCHIATRIST: Like?

BARTODZIEJ: Well, differently.

PSYCHIATRIST: You want him to continue choking, kicking, and persecuting you in every conceivable fashion. Is that it?

BARTODZIEJ: Something like that.

PSYCHIATRIST: Everything's beginning to come together. It is your conscience.

BARTODZIEJ: Just a bit, yes.

PSYCHIATRIST: Sometime in your life you committed an act of which you're ashamed. This happened more than ten years ago, let's say eleven, or maybe even longer ago than that. And it must have been something drastic to cause a psychiatric illness of such intensity. The only chance of a cure is if you tell me what happened all those years ago.

BARTODZIEJ: Is that necessary?

PSYCHIATRIST: You'll never get rid of him otherwise.

BARTODZIEJ: You're immoral.

PSYCHIATRIST: What do you mean by that?

BARTODZIEJ: You want to rid me of my conscience? You want me to forget the terrible thing I did? What are you trying to make me do?

PSYCHIATRIST: It is my duty to . . .

BARTODZIEJ: You want me to do something disgusting and then feel good about it? First a man murders another man, his own father, for instance, then sleeps with his mother or I don't know what else, and then he's supposed to feel all right, as if nothing had happened? Nice and healthy? What are you driving at? What are you up to?

PSYCHIATRIST: I am a psychiatrist and it's my duty to . . .

BARTODZIEJ: I won't tell you anything. I'm not such a bastard as to not feel that I'm a bastard. And I won't let anyone take the only thing I've got left: my conscience.

PSYCHIATRIST: Science is above morality. It's morality that's the object of scientific inquiry, not the other way around. We scientists examine morality scientifically.

BARTODZIEJ: I'm not talking about science, or morality, I'm talking about myself. I am a living human being, doctor, not a scientific object. And I want to feel that I'm alive. You won't make anything scientific out of me. Get yourself a rabbit for your science, but I wouldn't recommend that, either. Even a rabbit is too much alive.

PSYCHIATRIST: Your resistance is a typical symptom which always appears at the start of treatment and is in direct proportion to the intensity of the sickness. The more severe the case is, the more the patient resists the intervention of a psychiatrist. Your behavior is absolutely correct.

BARTODZIEJ: Really?

PSYCHIATRIST: Yes, really.

BARTODZIEJ (to ANATOL): Shall we demolish something?

ANATOL: We could.

BARTODZIEJ: The cabinet?

ANATOL: Not enough. It would be better to smash the table, or break the chairs.

BARTODZIEJ: That'll be hard. They're metal.

ANATOL: It can be done.

PSYCHIATRIST: If you gentlemen demolish my office it will only prove that I am right. A patient's aggression toward his psychiatrist is the best proof that the diagnosis which the psychiatrist has made is correct.

BARTODZIEJ: We'll ignore it, then.

ANATOL: Pity.

BARTODZIEJ: You heard what she said. Why should she be right?

ANATOL: Let's go, then.

PSYCHIATRIST: We'll be in touch, won't we?

BARTODZIEJ: Let's go, before I kill her.

SCENE 4

A table and two chairs. BARTODZIEJ *and* ANATOL *wearing identical dressing gowns are sitting at the table playing chess.*

BARTODZIEJ: Check! (*Pause.*) Did you hear what I said? Check.

ANATOL *moves a piece on the board.*

BARTODZIEJ: Take that back or I'll take your knight.

ANATOL *takes his move back, thinks. Pause. He moves another piece.*

BARTODZIEJ: You'd do better to protect yourself with the bishop.

ANATOL *makes the move suggested by* BARTODZIEJ.

BARTODZIEJ: Not with your rook! The bishop, I said. You've got a bishop on the other side there, look.

ANATOL *takes his rook move back and makes a move with a bishop. Pause.*

BARTODZIEJ: No, the rook's better.

ANATOL: Make your mind up.

BARTODZIEJ: Wait, let me think.

ANATOL: What do you need me for anyway?

BARTODZIEJ: Stop interrupting.

ANATOL: Why don't you play against yourself? It'd be simpler.

BARTODZIEJ: Yes, move the rook.

BARTODZIEJ *moves his opponent's piece.*

BARTODZIEJ: What were you saying?

ANATOL: There'd be no one to interrupt you if you played on your own. And I don't enjoy it anyway.

BARTODZIEJ: Don't you like chess?

ANATOL: I don't like pretense. You play on your own but you pretend you're playing against me. You move my pieces. Why don't you just play against yourself, honestly and openly, and stop pretending?

BARTODZIEJ: Because playing against yourself is not really playing. You need an opponent.

ANATOL: That's what I thought.

BARTODZIEJ: There's got to be two for it to be a game.

ANATOL: But why play?

BARTODZIEJ: What else can I do? I'm playing chess with you because there's nothing else I can do with you anymore. We've got to do something during these evenings together.

ANATOL: Playing chess with your own conscience . . .

BARTODZIEJ: You don't like it? Well, then, beat me, bite me, torment me, by all means, that's what you're here for. But since you don't want to, stop complaining and play chess with me.

BARTODZIEJ (*contemplating the chess board*): No, the bishop's better. (*He moves the rook back and moves the bishop. Thinks.*) Tell me, why don't you torment me anymore?

ANATOL: Time, dear boy, time. Everything wears out in time, even conscience. You know that as well as anyone. To begin with I did try, but how long can one go on?

BARTODZIEJ: It has been a long time, that's true . . .

ANATOL: Conscience is a spiritual matter, but I'm acquiring substance as a result of repetition, I'm consolidating myself. When the spiritual hardens it becomes material and loses its spirituality. The more physical I am, the less ideal I become.

BARTODZIEJ: You don't need to tell me about that.

ANATOL: Then why are you surprised? It's been a year since I saw my reflection in the mirror for the first time.

BARTODZIEJ: And . . . ?

ANATOL: I was disillusioned. I thought I was better looking.

BARTODZIEJ: So did I.

ANATOL: Before that if I stood in front of the mirror, it was blank.

BARTODZIEJ: I always envied you that.

ANATOL: No need to anymore. Now I see myself. Which means I've finally materialized.

BARTODZIEJ: Thanks to me.

ANATOL: Thanks to you, but it doesn't alter the fact that I'm no longer a delusion of yours.

BARTODZIEJ: What about me?

ANATOL: That's your problem, not mine. The effect has become separated from the cause. It has assumed an individual existence. Do you know how much I weigh?

BARTODZIEJ: No.

ANATOL: A hundred and eighty-seven pounds.

BARTODZIEJ: As much as that?

ANATOL: Yes. And I've been putting on weight lately.

BARTODZIEJ: Are you sure?

ANATOL: I weigh myself every day now. And there's no doubt about it, I'm afraid. I'm putting on weight. I'm getting heavier and heavier.

BARTODZIEJ: Because you don't do anything. You take no exercise. If you were to beat me, torment me, bite me . . .

ANATOL: Layoff that biting, will you? I exist sufficiently independently to have my own views.

BARTODZIEJ: And according to your views you no longer have to do your duty. You don't have to . . .

ANATOL: I know, I know: torment, bite, and so on and so forth! But then, what's it for? Why do you want it?

BARTODZIEJ: What a stupid question. I deserve it. For moral reasons.

ANATOL: I know. I heard. You spoke beautifully about morality at the doctor's. About how conscience is essential to you for moral reasons. You were magnificently outraged when she wanted to cure you of your conscience. I listened to your peroration and I thought to myself: that speech is much too pretty.

BARTODZIEJ: I spoke the truth.

ANATOL: But was it your truth? I'm beginning to wonder if you don't perhaps need me for something else as well. Maybe you need me just for that something else . . .

BARTODZIEJ: And what would that be?

ANATOL: It's quite straightforward: for something to do. To have a pastime, a conviction that something in life still matters. To feel something, to think something, to be afraid of something, to miss something . . . In other words, to stop yourself getting bored.

BARTODZIEJ: That's reductionism.

ANATOL: It's just a suspicion I've got.

BARTODZIEJ: You think I've nothing better to do than talk to you?

ANATOL: You haven't. Not anymore. Everything's gone: youth, ambitions, career, love . . . What's left? Just me.

BARTODZIEJ: You are a very vicious conscience.

ANATOL: Don't confuse me with nostalgia. And since we're on the subject of love, why did you love him so much in those days?

BARTODZIEJ: That was a long time ago.

ANATOL: Agreed. But why? What did you see in him?

BARTODZIEJ: I wasn't alone.

ANATOL: That doesn't excuse you. Was it the moustache? It's true, he did have a nice moustache, but that's no reason.

BARTODZIEJ: It wasn't the whiskers, it was the idea. He was the personification of an idea.

ANATOL: And you couldn't live without an idea?

BARTODZIEJ: Not then—no. (*Pause.*) At least, that's what I thought.

ANATOL: Exactly. You always needed something from outside, something ready-made, some ready-to-wear suit. You put it on and there you have it, and you feel really good right away. You can't sew it yourself. (*Pause.*) Or maybe you were missing something? A limb, perhaps? Maybe you needed an artificial limb. (*Pause.*) If it wasn't an idea, then it was a career you needed, and best of all a career with an idea.

BARTODZIEJ: No, it wasn't for a career.

ANATOL: But somehow it fit together, didn't it? The one with the other. That love of yours paid off.

BARTODZIEJ: I really did love him!

ANATOL: And is that why you denounced your best friend? (*Pause.*) As it is, he was quite lucky. He'll never find out who put him six feet under. The denunciation was discreet. (*Pause.*) You condemned him to death.

BARTODZIEJ: Not me.

ANATOL: That was the result.

BARTODZIEJ: No, that's not what I wanted.

ANATOL: But that is how it panned out, isn't it? You knew only too well what the consequences would be, what those times were like.

BARTODZIEJ: No. I mean, I did know but . . .

ANATOL: . . . but knowing, you didn't really know. And you're supposed to be intelligent. It's all right, I'm not accusing you, I'm too old for that. I'm asking out of sheer curiosity, that's all.

BARTODZIEJ: Ask whatever you want.

ANATOL: I don't want to anymore. I'm going to sleep.

BARTODZIEJ: Wait!

ANATOL: Since putting on this weight I've become sluggish and sleepy.

BARTODZIEJ: Don't leave me alone.

ANATOL (*yawning*): Tough, dear boy, we're both growing old and so is our last mistress, Schizophrenia.

SCENE 5

BARTODZIEJ *is getting ready for a trip: an open suitcase, bags, etc. Upstage there is a screen.*

OCTAVIA: Your pills. Don't forget to take them.

BARTODZIEJ: No danger of that.

OCTAVIA: I don't mean your sleeping pills. I mean your stomach pills and your heart pills. I've written which ones you're to take when on this piece of paper. You won't forget, will you?

BARTODZIEJ: Of course I won't. (*He kisses her on the forehead.*) Thank you.

OCTAVIA: Where will you eat?

BARTODZIEJ: In a restaurant.

OCTAVIA: Restaurants are horrible.

BARTODZIEJ: It's only for two or three days.

OCTAVIA: That's long enough to get sick. Try to eat veal. And no sauces.

BARTODZIEJ: I'll do my best.

OCTAVIA: Promise?

BARTODZIEJ: Yes.

OCTAVIA: Avoid stews and minced meats, you never really know what's in them. It's best to steer clear of meat altogether. There must be some vegetarian restaurants there.

BARTODZIEJ: There should be.

OCTAVIA: It's best not to go to dairy bars. They're dirty.

BARTODZIEJ: I won't.

OCTAVIA: And be careful with sugar. You know you're not allowed sugar.

BARTODZIEJ: I'll be careful.

OCTAVIA: I'll make you some sandwiches for the journey.

SCENE 6

BARTODZIEJ *moves the screen aside, revealing* ANATOL *behind it. He's sitting on a chair, in his dressing gown and he's reading a newspaper.*

BARTODZIEJ: Aren't you ready yet? Our train leaves in an hour.

ANATOL: I'm not going with you.

BARTODZIEJ: What do you mean you're not . . .

ANATOL: I'm staying here.

BARTODZIEJ: Get dressed this minute!

ANATOL: Gently, gently does it. Don't shout. When I say I'm not going, I'm not going.

BARTODZIEJ: Why not?

ANATOL: Because I also deserve a—hush!

He uses the screen to hide ANATOL *as* OCTAVIA *enters.*

SCENE 7

OCTAVIA: Would you rather have ham or cheese?

BARTODZIEJ: Cheese. Ham.

OCTAVIA: Are you sure you don't want me to come with you?

BARTODZIEJ: I'd like you to come, I'd like it very much indeed, but I don't want you to be exposed to any unpleasantness. After all, the man's only just come out.

OCTAVIA: I'm not frightened.

BARTODZIEJ: But he may be. His kind are afraid of people.

OCTAVIA: And won't he be afraid of you?

BARTODZIEJ: We've known each other since we were children.

OCTAVIA: I wouldn't get in your way. I'd wait in the hotel.

BARTODZIEJ: We haven't seen each other for fifteen years.

OCTAVIA: But you'll go back to the hotel at night.

BARTODZIEJ: Conversations with old friends are best when they're at night.

OCTAVIA: I'll make them with margarine. It'll be better for you.

Exit OCTAVIA.

SCENE 8

BARTODZIEJ *draws the screen back.*

BARTODZIEJ: So what's up? Why don't you want to go?

ANATOL: Because I deserve an amnesty, too.

BARTODZIEJ: How do you know about the amnesty?

ANATOL: I read your newspapers.

BARTODZIEJ: The amnesty changes nothing.

ANATOL: It changes everything. The death sentence was never carried out.

BARTODZIEJ: But who could have known that? Nobody knew.

ANATOL: But we know now.

BARTODZIEJ: Only now.

ANATOL: Our man's alive.

BARTODZIEJ: But he was condemned.

ANATOL: He survived.

BARTODZIEJ: No thanks to me.

ANATOL: But you didn't kill him.

BARTODZIEJ: Quite by chance.

ANATOL: That's nothing to do with me.

BARTODZIEJ: So I'm innocent? Just because he survived?

ANATOL: I didn't say that.

BARTODZIEJ: Did I or did I not denounce him?

ANATOL: You did.

BARTODZIEJ: Was it or was it not through me that he was sentenced to death?

ANATOL: It was.

BARTODZIEJ: What else do you want, then?

ANATOL: Have it your own way . . .

BARTODZIEJ: Sshh!

BARTODZIEJ *hides* ANATOL *behind the screen.* OCTAVIA *enters, carrying some sandwiches.*

SCENE 9

OCTAVIA: And don't put them into your suitcase or keep them in your pockets because you'll make them all messy. Keep them separate.

BARTODZIEJ: I'll do that.

OCTAVIA: It must have been terrible for you.

BARTODZIEJ: It was.

OCTAVIA: Were you at the trial?

BARTODZIEJ: No. It wasn't public.

OCTAVIA: I thought maybe as a witness.

BARTODZIEJ: No. I wasn't involved.

OCTAVIA: I can imagine what his family went through.

BARTODZIEJ: His family was taken away long before then.

OCTAVIA: What about his wife?

BARTODZIEJ: He wasn't married.

OCTAVIA: His girlfriend, then.

BARTODZIEJ: He didn't have a girlfriend.

OCTAVIA: What do you mean? Why not?

BARTODZIEJ: He was too busy for all that.

OCTAVIA: Doing what?

BARTODZIEJ: Anti-state activity.

OCTAVIA: An idealist?

BARTODZIEJ: Perhaps. But it was called something different in those days.

OCTAVIA: Are you taking the umbrella?

BARTODZIEJ: I don't like umbrellas.

OCTAVIA: Take it. The weather's unsettled. Only don't lose it.

BARTODZIEJ: If I don't take it, I won't lose it.

OCTAVIA: I'll bring you the umbrella.

Exit OCTAVIA.

SCENE 10

BARTODZIEJ *draws the screen aside to reveal* ANATOL.

ANATOL: . . . so you can have any kind of pang of conscience you like, but count me out. I'm withdrawing. My specialty is murder, not minor crimes. I'm a royal, Shakespearean, mythological conscience. I'm king over all other types of conscience. And now I've been made to look ridiculous.

BARTODZIEJ: Come with me, I beg you.

ANATOL: Only murderers are haunted by ghosts and visions. Other criminals have to do without all that. Now that it's transpired there was no corpse, there can't be a ghost, either.

BARTODZIEJ: But maybe there . . .

ANATOL: I'm not going to bother myself with trivia.

BARTODZIEJ: You call fifteen years incarceration trivial?

ANATOL: I'm not saying it's trivial. But it's not the same as death.

BARTODZIEJ: Judas in the Olive Garden trivial?

ANATOL: There's been no corpse.

BARTODZIEJ: Don't leave me.

ANATOL: Give me a corpse and I'll stay with you.

BARTODZIEJ *hides* ANATOL *behind the screen.* OCTAVIA *enters, carrying an umbrella.*

SCENE 11

OCTAVIA: You will call, won't you?

BARTODZIEJ: Of course I will. As soon as I find a hotel.

OCTAVIA: I'll worry about you.

BARTODZIEJ (*embracing* OCTAVIA): I know, and I do appreciate it. Who would worry about me if you weren't here?

OCTAVIA: This is the first time you've gone alone since we've been together.

BARTODZIEJ: I must.

OCTAVIA: I know. I know, and I'm not complaining. But you do need looking after.

BARTODZIEJ: I'm not ill.

OCTAVIA: But you catch colds easily.

BARTODZIEJ: That's not serious, is it?

OCTAVIA: And you're on edge. You've always been on edge, even when I first knew you.

BARTODZIEJ: It's the age we live in.

OCTAVIA: It's not the age, it's your nerves. But that's what I liked about you. When I first saw you, I thought: he's so fragile.

BARTODZIEJ: I wasn't then, not yet.

OCTAVIA: You always were. Fragile, sensitive . . . I remember the first time you took my hand.

BARTODZIEJ: So do I.

OCTAVIA: No, you don't remember anything. It was on that small bridge.

BARTODZIEJ: Ah, the ferns.

OCTAVIA: It was raining.

BARTODZIEJ: And I didn't have an umbrella.

OCTAVIA: But I did.

BARTODZIEJ: November.

OCTAVIA: No, September.

BARTODZIEJ (*hums*): "Come to me and I will give you a flower of the fern . . . " That was popular then. And before that it was (*hums*): "We are building a new house, yet another brand new house . . ."

OCTAVIA: Have I changed a lot?

BARTODZIEJ: You? Not a bit.

OCTAVIA: You're lying. But it's nice of you to. Did you love anyone before me?

BARTODZIEJ: No. There was nobody before you.

OCTAVIA: Really?

BARTODZIEJ: Yes, really.

OCTAVIA: I don't believe you.

BARTODZIEJ: Then why ask?

OCTAVIA: Because I want to hear it.

BARTODZIEJ (*hums*): "Hey, you tractors, iron stallions . . ."

OCTAVIA: What tractors?

BARTODZIEJ: I got it mixed up. I meant something else. This, for instance (*hums*):

"Do you remember that autumn,
And that small hotel, 'Beneath the Roses,'
The old hall porter . . ."

OCTAVIA: He wasn't ancient.

BARTODZIEJ: He was seventy.

OCTAVIA: Who was?

BARTODZIEJ: It doesn't matter.

OCTAVIA: Ah, a joke. That means you're in a good mood, anyway.

BARTODZIEJ: Marvelous!

OCTAVIA: Are you glad you're going to see him?

BARTODZIEJ: Of course.

OCTAVIA: Maybe you're just glad you won't be seeing me for three days.

BARTODZIEJ: I'm absolutely delirious with joy.

OCTAVIA: It's lucky I know you're a habitual liar.

BARTODZIEJ: Not at all. Not habitual. I only lie from time to time.

OCTAVIA: That's a lie, too. I'll iron you a shirt.

Exit OCTAVIA

SCENE 12

BARTODZIEJ *draws the screen aside. There is no one behind it:* ANATOL *has disappeared.* BARTODZIEJ *calls to* OCTAVIA, *who is offstage.*

BARTODZIEJ: Octavia!

OCTAVIA (*off*): What?

BARTODZIEJ: Maybe you should come with me after all.

OCTAVIA (*off*): No. Go on your own.

BARTODZIEJ: But why not?

OCTAVIA: I don't want to be in the way.

ACT TWO

SCENE 1

BARTODZIEJ *is in a large apartment, not yet fully decorated. Instead of chairs there are pouffes, soft and modern foam rubber bricks, very uncomfortable to sit on. There is a telephone on the floor. A bar plentifully equipped with various alcoholic drinks. A three-branch candlestick with candles. Next to that there is a raincoat, a suitcase, and an umbrella.* ANNABELLE *enters.*

SCENE 2

ANNABELLE *has a towel around her head; she has just had a shower and is drying her hair with the towel.*

ANNABELLE: He's not in.

BARTODZIEJ: I'm sorry, I . . .

ANNABELLE: Did anyone call?

BARTODZIEJ: When will he be back?

ANNABELLE: He should be back now. He's late.

BARTODZIEJ: Maybe I should come back later, too.

ANNABELLE: Had you fixed a time?

BARTODZIEJ: Yes.

ANNABELLE: For when?

BARTODZIEJ: For ever.

ANNABELLE: You'd better wait, then.

BARTODZIEJ: I wouldn't want to get in your way. I had no idea . . .

ANNABELLE: You're not in my way. (*Pause.*) Why don't you sit down.

BARTODZIEJ *sits down.*

ANNABELLE: Would you like a drink?

BARTODZIEJ: If you'd be so kind . . .

ANNABELLE: Tea, coffee, or something else?

BARTODZIEJ: Coffee, if I may . . .

ANNABELLE *turns on the hi-fi, smiles at* BARTODZIEJ, *and goes out. The music from the hi-fi plays.*

SCENE 3

BARTODZIEJ *is still sitting. The phone rings.* BARTODZIEJ *stays seated. The phone stops ringing.* BARTODZIEJ *continues to sit. The phone rings again and rings persistently.* BARTODZIEJ *stands.* ANNABELLE *runs in and picks up the receiver.* BARTODZIEJ *sits down.*

SCENE 4

ANNABELLE (*on the phone*): Yes? No, he's not back yet. Soon. Of course I will. I'll make a note. (*She does so.*) No trouble.

ANNABELLE *replaces the receiver, gives* BARTODZIEJ *a friendly smile, and leaves.*

SCENE 5

The phone rings. BARTODZIEJ *sits.*

ANNABELLE (*off*): Please answer it!

BARTODZIEJ *stands up and answers the phone.*

BARTODZIEJ (*on the phone*): Yes. No. A friend. He's not back yet. Soon. Could I what? (*The music is hindering him somewhat.*) Yes, of course. I'll just make a note. (*Clumsily, he starts to prepare himself for making a note.*) Three-five . . . four-oh . . . Three what? Six? Yes, yes, I can hear you. When? Immediately? You mean today? Right away today? Yes, yes, three-six, I've got it down. I'll repeat it: five-nine-seven-three-five-four-oh. No? Three-six? Don't mention it.

BARTODZIEJ *replaces the receiver and sits down. The phone rings.* BARTODZIEJ *stands up and at the same time the phone stops ringing.* BARTODZIEJ *sits down.* ANNABELLE *enters.* BARTODZIEJ *stands up.*

SCENE 6

ANNABELLE *is carrying a large china mug.*

BARTODZIEJ: That was the . . .

ANNABELLE (*interrupting*): Coffee's ready! (*Hands him the mug.*) I forgot the sugar!

BARTODZIEJ: Thanks, I . . .

ANNABELLE *runs out.*

SCENE 7

BARTODZIEJ *stands with the mug in his hand. Eventually, be sits down.* ANNABELLE *runs in with a large paper bag containing sugar.* BARTODZIEJ *stands up.*

ANNABELLE: Spoon!

She runs out.

SCENE 8

BARTODZIEJ *stands with the mug in one hand, the bag of sugar in the other.* ANNABELLE *runs in with a coffee spoon.*

SCENE 9

ANNABELLE *pours one spoonful of sugar after another into* BARTODZIEJ's *mug.*

BARTODZIEJ: Thanks, I . . .

ANNABELLE (*adding more sugar*): Another spoonful?

BARTODZIEJ: No thanks, I don't take sugar.

ANNABELLE: But do sit down, please!

They both sit. BARTODZIEJ *puts bag of sugar down on the floor. The music from the hi-fi is slightly less aggressive.*

BARTODZIEJ: It was from some committee.

ANNABELLE: What was?

BARTODZIEJ: The phone call.

ANNABELLE: Which committee was it?

BARTODZIEJ: Something to do with cooperation with . . . with something. I've forgotten.

ANNABELLE: With what, though?

BARTODZIEJ: I arrived this morning, and I haven't had enough sleep. That's why. But I've made a note of the telephone number. I'll bring it to you.

He puts the mug on the floor and stands up to bring the note.

ANNABELLE: Please don't get up.

BARTODZIEJ *sits down.*

BARTODZIEJ: It was a very bad connection.

ANNABELLE: It must have been long distance. They'll call again. So when are the celebrations?

BARTODZIEJ: Celebrations?

ANNABELLE: The ceremony.

BARTODZIEJ: I'm sorry, but I don't think I understand.

ANNABELLE: You know: the anniversary. You are from the committee, aren't you?

BARTODZIEJ: What committee?

ANNABELLE: The anniversary committee.

BARTODZIEJ: Could we turn that off?

He points to the hi-fi.

ANNABELLE: Of course.

She gets up and turns the hi-fi off.

BARTODZIEJ: I'm sorry, but I've spent the whole night in a train. And I've got trouble with my hearing. At my age, you understand . . .

ANNABELLE: What do you mean? You're no older than Anatol.

BARTODZIEJ: No. We're the same age.

ANNABELLE: Do you know him personally?

BARTODZIEJ: Since childhood.

ANNABELLE: And I thought—so you're not from the committee?

BARTODZIEJ: No. I'm here in a private capacity. Quite private.

ANNABELLE: Well, I never . . . We've not had many private visits yet. Have you come from the provinces?

BARTODZIEJ: You can tell, can't you?

ANNABELLE: No, but you said something about a train.

BARTODZIEJ: Yes. Nowadays I live in a small town and . . .

ANNABELLE: Would you like some music?

BARTODZIEJ: No, thank you. I've been there a long time now and when I read in the papers . . .

ANNABELLE: And you came specially for his sake?

BARTODZIEJ: Yes, and . . .

ANNABELLE: He'll be very pleased.

BARTODZIEJ: I hope so.

ANNABELLE: Of course he will! So far we've only had official invitations. Celebrations, committees . . . Nothing private. More sugar?

BARTODZIEJ: No, thank you.

ANNABELLE: You're the first of his old friends who's come to visit him. Were you with him, too . . . when he . . .

BARTODZIEJ: No. No, I wasn't.

ANNABELLE: Not at all?

BARTODZIEJ: Not at all. I wasn't involved in any of that.

ANNABELLE: That makes it all the nicer of you to visit him. I thought that maybe you were one of those who . . .

BARTODZIEJ: Not me. So none of them have . . .

ANNABELLE: So far there's been no one.

BARTODZIEJ: That must mean there is no one . . .

ANNABELLE: I don't know anything about all that . . .

BARTODZIEJ: You're right. You can't remember any of it.

ANNABELLE: What do you do?

BARTODZIEJ: Nothing, really. To be honest, I'm retired.

ANNABELLE: Really? So early?

BARTODZIEJ: That's just the way it turned out.

ANNABELLE: But you must do something, surely?

BARTODZIEJ: I breed rabbits.

ANNABELLE: For export?·

BARTODZIEJ: Not really. Actually, I'm only intending to breed rabbits.

ANNABELLE: For industry?

BARTODZIEJ: No, as a private business.

ANNABELLE: Minks are better. But silver foxes are best of all.

BARTODZIEJ: I'm sure you're right. Could I ask . . .

ANNABELLE: Only they need a big investment to get started.

BARTODZIEJ: How long have you known Anatol?

ANNABELLE: Ten days.

BARTODZIEJ: Is that all?

ANNABELLE: I couldn't know him earlier.

BARTODZIEJ: Of course not. Of course not . . . But in that case how did you meet him?

ANNABELLE: Anatol's been undergoing treatment. And I used to work in the clinic.

BARTODZIEJ: And you don't any longer?

ANNABELLE: Somebody has to look after the home.

BARTODZIEJ: Yes, of course. You mean, you're a nurse . . .

ANNABELLE: No! I was in administration.

BARTODZIEJ: That's a good career, too.

ANNABELLE: What career? I was part-time and doing it as cover for a friend. Actually, I'm an actress.

BARTODZIEJ: Oh!

ANNABELLE: I've got a screen test on Monday.

BARTODZIEJ: That's wonderful. Wonderful . . .

ANNABELLE: Forget about the rabbits. Anatol will find you something. You're a very nice person.

BARTODZIEJ: Oh, I'd never have thought that.

ANNABELLE: Here he is!

ANATOL *enters.*

SCENE 10

ANATOL *is carrying a bunch of red roses in one hand and a plastic bag in the other.*

ANATOL: Guess what her little elephant has brought his little froggy . . .

He notices BARTODZIEJ *and stops.*

ANNABELLE: They're beautiful! (*Kisses* ANATOL *on the cheek, takes the roses and plastic bag from him, and looks into the bag.*) No! I don't believe it! (*Kisses* ANATOL *on the other cheek.*) You've got a visitor. (ANATOL *and* BARTODZIEJ *stand facing one another.*) He arrived this morning. He breeds rabbits . . . (*Pause.*) Don't you know each other? (ANATOL *takes a step toward* BARTODZIEJ *and stops.*) He told me he knew you . . . (*Pause.* ANATOL *stretches his hand out to* BARTODZIEJ. BARTODZIEJ *approaches him. They shake hands.*) I'll fetch a vase, then. (*Runs out.*)

SCENE 11

ANATOL: How did you find out?

BARTODZIEJ: From the newspapers.

ANATOL: Are they writing about me?

BARTODZIEJ: It was on the radio, too. And the television.

ANATOL: That's true.

BARTODZIEJ: Full rehabilitation.

ANATOL: That's right.

BARTODZIEJ: I'm very glad.

ANATOL: Don't mention it.

BARTODZIEJ: Not about the rehabilitation. Just that . . . (*Pause.*)

ANATOL: What?

BARTODZIEJ: That you're alive.

ANATOL: Looks like it.

BARTODZIEJ: A lot has changed.

ANATOL: That's true. A lot has.

BARTODZIEJ: I've changed, too.

ANATOL: You mean that you're . . . that you're no longer . . .

BARTODZIEJ: That's right, I'm not. (*Pause.*)

ANATOL: I couldn't have known that. Sit down.

They both sit down.

BARTODZIEJ: I withdrew. From everything. I live in the provinces now and I have nothing to do with politics.

ANATOL: And you want me to congratulate you on that?

BARTODZIEJ: No. That's not why I wanted to see you.

ANATOL: Why, then? To tell me you made a mistake and you regret it? And that you apologize? Have you come to tell me that there are no longer any differences of opinion between us? And that you want me to give you absolution?

BARTODZIEJ: No. I know it might look like that, but that's not what this is all about.

ANATOL: And to praise you for being an old, unbending reactionary?

BARTODZIEJ: No.

ANATOL: Why not? I can do it: I'm a martyr, a holy victim of the errors and distortions of the past.

BARTODZIEJ: No, that's not why I . . .

ANATOL: An official remission giver, that's me; I can give you remission for your sins, I can even bless you, why not? At your service day and night, be my guest.

BARTODZIEJ (*standing up*): I'll go now.

ANATOL: Where to?

BARTODZIEJ: I'll go back home. That'll be best.

ANATOL: Stay.

BARTODZIEJ: It'd be best if I didn't . . . I'm sorry.

ANATOL (*standing up*): No, I'm sorry.

BARTODZIEJ: I started like a fool and so it had to end stupidly. It's my fault.

ANATOL *puts his arm round* BARTODZIEJ *and leads him back.*

ANATOL: Nonsense. I'm just a bit on edge, that's all. I've had a hard day. Sit down. We'll have a drink, chat. Have you had anything to eat?

BARTODZIEJ: No. I arrived in the morning.

ANATOL: We'll go out for dinner. You'll stay a few days, won't you . . . ?

BARTODZIEJ: That depends . . .

ANATOL: Of course you will. Where are you staying?

BARTODZIEJ: I don't know yet. I'll find a hotel.

ANATOL: No, you won't. You'll stay with us. We've plenty of room, too much room, in fact. Is this your suitcase?

BARTODZIEJ: Yes.

ANATOL (*picking up the suitcase*): We'll get you unpacked. (*Puts the suitcase down on the floor again.*) Or better still, we'll have a drink first. Make yourself at home. Why are you standing? Sit down, sit down, sit down! (*Pushes* BARTODZIEJ *down almost by force.*) You haven't changed a bit. Do you want some music?

BARTODZIEJ: Not really.

ANATOL (*starting the hi-fi*): I've got a bit thin on top, nothing unusual in that, but you, I promise you . . . Just the same, exactly the same. Your birthday's in July, or was it June, I've forgotten . . .

BARTODZIEJ: October.

ANATOL: Mine's June. Younger than you, but that'll even itself out, won't it? Everything will be evened out, it's already starting to even itself out. What do you want? This? Or that? (*Offers* BARTODZIEJ *various bottles.*) Or something else altogether.

BARTODZIEJ: This will do.

ANATOL: Don't stand on ceremony, what's mine is yours, a guest in the home brings God with him, as our forefathers used to say, and welcome. Like in the good old days. In unity strength, so let's be friends. Whoever is not with us, I mean not against us, *ora pro nobis, fiat voluntas tua*. Were you an altar boy?

BARTODZIEJ: No.

ANATOL: I was. Before the war. No, during the war, no, after the war, or Was it before the war? That's it, take it by the neck, and now the glass, from the bottle into the glass, like . . . thaaaat's lovely . . . (*He hands the full glass to* BARTODZIEJ.) Take it by the neck again, the glass, tilt it like . . . so . . . that's it, we'll close the bottle for the time being . . . Right, it's ready! (*Sits opposite* BARTODZIEJ *with his glass raised as if proposing a toast.* BARTODZIEJ *stands up and turns off the hi-fi, and sits down again.*) Here's to our . . . (*They drink.*) . . . to our, to your, and to your whatever. No, I swear you . . . (*He stares at* BARTODZIEJ.)

BARTODZIEJ: What's the matter?

ANATOL: You've gone a little bald, too.

BARTODZIEJ: That's not surprising, is it?

ANATOL: I thought only I had.

BARTODZIEJ: That's because we used brilliantine unnecessarily.

ANATOL: And had our hair cut in a duck's ass. At least I did: you changed your style.

BARTODZIEJ: That wasn't very hygienic, either. Neck shaved clean, and a haystack on top.

ANATOL: Dutifully unwashed.

BARTODZIEJ: But thoroughly combed.

ANATOL: Smoothed back.

BARTODZIEJ: The brilliantine was nothing. Sugared water was better. Came up like varnish.

ANATOL: There was plenty to varnish then.

BARTODZIEJ: There was.

ANATOL: I'm glad to see you, you old so and so.

BARTODZIEJ: Less of the old, less of the old.

ANATOL: Let's have another, then.

BARTODZIEJ: Maybe we shouldn't.

ANATOL: Why not?

BARTODZIEJ: It's bad for me.

ANATOL: Me, too. (*He pours into the glasses.*)

BARTODZIEJ: You didn't use to drink at all before.

ANATOL: I didn't after, either. Not for a very long time. All my life I didn't. Have to make up for it now. (*The telephone rings.*) Let it ring. I'm not answering it. I've had enough.

ANNABELLE (*off*): Anatol!

ANATOL: Yes, froggy?

ANNABELLE: Telephone!

ANATOL *picks up the receiver.*

ANATOL: Anatol the First. Yes . . . I'm afraid I can't. No, not possibly.

ANNABELLE *enters carrying a vase with the roses.*

SCENE 12

ANATOL: I can't today, I can't tomorrow, I can't the day after tomorrow, and in fact I can't at all ever.

ANNABELLE: Who is it?

ANATOL (*to* ANNABELLE): The Committee of Cooperation. (*Into the telephone.*) The fact is I never could . . .

ANNABELLE: The Committee of Cooperation with whom?

ANATOL (*to* ANNABELLE): With abroad. (*Into the telephone.*) So help me God.

ANNABELLE *puts the vase with the flowers down on the ground and takes the receiver from* ANATOL.

ANNABELLE (*into the telephone*): Please hold on. (*To* ANATOL.) What's it about?

ANATOL: Some meeting.

ANNABELLE: And why don't you want to go?

ANATOL: Because I'm talking to a friend. A childhood friend.

ANNABELLE (*into the telephone*): One moment, please. (*To* ANATOL.) Are you mad?

ANATOL: Not me. Everyone's gone mad, but I haven't. I've got my feet firmly on the ground and unbowed I continue to . . .

ANNABELLE: Anatol!

ANATOL: Hang on. What exactly am I continuing to do?

ANNABELLE (*into telephone*): Yes, I'm listening . . . yes . . . yes . . . What time? Of course. Of course not, there are no problems. Please send the car around. (*Replaces the receiver.*) They're coming round to collect you.

ANATOL: Yes, Froggy. They're always coming round to collect me.

ANNABELLE *takes his glass from him.*

ANNABELLE: You can get drunk later.

ANATOL: When? Life is short.

ANNABELLE: We'll go for supper to the Cristal when you get back.

ANATOL: What about my friend?

ANNABELLE: He'll come with us. And then we'll go to the Bowler Hat afterward.

ANATOL: Why the Bowler Hat?

ANNABELLE: Because the Pink Panthers are playing there.

ANATOL: Ah, that's different.

ANNABELLE (*to* BARTODZIEJ): Let's call each other by our first names. (*To* ANATOL.) You surely don't want me to be on formal terms with your friend?

ANATOL: Oh, no. Of course not!

ANNABELLE: I won't be a moment. (*Leaves.*)

SCENE 13

ANATOL: That's life, eh?

SCENE 14

BARTODZIEJ, ANATOL, *and* ANNABELLE *are returning from the Bowler Hat night club.* BARTODZIEJ *and* ANATOL, *both tipsy, are singing.*

BARTODZIEJ *and* ANATOL:

"The Party conqueror of fascism,
The Party leader of the masses,
The Party leading us all
To Socialism."

BARTODZIEJ: You're off-key.

ANATOL: What do you expect? I've never sung it before. This is the first time in my life.

BARTODZIEJ: Why now, then?

ANATOL: For the company. What about you?

BARTODZIEJ: It's different for me. That was my favorite tune.

ANNABELLE: Stop messing about, both of you.

ANATOL: Silence, child, when your elders are singing.

BARTODZIEJ: Don't let it upset you, pussycat.

ANATOL: Not pussycat. Froggy.

BARTODZIEJ: Don't let it upset you, Froggy. Your little elephant's got a weak head. He's not used to it.

ANATOL: But I will get used to it. I give you my word of honor: I'll get used to it.

BARTODZIEJ: He'll do everything he can. He's already started.

ANNABELLE: Do you want some coffee?

BARTODZIEJ: We don't want coffee. We want happiness for the whole of mankind.

ANATOL: I don't. Count me out.

BARTODZIEJ: That's true, my little cricket. He never did want happiness for the whole of mankind.

ANATOL: I had an evil character. Whereas he did want it. He was always jumping out of his pants with happiness. "An Angel in Trousers."

BARTODZIEJ: Where's that from?

ANATOL: Mayakovsky.

BARTODZIEJ: It's not.

ANATOL: You've forgotten. You expect me to remember for you?

BARTODZIEJ: Not "An Angel in Trousers." It was "A Cloud in Trousers." Besides that was one of his pre-revolutionary poems, so it was still decadent. Vigor came after decadence in accordance with the inexorable laws of dialectical materialism.

ANATOL: Certainly, I agree with that.

ANNABELLE: You're both boring. (*She leaves.*)

SCENE 15

ANATOL (*calling after* ANNABELLE): I'll be through in a moment! (*To* BARTODZIEJ.) Not bad, eh? I'll show you something. (*He takes a few snapshots out of his wallet and hands them to* BARTODZIEJ *one by one.*) On the beach. (*Hands him the next one.*) That's her with a girlfriend. Not bad either, eh? The one in the one-piece. I prefer a bikini. (*Hands him the next one.*) Eating ice cream. And here . . . (*Hands him the next one.*) Without a bra.

BARTODZIEJ: Did you make her take it off?

ANATOL: She did it herself. (*Pause.*) Not bad, eh?

BARTODZIEJ: Very nice.

ANATOL (*searching through the photos in his wallet*): Here it is! (*Hands it to* BARTODZIEJ.) On a bike.

BARTODZIEJ: What's so special about a bike . . . ?

ANATOL: What do you mean? Look at it closely. (*Pause.*) See?

BARTODZIEJ: Did you take it yourself?

ANATOL: Who else? Not bad?

BARTODZIEJ *gives* ANATOL *back all the photographs.*

BARTODZIEJ: Not bad.

ANATOL: That's nothing. Wait, I've got some more, a whole series. Six by four . . .

BARTODZIEJ: Where are you going?

ANATOL: They're in my desk. I've got a desk now, you know.

BARTODZIEJ: Never mind.

ANATOL: Don't you want to see them?

BARTODZIEJ: I'd rather talk.

ANATOL: Let's have a drink, then.

BARTODZIEJ: You've had enough.

ANATOL: What about you?

BARTODZIEJ: Me, too. We're not twenty anymore.

ANATOL: I am.

BARTODZIEJ: I'm not, though.

ANATOL: You've lived longer, of course you have. But they knocked fifteen years off me and I'm like new.

BARTODZIEJ: Do you bear me a grudge?

ANATOL: Why should I?

BARTODZIEJ: That they knocked those years off you but not off me? It was quite the opposite for me: those were the most beautiful years of my life.

ANATOL: Do you have to say that?

BARTODZIEJ: Yes, I do. I mean, I do understand.

ANATOL: What? What can you possibly understand?

BARTODZIEJ: Those fifteen years of yours.

ANATOL: Really? What else?

BARTODZIEJ: And my, let's call it, scientific worldview.

ANATOL: A bit late.

BARTODZIEJ: You've the right to say that.

ANATOL: Yes, I have. So what?

BARTODZIEJ: I believe I ought to explain why in those days I had this . . .

ANATOL: Scientific worldview.

BARTODZIEJ: Exactly.

ANATOL: Forget it.

BARTODZIEJ: But I ought to . . .

ANATOL: You explained it to me then. It made me want to throw up. You couldn't stop explaining. You went on and on. You wanted to convert me. Why repeat it all now? I knew it all by heart even then.

BARTODZIEJ: Because in those days I believed it was the only . . .

ANATOL: I know, I know. I've just told you I know. The only correct solution for us, for the whole of mankind, and so on. What can you tell me that's new?

BARTODZIEJ: That I've changed.

ANATOL: So what?

BARTODZIEJ: So I look at it differently now.

ANATOL: So what?

BARTODZIEJ: So I wanted to tell you I wasn't right then.

Pause.

ANATOL: I wouldn't say that.

BARTODZIEJ: What?

ANATOL: I wouldn't turn your back on it completely. After all, there have been certain achievements. We've rebuilt the country . . .

BARTODZIEJ: The country?

ANATOL: Schools, heavy industry . . . Especially heavy industry.

BARTODZIEJ: Are you serious?

ANATOL: Not to mention our international position . . . You can't disregard that. But most of all the leveling out of social differences, the restructuring of society, the removal of the last vestiges of feudalism.

BARTODZIEJ: Give me a drink.

ANATOL: Certainly. This, or that.

BARTODZIEJ: That.

ANATOL *pours into the glasses.*

ANATOL: Do you know what a solitary cell is?

BARTODZIEJ: I can imagine.

ANATOL: That's not enough. In that case, let's start another way: how long were you a virgin?

BARTODZIEJ: Do you mean a political virgin?

ANATOL: Not political! I'm asking you how long it was before you finally had it? The first time?

BARTODZIEJ: Who, me?

ANATOL: Stop pretending. In those days we pretended we were a pair of old rams. You pretended in front of me, and I pretended in front of you. But now we're grown-ups. When did you start?

BARTODZIEJ: Me? The usual time, I think.

ANATOL: Before you left school?

BARTODZIEJ: About then. I married early.

ANATOL: Who?

BARTODZIEJ: You don't know her. They took you in '49. I met her after that.

ANATOL: Me, I was a boy scout. Pure in speech, thought, and deed. Well, actually only in deed, and then not always. I saw a lot of things in the woods, but I didn't participate. I was good in action, but apart from that I was a boy scout. And God-fearing, one of those wearing a scapular.

BARTODZIEJ: You weren't like that when I knew you.

ANATOL: That's because it was later, after the war. I had a foul mouth then. I'm talking about the early forties now. First I wanted it to be pure, then I wanted it, but I wanted it to be romantic. That is to say, with love. You're laughing at me.

BARTODZIEJ: I'm not.

ANATOL: You would have laughed then. In short, it was only in the uprising in '44 that I very nearly got to anything. Her name was Halina and she was a liaison officer, of course, only a little older than me, but quite experienced, so everything was perfect. Very pretty. I liked her a lot and she liked me and it was romantic.

BARTODZIEJ: You were lucky, then.

ANATOL: But before it happened she was hit in the stomach with splinters from a Nebelwerfer 105. We carried her to first-aid, I carried her, I was at the back of the stretcher so I was able to see, I could see the guts, a whole mass of guts, she was wide open from the waist down and I looked and looked.

BARTODZIEJ: Couldn't you have changed places?

ANATOL: I could have, but I didn't want to. I wanted to see. It was all over before we got her to first-aid. And after that I couldn't. The war was over and I still couldn't. But I wanted to. I really wanted to. When you met me, I couldn't and later I still couldn't, and then they put me away. And I was inside for fifteen years. (*Pause.*)

ANNABELLE (*off*): Anatol!

ANATOL: Yes, pussycat! I'll be there in a moment! . . . At the trial I knew they were going to string me up and I thought: that'll be best. I was wrong. When they announced the verdict, it was worse. To die and not even to know what it's like . . . I was a virgin, but not like the Maid of Orleans. Two years I kept waiting for the noose, day in day out, night in night out, and it was bad. When they finally changed it to life I thought: it's better this way. I was wrong: it was worse again. I kept thinking: how much longer—ten, fifteen, maybe thirty years—can a man live? But did that mean I didn't want to live? Not that, either. As you can see, it's not easy to satisfy me. I got used to it, but I couldn't get used to having got used to it. (*Pause.*) What do you think I thought about during those fifteen years? Ideals? The third of May? A Poland that stretched from sea to sea? Maybe I did a bit at the beginning, maybe I did during those first two years. But afterward? Guess. And do you think I liked myself for it? I spent one year with one guy, a non-political, who said he only approved of one party, the E.D.F. You know: Eating, Drinking, and Fucking. I wanted to kill him. But what was I thinking about? Was I any better than him?

BARTODZIEJ: Surely you were better.

ANATOL: What do you know about it? You with your wife in a little house, probably with a garden. What dreams could you have had?

BARTODZIEJ: Not like your dreams.

ANATOL: Of course not.

BARTODZIEJ: But not bad, either. If you think I slept peacefully . . .

ANATOL: . . . then I'm not mistaken. You and your pangs of political conscience . . . Political conscience, what is that? It only makes me laugh.

BARTODZIEJ: Not just political.

ANATOL: What, then? You were always political. That's what your head was all about. You were all head and no stomach. And no guts.

BARTODZIEJ: Not just political.

ANATOL: An abstraction!

BARTODZIEJ: There were guts. And there still are.

ANATOL: Bullshit.

BARTODZIEJ: It was I who denounced you.

ANATOL: What?

BARTODZIEJ: I denounced you. I knew what you were doing and I denounced you. You got that death sentence, those two years in death row and those fifteen years inside thanks to me.

Pause.

ANATOL: Why are you telling me this?

BARTODZIEJ: I've always wanted to tell you.

ANATOL: No. Not always.

BARTODZIEJ: All right, not right away, but soon . . .

ANATOL: How soon?

BARTODZIEJ: Very soon afterward.

ANATOL: How soon?!

BARTODZIEJ: Well, a few years later.

ANATOL: How many years?

BARTODZIEJ: Two, three . . .

ANATOL: Four? Or maybe five? Or exactly seven? When could one start having a conscience? Or even should have one.

BARTODZIEJ: All right, not right away, but sooner than you think. I'm not that much of a sheep and I started to see what was happening for myself.

ANATOL: I see. First you started to see, and only then did you remember about me. Before that you thought you were all right. A delayed reaction conscience.

BARTODZIEJ: Anatol, I don't know how I can explain it to you. I don't know myself what came first, the change in my convictions or your ghost. Did I change my convictions because of your ghost, or did your ghost appear because I'd changed my convictions? I'll never unravel it now. I'm being honest with you.

ANATOL: Possibly.

BARTODZIEJ: And that's why I don't know how to explain it to you.

ANATOL: Am I asking you to?

BARTODZIEJ: But I'd like to explain it to you.

ANATOL: But I couldn't care less!

BARTODZIEJ: You couldn't care less about why I . . .

ANATOL: Not one iota! Why you did it is your business. All I'm asking you is: why are you telling me about it? Now. Today. Here. At this moment. To my face.

BARTODZIEJ: I came here specially to do it.

ANATOL: Better and better. That makes me even more curious.

BARTODZIEJ: Because I want you to know.

ANATOL: Precisely! Why? Why do you want me to know?

BARTODZIEJ: I want you to judge me.

Pause.

ANATOL: All right. Let's assume I do judge you. You surely don't expect the judgment to be mild?

BARTODZIEJ: I don't. And that's not what I want.

ANATOL: Very good. I've judged you. It's done. Judged. What now?

BARTODZIEJ: Pass sentence.

ANATOL: What sentence?

BARTODZIEJ: That's up to you. Up to your judgment.

ANATOL: What is this game? I'm not a judging institution.

BARTODZIEJ: Exactly! No institution will do anything in my case. There won't even be an indictment. So we must do it ourselves, between ourselves. You are the man who's been killed, and I'm the man who's killed you. "Man to man"— "*cheloviekom cheloviek.*" Remember that Russian song?

ANATOL: How could I forget?

BARTODZIEJ: In other words, just between us two, unofficially. You've judged me already, so now it's time for the sentence. What is the tariff for murder?

ANATOL: There is none. After due consideration.

BARTODZIEJ: There is. There must be. You know there is.

ANATOL: You want me to hang you, or what?

BARTODZIEJ: What if I did?

ANATOL: Are you some kind of lunatic?

BARTODZIEJ: No. Just a murderer.

ANATOL: What is it you want from me?

BARTODZIEJ: Justice.

ANATOL: Meaning what . . .

BARTODZIEJ: I want you to carry out sentence on me.

ANATOL: I've had enough of sentences!

BARTODZIEJ: Do it!

Pause.

ANATOL: Sentence my foot. You just want me to take vengeance on you.

BARTODZIEJ: That's right.

ANATOL: I know it is. I see what you're up to. You talk about a sentence, courts, justice, but you just want me to give you a good old-fashioned punch in the mouth.

BARTODZIEJ: No. A punch in the mouth is not enough. It's got to be real vengeance.

ANATOL: Not like ours, more of the Corsican variety.

BARTODZIEJ: That's right.

ANATOL: Double-barreled shotgun? Buckshot? I could invite you to go hunting and then, apparently accidentally . . .

BARTODZIEJ: That's it! That's it!

ANATOL: Could be done. I could do it.

BARTODZIEJ: You agree, then?

ANATOL: But why?

BARTODZIEJ: So I can feel I've done something.

ANATOL: Are you a pervert by any chance?

BARTODZIEJ: I am not a pervert. I need it for something else, not pleasure.

ANATOL: In that case I don't understand.

BARTODZIEJ: You mentioned the solitary cell.

ANATOL: Yes.

BARTODZIEJ: I've got my own solitary cell, too. It's not large, but it's my own private one. I sit in it and somewhere out there the world passes by. From the day I was born I've been wanting to leave that solitary cell and join in with the world. But a solitary cell is a solitary cell—it isolates. It doesn't allow entrance from outside and it doesn't let you get out. And what I do in my solitary cell has no meaning for the world, and what the world outside does has no meaning for me. I did something dreadful and what is the result? There is none, except for a pang of conscience, in other words—a ghost. But in real terms? Absolutely nothing. But if you were to take vengeance for what I've done, then I would feel that I had done something. There would be some consequences outside, some relationship between one thing and another, and the isolation would crack.

ANATOL: So that's why, in your solitary cell, you kept a certain little portrait . . .

BARTODZIEJ: Yes. A small solitary cell with a large portrait on the wall. I thought that He, who was the leader of the entire world, would join me with the entire world, that looking at his portrait I'd see the living world. A delusion, of course. It was only a portrait.

ANATOL: Retouched, what's more.

BARTODZIEJ: The solitary cell isolates the future from the past. I did something once, but there is no connection between that once and today. If you were to take vengeance now for the something I did once, there would be a continuity from that once to now, and now and once would create some sort of whole. Because if there are no consequences, then there are no causes and if there is no ending, it means there was no beginning either. There was never anything before, and there is nothing now. Do you understand?

ANATOL: Only too well.

BARTODZIEJ: And you're no longer surprised?

ANATOL: I'm only surprised that you've never thought of me.

BARTODZIEJ: What do you mean? But that's exactly why I've specially come here . . .

ANATOL: To tell me.

BARTODZIEJ: . . . to tell you . . .

ANATOL: . . . that you did something terrible to me. But what makes you so sure I want to know? Did you consider the situation you'd be putting me in? No, you never took that into account. And what am I supposed to do now?

BARTODZIEJ: Shoot me.

ANATOL: Idiot. (*Pause.*) No, worse than that. Egoist.

ANNABELLE (*off*): Anatol!

ANATOL: Yes, pussycat, wait! . . . It's all right for you. Some joker comes along and serves up a nice one: "I've pulled a dirty trick on you, take vengeance." As if I've got nothing better to do than settle your problems with the solitary cell and so on. And what if I've got other things to do? I haven't been out of circulation for fifteen years just so that now, when I am around, I can devote myself to something which no longer exists.

BARTODZIEJ: But it should exist.

ANATOL: That's not my business. For a long time I didn't have a future. Now I've got one and I want to spend time on it. Exclusively! I want to live at last.

BARTODZIEJ: And you think I don't? But how can one live when the past won't let go? One has to settle the past before one can look after the future.

ANATOL: Your past may not be letting you go, but mine has. I've finished with mine.

BARTODZIEJ: That's what I thought. "There are certain achievements. Education, heavy industry, the leveling out of social differences." And all those committees of cooperation with . . . Is that what you make speeches about at anniversaries? Nice apartment. Large, and in the center of town.

ANATOL: One cannot live by negation alone. Life is an affirmation.

BARTODZIEJ: Of what?

ANATOL: Of whatever.

BARTODZIEJ: So it's all the same what?

ANATOL: Yes, it's all the same. Life doesn't ask about abstractions and ideals. Life is made up of concrete things, it's built up day by day with whatever material there is at hand and not from some material that should be there but isn't. Minute following on minute and you in it—that's what life is. Everything else is invention.

BARTODZIEJ: Is that what you learned in prison?

ANATOL: Yes, it is. And especially in death row. You count the minutes there. Even the seconds . . . That was good training.

BARTODZIEJ: And they trained you well.

ANATOL: So you want to teach me, do you? You, who've spent your whole life meditating on your sofa? I was active throughout my life and always against something. Five years in the war, four years after the war, and when they took me in . . . Do you honestly think I got the death sentence for nothing? I was the last political prisoner from that period. Others have been let out long since. They held on to me the longest because I held out the longest. When they sentenced me to death they had their reasons and I didn't hold it against them. I didn't expect mercy. It was something for something. Do you know what I was doing? You do, but not everything. No, I'm not a victim of the errors and distortions like those who were let out in '56 and I never was. I was a real enemy. Nobody can criticize me for not really fighting. And if I'm saying now that it's enough, then it is enough. How long can one live in opposition to everything? You can be against from time to time, but being against all your life, non-stop, is a perversion.

ANNABELLE (off): Anatol, what are you doing?

ANATOL: Yes, pussycat, one moment! . . . You had your share being for, you stuffed yourself full of the positive, now it's my turn. Go over to the opposition and be against if you want to, taste a bit of that if your body's short of it, but don't forbid me to have some of what you've had too much of. That is not fair.

BARTODZIEJ: And all that?

ANATOL: All what?

BARTODZIEJ: All of what was before, our past, yours, mine . . .

ANATOL: I've told you—it doesn't exist.

BARTODZIEJ: And it shouldn't? Everything has to pass by senselessly, without leaving a trace or meaning . . . It's to be swept away . . . Is that how you want it to be? For it to be like smoke, or dust, like nothing? For everything to be like nothing?

ANATOL: Leave me alone!

BARTODZIEJ: Anatol, if you don't do something now, everything that's ours will crumble. Everything that's yours and mine.

ANATOL: Too late. It's crumbled already.

BARTODZIEJ: I know, I can see that. But it's not too late yet.

ANATOL: Nothing can be done . . .

BARTODZIEJ: Punish me, take vengeance, carry out the sentence. Let there be some kind of right.

ANATOL: Right? Did you say "right"? You?

BARTODZIEJ: Yes, me. There must be something permanent in this mess that is our lives. Something which never changes, that remains.

ANATOL: There is something like that.

BARTODZIEJ: What?

ANATOL: Him!

BARTODZIEJ: Who? Where?

ANATOL: There!

BARTODZIEJ: I don't see anything.

ANATOL: Because you're looking too low. Look higher. There. Higher, higher!

BARTODZIEJ: But what is it?

ANATOL: The portrait.

BARTODZIEJ: I don't see any portrait.

ANATOL: It's there. Even when you can't see it, he's there and he's watching us. He was, is, and will be. Smiling. And he's right to smile. Because his creation lives on and does not pass away. He's in us, in you as much as in me. We're both his creation. It doesn't matter if we're right or left, whether we were for him or against him, but it was always through him, he was always at the center of all our affairs. You want to know what remains? He remains, even now he's in you and in me. You talked about our lives—well, look at our daddy.

BARTODZIEJ: You're drunk. I can't talk to you.

ANATOL: Yes, my brother—there is our parent. We're all his children. Whether you like it or not, we're his blood. Our blood was his, for him or against him but his. His. Bow to our father.

BARTODZIEJ: That's enough, Anatol.

ANATOL: Bow to him, I said! No respect for your father? The one who was, is, and will be?

BARTODZIEJ: But he's not alive anymore!

ANATOL: Who said that? Did I hear some blasphemy? His body may be dead, but his Spirit, his Spirit is eternally alive! The Spirit of History, the Zeitgeist. And that never dies. If you want, I'll prove it to you. Have you got any matches?

BARTODZIEJ *hands* ANATOL *a box of matches.* ANATOL *lights the candles.*

BARTODZIEJ: What are you going to do?

ANATOL: Invite him to come and sit down with us.

BARTODZIEJ: Anatol, this isn't funny.

ANATOL: Of course it's not! Would I make jokes at my own expense? Let him come down, let him sit down with you at his right hand or at his left and with me as well, and let him have a drink with us. They say he liked a drink when he was young.

BARTODZIEJ: Anatol, you can't do things like this.

ANATOL: Can't I practice a cult? My forefathers were allowed to practice their cults, and I'm not allowed to? (*He fills the glasses and hands one to* BARTODZIEJ.) Here, hold this, it'll come in useful. And now face the portrait and repeat after me.

BARTODZIEJ: I'm not repeating anything.

ANATOL: Wherever you are, in whatever corner of the world . . . No, that's not it. Start again. It's quite simple: I, Anatol, still alive though I was to have been dead, invite you, who are dead, but living through me, for a little drink. If you're an honorable man come and drink with the shit you shat on, in other words, me and with my friend who always was a shit. I call on you through the fire of a platoon and through individual fire. I call on you through the water, the colder water. Through the earth I call on you, or through that which is below the earth, which you know about. Come, appear and manifest yourself since you are summoned.

BARTODZIEJ: I'm not taking part in this.

ANATOL: Ssshh . . . Can you hear?

BARTODZIEJ: What?

ANATOL: Footsteps . . . On the floorboards . . . A long way away . . .

BARTODZIEJ: What footsteps?

ANATOL: He's coming!

BARTODZIEJ: You're imagining it.

ANATOL: Closer and closer!

BARTODZIEJ: There's no one coming.

ANATOL: Stone against stone and echo following echo . . .

BARTODZIEJ: Nobody's coming—nobody!

ANATOL: He's in the next room already.

ANNABELLE *enters behind* ANATOL.

SCENE 16

ANNABELLE: Anatol, what are you doing? Why haven't you come to bed?

ANATOL (*pointing ahead*): He's here!

ANNABELLE: Who's here? Where?

ANATOL (*backing away*): There, there. It's Him!

ANNABELLE: Who? What's going on here?

ANATOL: I'm on my knees!

He falls to his knees, tears his collar open, choking. ANNABELLE, *standing behind him, holds him up.*

ANNABELLE: Anatol!

ANATOL: I'm going to Damascus! I'm a sinner . . . I'm dust!

ANNABELLE: Is he drunk or what?

BARTODZIEJ (*next to* ANATOL, *opens his eyelids, inspects his pupils*): No, it's something more serious than that.

ANNABELLE: I knew this would happen!

BARTODZIEJ: Call an ambulance.

ACT THREE

SCENE 1

The BARTODZIEJ *home. Table, sofa.*

ANNABELLE: It's not about myself I've come.

OCTAVIA: I'll call him. Do sit down, please.

Exit OCTAVIA.

SCENE 2

ANNABELLE *sits down on the sofa and waits. She picks up the illustrated weekly, the same one which Octavia had been reading in Act One, Scene 2. She looks through it. Starts to read. Eventually, finding something that interests her, she takes a notebook out of her bag and copies something from the weekly into the notebook.* OCTAVIA *comes in.*

SCENE 3

OCTAVIA: He'll be down right away. He has to get dressed first. He always sleeps after lunch. (ANNABELLE *puts the notebook away and puts down the illustrated magazine.*) Please don't stop, by all means carry on. Only that one is last year's. I've got more recent editions if you'd like to see them.

ANNABELLE: I wouldn't want to be any trouble . . .

OCTAVIA: It's no trouble at all. I collect them because I have a subscription. This one happens to be out because of this knitted vest. Let me show you . . . (*She has sat down on the sofa next to* ANNABELLE *and now takes the magazine from her.*) Not this page, just a minute, where was it, here it is, see, it's a very good crochet pattern. In fact, I've started it, but I can't get it finished, something always comes up, if it's not one thing it's another. It's imported, isn't it, that coat?

ANNABELLE: I bought it a long time ago.

OCTAVIA: It suits you.

ANNABELLE: Do you like it?

OCTAVIA: It's just beautiful. You can't get suede, unless it's reject, they only do it for export, or privately, but that's very expensive. Yours is different, isn't it? There were a few models, I had a friend but she doesn't work in that field anymore. Were you writing something?

ANNABELLE: I was just copying something.

OCTAVIA: Do you knit?

ANNABELLE: No, I don't.

OCTAVIA: That's what I thought. You don't look as if you did.

ANNABELLE: My mother wanted me to learn but what with one thing and another . . .

OCTAVIA: What thing?

ANNABELLE: I started my studies.

OCTAVIA: So young?

ANNABELLE: Yes. As a child.

OCTAVIA: You were a student?

ANNABELLE: Exactly.

OCTAVIA: And what did you study?

ANNABELLE: Various things. But I can sew.

OCTAVIA: It's not that difficult, knitting. What were you copying, then?

ANNABELLE: Carrot cutlets.

OCTAVIA: A recipe?

ANNABELLE: Yes.

OCTAVIA: Do you cook?

ANNABELLE: A little. I started recently.

OCTAVIA: On your own?

ANNABELLE: On my own, yes.

OCTAVIA: I'm so glad I've met you. Bartodziej told me . . .

ANNABELLE: What did he say?

OCTAVIA: That his friend was taken ill. How is he now?

ANNABELLE: Not very well.

OCTAVIA: Is he your husband?

ANNABELLE: Yes. Nearly . . .

OCTAVIA: I'm sorry. I have no right to ask.

ANNABELLE: It doesn't matter. Really.

OCTAVIA: Female curiosity. But you're young. I've been with Bartodziej eleven years now. Didn't he tell you?

ANNABELLE: I didn't see him for long. My husband spoke to him.

OCTAVIA: They're friends.

ANNABELLE: They talked till morning.

OCTAVIA: What about?

ANNABELLE: I don't know. I was asleep.

OCTAVIA: Bartodziej wasn't too well when he got back, either.

ANNABELLE: I was woken by shouts and when I went into the room, Anatol had an attack. The ambulance came.

OCTAVIA: You don't say? Was it serious?

ANNABELLE: They took him to the hospital.

OCTAVIA: Was it as bad as that?

ANNABELLE: They kept him in for quite some time.

OCTAVIA: In the hospital?

ANNABELLE: In the neurological ward.

OCTAVIA: What was wrong with him?

Pause.

ANNABELLE: He's had a diagnosis.

OCTAVIA: I see. (*Pause.*) And now?

ANNABELLE: He's home.

OCTAVIA: What a misfortune. What do you think caused it?

ANNABELLE: He'd been ill before. You know that he was released . . .

OCTAVIA: Bartodziej told me. But an attack like that . . .

ANNABELLE: Bartodziej was there when it happened. I wasn't.

OCTAVIA: Something must have caused it. Didn't your husband say?

ANNABELLE: He can't.

OCTAVIA: Perhaps he doesn't want to say.

ANNABELLE: No, he can't.

OCTAVIA: Maybe he's got secrets from you. (ANNABELLE *shakes her head.*) They sometimes won't say. You're young yet, but I'm experienced. You have to do it skillfully. Have you asked him? (ANNABELLE *confirms by nodding.*) That's good. One has to ask, but not right away. You have to sense the moment. They tell you themselves eventually. He'll definitely tell you.

ANNABELLE: No, he won't tell me.

OCTAVIA: Why not? Is he as stubborn as that?

ANNABELLE: No, he won't tell me. (*She takes out a handkerchief and puts it to her eyes.*)

OCTAVIA: He will. He will with time.

ANNABELLE: He lost his sense of speech. (*She weeps and rests her head on* OCTAVIA'*s shoulder.*) He's a cripple now.

Pause.

OCTAVIA (*stroking her head*): There, there, child, there. It'll get better. It will. (*Takes the handkerchief, which* ANNABELLE *is holding tightly, from her hand and wipes her tears, then puts the handkerchief to* ANNABELLE'*s nose, as if she really were a child.* ANNABELLE *sniffles into the handkerchief loudly and helplessly.* BARTODZIEJ *enters.*) Ah, there you are!

SCENE 4

BARTODZIEJ: I'll come back later, then . . . (*Makes a move as if about to leave.*)

OCTAVIA: Come back!

BARTODZIEJ (*to* ANNABELLE, *uncertainly*): Good afternoon . . . How are you . . . ?

OCTAVIA: Stop playing the fool. Can't you see?

BARTODZIEJ: You know each other, then?

OCTAVIA: Bring some valerian. It's in my room, next to the bed. And put the kettle on. Make some tea, and make it strong. What are you waiting for?

BARTODZIEJ *leaves.*

SCENE 5

OCTAVIA: Sit down comfortably. Take your coat off. (*Helps* ANNABELLE *take her coat off.*)

ANNABELLE: I'm so sorry . . .

OCTAVIA: Don't be silly. I'll give you a clean hanky. The tea will be ready in a minute. I've got some good rowanberry tincture. And you're tired after your journey. Was it very crowded?

ANNABELLE (*still sniffling*): It was . . . To start with . . . Then they got off.

OCTAVIA: It wasn't too bad, then. Very few people come as far as here, and it's completely empty all the way to the border. Will you stay the night?

ANNABELLE: I don't know. I don't want to be any trouble.

OCTAVIA: Of course you'll stay, of course you will. Where else would you go? You'll be no trouble at all, there's plenty of room, you can sleep downstairs. We sleep upstairs. We'll give you something to eat, you can go back tomorrow. Or the day after. Whenever you want.

ANNABELLE: Not the day after tomorrow, I can't.

OCTAVIA: Why not?

ANNABELLE: Anatol.

OCTAVIA: No one to look after him?

ANNABELLE: A neighbor said she would but only till the day after tomorrow.

OCTAVIA: Can't he manage on his own?

ANNABELLE: He's in a wheelchair.

OCTAVIA: A wheelchair? Why?

ANNABELLE: He's paralyzed.

OCTAVIA: Oh, my God! (*Pause.*) I had no idea . . . And you're on your own with him?

ANNABELLE: He doesn't have anyone.

OCTAVIA: I see. Yes, I see.

ANNABELLE: I must go back tomorrow.

OCTAVIA: Of course you must. Of course. What a tragedy . . . You must tell me everything. Would you like to wash your hands?

ANNABELLE: Do I look terrible?

OCTAVIA: Of course not. Of course not. The bathroom's on the right.

ANNABELLE: Thank you very much.

OCTAVIA: There's no need to thank me. Go on. We'll talk.

ANNABELLE *leaves.*

SCENE 6

OCTAVIA *inspects* ANNABELLE*'s coat, puts it on, sees how it fits, then takes it off. Then she lays the table for tea.* BARTODZIEJ *comes in.*

SCENE 7

BARTODZIEJ: I can't find it.

OCTAVIA: Did you put the kettle on?

BARTODZIEJ: Yes, I did.

OCTAVIA: Then get the tincture.

BARTODZIEJ: Where is she?

OCTAVIA: She'll be back shortly. You've certainly done something to be proud of, haven't you?

BARTODZIEJ: When?

OCTAVIA: Then.

BARTODZIEJ: But I didn't do anything!

OCTAVIA: That's what I meant. Go on, bring the rowanberry tincture. Only hurry up.

BARTODZIEJ *leaves.*

SCENE 8

OCTAVIA *works around the table.* ANNABELLE *enters.*

SCENE 9

ANNABELLE: Where's Bartodziej?

OCTAVIA: He's gone for the tincture. I'm not interfering. I know you've come to see him about something. But if I can help you in any way . . . I do know him better.

ANNABELLE: It's about somewhere to live.

OCTAVIA: Somewhere to live? For whom?

ANNABELLE: Anatol.

OCTAVIA: What do you mean? Bartodziej told me you had . . .

ANNABELLE: We've lost that. We've got a small place now.

OCTAVIA: And it's too small, is it?

ANNABELLE: That doesn't matter. It's just that there's no elevator. I'd like to take him to the park from time to time, just so he can get some fresh air. But I can't manage the wheelchair up and down the stairs.

OCTAVIA: You must have a elevator. But what can Bartodziej . . .

ANNABELLE: I've heard people say that he's got contacts. He could help us.

OCTAVIA: Bartodziej?

ANNABELLE: He could arrange something, talk to someone who could . . .

OCTAVIA: It's too late, dear. He can't do anything now.

BARTODZIEJ: Doesn't he know anyone?

OCTAVIA: Not now. He's been out of circulation for a long time now.

ANNABELLE: But I thought . . .

OCTAVIA: Everything's changed. It's true he could have helped once. But not now.

ANNABELLE: What am I going to do, then?

OCTAVIA: Let me think about it. But just for now, sit down. (ANNABELLE *sits at the table.*) He didn't tell me anything at all about the illness, that Bartodziej of mine.

ANNABELLE: He couldn't have known. He left right away.

OCTAVIA: Right away?

ANNABELLE: Almost immediately.

OCTAVIA: You mean he didn't bother to go to the hospital?

ANNABELLE: It was all very confused.

OCTAVIA: And he didn't look after anything?

ANNABELLE: He had to catch the train. He didn't have enough time.

OCTAVIA: Yes, he's a busy man. He has no time at all.

ANNABELLE: The ambulance arrived, they took him down on a stretcher, he was unconscious. I thought it was the drink.

OCTAVIA: Did they drink?

ANNABELLE: Only a little.

OCTAVIA: Didn't he call later to find out?

ANNABELLE: Who?

OCTAVIA: That Bartodziej of mine, of course.

ANNABELLE: He might have. I wasn't home much, being with Anatol. He had a stroke and . . .

OCTAVIA: Yes, he's very sensitive.

ANNABELLE: . . . they wanted to operate on him for something else. They don't always know in the emergency room . . .

OCTAVIA: In other words, he ran away.

ANNABELLE: . . . but in the hospital they gave him a thorough examination. He'd been ill before, but nothing as serious as that and in fact he felt quite normal. He had so much energy . . . I never would have thought anything like that would happen.

OCTAVIA: He's got bad nerves, that Bartodziej of ours. I'll talk to him. As for the apartment, we'll think of something. It's not right the way it is.

ANNABELLE: You think it will work?

OCTAVIA: I know it will work.

ANNABELLE: But you said he no longer has any contacts.

OCTAVIA: Don't you worry about that.

ANNABELLE: How will he fix it, then?

OCTAVIA: I'll fix it.

ANNABELLE: How can you fix it . . .

OCTAVIA: That's my business. Don't you worry yourself about it.

SCENE 10

The scene is the same as in Act One, Scene 2: OCTAVIA and BARTODZIEJ are sitting at separate lamps, quite far from each other. OCTAVIA is reading an illustrated magazine.

BARTODZIEJ: Rabbits. (*Pause.*) I'm going to breed rabbits.

OCTAVIA (*not interrupting her reading*): No.

BARTODZIEJ: What?

OCTAVIA: I said no.

BARTODZIEJ: What do you mean "no"?

OCTAVIA: No, you will not breed rabbits.

BARTODZIEJ: I won't?

OCTAVIA (*putting her reading matter aside*): No, you won't. You will not be breeding any rabbits. And I mean none.

BARTODZIEJ: And why's that?

OCTAVIA: Because you're going to be too busy with a human being.

BARTODZIEJ: Do you know what you're saying, woman? Do you know what kind of responsibility you're taking on? Are you suggesting that I should abandon my project of studying the connections between social life and politics as they grow out of the primitive stage of common ownership and develop into the beginning of a relationship between them? If I don't do it, nobody else will. Things like that simply aren't done nowadays.

OCTAVIA: Shall I tell you what's not done? Leaving a friend who's sick is not done.

BARTODZIEJ: Oh, that's what you're going on about.

OCTAVIA: Not only that.

BARTODZIEJ: It's a difficult question.

OCTAVIA: You'd rather talk about rabbits, would you?

BARTODZIEJ: Not at all, why should I? In fact, they're connected.

OCTAVIA: Fancy that!

BARTODZIEJ: Maybe you don't see the connection.

OCTAVIA: You're not going to get out of it now.

BARTODZIEJ: I have no intention of doing so. I've done everything I could to get out of it a long time ago, but it was all in vain. I've lost hope.

OCTAVIA: You won't succeed. The man is incapable of doing . . .

BARTODZIEJ: That's what I'm saying.

OCTAVIA: He's sick, paralyzed, dumb, he can't move, he can't speak, they take him to hospital and you . . .

BARTODZIEJ: What about me?

OCTAVIA: And what have you done for him?

BARTODZIEJ: Nothing.

OCTAVIA: Nothing!

BARTODZIEJ: That's what I said. Nothing. I agree with you. Totally.

Pause.

OCTAVIA: And can you tell me why?

BARTODZIEJ: Because I'm sick, too.

OCTAVIA: Ah, I didn't know that.

BARTODZIEJ: Of course you didn't.

OCTAVIA: Does your little finger hurt? Or maybe you've a headache?

BARTODZIEJ: I'm sick like him.

OCTAVIA: You wouldn't dare say that again.

BARTODZIEJ: Why say it again? I keep saying it to myself, but nothing comes of it. Facts without consequences. Non sequitur.

OCTAVIA: Tell me, how can you be so insolent?

BARTODZIEJ: What do you mean?

OCTAVIA: How dare you compare yourself with him? Your situation with his?

BARTODZIEJ: There's no comparison. They're identical.

OCTAVIA: God will punish you for saying things like that.

BARTODZIEJ: I doubt if He exists.

OCTAVIA: That's probably why you're capable of such sins. It's either that or because you're idle. If you'd only do something . . .

BARTODZIEJ: I am too busy.

OCTAVIA: By what?

BARTODZIEJ: With my inner life . . .

OCTAVIA: Oh.

BARTODZIEJ: . . . which does require great effort. Unfortunately, without result.

Pause.

OCTAVIA: So it's true after all.

BARTODZIEJ: Yes, it is. I expected something else. But even expecting results didn't bring any results.

OCTAVIA: So, I've been living with a mummy.

BARTODZIEJ: Are you talking about me?

OCTAVIA: Yes, you. An Egyptian mummy.

BARTODZIEJ: This is something new.

OCTAVIA: There's nothing new. It's just that now I'm telling you what's on my mind. For a long time I said nothing. I expected you to understand it for yourself. I tried to make you understand. I waited patiently. I put up with everything, because I expected him to say something to me in a human voice. And he has— about his inner life.

BARTODZIEJ: Have I said something inappropriate?

OCTAVIA: It's not as if I had any delusions. I knew what he was like right from the start. But I thought he was alive, only a little anesthetized. I thought something had anesthetized him. I thought that beside me he'd awake, that he come back to life and he'd become a human being again. That's what I tried for sincerely. My intentions were good. I did love him, after all, even though I took him without any delusions, with no stupid romanticism. I knew what I was taking on and I agreed to it. Because I thought: he is a human being.

BARTODZIEJ: This is about me after all.

OCTAVIA: All those years together, but finally separate. I thought that my feelings and my efforts will make something in him stir, will reveal something, will make him notice me at last. A long and futile wait.

BARTODZIEJ: I'm not doing well.

OCTAVIA: But can he see a human being? Someone who isn't human cannot see a human being.

BARTODZIEJ: You think I'm not alive, is that it?

OCTAVIA: Why, are you alive?

BARTODZIEJ: I am a human being.

OCTAVIA: I have not seen any evidence of that yet.

BARTODZIEJ: So how can you tell?

OCTAVIA: That's exactly how. If there were any evidence, I'd have seen it.

BARTODZIEJ: What do you know about it, anyway?

OCTAVIA: Everything, I should think.

BARTODZIEJ: No, you know nothing. You think you have some idea about me. What do you know about the thoughts I have and what I'm doing when I put on my slippers and drink my tea? A house with a garden, so pretty, is that it? The peace of the home, a quiet life and good neighbors. Good morning—good morning. Everything in its place, nicely ordered. The jam on the shelves, the pickles in their jars, and me in my drawer. Floor polished especially at Christmas, a walk to the wood for one's health, a nap after lunch, the morning paper and evenings by the lamp. And everything's in order, everything's in its place, right? But here, here inside!

OCTAVIA: And you think I enjoy it? The kitchen and the pots and your socks are fun, are they? Am I doing it for myself? And sitting here in this God-forsaken hole is that what I wanted? You brought me here and here's where I sit. And I just watch the best years of my life going past. You wanted peace, I gave you peace. I did everything just the way you wanted, I gave you more even. I didn't say a word. Everything for you and what was left for me? Your inner life!

Pause.

BARTODZIEJ: You're right.

OCTAVIA: What?

BARTODZIEJ: You're right. But how do we get out of it?

OCTAVIA: Can't you see?

BARTODZIEJ: The way out? It's a labyrinth.

OCTAVIA: I think I'll kill him.

BARTODZIEJ: What can we do? Where can we go?

OCTAVIA: Ah—run away!

BARTODZIEJ: It's the same everywhere.

OCTAVIA: But in you, inside . . .

BARTODZIEJ: That's what's the same. Everywhere it's inside and inside is everywhere.

OCTAVIA: Oh, God, he's off again!

BARTODZIEJ: And it's always the same.

OCTAVIA: What is?

BARTODZIEJ: It's always the same inside.

Pause.

OCTAVIA: That time, on that small bridge, what were you thinking about?

BARTODZIEJ: What small bridge . . . ?

OCTAVIA: That time in September, when we were standing there . . . you must remember.

BARTODZIEJ: Yes, I do. It was raining.

OCTAVIA: Were you thinking about me? Only about me? Or was your mind full of something else? Is your head always full of this and that and something else and God knows what? Can you ever think of something or someone and not be thinking of something else at the same time? Can you? Or is that how it always is and always has been?

BARTODZIEJ: I remember. There were ferns . . .

OCTAVIA: What about me?!

BARTODZIEJ: You? You were there, too . . .

OCTAVIA: Let's leave it! Give it a rest.

BARTODZIEJ: I have no rest.

OCTAVIA: I can see that. Let's go back to what we should do. For your sake, primarily.

BARTODZIEJ: If only I knew that . . .

OCTAVIA: But I do know. Let the Anatols come and live with us.

BARTODZIEJ: Anatol? Here?

OCTAVIA: You'll take him in.

BARTODZIEJ: Is this supposed to be a . . . punishment?

OCTAVIA: Punishment? Why? He is your friend, after all.

BARTODZIEJ: But can I . . . ?

OCTAVIA: Are you starting again? We've had enough of that. You'll look after him. It'll do you good. And him, too.

BARTODZIEJ: Him, too?

OCTAVIA: Naturally.

BARTODZIEJ: To look after a human being . . .

OCTAVIA: That's settled, then.

BARTODZIEJ: But . . .

OCTAVIA: And I don't want to hear any "buts." I've had enough! They'll live here with us. (*Pause*) What did you say?

BARTODZIEJ: Nothing.

Pause.

OCTAVIA: Have you ever talked to a picture?

BARTODZIEJ: Why do you ask . . . ?

OCTAVIA: Because I'd like to know if you know the feeling. If you know what it's like when you talk to a picture. You can shout at the top of your lungs, and the picture . . .

BARTODZIEJ: Not even once?

OCTAVIA: That's right.

SCENE 11

BARTODZIEJ's *home. Night.* OCTAVIA *is sitting at the lamp and knitting a sweater, which she is halfway through. Every so often she stops and listens, waiting for something. At her side a glass of tea, which she sips from time to time. A large kettle and a teapot on a tray. A provincial quiet. The ticking of a wall clock. Distant barking of dogs, the distant bell on a church tower strikes two, a distant whistle of a locomotive, the tea is finished.* OCTAVIA *is waiting considerably beyond the time at which one usually goes to sleep. The sound of a car in the road, stops, the motor is switched off. A long silence, then the slamming of a car door, approaching footsteps on the gravel path, the ignition switched on and the car starting and driving away.* OCTAVIA, *who has stopped knitting her sweater and has been listening to the sounds outside carefully, now eagerly and with some ostentation returns to her work.* ANNABELLE *enters: she is wearing a tightly belted Burberry coat with a bag slung over her shoulder. She is carrying a traveling case.*

SCENE 12

ANNABELLE: The train was late.

OCTAVIA: I've unstitched what you started.

ANNABELLE: They didn't even announce it would be late.

OCTAVIA: I had to do it because the sleeves were completely crooked.

ANNABELLE: It's not my fault.

OCTAVIA: And the pattern was all wrong. It's got to be started from scratch.

ANNABELLE: Good night. (*Goes toward the interior of the house.*)

OCTAVIA: Won't you have some tea? (ANNABELLE *stops.*) Surely you'd like some. (ANNABELLE *turns back, puts her case down on the floor, and sits at the table.*) Only the water's cold. It has to be heated up. (ANNABELLE *stands up, picks up the kettle, and moves toward the kitchen.*) I'd like some, too.

ANNABELLE *turns back, takes off her shoulder bag and hangs it on the arm of the chair, takes the glass from the table and puts it on the tray, takes the tray with the kettle, pot, and glass out into the kitchen.*

SCENE 13

OCTAVIA *sits and waits.* ANNABELLE *returns.*

SCENE 14

OCTAVIA: What was it like?

ANNABELLE: The usual.

OCTAVIA: Did you find anything?

ANNABELLE: No, but I've got something promised.

OCTAVIA: Something definite?

ANNABELLE: I think so.

OCTAVIA: Where?

ANNABELLE: In an office.

OCTAVIA: What kind of office?

ANNABELLE: An office. Planning.

OCTAVIA: In administration?

ANNABELLE: That's right. Administration.

OCTAVIA: And is it certain?

ANNABELLE: They're going to let me know.

OCTAVIA: So when are you going again?

ANNABELLE: Tuesday.

Pause.

OCTAVIA: Do you want something to eat?

ANNABELLE: Not really.

OCTAVIA: Only there is nothing. I didn't have time to do the shopping. I had to clear up in Anatol's room.

ANNABELLE: I'm not hungry.

OCTAVIA: It was very dusty. Did you eat?

ANNABELLE: No. But I'm not hungry.

OCTAVIA: Was it crowded?

ANNABELLE: A bit. As usual.

OCTAVIA: Why was it late?

ANNABELLE: I don't know. They didn't say. (*Pause.*) It was late without any warning. They might have announced it. (*Pause.*) They might make an effort on that line at least.

OCTAVIA: What line?

ANNABELLE: It's an international line.

The kettle's whistle can be heard from the kitchen. ANNABELLE *goes out into the kitchen.*

SCENE 15

OCTAVIA *waits.* ANNABELLE *returns.*

SCENE 16

ANNABELLE *is carrying a tray on which there is the kettle, teapot, two glasses, and tea bags.*

OCTAVIA: I didn't wash up because I didn't have time.

ANNABELLE: I'll do it tomorrow. (*Pause.* ANNABELLE *starts making the tea, pouring, etc.*) How does Anatol feel?

OCTAVIA: Same as usual.

ANNABELLE: Did he eat anything today?

OCTAVIA: Bartodziej fed him.

ANNABELLE: Did he sleep?

OCTAVIA: It's hard to tell when he's asleep. His eyes are closed but you can't tell if he's sleeping. Sometimes he just looks.

ANNABELLE: I know.

OCTAVIA: He just looks and looks. (*Pause.*) You know?

ANNABELLE: Yes, I do.

OCTAVIA: Does he see anything?

ANNABELLE: Did they go for a walk?

OCTAVIA: Bartodziej took him.

ANNABELLE: To the woods?

OCTAVIA: I don't know. I didn't ask. I didn't have time because I was doing the washing. I washed that blue thing of yours.

ANNABELLE: What about afterward? When they got back?

OCTAVIA: Bartodziej read him something.

ANNABELLE: The newspaper?

OCTAVIA: No, out of same book. Does he understand anything?

ANNABELLE: That'll be enough, I should think. (*Referring to the tea that has been made in the teapot.* ANNABELLE *pours the tea into the glasses.*)

OCTAVIA: Is it cold outside?

ANNABELLE: Not really.

OCTAVIA: Misty?

ANNABELLE: Only on the fields. And in the town, too.

OCTAVIA: Did you walk from the station?

ANNABELLE: No, I took a taxi.

OCTAVIA: You're looking well.

ANNABELLE: I'm tired.

OCTAVIA: You are a bit pale and you've got rings under your eyes, but it suits you. Did you sleep on the train?

ANNABELLE: Not a wink.

OCTAVIA: That must be why, then. (*Pause.*) That blue thing was so dirty, I can't tell you. It would have got right into the fiber.

ANNABELLE: I don't know how I can thank you.

OCTAVIA: There's nothing to thank me for.

ANNABELLE: There is, there is. You've got so much to do . . .

OCTAVIA: Not with Anatol. Bartodziej does all that.

ANNABELLE: I just don't know how I can pay you back.

OCTAVIA: That's up to you.

ANNABELLE: How I can pay you back for this great kindness. For all this goodness and for that blue thing and for this sweater for Anatol which I started off all wrong but you've put right and for the tea . . .

OCTAVIA: Nice bag.

ANNABELLE: Which one?

OCTAVIA: That one.

OCTAVIA *indicates* ANNABELLE*'s handbag which is hanging over the chair.*

ANNABELLE: Oh, that one.

OCTAVIA: Is it new?

ANNABELLE: No, I had it before.

OCTAVIA: I've never seen it before.

ANNABELLE: A long time now.

OCTAVIA: Who is he?

ANNABELLE: It's none of your business.

OCTAVIA: On the contrary. You're living in this house.

ANNABELLE: Fancy, I never knew.

OCTAVIA: Under my roof!

ANNABELLE: Really? Anything else?

OCTAVIA: Who brought you back?

ANNABELLE: A leprechaun.

OCTAVIA: You insolent slut. But you will tell me.

ANNABELLE: If I want to.

OCTAVIA: You must tell me!

ANNABELLE: Must I? And why's that? Respect for my elders, is that it?

OCTAVIA: I have a right to know!

ANNABELLE: Because you'd like to, too, is that why?

OCTAVIA: This is my house!

ANNABELLE: Not your fanny, though!

A coughing fit can be heard from inside the house. The two women fall silent. The cough is violent, that of someone who is very ill, not someone who has just choked on something. An asthmatic, painful, recurring, prolonged cough which only becomes quiet after a long time.

ANNABELLE: Anatol?

OCTAVIA: Yes.

ANNABELLE: Has he caught a cold?

OCTAVIA: He was all right during the day,

ANNABELLE: It's probably nothing serious.

Pause. A louder cough.

OCTAVIA: It sounds as if his lungs are infected or something. Or something in his throat.

ANNABELLE: Something's happened to him.

OCTAVIA: It looks like it.

ANNABELLE: I'll go to him.

ANNABELLE *moves off toward the rest of the house.*

OCTAVIA: Leave him! (ANNABELLE *stops. Pause.*) Or at least take your coat off. And have a wash.

ANNABELLE *turns back, and sits down on the chair helplessly.*

ANNABELLE: That won't help.

OCTAVIA: No, it won't.

Pause.

ANNABELLE: What can I do?

OCTAVIA: Don't you know?

ANNABELLE: No, I don't.

OCTAVIA: Then you'll have to think.

ANNABELLE: I have thought.

OCTAVIA: And?

ANNABELLE: And I can't do anything . . .

OCTAVIA: That's because you haven't thought long enough.

ANNABELLE: No. I keep on thinking.

OCTAVIA: Not long enough because perhaps you're only thinking about tomorrow, or Tuesday. But you haven't thought about what it'll be like later—in a year's time, or two years', or ten . . . (*Pause.*) Have you? But you must. Because it can't go on that long. Now you leave and come back to him. But one day you won't come back.

ANNABELLE: I won't leave him.

OCTAVIA: Why make futile promises?

ANNABELLE: Never!

OCTAVIA: It sounds good. (*Pause.*) He's a total cripple.

ANNABELLE: I'll take him away from here.

OCTAVIA: He likes it here.

ANNABELLE: I'll take him!

OCTAVIA: Where to? And what will you live on? His pension?

ANNABELLE: I can work?

OCTAVIA: In that office? That planning office?

ANNABELLE: It'll be enough for us.

OCTAVIA: And who'll look after him? (*Pause.*) You're telling yourself fairy tales which you don't even believe yourself, but something definite has to be decided. And it's not a question of keeping him and all the rest. This is about you. Today you still came back, but what happens next, and how long will you still be able to put up with all this? Is this the way it's going to be until death—his or yours? His sooner than . . .

ANNABELLE: Don't say that!

OCTAVIA: You've thought about it.

ANNABELLE: Never!

OCTAVIA: It's better to think about the things you've thought about, otherwise you can start having all sorts of thoughts. Sometimes a person can kill in order not to steal. The shame of it may be smaller, but the sin is greater.

ANNABELLE: Why are you talking like this?

OCTAVIA: Because I'm sorry for you. I can see you're being tormented by all these various thoughts. And because of us, because of me, and Bartodziej . . . We were living in peace, and that's how we'd like to end our lives . . . But now all sorts of things are beginning to happen . . . And all sorts of things can happen. I don't want that.

ANNABELLE: I'll take Anatol.

OCTAVIA: Anatol will stay here.

ANNABELLE: So you're throwing me out, are you?

OCTAVIA: But my dear child, why say that? Rather tell me: have you got anyone?

ANNABELLE: I've had offers.

OCTAVIA: I'm not asking you that, I'm not asking you about offers. Have you got anyone special?

ANNABELLE: He wants to marry me.

OCTAVIA: Really?

ANNABELLE: That's what he said.

OCTAVIA: Before or after?

ANNABELLE: After. All the time.

OCTAVIA: That means he really does want to. Who is he?

ANNABELLE: Mercedes Coupe.

OCTAVIA: Who's that?

ANNABELLE: He's forty, divorced, in very good shape. He lives abroad.

OCTAVIA: What's he do?

ANNABELLE: He's in stocks and shares.

OCTAVIA: Did he come on a package tour?

ANNABELLE: Of course not! On business. High level.

OCTAVIA: Is all this true?

ANNABELLE: I know what I'm talking about.

Pause.

OCTAVIA: And what about the most important thing?

ANNABELLE: Better than I could have wanted.

OCTAVIA: Now I understand.

SCENE 17

ANATOL *in a wheelchair. Next to him, sitting on a low stool, is* BARTODZIEJ, *in shirt sleeves, with an open book in his lap.* BARTODZIEJ's *jacket is hanging from the back of the chair which is at some distance from them both.* BARTODZIEJ *is reading.*

BARTODZIEJ (*reading*):

"And now he the poet has seen and recognized him,
A God that's much worse, to whom are enthralled
Both time and the fate of all one-day kingdoms.
His face is enormous like ten moons in full,
A chain round his neck of undried yet heads.
Whoever denies him is touched by his wand,
Begins to gibber and loses his reason.
And whoever bows remains but a servant.
His new lord will treat him with utter disdain.
(*Short pause.*)
Who are you, Mighty One? Nights are so long.
Do we know you as . . ."

OCTAVIA (*off*): Do you want some cherries?

BARTODZIEJ (*to ANATOL*): Do you want some cherries? (*Barely perceptibly, and with great difficulty, ANATOL moves his head away from BARTODZIEJ in much the same way as do people whose motor faculties are severely impaired. Into the wings.*) I do!

OCTAVIA (*off*): Then come and get some!

BARTODZIEJ *lays the opened book down on the floor, gets up and leaves.*

SCENE 18

ANATOL *remains motionless in his wheelchair.*

SCENE 19

BARTODZIEJ *is carrying a blue enamel mug. He sits down on the stool, puts the mug on the floor, picks up the book, and reads.*

BARTODZIEJ (*reading*):

"And you who wear sensible Hegelian tails
And like wild windgiven corners,

Have you taken only a name that is new?
In a green bag there are secret bulletins. The poet hears . . . "

Break.

BARTODZIEJ *lays the opened book down on the floor. He picks up the mug with the cherries, stands up, and walks up to the open window. He stands and looks out of the window. After a while he starts to speak, eating the cherries in the pauses, or at moments chosen by the actor. He spits the stones into the palm of his hand and puts them into the mug.*

BARTODZIEJ: Great . . . Maybe he was great . . . I don't know . . . I thought he was great, the Spirit of History. Only you could never get any toilet paper. "Storming the heavens they scorned matter." And you still can't. But what does that matter in the face of greatness, I thought to myself. And all those not dried out heads . . . Just the same. What do they matter in the face of that Spirit? They'll dry out one day and then it'll be pretty. And that's how everything got evened out. Severed heads were worth as much as toilet paper.

Pause.

VOICE FROM THE STREET: Mend your pots and pans!

A longer pause than before.

BARTODZIEJ: They're playing soccer. The other side of the river . . . (*Pause.*) And the result of the match was one to nothing. No numbers other than one. Count to one. (*Pause.*) We had nothing and he had one.

VOICE FROM THE STREET (*nearer than before*): Mend your pots and pans!

BARTODZIEJ: They say that being a whore is not a profession, it's a character trait. And Socrates said: "Know thyself." To this day I don't know what he meant by that. All I know is that people know me. "He who doesn't know me will get to know me very soon," as Captain Ziółkowski used to say. Maybe one person won't manage to get to know another, but two or three together . . . Not to mention when there are more of those who know you. Let's say a hundred thousand. No, I've exaggerated a bit there. You have to know someone at close quarters. We knew Captain Ziółkowski personally.

VOICE FROM THE STREET (*near*): Mend your pots and pans!

BARTODZIEJ (*watching the amateur soccer match across the river*): Goal!

BARTODZIEJ *puts the mug down on the floor near the window, goes over to the chair, takes a glasses case out of the pocket of his jacket, takes the glasses out, puts them on, puts the case into his trouser pocket, and returns to the window.*

BARTODZIEJ: There are so many of them there! All tiny tots. More than you need . . . More than twelve a side, much more . . . (*Counts.*) One, two, three . . . five . . . eight. Eleven . . . thirteen, fourteen, fifteen . . . nineteen, twenty, twenty-one, two, three, four, yes! Twenty-five, twenty-six . . . Thirty! Thirty-one. Thirty-two, they all want to play, thirty-three, four . . . (*Turns back toward* ANATOL.) I can't count them, they just flash past. (*Back to the window.*) They're really kicking it! (BARTODZIEJ *takes his glasses off, takes the case out of his pocket, and puts the glasses into their case.*) Mind you, they've got a real ball. Not like we used to have. We used to play with a rag ball. (*He puts the glasses case into his pocket and turns to* ANATOL.) Shall we read something, then? (*He moves away from the window and sits down on the stool again next to* ANATOL. *He picks up the book, turns over a few pages, and reads.*)

"Red citadels and capitals that fall
Wings in the skies and rivers of wire
Are there for a moment and turn into dust.
Where is the fire's heat, the moving whips of fire,
Where are the rust-red towers? I see clouds
And a day like the one that was before time."

VOICE FROM THE STREET (*moving away*): Mend your pots and paaans!

Comments about Chronology

The time in which the play is set—both its own historical time (separate from the time of the action on stage, or the time of its theatrical presentation) and the references contained in it to the historical time outside its own historical time— is set out below. However, before a designated person (actor or director) or simply an interested person (the general reader) starts looking at it, the author would like him or her to take into account that though the coordination of times and actions of the play passes any tests of probability, this play is not to be categorized as a historical document. For instance, the author knows of no case of a spectacular amnesty in the People's Republic of Poland in 1964. This does not mean that such a case did not, or could not, have happened. Similarly, the character of Anatol is entirely the author's creation which does not rule out the possibility that certain of its elements could be real, and some most certainly are real.

Historical time is shown most clearly—in visual terms—through dress. The extent to which a production of this play is set in a precise historical time is left to the performers: it can be very precise, more or less, or completely imprecise. The history (in the sense of the story) of this play is sufficiently synthetic to be real regardless of the decision chosen.

The historical time of the play (its own):

Act One

A. BARTODZIEJ (Scene 1)—spring 1964, the prologue and a particular correspondence with the end of Act One land simultaneously with the beginning of Act Two.
B. BARTODZIEJ, OCTAVIA (Scene 2)—autumn 1962.
C. BARTODZIEJ, ANATOL, PSYCHIATRIST (Scene 3)—winter 1964.
D. BARTODZIEJ, ANATOL—the game of chess (Scene 4)—winter 1964, shortly after the visit to the Psychiatrist.
E. BARTODZIEJ, ANATOL, OCTAVIA (Scenes 5 to 12)—spring 1964.

Act Two

BARTODZIEJ, ANNABELLE, ANATOL—the day after the last scene of Act One, through one day and one night.

Act Three

A. OCTAVIA, ANNABELLE (Scenes 1 to 9)—autumn 1964.
B. OCTAVIA, BARTODZIEJ (Scene 10)—shortly after the previous scene.
C. OCTAVIA, ANNABELLE (Scenes 11 to 16)—spring 1965.
D. BARTODZIEJ, ANATOL - the ending (Scene 17)—summer 1965.

The whole: from autumn 1962 (Act One, Scene 2) to summer 1965 (the ending).

References outside the play's own time and defining some of the contents of its own time:
The Warsaw Uprising—1944
The end of the War—1945
Anatol's arrest—1949
Bartodziej's wedding—1953
Anatol's amnesty (in the play's own time)—1964
Bartodziej's anxieties, 1st phase—1955-1957
Bartodziej's anxieties, 2nd phase—1957-1962
Bartodziej's anxieties, 3rd phase (in the play's own time)—1962-1964

Sławomir Mrożek

MILITARY SECRET

Dušan Jovanović

DUŠAN JOVANOVIĆ
Photo courtesy of Dušan Jovanović

MILITARY SECRET AND THE ENGAGED THEATRE OF DUŠAN JOVANOVIĆ

Ivan Talijančić

Dušan Jovanović (b. 1939 in Belgrade, former Yugoslavia) is a writer, director, and educator, who has challenged, awed, influenced, and taught generations of audiences and theatre artists in his homeland. His work has nonetheless made its mark well beyond Slovenian borders as his plays and productions have been extensively translated, produced, and toured internationally for the past three decades, even reaching the epicenter of the American theatre—New York—when a touring production of his play *Liberation of Skopje*, presented at La MaMa, was honored by the Obie award jury with a Special Mention in 1982.

From the very beginning of his theatrical career, Jovanović has been endowed with an uncanny ability to embody and transcend the complexities of his time. Upon completion of his studies at the Ljubljana Academy of Dramatic Art, Jovanović pursued directing and playwriting, co-founding two theatres in the 1960s, the Theatre Pupilija Ferkeverk and the Glej Experimental Theatre. This early period of his career was characterized by performative experiments in line with the renegade, anti-bourgeois spirit shared by many of the neo-avant-garde theatre artists of his generation. His aesthetics were not dissimilar in nature to the work being developed by his American contemporaries in the Open Theatre and the Living Theatre—the parallels being nothing short of extraordinary given how sheltered many Yugoslavian theatre artists were under communist rule.

Despite Jovanović's commitment to radical experimentation and his kinship with members of the avant-garde theatre movement of the sixties and seventies, he has remained generally cautious of ideology, hyper aware of its potential power to corrupt and distort. In his 1971 piece, *Play Out of a Tumor in the Brain, or Polluting the Air* (*Igrajte tumor v glavi ali onesnaženje zraka*), he addresses directly the role of ideology in the theatre. A metatheatrical work dealing with the conflict between the traditional and the innovative, the play focuses on the actions of a small group of avant-garde artists from a local theatre ensemble who have forcibly taken over the central theatre building, barricading themselves in. Their action, intent on driving out the conservative artists and redirecting the theatre's course, escalates into a political affair at the national level. As the group's lack of cohesion and instability becomes manifest, authoritarianism, revolt, and murder ensue. *Play Out of a Tumor in the Brain* successfully dodges the assumption that Jovanović may have intended to champion the values of the neo-avant-garde over the traditionalists. Instead, it becomes a meditation on how utopian ideologies implode, becoming sites of inevitable violence—a theme that Jovanović will continue to explore throughout his oeuvre.

Though Jovanović's work at both the Theatre Pupilija Ferkeverk and the Glej Experimental Theatre brought him significant critical attention, his experimentation during the 1960s and 1970s was not to be limited to what he could accomplish within the confines of his own independent theatres. In 1969, the Mladinsko Theatre, itself an emerging center for theatrical innovation aimed at young audiences, invited Jovanović to direct a production of Aleksandar Popović's *Little Red Riding Hood*. With this initial project, a collaborative relationship was forged. As a result, numerous productions directed by Jovanović were staged at the Mladinsko over the next decade, including his groundbreaking work *Victims of Bang Bang Fashion*—which demanded an innovative rehearsal process rooted in improvisation. Jovanović's active presence at the theatre gradually transformed it—philosophically as well as organizationally—and by 1979, he became the theatre's artistic director.

During his leadership, Jovanović instituted formal changes to the Mladinsko, positioning it to become a leading forum for political theatre in the country. Organizationally, he eliminated seasonal subscriptions in order to make room for more flexible rehearsal periods that could accommodate touring. He made substantive changes to the ensemble and technical staff to allow for an influx of new ideas and to raise the level of professionalism. He expanded the physical space by acquiring more non-traditional performance areas. The theatre's repertory was rethought—with a particular effort to include more new Slovenian drama. As a result of the changes and the nurturing of relationships with theatres outside of Ljubljana, the Mladinsko became, according to Jovanović, a "reference point" for what theatre in Yugoslavia could become once the old systems were displaced.

Under Jovanović's tenure, Mladinsko not only forged new paradigms for theatrical expression—so much so that it became the most progressive institution in the former Yugoslavia—it also became a veritable incubator for emerging innovative directors, producing a generation of visionaries (such as Dragan Živadinov, Tomaž Pandur, and Vito Taufer) who are now among the most prominent theatre artists in the region.

During the 1980s, the Mladinsko Theatre has been appropriately called a "political theatre" and an "engaged theatre"—not necessarily for what it promised but for what it exposed. Its political efficacy lay in its multifaceted nature—the panoply of perspectives, consequences, and possibilities it offered to counter the illusion of unity propagated by the state. Audiences who were. to quote Jovanović, "already imbued with viruses of doubt, boredom, apathy, and hidden resistances to totalitarianism" reacted with fervent enthusiasm. Rather than espousing an alternative ideology, the theatre served as a site of diversity, a space to gather in and expose "the crack in the dam."

Jovanović's commitment to a political theatre that serves to challenge existing ideological systems rather than advance alternative agendas can be observed not only in his directorial choices at the Mladinsko but also in the playscripts, which often center on the erosion of utopian microcosms. His narratives are explorations of apparently inevitable processes, journeys from utopian myth to a dystopian reality.

Jovanović's 1983 play *Military Secret* (*Vojaška skrivnost*) charts such a journey—from ideological promise to chaotic violence—through allegory and satire. The play, less experimental in form than his early work, is crafted more in keeping with the Western theatrical canon, using a classical dramaturgical structure. Set in a zoological institute where research in animal languages is being undertaken, Jovanović uses anthropomorphized animals alongside human scientists to illustrate how an ideological system, fractured by conflict and personal agendas, descends into brutal chaos.

The play remains a testament to Jovanović's eerily prescient understanding of the turn of political tides in the former Yugoslavia. At times reminiscent (in terms of genre and subject matter) of works by such literary luminaries as Eugène Ionesco and George Orwell, the play could be interpreted as a veiled allegory of the Yugoslavian society at the time, and its imminent fate. In the wake of Tito's death in 1980, his largely successful efforts to maintain harmony among the federation's culturally and economically disparate republics were beginning to disintegrate, and the strife between the ruling intelligentsia (represented by the scientists in the play) and the general populace (i.e. the animal characters) was beginning to rear its ugly head. Beginning with cheerful escapism, and gradually escalating to dissent and chaos, the play anticipates the civil war that marked the following decade's fall of communism and the devastating dissolution of the former Yugoslavia of the early 1990s.

Military Secret remains a chillingly foreboding testament to the end of an era, while also serving as a prototype for a particular form of political theatre that works to avoid the ideological systems it is critiquing. Curiously, the play resonates well beyond the historical period in which it was written: it taps into global concerns of the early twenty-first-century—anticipating the current environmental crisis and warning about the cataclysmic consequences

MILITARY SECRET

A ZOOLINGUISTIC MIRACLE IN THREE SEQUENCES AND TWO PAUSES

Dušan Jovanović

Translated by Ivan Talijančić

CHARACTERS Of ANIMAL ORIGIN

ROCKY—a racehorse
FLO—a donkey
BLACKY—a stray dog
DOLLY—a poodle
BO—a black bear
GOLDIE—a boar
TOM—a village tomcat, black
DOT—a parakeet
STELLA—a cow
MARY—a white Persian
FANNIE—a goat
IKA—a sheep
VITO—a chimpanzee
RAT

CHARACTERS Of HUMAN ORIGIN

ALICE—a six-year-old girl
VERONICA—her mother, a nurse
LIZZY—a cook
DOCTOR LEPTIN—a scientist
DOCTOR GOODMAN—a scientist
DOCTOR HITMAN—a scientist
PROFESSOR HEGEL—a law professor
DOCTOR HORNER—a scientist
FRANKIE—a janitor, no qualifications

Hallucinations and dream characters are enacted by the individuals of animal origin.

The action takes place at the Zoolinguistic Institute at the Veterinary Clinic. The playing space is divided into three parts. The largest one is dedicated to the convalescence of the sick patients of animal origin, and we refer to it as the Patients' Ward. The second part suggests a study/laboratory/office area: we refer to it as the Headquarters. The third playing area is, indeed, just a corner. We call it the Surveillance Room.

The only caged animal is BO the bear.

FIRST SEQUENCE

HEADQUARTERS

The opening credits of a film scroll in the darkness, acknowledging, among others, that the text was written by Doctor A. Polanec. The film is shot in the typical scientific documentary style—the visuals are closely illustrated by the speaker's voiceover.

SPEAKER: One of the first—if not *the* first—to speak with animals was our fellow citizen, one of our most prominent scientists, Doctor Ivan Regen—born in 1868, deceased in 1947. As we all know, Regen studied the sound of crickets and grasshoppers. He sought to discover how and why they chirp. The conclusion he reached is that the male's song is the road sign for the female to find her mate in the thick grass. By the means of a very rudimentary experiment, he proved that what matters to the female is indeed only the voice of the male and not his external appearance. He lured a female cricket by phone by transmitting the male's chirping from a remote location to the room where the female had been. Once he placed the receiver on the floor, the female immediately rushed to it, circled around it, tried to get inside, and behaved as if the male had been inside. With this and other equally original experiments, Regen discovered that crickets and grasshoppers communicate amongst themselves. By studying the world of small insects, our scientist went even further with his discoveries. For instance, he learned that some of these six-legged musicians play in duets; and, if three males find themselves on a sunny slope, they sing in a trio, and if there are even more around, they form a chorus . . .

Having become deeply acquainted with insects, and once it was evident that the grasshoppers communicated with each other, it occurred to the scientist that he could learn their language and begin conversing with them. Day in and day out, he would record their music and transpose it into notes. After a thorough analysis of these scores, he decided to play this music himself in order to establish contact with a grasshopper. His desire was to answer its song with a song.

At last, one late evening, on August 31, 1925, two young males were chirping in an astonishing canon. When their song reached the peak of its beauty, Regen pitched in with a chant of his own. The accompanying singer went silent, while the lead went on to sing with Regen, and thus began the amazing game between the man and the insect . . . The male who chirped with Regen had for sure taken him for one of his own kind—he treated Regen as a bug. Our scientist himself was said to have nearly swooned from excitement.

Until that fateful moment, one sweltering August night in 1925, no man had ever come closer to an animal. The ice was broken.

HITMAN *turns the projector off and switches on the lights.* LEPTIN *stands by the door.*

LEPTIN: My name is Leptin. I am in charge of the surveillance department.

HITMAN: Part soldier, part physician. In brief: a belligerent doctor.

Mooing, barking, and parrot's screeching is heard from the Patients' Ward.

HITMAN: Your resignation comes at a most inopportune time. I am aware that many are vying for your services, but you have a crisis at hand at your home base.

LEPTIN: I am due to take office at the Biological Institute in Cologne as of July 1.

HITMAN: You will stay here and see to it that things get back to normal.

LEPTIN: I intend to get married.

HITMAN: You are speaking to an unrepentant bachelor.

LEPTIN: The liaisons in the Institute are such that there isn't a whole lot that can be accomplished. I'd rather go someplace where there is an opportunity to get the work done.

HITMAN: Goodman is the only person left from the first prewar generation of biologists who concerned themselves with the decoding of speech of certain animal species. The younger ones are . . . Well, you know as well as I do. It's a desert out there. You just have to remain patient for a while longer.

PATIENTS' WARD

HORNER *and the nurse* VERONICA *make rounds, with the six-year-old* ALICE *roaming around in close proximity.* HORNER *goes from one patient to the next without much interest. He checks their charts, waves his hand here and there, which can be interpreted as a chronic display of desperation.*

HORNER: Addison's disease, oligophrenia, orchitis, various fractures—and so on! What kind of a concept is that, for crying out loud? It's, more or less, as if we were planting fruit, grains, and spring vegetables in the same patch of dirt! This is unheard of anywhere else in the world! The Clinic is one thing; the Institute's research project is something entirely different!

VERONICA: Alice, get out of there! (*To* HORNER.) Pardon me.

HORNER: Can't you get someone to baby-sit that child?

VERONICA: Mother got sick.

HORNER: Whose mother?

VERONICA: *My* mother. Leptin's went to the baths.

HORNER: At her own expense, I hope?

HEADQUARTERS

HITMAN *and* GOODMAN, *alone.*

HITMAN: We received your letter.

GOODMAN: Yes.

HITMAN: It was quite a surprise for us all.

GOODMAN: I can imagine.

HITMAN: And quite a disappointment, I might add.

GOODMAN (*hurt*): I know, I know, I know!

PATIENTS' WARD

HORNER: While working at the division of odd-toed ungulates, at least I knew what I was doing, I was professionally equipped to handle my job. My thesis encompasses a wide spectrum of issues from the health insurance of all animals to non-infectious, organic, developmental and metabolic diseases, deficiencies, intoxications . . . One cannot say that I am not sufficiently educated. I just simply can't get my bearings straight in this chaos.

HEADQUARTERS

HITMAN: What is the matter with you?

GOODMAN: I put it all in writing. I am no longer capable of handling these things. I long for the contact with animals . . .

HITMAN: Are you tired?

GOODMAN: I paddle away, and the boat won't budge. There are no sails . . . no winds . . . no sea. I feel like I am rolling in place on the eyeball of a blind horse.

HITMAN: Oh please! Why such resignation? (*Firmly.*) The dissolution of the Institute is out of the question!

GOODMAN: Let someone else take over. I can't do it anymore.

HITMAN: Your proposal is absurd . . . Downright crazy! Your Institute is amongst the world's best in the field of zoolinguistics—undoubtedly, much to your credit. The eyes of the world's scientific establishment are gazing intently upon us. There is no going back.

GOODMAN: I am old . . .

HITMAN: You must endure.

GOODMAN: Find some younger zealot.

HITMAN: It is *you* who must forge ahead.

GOODMAN: Ahead, where?

HITMAN: Ahead, period! Everything but the resignation! You put in decades of work into this! We have no choice! This is a capital project. We must dig further, deeper, we must take risks . . . leaps of faith!

GOODMAN: Is there anyone left who still cares? We are no longer a team, everyone is running off, throwing in the towel . . .

HITMAN: You care, I care—that *is* enough. You will get all-encompassing support. If all else should go down the drain, so be it. But this—no way! End of story.

PATIENTS' WARD

VERONICA: The work never stops here, you know?

HORNER: Veronica, listen! I filed a complaint. I asked Goodman directly, if we truly are what we are—meaning, a research project—why do we harbor *sick* animals? Isn't that at odds with our mission? Wouldn't it be easier to give up the therapeutic approach and devote ourselves exclusively to prevention?

LEPTIN *enters the Ward. It is clear that he overheard* HORNER.

LEPTIN: Horner, you don't get it, as usual! For starters, we made a conscious choice in selecting the patients who, under the ordinary circumstances at the clinic, certainly would not fit. Secondly, our program intentionally targets critical cases, as they require considerably longer treatments. And why is that? Medication time is also the time it takes us to form a community. It is within the collective destiny of a community that the factor of individual crises encourages the process of socializing, the latter being a prerequisite for dialogue. The dialogue being *the* subject of our investigation!

HORNER (*aggressively*): Well if we're talking therapy, let's roll up the sleeves and go at it!

LEPTIN (*interjecting*): Please—not in front of the clients!

HORNER (*sardonically*): You think they understand me too?

LEPTIN: Perhaps you underestimate them.

HORNER (*furiously*): You're out of your mind, I swear.

HORNER *rushes out, while* FRANKIE *comes in through the other door.*

FRANKIE: Hey. So, wassup with our comrade head doctor? No morning rounds for him, eh? Isn't that in his job description?

VERONICA: Comrade Frankie, that is not your concern!

FRANKIE: In this moment, I am not just your Comrade Frankie, but the representation of the workers' inspectoration. And that's a certain organ, in case you didn't know.

LEPTIN (*takes* VERONICA *by the hand*): It's alright. Of course we know.

VERONICA: Doctor Goodman is in his office. He is talking with Doctor Hitman.

FRANKIE: Who's that dude?

VERONICA: He came to us from the Military Medical Academy.

FRANKIE: For good?

LEPTIN: More or less.

FRANKIE: Holy cow! (*Shortly afterward.*) So you're tellin' me we got emergency management?

HEADQUARTERS

LIZZY, HITMAN

LIZZY: You know I adore these beasts, but the meals are a headache. With birds and ruminants it's okay, but carnivores—it's always a bunch of problems. Meat's just expensive as hell, and sometimes you can't even get it!

HITMAN: Which animal is nearest to your heart?

LIZZY: Well I am a country girl, I am used to the domestic kind, but these tropical ones are somethin', aren't they?

PATIENTS' WARD

ALICE (*suddenly*): But I know you!

MARY: From where?

ALICE: I saw you at the fur boutique . . . Granny was buying a fox choker . . .

MARY: Ah, the boutique living!

ALICE: You didn't like it?

MARY: It was interesting at first, but little by little it became unbearable.

TOM: What could have possibly been that bad?

MARY: How would you like to live in a morgue, 24/7?

ALICE: A morgue?

MARY: Yes, with dead animals hanging all around you? Men mass-murder innocent animals so they can adorn themselves with their furs.

TOM: You think I don't know that? I do, and my mental health is still intact. I got nerves of steel.

MARY: But for how long?

TOM: Nerves are forever.

MARY: Yours may be. The mice ate mine.

ALICE: Oh!

MARY: Plus, this polio that struck me, it's all nerves . . .

MARY *freezes and screeches in fear.*

MARY: There he is!

RAT: Don't worry, I am the rat mama, a friend of your sister's!

MARY: I don't have any sisters!

RAT: What a beauty. She's got a silky, pure, white coat, fleshy lips and pink paws. Is she the one?

MARY: Only the four of us were entitled to a pedigree—my three brothers and myself. They tossed my sister in the water.

RAT: I found her at the landfill.

MARY: Oh!

RAT: She was still alive. I took her for a walk through the city's sewer system.

MARY: Oh!

RAT: I tanned her skin . . . I brought it so I can show you.

MARY: Oh!

RAT: Your mistress Laura may want to sell it, perhaps?

MARY: Oh!

RAT: Or *you* could sell it—under the table! No one will ever know.

MARY: Oh!

RAT: We can split the booty fifty-fifty. Deal?

APPARITION OF A LADY: Ohhh, she's so adorable!

APPARITION OF A GENTLEMAN: Bye-bye, kitty!

APPARITION OF A LADY: Bye-bye kitty!

MRS. LAURA'S GHOST: Mary . . . ! Pussycat . . . ! My sciatica is killing me, come lie on my back!

MARY: Yes, ma'am!

MRS. LAURA'S GHOST: Why aren't you purring, my darling? I can't fall asleep when you aren't.

MARY: But I am purring, ma'am!

MRS. LAURA'S GHOST: You're gurgling, Mary . . . Gurgling . . .

MARY: Oh!

ALICE: Ouch!

BO: They threw teargas in my den. I had to get out so I could breathe. I saw a rifle right in front of my face and I cried like a cub. You see, Mary, I am a fur now. They douse me with mothballs, so I don't need to itch or scratch. And in the wintertime, I proudly shroud the President of Friends of Youth at the Municipal Council. Everything's the same as it was before, except now I sleep in the summer and I don't ever feel the hunger again.

"No hunger, no thirst, no memories left.
Sweet bees, celebrate!—no more honey theft!"

ROCKY: Here's to our poet!

ALL: Cheers! To our poet!

MARY: Oh!

BO: Life is a prison cell, Mary, and the song that echoes within it—a dream about freedom!

ALICE: Wow!

BO: Mary, it's almost morning, I gotta get to the closet!

MRS. LAURA'S GHOST: Mary, if you can't purr nice and even, you may as well go sleep in the closet.

MARY: Bo, wait!

BO: Bye, Mary, see you in the closet!

APPARITION OF A LADY: Bye-bye, kitty!

RAT: Bye-bye kitty . . .

HEADQUARTERS

Telephone rings.

GOODMAN (*picks up the receiver*): Mary, who? Oh, yes, the Persian. Of course, we are running tests. Yes, ma'am, these things take some time. (*Moments later.*) My opinion? My opinion is that she's sick with something that's very similar to polio. Yes, those are the symptoms. By all means, feel free to call next week . . . (*Hangs up, to nurse* VERONICA.) Has the tocopherol been delivered?

VERONICA: Yes, but only the thousand-milligram vials. (*Goes to the adjacent room.*)

GOODMAN: At least something.

VERONICA (*from the adjacent room*): Aren't you going to the Council meeting?

GOODMAN (*telephone rings at his desk, he answers*): Yes, operate!

Sounds of a cat and a dog fighting are heard from the Patient's Ward.

GOODMAN (*slamming the receiver down*): I simply can't stand listening to Horner any more!

VERONICA (*from the adjacent room*): Leptin could substitute you! (*Enters carrying a phone.*) You got Moscow on the line.

GOODMAN (*nervously*): Don't you know how to transfer?

VERONICA: That button is broken, as you know.

GOODMAN: So why don't you call the phone company?

VERONICA: I called at least five times, but they never came!

GOODMAN: *Allo? Oui, c'est moi. Bonjour,* Comrade Pčelov. *Ça va? Parfaitement! Notre* black bear *vous attend impatiemment* . . . No, no—his name *Bo* . . . *Oui.* Good. *Khorosho.* We will come meet you at the airport. *Zdravstvuyte.* Good-bye! (*Hangs up.*)

HITMAN *enters the room.*

HITMAN (*dryly*): Call Moscow and tell them they have no reason to come here.

GOODMAN: What should I say?

HITMAN: Tell them the bear croaked.

GOODMAN: When?

HITMAN: Don't play dumb, please . . .

PATIENTS' WARD

GOLDIE: I figured out that words that represent the most beautiful things in the world all begin with "pi": "pink," "pint," "pipe," "pillow," "pizza," "pig." "Pig"—sounds so rapturous!

ROCKY: You're making it sound like you're proud of being a pig.

GOLDIE: I am a purebred Yorkshire, dumb ass . . .

ROCKY: As if a Yorkshire wasn't a pig!

GOLDIE: A Yorkshire is a Yorkshire. Don't you get it?

BLACKY: So what is the difference between a Yorkshire and an ordinary pig?

DOT: Porco vulgaris!

GOLDIE: A mature Yorkshire is not a pig for slaughter.

ROCKY: You mean, they won't make a goulash out of you?

GOLDIE: A friend of mine, Doctor Porcini, prefers horse goulash.

ROCKY (*sarcastically*): You don't say?

MARY (*naively*): They eat horses too?

GOLDIE: They go apeshit for colts.

BLACKY: Let's face it: Italians do cat roasts.

TOM: I don't buy it.

BLACKY: Grilled cat . . . it's a delicacy.

DOLLY: Garnished with rigatoni.

GOLDIE: I told you, horse goulash is what Doctor Porcini likes best.

ROCKY (*getting worked up*): Chopping up a racehorse to make goulash? This is unheard of! They grind up bears and donkeys to make sausages.

GOLDIE: It's a well-known fact that two-legged creatures adore horse burgers!

ROCKY: For the record, my fine-feathered friends: these gams are worth a million on the European market.

VITO: Ha-ha!

ROCKY: Eeee-ha-ha!

DOT: The word on the street in Nairobi is that ape meat is rather delicious.

VITO: Liar!

DOT: That came straight out of the British Consul's mouth, if you really care to know!

VITO: I know, that guy who ends up looking like my ass when he goes sunbathing.

DOT: You brute!

SURVEILLANCE ROOM

LEPTIN *and* HITMAN.

HITMAN: Can you tell me, at least roughly, what they are talking about?

LEPTIN: Judging from graphs on this screen, I'd say we are dealing with some sort of intolerance. The dialogue is rather stalled . . . insidious. This frequency up here seems to indicate something downright obscene . . . Recurring patterns are interesting . . .

HITMAN: Right. Wouldn't you say that's a bit general?

LEPTIN: The main difficulty in translating this language is that it is too spontaneous, unguarded, natural . . . Secondly, the trouble is that we have no sync between sound and movement.

PATIENTS' WARD

DOLLY: After lunch, Mrs. Jolly's paramour would always burp, stick a toothpick between his canines, and say: "Piggy is the most beautiful bird of them all!"

BLACKY: For sure he was referring to your lecherous mistress.

GOLDIE: Piggies are the sexiest bitches. No doubt about it.

TOM: Well, with cats, there is just no comparison.

GOLDIE: I wouldn't screw a cat if you paid me.

STELLA: Cows make bulls horny.

BLACKY: You know that expression "fucks like a cow?"

STELLA: No, what does it mean?

BLACKY: Means you are a lousy fuck.

STELLA: Oh really? Pardon me.

ROCKY: Hence the expression: "He is such a stallion!" I could do you anytime.

DOT: Bitches are the meanest and nastiest of them all.

BLACKY: Shut up, scarecrow!

DOT (*standoffishly*): Bitches ride your ass!

VITO: If you've never screwed a cute monkey, you don't know what you're missing.

SURVEILLANCE ROOM

LEPTIN: You see, I normally interpret these ornate peaks above the axis as some sort of a patriotic statement . . . metaphorically speaking, of course . . .

PATIENTS' WARD

GOLDIE: So you're saying I'd be better off screwing a woman?

DOLLY: You're all talk. A wagging tongue never knocked anyone up.

BLACKY: If I weren't so out of it because of all these pills, I'd be giving it to you good and hard.

DOLLY: I'm not *that* desperate.

BLACKY: No, you're not that lucky.

DOLLY: Listen, the studs who hit on me are of a different kind.

BLACKY: *Hugely* different, I bet.

GOODMAN *enters. He injects the poodle with a syringe.* LIZZY *enters behind him.* DOLLY *yelps in fear,* GOODMAN *tries to calm her down.*

LIZZY (*with hesitation*): Comrade Doctor, I don't mean to interrupt, but I just can't help myself . . .

GOODMAN: Don't go around in circles, Lizzy. What seems to be the problem?

LIZZY: That no-good, Frankie . . . I got a feelin' it's all his fault!

GOODMAN: Calm down, Dolly, be a good girl . . . ! (*To* LIZZY.) Frankie who?

LIZZY: Well, you know, Comrade Frankie, the janitor with no qualifications, pretends that I am after him . . .

GOODMAN: Lizzy, I am busy, can't you be brief?

LIZZY: He constantly loiters around the kitchen, even though I told him a hundred times it's none of his business!

GOODMAN: Throw him out, then!

LIZZY: I swear, Comrade Doctor, whatever I can get my hands on, I throw on his head . . . but it's no good, he just grins at me!

GOODMAN: He must be in love with you . . .

LIZZY: Comrade Doctor! He stole my recipes for Vito! I have no idea what to make him for lunch!

VITO *begins to show signs of agitation.*

GOODMAN: Excuse me, but who is Vito?

LIZZY: The monkey! This funny chimp with skin cancer or whatever it is . . .

VITO *shows further signs of agitation, while* GOODMAN *observes him with interest.*

GOODMAN: Aha, of course. And why do you suspect Frankie would steal your monkey recipes?

LIZZY: No one else is capable of such unsavory jokes, Comrade Doctor, no one else! He has no respect for the animals! He comes to the kitchen acting all high and mighty and—get this—he *spits* into the cats' stew! (MARY *and* TOM *hiss angrily.*) You know what I mean? Then he says: "A bit of spice goes a long way!" What can one do with a man like that? A janitor who is clueless about hygiene! We should at least enroll him in some kind of a course! This can't go on!

GOODMAN: Alright, I will call him and talk to him. As far as monkeys are concerned, you need to cook . . .

LIZZY: I beg your pardon, Comrade Doctor, gotta write this down . . .

LIZZY *is looking for a pencil.* GOODMAN *takes turns petting different animals and looking at them with concern.*

GOODMAN: So then: different fruits, bulbs, roots, tubers can be the basis of their daily meals, to be supplemented with roots, seeds, and nuts—once a week, whole, not minced—as well as buds, such as cabbage, leafy greens, spinach, juicy stems, string beans, rhubarb, and all kinds of fruits, of course . . . Though, they generally prefer bananas.

LIZZY: With a pinch of salt?

GOODMAN (*exiting*): That's not necessary!

LIZZY: Thank you, Comrade Doctor!

A short and scrawny man in rubber boots and filthy overalls appears at the door. Under his moustache, he sports a wide, stupid grin.

FRANKIE: Twice a day, I like to come here where it's nice and warm to let it rip in peace. How about that? (*Walks toward* LIZZY.)

LIZZY: Don't you dare come near me!

In that moment, something unexpected occurs. The animals begin to hiss, growl, and threaten. The atmosphere is tense and aggressive. FRANKIE stops in his tracks, begins to withdraw, then runs for the door. LIZZY slips the notebook in her pocket, nods to VITO, and exits. HORNER enters through another door. Silence.

HORNER (*after a brief pause, pensively*): A wolf comes into a restaurant, and a waiter runs to him immediately: "Mister Wolf, your honor, what can I get for you?" And the wolf goes: "An innocent lamb for starters, then we'll see." "Would you like some salad, Mister Wolf, or something to drink?" "Salad? No," the wolf growls. "And to quench my thirst, bring three bottles of blood, preferably fresh and not too chilled."

A protracted silence ensues. HORNER tensely observes the animals.

HEADQUARTERS / SURVEILLANCE ROOM

VERONICA (*on the intercom*): Darling, Goodman is asking what Horner is doing in the patients' ward.

LEPTIN: He provokes the patients, dear. He is trying his best to disgust them as much as possible.

GOODMAN: (*as* VERONICA *switches off the intercom*): If something goes wrong, intervene.

LEPTIN: Fine.

PATIENTS' WARD

HITMAN *and* ALICE *carefully sneak into the room, each from a different entrance. Not noticing them,* HORNER *takes a chug from the flask he always carries in his inside coat pocket.*

HORNER: Well, one fine day, the wolf decides to go for liquor. After drinking all day and well into the night, and getting properly sloshed, he stumbles into some chi-chi nightclub. The whores scream in fear, the drunkards go numb, the orchestra stops, the dancing girls run for cover. So, the maître d' musters up his strength and approaches the wolf's table with a double scotch on his tray. "I beg your pardon," says he, "but we are left without entertainment because our ladies are terrified of you, I am afraid you'll get bored in this establishment." "Under no circumstances," says the wolf, "will I allow you to be left without entertainment. I will get up on the stage myself!" "Wonderful, beautiful," says the maître d'. "Shall I tell the orchestra to accompany you?" "Naturally," says the wolf, "Let them play the good old 'Dream on, Vegetarians!'"

HORNER *incessantly stares at the animals, who pay no attention to him.*

ALICE (*with a strange detachment in her voice*): That joke's not funny at all!

HORNER *starts to leave, but* FANNY *finally caves in and bursts into tears, hysterically. This escalates to a nervous breakdown. Abhorred,* HORNER *retreats, and* HITMAN *runs after him.* LEPTIN *enters through another door in haste.*

LEPTIN: How many times did I tell you not to listen to that provocateur? He is clueless when it comes to wolves! He made it all up! Calm down, Fanny! Come here, let's go for a walk! Off we go, to the garden! Off we go, sweetie, come along, you'll feel better, it's spring outside, everything's green . . . Let's all go!

ALICE: To the garden! To the garden!

The animals follow ALICE *and* LEPTIN, *except for* BO *and* TOM.

TOM: Is your mother still alive?

BO: She died in childbirth.

TOM: When you were born?

BO: Me and my brother Mo.

TOM: And your father—was he born in a zoo, too?

BO: The hunters caught him and put him in a cage while he was still a cub.

TOM: Was it hard to get used to the cage?

BO: You can't imagine. He cried his heart out.

TOM: And now?

BO: He doesn't cry anymore.

TOM: You got it easier: you weren't born in the woods, you never tasted wilderness.

BO: The wilderness is in you. It rises every morning in your muscles, your belly, your nostrils, your claws, your jaw, your fur . . .

VERONICA *enters, looking for* ALICE.

VERONICA: Alice! Alice? Has anyone seen Alice? (*Exits.*)

TOM: Where there is a man, there is no freedom—right?

BO: None.

TOM: But why? Why does it have to be like that?

BO: It's a by-product of the intellect. The intellect seeks to arrange things so that it's all shiny and good for those who got it, and for those who haven't . . . it's all rotten and sad.

TOM: So, the intellect is selfish?

BO: Indeed. The intellect cares only about its own offspring, and ignores the others'.

TOM: And what if either of us were to become . . . intellectual?

BO: We can't.

TOM: Too late?

BO: We can't.

TOM: But we can learn.

BO: Learn? We just have to say no.

TOM: No?

BO: Just say no.

TOM: If the opportunity were to present itself, would you escape from the zoo?

BO: Oh yeah.

TOM: And risk death?

BO: And risk death.

TOM: Would you escape from here?

BO: I don't know . . .

TOM: You wouldn't?

BO: For some time, I used to think that this clinic was the ideal place . . . for all of us.

TOM: And now, what do you think?

BO: Ah! It would be better for me to think nothing at all.

HEADQUARTERS

HITMAN *and* HORNER—*the latter being rather drunk.*

HORNER: Goodman is the biologists' old guard. The lover of the laws of nature. A dreamer. Attracted to the impossible.

HITMAN (*ironically*): I can't imagine what it'd take for a man to become like that.

HORNER: I bet his granny told him stories when he was a kid . . . told him he could hear the animals talk on the Midsummer's Eve, provided that someone secretly slipped fern seeds in his pocket. That seems to have had a life-long effect on him. He is a lonesome weirdo, a dreamer. He carries on talking with bears, and can't spare a word for his collaborators. What a peculiar breed! But I don't blame him. I pity him, to be honest.

HITMAN: And Leptin?

HORNER: Welllllll—Leptin is a bird of a different feather. The kind that knows what he wants. He'll squeeze the last drop out of Goodman, then get the hell out of here. No worries, he'll manage to convert Goodman's ravings into hard currency. Otherwise, they wouldn't be calling him from Japan and Germany at least twice a week. They have a nose for his kind over there.

HITMAN: It seems you don't care much for this project.

HORNER: On the contrary! And yet, you know what? I believe in these . . . *domestic* kinds, you understand? One could manage just fine with them, always! But these southern species—it's a different language, customs, *everything*! It just doesn't fit! They are so savage and misbehaved . . . need I say more? Just look at that monkey and that parrot! They scare you shitless . . . if you'll pardon my expression.

HITMAN: And what would be the solution?

HORNER: Segregation! Two departments! No time like the present! It would make our work so much easier.

VERONICA *enters.*

VERONICA: Doctor Horner, pardon the interruption. Stella has diarrhea.

HORNER: Without any pills to prescribe, my hands are tied!

VERONICA: Well, I thought perhaps, with Doctor Hitman being with the Military Medical Academy . . .

HITMAN (*grinning*): I am not from the Military Medical Academy.

PATIENTS' WARD

TOM: And what do you do at the zoo at night?

BO: I think. I dream. I stare into the darkness. Sometimes I grab the bars and try to rip the fence out. I rest my head on the ground and listen. I compose poems.

TOM (*pondering*): How did you become so withdrawn?

BO: Sooner or later, everyone turns odd here. Either you lose your mind or you withdraw completely in hopes of croaking as quickly as possible. (*A moment later.*) Take Val, the monkey—she's a typical example.

TOM: What happened to her?

BO: She miscarried a cub. Next day, she pulled in a two-year-old female through the bars.

TOM: She kidnapped her?

BO: Yes. She nestled her close, played with her, and nursed her for a few days.

TOM: And then?

BO: A shooter fired a sedative projectile into her rump. And now they are lacing her food with god-knows-what—all day long she just lounges on her back and masturbates.

TOM: Holy cow!

BO: There's never a shortage of revolting stories around here. That's just the way it is. Domestic animals can't stand being without people, and the wild ones can't stand people at all.

TOM: Perhaps the solution would be to . . . domesticate all of us.

BO: You are raving.

TOM (*pondering*): When I stop and think about it, you are half-domesticated yourself. And you have many good friends amongst the guards.

BO (*incisively*): Honey, the main deal here in the zoo is: independence for the guards, and slavery for the bears. Everything else is just window dressing.

HEADQUARTERS

HITMAN *and* GOODMAN. ALICE *sits in* GOODMAN*'s lap.*

HITMAN: What is your end goal for this project?

GOODMAN: Understanding, togetherness, *limitless communication*. Scientifically speaking, this project is open-ended.

HITMAN: We'll have to close it.

GOODMAN: Meaning?

HITMAN: We'll have to define its technological end.

GOODMAN: And what would that be?

HITMAN: Computerized translation of animal speech to human language.

GOODMAN: We have to look before we leap! We can't walk through a wall! Until now, with every single attempt to simultaneously translate animal language to ours, we stumbled, we still stumble, and we'll continue to stumble in the future!

HITMAN (*stoically*): We'll keep stumbling for a while longer, then we will stumble no more.

GOODMAN: In this country—such as it is—such a giant leap is just . . . impossible! Any which way you look at it, we are simply not ready for it!

HITMAN (*furiously*): Who is not ready? Your team of scientists? Your administration? The animals? Who? Who is sabotaging things here?

GOODMAN: You misunderstood me. I meant not ready, as in *not equipped*.

HITMAN (*conciliatory*): I read all of your works, even those scattered around various journals, and I can tell you that I am very much apprised of the overall situation. I know what I speak of when I say that you have already completed the experimental phase! All it takes is a small step, a tiny passage from abstraction and intuition toward concreteness, liveliness, and fruitfulness.

GOODMAN: That was my thinking for the past twenty years. And now, I believe I exhausted all possibilities.

HITMAN: You will never be able to convince me that you don't know what is happening with them, what they want, what they think, what they say. You know.

GOODMAN (*calmly*): Me personally—of course I do, but us as a whole, no. We never will!

HITMAN: What do you mean, "us as a whole"?

GOODMAN: *Us*—as in this Institute, *us*—as in this science, *us*—as in *us* . . . as in—the whole lot of us!

HITMAN (*quietly, very quietly*): But why?

GOODMAN: In the animal language, audio-track is just one of the speech components. Other, equally important ones are contained within a descriptive expression of the body, within a meta-speech. Unbridled body moving freely— that is the message. That's the crux of the problem.

HITMAN: Then, the problem with the translation is really a technological one. We need a *mixing board* of sorts. We need to synchronize the *image* with the *sound*. If you shoot the animal in motion, record the audio-track, and gang up a series of well-programmed computers, you should end up with a fairly accurate translation. I mean, *useful information*.

GOODMAN: Forgive me, but what useful information would you end up with if you were to transcribe Schönberg's atonal music to a traditional octave? You think there'd be anything left of his music?

HITMAN: There'd be nothing left of his music, Goodman! You'd get what you want—you'd get *do-re-mi-fa-sol-la-ti-do*! That's the trick!

GOODMAN: I don't play that game.

HITMAN: Don't be nervous.

GOODMAN: I am not nervous. I used to be. Now, it's a different story. Say, I place a cat on the table. Then I transfer into him. And I purr. What joy! What bliss! Seems simple, but it's not. Though I've been trying for twenty years, I still haven't managed the cat passage on a first try. Wonder why? Perhaps inside it, in spite of everything, I still feel neglected, considering its tiny stature and slow, dull existence. Perhaps thoughts of the lower order rarely get to be the dominant ones. Perhaps that's it. I don't know.

HITMAN: What are you in Chinese horoscope?

GOODMAN: A cat. Always been.

HITMAN: Me too. (A *moment later.*) What I do here is not a hobby. I devoted my life to it. You should try to crawl under *my* skin sometime.

GOODMAN: You should never offer your skin to anyone—you may end up empty handed.

HITMAN *slowly rises and exits.* GOODMAN *gives* ALICE *a kiss.* FRANKIE *enters shortly afterward.*

FRANKIE: Ya call me?

GOODMAN: Yes. Lizzy complained. She says you bother her in the kitchen.

FRANKIE: Mister Doctor, may I be frank?

GOODMAN: I wouldn't expect anything else from the likes of you.

FRANKIE: May I be direct, and tell you, man to man, what the deal is?

GOODMAN: Go ahead.

FRANKIE: The truth hurts!

GOODMAN: Out with it.

FRANKIE (*sighs*): Lizzy and that chimp, Vito, they . . . (*Gestures.*) Ya following me?

GOODMAN: No.

FRANKIE: They have relations.

GOODMAN: What kind of relations?

FRANKIE: 'Scuse me, don't wanna vulgarize in front of children . . .

GOODMAN: Alice, go play . . .

ALICE *exits.*

GOODMAN: For crying out loud, Frankie, what are you talking about?

FRANKIE: They fuck, get it? They fuck!

GOODMAN: Impossible!

FRANKIE: She hooked up with the monkey, I'm tellin' you! They nuzzle like the French—mouth to mouth! I'll kill him!

GOODMAN: Please, calm down!

FRANKIE: Friggin' gypsies, I'll butcher them all!

FRANKIE *slams the door.* GOODMAN *sits down.*

PATIENTS' WARD

The animals arranged the space according to their wishes and prepared it for a roundtable discussion. They applaud DOT *as he approaches the podium.*

DOT: Dear animals! Under the auspices of this roundtable at the Veterinary Clinic also known as the Phoenix Clinic, named after the mythological bird, that eternal icon of the animal kingdom's holocaust, I speak to you this evening about the subject we presently find of burning importance. The title of the lecture is: Introduction to the Philosophy of Animal Domestication.

FLO: He's so smooth!

BO: Like butter!

DOT: Domestication of animals, as we are well aware, is the biggest crime committed by the human race in the course of history.

ROCKY: I disagree!

VITO: Don't interrupt! You can express your opinion later, in the Q & A.

DOT: By domesticating certain animal species, man obtained an unpaid workforce—slaves who, with no rights whatsoever, carry out the hardest of tasks including transportation, agriculture, protection of man's properties . . .

DOT *takes a sip of water.*

BLACKY: Bastard! That one was aimed at me!

DOT: . . . as well as provide an endless stream of offspring which man thoughtlessly consumes for his abundant daily and—often equally extravagant and copious—nightly meals!

BO: That's right!

DOT: Naturally, many questions of legal and ethical nature arise in conjunction with this issue. For instance: what gives men *the right* to change the world according to their liking, to suppress and abuse other living creatures? Who gives them the right to alter and extinct certain species, and create new ones?

FANNY: No one!

DOT: I would like to emphasize that domestication—as some animal theoreticians would like to prove—is not a "deviation from animalistic habits of primitive bestiality"! The practice of domestication reduces animals to the level of obedient tools, it develops within animals a degrading dependency on men, it alters the laws of nature and the animal character—it paves the road to even greater and more shameful domination of men over animals!

FLO: He's sharp as a razor!

STELLA: And pretty damn courageous too!

DOT: We have not sufficiently considered nor discussed the deadly and devastating effects of domestication. We are not, nor can we afford to become hypocritical; therefore, I will leave no stone unturned as I enumerate certain unfortunate deformations that multiplied amongst the domesticated species. In the process, I am afraid I will be unable to avoid bringing up some concrete examples.

He takes a sip of water.

VITO: Hit me, baby!

GOLDIE: Here's to Dot!

DOT: Not so long ago, goat used to be a lively, curious, mischievous, and entertaining creature. Since man drove it to submission, she became the symbol of stupidity and narrow-mindedness, of idiotic pranks and gullibility. These traits are hardly something any self-respecting animal could be proud of! All too often, goat has been known to follow unknown mountaineers for hours, to endear herself to them, and to bother them, with the sole purpose of begging for food! I ask myself, why is this so? Is it worth it? Doesn't nature offer us plenty of sweet and nutritious fruit? Must we lick the hands of the two-legged murderers in submission? (*The speaker coughs, while the audience claps in delight.*) The following fact goes to show just how degraded and perverted the goat's character has become: if she feels like she hasn't won the heart of her master, she becomes as jealous as a rabid dog and chases away fellow goats if she feels they spend too much time around him!

FANNY (*in tears*): Up yours, for attacking me so much!

DOT: Meanwhile, men use goats—their skins, that is—to make parchment and wineskins.

MARY: Right! What kind of logic is that?

As the agitation escalates, animal voices and noises are heard. Someone exclaims "shhhhhhh," the audience settles down, and DOT continues.

DOT: Pigs' gluttony is a well-known fact, and as such it is hardly necessary to waste much time discussing it.

GOLDIE: When bellies are full, everyone's happy!

DOT: And yet, the domestic pig by far exceeds all living creatures in that regard—besides, possibly, her two-legged master. The lack of good taste, moderation, and selectiveness pigs manifest in fulfillment of their overindulgence is so extreme that they are unable to forgo even putrefied remnants of synthetic foods, trash from people's kitchens and similar dross that every other animal would reject in disgust! Which is the reason why domestic pigs accumulate an abundant layer of fat under their skins—up to the record-breaking three feet in thickness!

The animals are in a state of amazement.

TOM: Three feet of fat?

DOT: That fat is what men ultimately feast on, and thanks to that very same fat they gather strength to torture, subdue, and terrorize other animals!

GOLDIE (*bitterly*): They couldn't even season a salad with your feathers, not to mention anything else!

DOT: By domesticating the pig, man has reduced the dignity of animals to the lowest possible degree of morality!

GOLDIE: Fuck you, Dot!

VITO: Silence!

DOT: Whichever way we turn in the world of domesticated species, we see only submissiveness, decadence, displacement, even brainlessness. Take Ika, for example! The effect of domestication within sheep is more evident than in any other animal species. What used to be a sprightly, quick, deft, and defiant animal capable of climbing everywhere, adept at valiantly confronting any danger, has now become a listless, dull creature devoid of spirit. Poor Ika is a slave with no opinions to speak of—a veritable sheep. Her fatalism, her obedient attitude toward everything that comes her way is unparalleled!

IKA: I am a faithful animal.

VITO: What?

IKA: I am faithful.

DOT: You mean—*religious*?

IKA: Yes, religious.

DOLLY: Unbelievable, we have a believer in our ranks!

FANNY: That is indeed a rarity in these godless times.

MARY: She must be a Quaker!

IKA: No, I am the disciple of an ancient religion that men have destroyed and animals have forgotten. It is the *ruminants'* faith, the faith of matter, of stars, planets, the faith of our universe.

STELLA: Holy cow!

FANNY: So, you pray while you chew?

IKA: It is not I who prays. My body devotes itself to prayer while the cud dissolves into nutritious matter and invigorating juices on the ceremonial journey through the stations of the Almighty. Four are the altars: rumen, reticulum, omasum, and abomasum. Holiness of life burns in the matter that transforms into power so that the eyes may see the light, the extremities move, the heart pump blood through the veins, for the matter to gain consciousness of its movements within the tremor and flow of other matters.

ROCKY: Interesting . . .

BO: Very poetic.

STELLA: So you are saying the Earth practices ruminants' faith too?

IKA: The Earth prays to earthquakes, to volcanic eruptions, to hot springs and invisible gases. Mother Earth is the daughter of the Sun, which is the child of the universe.

BO: And the stars?

IKA: The stars are the Sun's sisters.

DOT: In principle, if I understand correctly, this is some kind of pantheism?

IKA: It isn't: you must first and foremost listen to yourself, the time and the movement of the matter that makes you what you are.

VITO: So, rumination is a meditation of sorts?

IKA: It's more. Rumination is built on a principle of fours. Four altars: rumen, reticulum, omasum, and abomasum; four elements: earth, fire, water, air; four seasons: winter, spring, summer, and fall; four dimensions; four-step engine; four sizes: stone, rocks, gravel, sand. Animals have four legs, cars have four wheels, four count makes the most beautiful music. The principle of fours is in the nature, the principle of threes is man-made: the Holy Trinity, the waltz, the TNT. All that grows and yields, all that comes and goes, all of it lives and dies in fours: tornado, storm, wind, breeze—that's us and our destiny. And now, for the Big Mass—stuff your mouths: one, two, three, four. Chew! Give it a try!

ALL ANIMALS (*chewing and counting at the same time*): One, two, three, four; one, two, three, four; one, two, three, four . . .

VITO: Stop! Stop! (*They all stop, except for* STELLA.) Shame on you! I am making an extraordinary effort here to gather the illuminated vanguard, I organize a roundtable about our burning issues and irregularities with what appears to be a handful of like-minded fellows, and you end up catering to the ghastly provocations of the clerics and fall into a trance like regular fanatics!

STELLA: One, two, three, four—*I feel!* Two, three, four—*I feel!* Two . . .

BLACKY: Will you stop it?

STELLA: I am so happy. So happy.

VITO: You see? Look at Stella. What is one to do with such individuals? How do you awaken them?

FANNY: You know what, Dot? We are all messed up and busted in our own ways, so no need to shove this crap down our throats. You go on and on and criticize, when you yourself are in the same shit.

GOLDIE: Ika's ideas *are* fresh, one has to give it to her. I am an atheist, I believe in neither God nor Devil, but I feel the need for, you know, some principle of harmony . . . So as not to be so distracted and rejected . . . superfluous to myself, burden to others, you know, after all the faith, the faith . . .

STELLA: The faith unites, the faith illuminates, it helps us live!

VITO: The faith is the opium for those who'll end up in the slaughterhouse! Don't you get it?

IKA: May I propose something?

DOT: Go ahead!

IKA: Since I am aware that there is a considerable interest here in the principle of fours, I will hold an abbreviated course in the history of ruminants' movement four times a week. I wouldn't call it Religious Studies yet, just the Introduction to the Spiritual Exercises for Beginners. Whoever won't listen, won't have to. Everything would be on a voluntary basis.

DOT: I am against it.

GOLDIE: Let's vote then!

VITO: Voting is absolutely unacceptable.

STELLA: Would you be so kind as to explain why not?

VITO: Look. We are in a clinic here. We are sick, patients with serious injuries. We are plagued by ailments, health issues, depression. So now, I ask you: is it possible to maintain a clear conscience and a strong will, is it possible to actively participate in our healing process if we count to four in unison like poor lambs, and obediently wait until we croak?

BLACKY: It's not possible.

VITO: That is why I am against voting, against religious studies and spiritual exercises, and against rumination.

DOLLY: Correct.

BLACKY: Health comes first, it's true.

FLO: Help yourself and God will help you along the way.

VITO: We must reject fatalism—that is our common task and responsibility. There is no healthy community without healthy individuals! Do you agree?

TOM: We agree!

DOT: However, the opposite holds true as well: there are no healthy individuals without a healthy community. That is why I propose that we re-educate Ika—that we, as a healthy community, help her, that we save her from the mouth of the ruminants, from the four-counts, and similar . . .

ALL: Let's save her!

IKA: I will not let anyone take my faith away.

BLACKY: She is incorrigible!

FLO: You'll die before you see the light.

IKA: Leave me in peace.

VITO: Alright, but you have to promise not to do any four-count propaganda.

IKA: I promise.

DOT: So, we are in agreement. Let's go to sleep. I hereby conclude this evening's roundtable discussion at the Phoenix Clinic and thank you for your cooperation. Good night.

ALL: Good night.

As the space sinks into a sleepy twilight, BO *the poet sings to his fellow sufferers. It's a lullaby inspired by the literary giant that is Lermontov.*

BO (*singing*):

"Under the golden crest of corn,
The fields are sleeping.

Smoke rises from the distant village,
The fog is creeping,
Light and blue.

But dark is the forest! Within its cover, the stars shimmer
Murmuring by my weary feet—look!—a silver stream!

Oh, it is true . . .

My limbs shiver,
From this foreboding, I must escape in a dream!"

The stage sinks into the darkness.

End of FIRST SEQUENCE.

SECOND SEQUENCE

PATIENTS' WARD

Morning.

IKA: By god, what kind of a name is that—*Dolly*?

DOLLY: It's a diminutive English version of the Spanish name Dolores. As my mistress's name is *Jolly*, everyone calls me *Dolly*. As in: doll, sweetie, girlie . . .

FANNIE: It rhymes with *Jolly*: Dolly—Jolly.

DOLLY: So-so. Still, the two of us are truly inseparable. We're always together. During travels, visits, at home . . .

MARY: You sleep together too?

DOLLY: We sleep in the same bed, the same music lulls us to sleep, the same ruby-red canopy in pure silk flutters above us in luscious frills. And if my bedtime ribbon is turquoise, you better believe that lace on my mistress's nightie will be the same color.

GOLDIE: So, it is safe to say that you and your mistress are quite intimate.

DOLLY: No doubt.

FLO: And what is your mistress's profession?

DOLLY: She is a prima ballerina at the National Theatre.

BLACKY: Actually, she's a second-class member of the *corps*.

DOLLY: Blacky! How dare you!

BLACKY: She hasn't had a solo on the boards since she was signed two years ago, upon recommendation of that choreographer on Steep Street—what's his face?—you know, the one who used to have that stuffy Terrier, and is now roaming around with some loopy Dalmatian.

DOLLY: Mr. Tolstonosovski *did* indeed recommend Madame Jolly, but that has absolutely nothing to do with what you're aiming at.

BLACKY: I am not aiming at anything. I am just corroborating your information with facts. Facts I heard from your friend Marko.

DOLLY (*to the group*): Marko is a useless bookworm who scribbles radio plays for kids, a drunkard and a loudmouth! Otherwise, Blacky's lucky owner . . . he beats him like a cat, twice a week.

TOM: Miss, you don't say "he beats him like a cat," but "he beats him like a rented mule."

STELLA: Or, better even, "like a dog!"

BLACKY: Marko is not a "useless bookworm," but a lead artist on comics and graphic novels for children and young adults. Besides, I am compelled to point out that Marko is not a drunkard but a man who drinks occasionally, like everyone else.

FANNIE: True, all men drink a bit, all of them!

BLACKY: And last but not least, I want to alert you to a certain philosophical superficiality that I fundamentally cannot tolerate. I am not, nor do I want to be, anyone's *property*, unlike many of you who are proud and grateful to *belong* to somebody. I am *my own master*, so it follows that no one, including my friend Marko, can ever be my *owner*. And this affair about "the beating" twice a day, let me just say this: if someone *kicks* someone because they were being provoked, or they are angered to the point of throwing, say, Tolstoy's *War and Peace* at someone, that still doesn't mean that they are receiving corporal punishment, or—as our charming blonde puts it—a beating.

DOLLY: Then, why do you squeal so often in that desolate backyard of yours?

BLACKY: Well, *that*, if you don't mind, is none of your damn business.

DOLLY: All I know is that Miss Jolly often says: "See, Dolly, some puppies are so unlucky in life! Poor Blacky, they must've beaten the living daylights out of him again."

BLACKY: I won't tolerate a former stripper blabbering nonsense about my "poor" self!

DOLLY: What stripper?

BLACKY: Stripper at the Elephant Bar! Don't act dumber than you already are!

STELLA: What's a stripper?

ROCKY: A bitch who strips.

GOLDIE: You know, she takes off her clothes for money until she is buck naked, and dances in front of people who watch her.

STELLA: What's so special about that? Us four-legged ladies, we are always naked, and no one ever bothers to look at us!

DOT: Yes, but you don't dance.

FLO: What about nudists?

ROCKY: Nudists are strippers who don't dance.

GOLDIE: As far as I know, they don't get tips either.

DOLLY: Striptease is an art form, and nudism is a hobby—that is the difference.

BLACKY: A-ha! So, you admit—Jolly *is* a stripper!

DOLLY: *Was*. For a while. So what? We even performed together in a number called "Yearning."

BLACKY: That's news to me.

DOLLY: Yes. It was set to Schumann's *Dreaming*.

MARY: I am not familiar with that piece.

DOLLY: Even if you were—it was a success beyond all expectations.

BLACKY: I am sure the number was peppered with obscenities.

DOLLY: It didn't seem the least bit scandalous to me. On the contrary, it was a truly exciting story.

FANNIE: What story?

DOLLY: Well, you know, it all starts with Miss Jolly as a lonesome, unhappy woman who—as the title suggests—yearns for love, understanding, sweet home, and warm embrace. In short, she shows all this with her fantastic movement:

she twists and turns, and strikes various poses, and the dudes are just staring, mouths open wide, and they can't believe that such a smoking bitch can't find anyone who'd take her under his wing and give her the comfort she deserves.

GOLDIE: It's a curse. Really.

DOLLY: Anyway, so she dances on and on, and still there's no help in sight . . .

BLACKY: And where are you all this time?

DOLLY: Hold on, I am on the stage behind the string curtain and I am watching, although it's not my turn yet.

FLO: When is your turn?

DOLLY: As I was saying—when Jolly collapses on the white fur rug . . .

MARY: My god, the white fur again!

DOLLY: . . . and her entire body starts to shiver as she bursts into tears and moans . . .

FLO: Real tears?

DOLLY: She's acting, *comprende*? Where was I?

ROCKY: She moans . . .

DOLLY: Right, so she moans, and chokes up, and when she reaches the peak of her misery and solitude and all that, she yelps: "Dolly! DOLLLYYYY!"

VITO: She calls you?

DOLLY: That's right.

GOLDIE: And what do you do?

DOLLY: I leap from the Rococo love seat, peak through the string curtain, and skip along toward her.

DOT: And?

DOLLY: And with my cherry-red tongue I begin to lick her left nipple for starters . . .

TOM: What covers it?

DOLLY: Just the Cuban sugar syrup, to keep the silver pasty in place during the dance . . .

TOM: Yes, and then?

DOLLY: Then I lick the right nipple. This calms her down, she relaxes, pets my head, nuzzles my nose, and covers my eyes. I go on and jump on her belly, walk on it a bit—as if I was searching for a place to lie down—I turn my head, go toward her hips, and finally, I curl up on her Venus mound. I stay there for a few moments, I balance myself to avoid sliding down further. Lastly, she lifts herself, sits up, hugs and pulls me to her knees, and rests her hot, sweaty brow against them so her long, lightly curled hair covers me, her face, her legs, everything. Music plays on, lights slowly fade. (*A moment later.*) That's it.

ROCKY, GOLDIE, FLO, TOM: Bravo! Bravo! Incredible! Thank you!

DOLLY: Everyone was stunned, amazed, the applause went on for ages . . .

BLACKY: And the point of the story is . . . ?

DOLLY: Excuse me?

BLACKY: What did the artists intend to express through this performance?

DOLLY: You mean, you don't get it?

BLACKY: No, I am afraid I don't.

VITO: I don't either, but it sure is impressive.

GOLDIE: For me, the message is that man and dog can understand each other quite well, provided they are both fucked up.

FLO: Whatever! The trick is that *she* . . .

BLACKY: *She*, who?

FLO: Dolly, of course . . . that when things get tough, *she* is the only one who understands *her*! Isn't that right?

BO: The ending's no good . . . too happy somehow.

VITO: Where did you see a happy ending?

TOM: Nobody cried here!

STELLA: If some handsome hunk came along, that would be a happy ending . . . This way, she is stuck with a puppy, which makes her burden even greater.

VITO: Why don't you let her speak for herself?

FLO: That's right, let her speak for herself.

DOLLY: What is there to say? Ballet as an art form has no agenda. Dance speaks the language of emotions, of bodies' and souls' pleasures and sufferings. Everyone interprets the movement language at his own discretion. It would be unfair if someone tried to impose a single way to experience it or observe it.

FLO: Of course, everyone knows for himself what he ought to think.

DOLLY: Actually, Miss Jolly and I just wanted to weave the truth about our own lives into that story. About our loneliness and our yearning.

BLACKY: I don't know about Mrs. Jolly, but don't you try to moan about being lonely.

DOLLY: I am, for the record.

SURVEILLANCE ROOM

HITMAN *listens to the recording of the "animal version" of the conversation from the previous scene as* FRANKIE *enters.* HITMAN *lowers the volume slightly, but the sound of the recording is nonetheless present throughout the following scene.*

FRANKIE: Boss, you got five minutes for my lil' self?

HITMAN: Have a seat, Frankie.

FRANKIE: You know that, before coming here, I was at the Institute for Thinking?

HITMAN: In jail?

FRANKIE: Double-bolted.

HITMAN: I didn't know.

FRANKIE: Yes, you do, you know everything.

HITMAN: What was the reason?

FRANKIE: That chiquita cried wolf about rape, but—never mind, only I know what she had going on in her head, and how much she "resisted," if you catch my drift.

HITMAN: Alright, but this is behind you now, you served your sentence . . .

FRANKIE: I was gonna say something else: at the Institute for Thinking, a man really learns how to use this! (*Points to his forehead.*) Swear to god!

HITMAN: I believe you!

FRANKIE: I am all eyes and ears, I follow what's cooking around here . . . Lots of stuff don't work right, it's all upside down! Right? You got rats everywhere, we are missing this, that, and the other, Goodman's got migraines, and the beasts are running around unchecked, everyone doin' what they want . . . it's all so unfair!

HITMAN: Really?

FRANKIE: Damn right, bro! I'm so happy you are taking it over!

HITMAN: I am not "taking over" anything.

FRANKIE: The main thing is, you *got* here—that's already, like, wow! But I was gonna say: I train my brain! I got used to it at the other institute, a half-hour of mental workout every day. There you go! See the result?

HITMAN: Get to the point!

FRANKIE: You are a big military man, I bet you know what a "talker" is.

HITMAN: A talker can be defined as a person from the enemy ranks who is in possession of confidential—or at least useful—information that, when captured, he or she releases to the opposition either voluntarily or by force.

FRANKIE: Bingo! In plain talk, a talker is an involuntary snitch.

HITMAN: That was well put.

FRANKIE: See now, where there's no war, it's damn hard to catch a talkative talker on a foreign nation's territory. You know, someone who'd spill something important. Am I right?

HITMAN: Indeed, this becomes quite complicated in peaceful circumstances. That is to say, isolation and consequent exploitation are insurmountable obstacles.

FRANKIE: That's it! But! What if the talker was of animal origin? (*Triumphantly.*) What do you say to that?

HITMAN: You mean, kidnapping well-informed animals?

FRANKIE: That's it, boss!

HITMAN: I am not your boss.

FRANKIE: I'll give you a concrete example. What if a high-ranking NATO general were to have, say, a Doberman? Those are sharp puppies, no doubt! The beast would always hang around when Americans and Germans are brainstorming how to screw Russkies over! You got the generals lounging in the garden, wining, dining, and fantasizing, and the Doberman perks up his ears and waits for his bone!

HITMAN: Meaning, this Doberman would know NATO's military plans?

FRANKIE: No kidding!

HITMAN: So far so good, but let's say the dog is in Berchtesgaden, Germany. How do we get him?

FRANKIE: Now listen to me. Say, our little Doberman goes for a walk with one of the general's bodyguards, every evening from 9 to 10, to piss and such. Then, some 200, 300 yards away, you put a bitch in heat. You got the wind blowing the right way, our puppy's gonna sniff her a mile away. And when he does, it'll be easy to lure him into a car and snatch him across the border the same night.

HITMAN: Directly to us, to the surveillance headquarters?

FRANKIE: Your wish is our command, boss.

HITMAN: So our animals could unknowingly interrogate him while we, in utmost secrecy, record and select the information unbeknownst to them?

FRANKIE: That's right.

HITMAN: It is a brilliant idea. Unfortunately, it is unacceptable.

FRANKIE: But the Doberman could be from the Eastern Bloc!

HITMAN: Is this the perception you have about our military? Where do you live, Comrade Frankie? Ours is not the kind of army you have in mind! The use of zoolinguistics for military purposes is out of the question! No way!

FRANKIE: But everybody's doing it . . . I read about it!

HITMAN: I know what everybody's doing, thank you very much, I am in the loop. Have you heard of the biological weapons? Of course you have. Do you know that the US Navy has kamikaze dolphins? And that the Swedes deploy reindeer units to eliminate minefields? Are you aware that the Israeli-trained bees can destroy up to two million Arabs per day? Can you even begin to imagine what kind of havoc East Germans are able to wreck with their Tsetse flies if the winds are favorable? And the Bulgarians with their snakes? The list goes on! We are talking about mass murder, my dear. Our hands shall not be stained with zoo-weapons!

FRANKIE: Information is a *currency*, not a weapon . . .

HITMAN: What do you know about *information*?

FRANKIE: Not an iota.

HITMAN: And about currency?

FRANKIE (*after a pause*): Money makes the world go 'round.

HITMAN: And what about: "If you work hard, you'll get rewards?"

HEADQUARTERS

GOODMAN *has a (live) cat on his desk.* LIZZY *enters. They both look confused.*

LIZZY: I really am not a whistleblower, I just felt that I had to tell you . . .

GOODMAN: What?

LIZZY: About the pills . . .

GOODMAN: What pills?

LIZZY: Dr. Leptin gave them . . . so I could grind them into the gingerbread cookies for the bear . . .

GOODMAN: And . . . ?

LIZZY: I am afraid I am gonna die!

GOODMAN: Did you have one of those cookies?

LIZZY: They were just too good . . . I had seven.

LIZZY *holds her head and gets dizzy—and a bit flirtatious.*

LIZZY: Horror. Up where the low ceiling of my kitchen used to be, there is a huge ravine, thousand yards deep, and I am evaporating into it—the more I resist, the more of me disappears. What little is left of me is a tiny shriveled-up creature: an ant—a pitiful, scared, little red ant who carries his larvae into the lungs and belly of the one who is soon to be no more. The sound of pumping blood deafens me in those immense caverns, they reek of mold, I am choking. I am surrounded, I want to strangle but have no hands . . . I want to scream but have no voice . . . I strain myself to crawl up to the peaks of ecstasy, but then I collapse to the bottom of the abyss, helpless. Gross! Do I really have to turn to pus in order to release myself?

GOODMAN: I'll give you an injection. Come along, you took a strong hallucinogen . . .

GOODMAN *escorts* LIZZY *out of the office.*

PATIENTS' WARD

HORNER *and* VERONICA *enter.*

HORNER: Come on, let's go! Get your asses up! Goldie, Blacky, Rocky, Ika, Stella, Fannie—vaccinations; Dot—X-rays; Vito, Flo, and Tom—blood samples; and you, Bo, we need your urine! What are you staring at? It's just *water*, just some *water* you'll have to pass! Let's go!

HORNER *and* VERONICA *are pushing the animals out of the ward.* MARY *and* DOLLY *are left behind.*

MARY: May I ask you something?

DOLLY: Sure. Go ahead.

MARY (*shyly*): Have you tasted love's sweetness on more than one occasion?

DOLLY: I may come off as being utterly shameless, and yet the volume of my erotic experiences is rather modest. While I was a young bitch still, I hopelessly fell for a fire-red Irish Setter who wasn't really giving me the time of day. Needless to say, this was strictly platonic. A one-way street. Water under the bridge. The first awakening of youth's fever. After that, a few flirtations grazed me—such superficial relations that leave no trace in a dog's heart. In the whirlpool of remembered feelings, they are like cold reflections of white lilies. That's the way it is—the flower that glides like a kiss across the water's surface barely blossoms, barely moves . . .

MARY (*after a pause*): I am still a virgin.

DOLLY: That's nothing to be ashamed of.

MARY (*quietly*): I know.

DOLLY: Virginity is essentially a virtue.

MARY (*quietly*): I have a terrible craving for love's warmth. I am a cat that nobody caresses, pets, or hugs . . . A cat that serves as a decoration. I want to love and be loved.

DOLLY (*a moment later*): You have the whole world ahead of you. I have nothing. Just emptiness.

MARY: Ah. You're just saying that.

DOLLY: I can't have children.

MARY: Oh.

DOLLY: Yes . . . They are running tests now, you know . . . Maybe they'll discover something . . .

MARY: I am sure they will. And I sure hope you'll get pregnant.

DOLLY: You are a kind and charming creature. I am happy we became friends . . .

MARY: I never had a real girlfriend—you can't imagine how happy our time together makes me. I never talked like *this* to anyone.

DOLLY: Mary, I can't begin to describe how much I want children. This is *insane*! It's all I think about.

MARY: Me too.

DOLLY: You'll have them, for sure.

MARY: Problem is, there aren't any respectable Persians with a pedigree in our town. And Miss Laura is very . . . easy-going . . .

DOLLY: I know, she hates to make an effort, she hates to travel, to pick up the phone . . .

MARY: And, she hates to pay . . . It costs money, you know?

DOLLY: And then she goes: "Who is going to care for the newborns, you'll have to lock yourself up in the house, who'll take care of them, it's so complicated . . ." I know that one by heart.

MARY: See? And with this polio on top of everything . . .

DOLLY: Please, have faith in these doctors. They are specialists, believe me, they know what they are doing.

MARY: This clinic, Dolly, is an assembly line.

HEADQUARTERS/SURVEILLANCE ROOM

GOODMAN *and* LEPTIN *speak over intercom.*

GOODMAN: I found traces of lysergic acid diethylamide.

LEPTIN (*a moment later*): What possessed that cow to devour those cookies?

GOODMAN (*angrily*): A much more serious question, Leptin, is: why did you use LSD? And under whose authority? What did you think you were doing?

LEPTIN (*slowly*): What I am doing at the moment is directly connected with the sixties research phase. Back then, it was all based on Bingel's hypothesis that the brain structure of all mammals was a "black box" of sorts, that all those bio-energies released by one system could get attached and saved to another. Therefore, even speech. I wanted to allow the community to face, through God, the uncensored type of emotionality which enables and produces language on the level of abreaction. Bo seemed to be the most suitable guinea pig. I wanted to check and see how it would work. That's all.

GOODMAN: You are getting further away from the goal, Leptin! We agreed on what we'd work on, we have a plan! No one is at liberty to change it of his own accord! (*A moment later.*) You acted thoughtlessly. I don't want any kind of uncontrollable euphoria in this group!

LEPTIN: We must take risks! Without euphoria, there's nothing!

GOODMAN: No!

LEPTIN: We're running in circles, Goodman!

GOODMAN *turns the intercom off. Phone rings.*

GOODMAN (*in the receiver*): Where is he? I am coming to the waiting room.

PATIENTS' WARD

The animals return to their places like well-behaved patients. VERONICA *does an exemplary job of being a nurse.* HORNER *offers a sip from his treasured flask to* FRANKIE. *A confidential conversation ensues, properly fueled by booze.*

HORNER (*whispers*): Whatever you do is too much already for that lousy paycheck. It's a different ball game when you know you work for *yourself*.

FRANKIE: Easy for you to say, you travel abroad whenever you want . . .

HORNER: I told you: I'll start a pig farm, and I'll take you in. You'll be a *partner*!

FRANKIE: Me, a partner? I got no dowry.

HORNER: You'll be a partner. We'll join forces.

FRANKIE: You got land, stables, everything. I don't even have dirt under my fingernails.

HORNER: Are we buddies?

FRANKIE: Damn right we are!

HORNER (*even more confidential*): This piglet . . . (FRANKIE *turns to look at* GOLDIE.) Don't look! . . . Would be good to have . . . He's worth his weight in gold . . .

FRANKIE: Leave it to me, I already know what I'm gonna do!

HORNER: That'll be your dowry!

SURVEILLANCE ROOM

LEPTIN *and* ALICE.

ALICE: Lizzy says you're not my father.

LEPTIN (*after a pause*): I think that I am and that I'm not. (*Another pause.*) What do you think?

ALICE: I think my dad is Uncle Goodman.

LEPTIN: Why do you think that?

ALICE: Because Uncle Goodman is a father to Mom, father to you . . . He's a father to all of us.

PATIENTS' WARD

GOODMAN *and* PROFESSOR HEGEL *enter and head toward* DOT *in haste.*

GOODMAN: No, we only just examined him.

HEGEL: Do you have the X-rays?

GOODMAN: They're in the office. (*He taps the parakeet's throat.*) See, your bird is holding up valiantly.

HEGEL: He's apathetic, that much is clear! Armed assault on one's personal integrity is no small thing.

GOODMAN: This "armed assault," as you define it, how did it happen?

HEGEL: The clock had struck five. My wife and I were in the living room, listening to Vivaldi and drinking black Georgian tea. Anna was engrossed in her needlework and I was browsing the addenda to the Unified Labor Laws. Though I am retired, I like to be apprised of all things new. I like to be in the loop. We were positioned in such a way that we could take a peek at the balcony from time to time. Our balcony is six by twenty feet, facing the garden. Dot was sunbathing on the balcony.

GOODMAN: Was he in his cage?

HEGEL: He was calm and poised as a statue on his wooden bar, when all of a sudden—I couldn't believe my eyes—I see feathers flying in the breeze, I hear a squeaking cry, and Dot collapses to the ground, unconscious.

GOODMAN: You didn't hear a gunshot?

HEGEL: No.

GOODMAN: Unbelievable. (*A moment later.*) All I can tell you with certainty at the moment is that your parakeet's right wing is broken. I can't tell you anything about potential internal injuries. Naturally, we'll have to operate, and we'll go from there.

HEGEL: And he'll live?

GOODMAN: Provided that there are no complications, yes.

HEGEL: He is all Anna and I have.

GOODMAN: Please come with me. I believe our chief of police, who is otherwise the court's medical expert, Doctor Hitman, would like to speak with you.

They leave.

DOT: Hit men are usually anonymous lunatics who shoot at respectable victims with the intention of becoming famous themselves by the way of a bloody crime.

FLO: To write themselves into history books.

DOT: Indeed.

ROCKY: In your case, then, one couldn't say that the attacker was a hit man.

DOT: Why not?

GOLDIE: You are not famous, that's why.

DOT: I am a victim of an assassination attempt.

ROCKY: A victim, yes; a celebrity, no.

VITO: What if the hit man who targeted Dot was a famous lunatic who assaulted an anonymous victim?

GOLDIE: No one knows, he hasn't been apprehended yet.

VITO: When they shoot at the American president or the Pope, they catch them in the blink of an eye.

IKA: Terrorism is the disease of the modern world.

TOM: When you stop and think about it, Bo and I are both terrorists' victims too.

DOT: How funny!

TOM: What's funny?

DOT: The neighbor's kid lured you into his backyard with a delicious sweet water trout, then mauled your back with a heavy bat from his hiding spot. Right?

TOM: Right.

DOT: And that prankster aimed his slingshot at Bo and hit him in the eye—am I right?

BO: Right you are.

DOT: And you two call this "terrorism"?

BO: How else would you call it?

DOT: Sadism.

TOM: Sadism?

DOT: Slings and bats—that's just plain sadism.

GOODMAN, PROFESSOR HEGEL, *and* HITMAN *enter. They approach* DOT *with determination.*

HITMAN (*to* GOODMAN): Is this the victim? Remove the bullet from his wing.

GOODMAN: You mean—just like that . . . no anesthesia?

HITMAN: For Christ's sake, don't make this complicated! Here are some tweezers! (*To* PROFESSOR HEGEL.) You didn't see the assailant?

HEGEL: No. (*To* HITMAN.) Didn't the two of us already meet elsewhere?

DOT *screams.* GOODMAN *passes the bullet to* HITMAN. PROFESSOR HEGEL *is looking at* HITMAN.

HITMAN: I wouldn't say so. (*He rolls the bullet between his fingers, lifts it toward the light.*) This lead is for a small-caliber Flobert.

HEGEL: A hunting rifle?

HITMAN: It's a sport gun.

HEGEL: Would it be safe to assume, then, that the assailant is a member of a shooting club?

HITMAN: Have you ever sentenced such a character?

HEGEL (*shocked*): Are you saying that I was the bullet's intended target?

HITMAN: Don't you think people have better things to do than loiter around gardens and shoot at parrots?

HEGEL: The unemployment *is* rather high.

HITMAN (*shakes his head*): For the time being, the unemployed aren't running loose with rifles just yet.

HITMAN *makes a sharp turn,* PROFESSOR HEGEL *and* GOODMAN *rush after him and exit the ward.*

BLACKY: I would gladly go on a search for your hit man if I weren't ill. Your neighborhood is not that big. One, two, three—bam!—I'd catch him just like that.

DOT: Are you a hunting dog?

BLACKY (*with sadness*): My mother was a purebred retriever.

DOT: And your father?

BLACKY: Well, you know how it is: mom was on a leash, and dogs would come and go. (*Changing the subject.*) Do you suspect someone?

DOT: To be perfectly honest, I have no idea who it could be.

BLACKY: Tell me about the couple with whom you lived.

DOT: Professor Hegel is a retired judge of the Constitutional Court, and Anna, also retired, a former bank clerk; both are tiny, insignificant, modest people. They lead quiet, microcosmic lives, without relatives, friends, or foes.

BLACKY: You've been with them for a long time?

DOT: Five years.

BLACKY: Where were you before that?

DOT: That is a long story. (DOT *dwells on the past.*)

BLACKY: Well, never mind, if you'd rather not say . . .

DOT (*after a pause*): I came from Nairobi. I lived for several years with my friend Darko, a third secretary at the Embassy of the Socialist Federate Republic of Yugoslavia. It was fun, easy living.

BLACKY: Lots of visitors?

DOT: Here and there, mostly just some black bitches I wouldn't even spot in the dark. Otherwise, it was mainly diplomats and lots of blabbering.

BLACKY: About politics?

DOT: About the Third World, investments, arrests, interventions, Stalinism, Berlinguer, Castro, weapons trafficking, loans, everything!

BLACKY: Ah!

DOT: Blah-blah-blah . . .

BLACKY: You were eavesdropping?

DOT: I know everything they said by heart.

BLACKY (*after a pause*): That may very well be the point!

DOT: The point of this attempt on my life, you mean?

BLACKY: Of course. Maybe you heard something that you weren't supposed to. Something you are supposed to forget forever and ever. And you'll forget most easily if you're not around anymore.

DOT: I am not an informant!

BLACKY (*harshly*): You blabber on, whatever comes to mind.

DOT: I am not a traitor!

BLACKY: Perhaps not consciously so.

DOT: I'll be quiet as the grave!

BLACKY (*cynically*): *In* the grave, you mean?

DOT: Blacky!

BLACKY: Calm down!

DOT: *Blacky!*

BLACKY: Calm down, I tell you. (*A moment later.*) You are in deep shit, you know that?

DOT: I do.

BLACKY: Where is your friend Darko now?

DOT: In Moscow . . . as a second secretary.

BLACKY: Why didn't he take you with him?

DOT: He said it was freezing there.

BLACKY: Freezing? They have central heating, don't be an idiot!

DOT: I don't know . . . I don't know . . . He said that it often broke down . . . That I would wither and die in the cold.

BLACKY: You'll wither and die because of something else.

DOT: You mean, poison?

BLACKY: How should I know?

DOT: Or another bullet?

BLACKY: Calm down, I said.

DOT (*sings*): *O partigiano, porta mi via, o bella ciao, bella ciao, bella ciao ciao ciao . . .*

BLACKY: Shut up, idiot!

DOT (*screeches*): *Viva il socialismo e la libertá!*

BLACKY: What's wrong with you? What's with the screaming?

DOT: Why, is it not allowed?

BLACKY: Don't you know where you are?

DOT: Where am I?

BLACKY: In the Veterinarian Clinic

DOT (*sings*): *Rule, Britannia, Britannia over the waves* . . .

BLACKY: Stop it, right now! (DOT *stops singing.* BLACKY *now definitely assumes the role of an interrogator.*) Where did you learn that song?

DOT: In Australia.

BLACKY: What town?

DOT: Sydney.

BLACKY: Where at?

DOT: At the house of Lord Boxtrottle, a relative of the British Queen Victoria, the Assistant Governor of Her Majesty's. It was in his salon that I listened to the stories about the British Empire, about the conquest of Africa, India, America, and Guinea.

BLACKY: I see. You mingled with imperialists.

DOT: I was in a cage. They were in armchairs.

BLACKY: You were under their influence, admit it!

DOT: I wasn't!

BLACKY: They poisoned you ideologically!

DOT: I am a staunch socialist!

BLACKY: Liar!

DOT: I am a social-democrat!

BLACKY: Nonsense!

DOT: I am a democrat and a liberal and a radical!

BLACKY: No way!

DOT: I am a Euro-Trotskyist!

BLACKY: Not true!

DOT: What am I then?

BLACKY: A parakeet.

DOT (*after a pause*): That won't do.

BLACKY: Okay then—a parrot.

DOT (*after a pause*): That wouldn't be accurate either.

BLACKY: Why don't you say what you think you are, then?

DOT (*slowly*): I think I am a *ruined* parrot.

BLACKY (*moments later, in Australian accent*): How old are you, Mike?

DOT (*slowly*): I was born in 1701.

BLACKY: O, Gosh! As old as that?

DOT: Yeah.

BLACKY: You look good for your age!

DOT: That's the look of a parrot Death has set her sights on already.

HEADQUARTERS

HITMAN *and* PROFESSOR HEGEL.

HITMAN: I am trying to protect you. That's all.

HEGEL: From whom?

HITMAN: There will be another attempt.

HEGEL: By whom?

HITMAN: Move in here with us temporarily. There is plenty of room, and you may bring your companion along. Your parrot, a garden, and a library are all here, we have a cinema in the other building, but most importantly—you will be *safe* here.

HEGEL: But, I really don't understand any of this! I retired several years ago!

HITMAN: Lucky you!

HEGEL (*pulling himself together*): I will consider your offer. For the time being— thank you kindly!

SURVEILLANCE ROOM

LEPTIN: Quickly, let's talk. I eavesdropped on the animals' conversation.

GOODMAN: Yes, and?

LEPTIN: I believe that Hitman himself prevented Darko taking Dot to Moscow. Then, he personally saw to it that the parrot should end up in the hands of Judge Hegel and his wife Anna. And finally, I think it was him who shot Dot in order to have him brought here.

GOODMAN: Why would he do all that?

LEPTIN: Because he believes that the parrot will provide him with information about the political activities of the third secretary in Nairobi, about influential protégées of our prematurely retired Judge, and Anna's business secrets from her investment banking days. (*After a pause.*) Do you understand what his ultimate goal is?

VERONICA: Total surveillance of all institutions, people and their lives aided by an animal police force. Dogs, cats, cows—all manipulated as spies.

GOODMAN: That's ghastly. That's inhumane. So, it is not only the matter of the country's border security? (*After a pause.*) The only way out is to dissolve this Institute, urgently and unconditionally.

LEPTIN: He won't allow it. We'll have to get rid of him first. We are dealing with a forceful madman who's becoming more dangerous by the hour. Can't you fire him?

GOODMAN: How?

LEPTIN: Just kick him out! And if that doesn't work—eliminate him.

VERONICA: Our friendly client could take care of that—it'll be calm, clean, and scandal-free.

GOODMAN: Who?

VERONICA: Bo, the bear. He could shred him apart.

GOODMAN: He is a poet. I doubt he'd be willing to stain his claws with the blood of a cop.

LEPTIN: He is as much of a poet as he is a beast and a freedom fighter.

PATIENTS' WARD

ALICE: Dottie . . . Dottie . . . I think it would be nice if you could apologize to Tom and Bo. What do you say?

DOT: I apologize to you, Bo, and to you, Tom. I didn't mean to offend. You two were also victims of terrorism.

TOM: Thanks.

BO: Fine. No need to apologize. We are all sick and irritated and our nerves are on a short fuse.

DOT: I am a pitiful, neurotic little geezer.

TOM: Whatever.

GOLDIE (*a moment later*): Guys, these days, one can get a young Yorkshire pig in the countryside in exchange for six pounds of coffee. This is how far along our country's gotten in its "development."

DOT: Please, don't be angry with this ruffled, old, feathered monkey.

BO: Come on, nobody's angry with you.

DOT (*in despair*): I always voiced myself loudly and cheerfully, I was a joker and a gossip, but I never offended anyone! But now, I've crossed that line.

BO: Let's forget about it, it's water under the bridge. Period.

DOT: I can't forget anything. I am over 180 years of age, and I still remember my parents. Are you aware that parakeets get married? Are you aware they know the meaning of marital bond and faithfulness? Can you even begin to imagine how my elders loved and cared for each other? How they kept falling into each other's feathery embrace? I didn't forget! I didn't forget how they ground seeds in their beaks for me, how they kept me from harm!

TOM: Dottie, no one resents you!

BO: Really, we love you.

DOT: You forgave me?

TOM: I swear.

PATIENTS' WARD

Night.

HORNER *and* FRANKIE *enter—they are quite drunk. At first, they just meander and stumble around the animals, but then they take their anger out on them. Kicking and hitting abounds. The panic among the animals escalates.*

FRANKIE: Come, another sip of schnapps. It's homemade, it won't do no harm.

HORNER (*drinking*): Curse the day I chose to become a veterinarian! What a disgusting job! Puss-filled entrails, stench and shit, festering wounds, rotten breath . . . Day in and day out.

FRANKIE: What about me? I deal exclusively with shit and piss. You think I am a dung-lover by nature? You think I was born that way? No qualifications, no school, lowest salary in the entire organization, so whoever wants to spit on me can go right ahead. Come on, partner, we'll settle this, I tell you!

HORNER: Goldie, my sweet boy! In 1958 my dad was in jail, my brother in the military—howling with the wolves on the Albanian border—and back home, my arthritic mother and pregnant little sister with one little bastard on her hands already that no one would provide for. The priest suggested that I study theology, and an assistant in the mayor's office, an uncle-in-law, offered a restricted scholarship for veterinary studies. There. That's how I forsook the Lord and sold my soul to the cattle!

FRANKIE: The cattle is our salvation, partner! It's the future!

HORNER: Damn, how I hate these beasts, and that Goodman, and his stupid theories about talking animals!

FRANKIE: You got some poison on you, for the chimp?

Someone fires a gun at the door lock from the outside and blows it open. HITMAN *rushes in, with* LIZZY *at his heels.*

HITMAN: Are you out of your minds? What are you doing?

LIZZY: You are drunk.

HORNER: We wanted to dedicate a few moments to these asses . . . disciplinary measures, so to speak!

LIZZY: You beat them?

FRANKIE: Well if they can really talk, they should also learn to ask: "May I go to the toilet?" Or what? Am I right?

GOODMAN, VERONICA, *and* LEPTIN *run into the ward.*

HITMAN: Well, well, what a party! Dumb quasi-revolutionaries and drunkards on one side, and on the other, the intellectual intelligentsia in the last stages of cynicism. Boycott, mutiny, and sabotage! Is it possible to talk *at all*? We live in the midst of a language hell. Our house of words is cursed and sick! It no longer serves its purpose! I don't believe in palaces with walls made of words! The word's no more! Those dead heaps of sound without weight, smell, and taste disgust me! May the laughter, gasping, hiccups, choking, and human cries be the only sounds left echoing within quantum physics! May only chirping, mooing, roaring, and meowing be heard within cybernetics. What is the voice of a living creature, anyway, in comparison with the sound of the factory sirens and the cannons' thunder? What are excuses in comparison with action? The apex of thought is a dumb act. Work and be silent! Shut your mouths, understood? Randomness and incompleteness, approximation, lies and confusion are all consequences of language. Errors of the loudmouths are threatening the balance of the world's powers! Each attempt at articulation is only an accumulation of egotism and nonsense, the spread of panic, an unbearable noise! I repeat: shut your mouth! Put a cork in it! I don't believe in the possibility of communication though language! I don't believe it's possible to convince anyone of anything! Every negotiation is a stillborn of a schizoid utopia. Conversation is a miscarriage of the will to change the world. Dialogue is a crime against the dictate of necessity! Make no mistake! I am not curious, I am not interested in what you think, I feel no need whatsoever to find it out, because your thoughts in any case are not going to be taken in consideration. About our common effort here, know this: zoolinguistics is a science of an extraordinary importance to the society. You will understand that in due time. I am announcing a moratorium on the circulation of information, and strict surveillance of people's movements, material goods, and research procedures. Everything that takes place here from this moment on is highly classified! *A military secret.* Dismissed!

End of SECOND SEQUENCE.

THIRD SEQUENCE

PATIENTS' WARD

HITMAN *and* PROFESSOR HEGEL, *shoulder to shoulder.* PROFESSOR HEGEL *holds paperwork of some sort in his hands. Opposite them, the Institute staff huddles together.* GOODMAN *is the only one missing. The atmosphere is rather tense. Animal sounds are heard, here and there.*

HEGEL (*clearing his throat*): Due to numerous infractions and irregularities that have lately become so frequent as to seriously endanger the existence and the ongoing work of the Institute, we had no choice but to take certain disciplinary measures and implement certain changes in the house rules and the staff structure of this institution. Doctor Hitman will now inform you of the decisions made.

HITMAN: So: the Institute is now a boarding-style facility. Practically speaking: going forward, we will not only work, but also live and eat here. No one is allowed to leave the premises without a special release, to be issued by Professor Hegel. Professor Hegel will prepare the new statute as well as the appropriate rules of conduct. I am responsible for the Institute's operations at large, including the Surveillance Center, effective immediately. Likewise, I am now also the chief physician and general manager. Sister Veronica has been named the head of kitchen, while Lizzy assumes responsibilities of the head nurse, going forward. Doctor Leptin shall oversee the animals' health insurance and his access privileges at the Surveillance Center have been revoked. Doctor Horner is relieved of his post as the head of treatment and shall focus exclusively on the hygienic needs, assisted—now more effectively than before—by Comrade Frankie. I am issuing strong citations of conduct to Frankie and Horner, and strong reprimands to everyone else. To work! Sister Lizzy, follow me! (*He stops, turns around.*) Disband without comment. I want no more conferencing under this roof.

Everyone leaves, and only HORNER *and* FRANKIE *stay behind amongst the animals.*

FRANKIE *devotes himself to cleaning the space, while* HORNER *disinfects certain animals. It is obvious that they are absorbed in work and conversation to the point that they pay no attention whatsoever to the animals.*

HORNER: The scant selection at the butcher's goes to show that the chains connecting the stables with kitchen tables are all rusty.

FRANKIE: Franks and cold cuts you can still get here and there . . . but fresh meat? Forget about it.

HORNER: In my opinion, the most important thing now is for the Federal Executive Committee to approve the proposed wholesale prices for cattle, and, based on that, the retail prices for meat.

FRANKIE: That's political blindness. What will the simple laborer put in his mouth? Say, a citizen of my caliber?

HORNER: Problem is, the prices of corn, feed, and above all, energy, are soaring, which significantly inflates farming costs. That's exactly why we are stuck with this dual pricing system.

FRANKIE: Without those calories, birth rates are going south, and so does a man's cock! Dammit, we gotta have meat, twice a week at least!

HORNER: The former were established by the federal government and should be in effect, according to the regulations . . .

FRANKIE: Hell if I care, let them regulate, even it it's by prescription only!

HORNER: . . . and the latter has to do with the market: the gap between supply and demand is getting wider and wider, since no one observes the decisions of the Executive Committee.

FRANKIE: Steak gives you the strength to endure all that bullshit!

HORNER: This is how we found ourselves in this peculiar situation: statistically, cattle farming appears to be thriving, but, understandably, the selection on the market is dwindling. As a result, stables are full, and slaughterhouses empty! The black market's blossoming!

FRANKIE: "All for one, one for all!" I live by that motto and I will never bow down to these shameless demands that we—brothers and fellows—from the Institute's unified labor organization get split into those with tiny frozen salaries and those with oversized freezers at home! Never!

HORNER: It is therefore hardly surprising that numerous confident predictions indicate that, due to the current circumstances in farming industry, it won't be possible to meet current goals, if the current pricing politics continues in spite of everything.

FRANKIE: In this situation, the little man will be forced to resort to unprecedented, unusual, somewhat controversial and suspect, and yet certainly tried ways of *bringing his own piece of meat to the table*! In the institutions that were never established as geriatric asylums, or social-service shelters for ruminants, odd-toed ungulates and poultry, we, the meat consumers, insist on our right to relieve the suffering of untreatable and seriously ill patients for humanitarian reasons. I assure you that the Institute's intelligent implementation of euthanasia will not only cover its own needs in the fresh meat department, it could even reach international acclaim with its competitive offerings and highly diverse selection.

HORNER *and* FRANKIE *forcefully stare at the patients who don't display any particular signs of distress this time around.*

HORNER (*quietly*): I am not sure they picked up on the meat of our conversation. (*A moment later.*) We used a multitude of uncommon terms.

FRANKIE: By the time they catch our drift, it will be too late . . .

HORNER: This was, as they say, the last opportunity for confession.

HORNER *and* FRANKIE *leave the ward.*

FLO: Folks, what is going on here? Could someone please explain this to me?

BO: The clinic is *no more*!

STELLA: What will happen to us? Where will we go?

DOT (*a moment later*): If we wish to survive, we must get organized!

HEADQUARTERS

LIZZY, *in her new role, and* HITMAN.

HITMAN: Where is Goodman?

LIZZY (*hesitating*): Oh, Comrade Hitman, it is quite unbelievable, I don't dare tell you . . .

HITMAN: Speak.

LIZZY: You'll think I am out of whack!

HITMAN: Speak!

LIZZY: I am not convinced myself of what I saw, exactly . . .

HITMAN: What did you see?

LIZZY: Actually, I don't believe in what I'd seen, and yet it seems to me it did happen . . .

HITMAN: What?

LIZZY: May I start from the beginning? (HITMAN *nods*.) Well, early this morning, while I worked in the kitchen, I was supposed to bring some salt to Fannie and Mary, two bananas to Vito, and milk to Mary. I put it all on a tray and went to the patients' ward. When I entered, I went straight to Vito and gave him the bananas, I turned around so as to give the milk to Mary, then I saw Doctor Goodman kneeling next to Tom. I was scared shitless, I thought maybe he wasn't well, that he collapsed, you know what I'm sayin'? I just stared at him for some time, I wasn't sure what to say or what to do! I froze, don't know how else to explain this to you! And the moment I was gonna dump the tray on the floor and get near him, oh horror, I saw him slowly, kinda invisibly, merging with Tom. And he vanished. There wasn't a trace of him left, just Tom.

PATIENTS' WARD

ROCKY: I am against these endless debates! I had it up to here with all of you!

DOLLY: He's right. Enough politics! Aren't we capable of talking about something more entertaining? After all, there are some aristocrats in our midst! We are not all commoners!

FANNY: *Who's* an aristocrat?

ROCKY: Me—for example! According to Arabian requirements, a horse must have good proportions; short flexible ears; heavy, but certainly healthy bones; a face that's not too meaty; and nostrils as wide as a lion's throat. It should be graced with dark, ever forward-facing eyes, resembling the eyes of a woman in love.

VITO: The day you look like a woman in love, I'll become Tarzan!

ROCKY: Its neck should be lean and long, its shoulders and buttocks wide, its calves curved, with very long even ribs and very short odd ribs, and a tight physique.

GOLDIE: The more I look at you, the less you fit the description.

ROCKY: Its thighs should be like ostrich's, its muscles like camel's.

FLO: That's absurd! A thoroughbred horse is a typical human invention. There is no such thing in the nature. In the nature, there are only wild horses.

GOLDIE: Rocky is actually a fake.

ROCKY: You don't seem to understand something very basic: the nature provides raw ingredients. A raw ingredient is considered to be of a lesser value. People value the most what they make themselves, in other words, what they obtain and manufacture from natural sources. In Budapest, Vienna, Madrid . . . everyone looked at me as if I were a god!

IKA: You swear to God?

ROCKY: I swear.

IKA: But—why is that?

ROCKY: Because I am a noble creature! That's what I mean! The raw material can be nice, useful, or precious, but it can't be noble! Processed gold increases its value tenfold! Renoir's *Landscape on the Coast Near Menton* is a hundred times more expensive than the plot of land in the painting!

FANNIE: How is that possible?

ROCKY: Cézanne's *Still Life* at MoMA is worth millions of dollars! And do you know what's in the picture?

FANNIE: What?

ROCKY: Twenty-three apples, a crumpled white napkin, and a clay pot with some dried-up grass in it.

IKA: That's all?

ROCKY: That's all.

FLO: So why is the painting so expensive?

ROCKY: Because it's art. Because it's unique. Because it's noble!

VITO: Do I sense that you might be comparing yourself to Cézanne's *Still Life?*

ROCKY: Not exactly, but if the current prices in the global marketplace are to be trusted, I don't lag behind a Cézanne that much.

FANNIE: So how much are you worth?

ROCKY: Enough for Mr. Richman, a private breeder, to cash me in and buy the Clinic with all of you in it, and still have enough for a decent-sized yacht.

IKA: I don't get it, how is it that all of us put together are worth so little?

FANNIE: What kind of stupid criteria are these?

BO: Racist criteria!

FLO: How is it possible that one life is worth more than another?

TOM: Isn't each one of us a unique living creature?

ROCKY: And yet, each of us has a market value.

FANNIE: Based on what?

ROCKY: Based on one's use value.

STELLA: And what is use value?

ROCKY: Your use value is that you give milk, Tom's is that he catches mice, Flo's is that he hauls the cart from the vineyard and back, Blacky's is that he watches over the house, Dot's is that he imitates and entertains people, and so forth. Each of us has a use value of one's own. Some more, some less.

Dead silence.

BLACKY: The only thing that baffles me in Rocky's case is that someone rides him his entire life. See, I wouldn't be able to tolerate that.

ROCKY: And I wouldn't be able to tolerate the chain and the muzzle.

BO: That's why they rein and saddle you!

DOLLY: Bo, you don't have a say in this matter. You've been caged in the zoo your entire life.

ROCKY: Consider yourself lucky for having made it to the Clinic. You are in decent company, for once.

BO: As if the stable was so much better than the cage!

BLACKY: It doesn't matter who's on a leash, who's on reins, and who's on a chain, or which one's worse than the other. That's the wrong question to ask. It's ALL so rotten, that it can't be possibly more rotten than it already is.

DOT: Beware the gloomy dog and his black paws!

BLACKY: I am a pessimist, I admit it. The reason why I am a pessimist is that all of you find your own destiny more acceptable than others'! Torture and humiliation are more easily tolerated on one's own skin than on that of one's neighbor: that's the ideology of the enslaved and the uneducated of this world.

MARY: I would never be able to settle for a dog's life, if someone were to make me this offer. You can't persuade me that each existence is equally pitiful.

DOLLY: No need to get personal, thanks!

BLACKY: Rocky unconditionally submits himself to the bloody dictatorship of spurs, reins, and whips. He is completely unaware of being a victim of soulless training, deserving of our compassion. On the contrary, he is convinced that he lives and works for his equine ideals!

ROCKY: Blacky, the situation with competitive sports these days is such that you can't accomplish anything without grueling efforts in training!

BLACKY: Richman takes advantage of you for his dirty business.

ROCKY: It is *I* who takes advantage of him!

BLACKY: WHAT? What did you say?

ROCKY: I am using his capital, his knowledge, his servants, and his connections for the benefit of personal gain and recognition.

BLACKY: And what does that recognition do for you?

ROCKY: The sweet taste of victory is impossible to explain to someone who is not an athlete. I am built in such a way that I feel the need to *race* deep within me. That's a passion: to run, run fast, faster, to be *the first*, far ahead of everyone else.

Dead silence.

FLO: I would never have imagined that a horse could sink so low.

HITMAN *enters, the animals get silent. He stops next to* TOM.

HITMAN: Doctor Goodman, please get out. (*Dead silence.*) I beg your pardon, this is an extremely painful situation. (*Dead silence.*) This behavior is unworthy of a scholar. (*Dead silence.*) Why are you doing this? What do you hope to accomplish? (*Dead silence.*) Meow at least, if you can't speak . . .

GOODMAN: I can speak.

HITMAN: Thank God! Then speak, please, tell me what's bothering you, tell me freely what it is I do that you disapprove of.

GOODMAN: You fool yourself by attempting to understand the phenomenon of speech in two different ways. Speech as a social reality is just a part of what we define with the word "truth." A single thought cannot encompass two kinds of truth because logic requires appropriate coordination. If we say that the Sun, according to perception, rotates around one visibility sector of the Earth, and we simultaneously claim that the Earth, understandably, rotates around the Sun—then there you have two truths you need to reconcile. If we claim that zoolinguistics attempts to understand the speech of animals, we cannot simultaneously claim that this speech doesn't exist, and even further, that all speech is useless, barely worth reducing to its basic biological dimension. Is it possible to uphold such a conflicting opinion in one's practice? Is it even acceptable?

HITMAN: If you are open to the critique of scientific discovery, and ready to keep epistemological results in mind, you are surely no stranger to Emile Boutroux's thesis about the Contingency of Natural Laws as a critique of ideals of absolute deduction and as an opposition to reductionism. In that sense, his thinking was validated by later scientific developments. It truly seems, more and more so, that in all situations leading to the reduction of high to low, from the more complex to the simpler, that the reduction becomes reciprocal, meaning that the lower becomes augmented by certain characteristic of the higher, and that "the simplest" becomes more complete. It was in such a way that Einstein reduced gravity to the curvature of space, and though this appeared as a reduction from a physical to a geometric plane, he was able to relate curvature to mass, which consequently implied reciprocal reduction. The day that *the vital* is reduced to the physical/chemical, according to Charles-Eugène Quye, the latter will become greatly enriched with as many heretofore unknown properties—and contemporary molecular biology is indeed getting closer to being able to verify this dual anticipation. Could the same not be said for languages as well? Reduced language is not necessarily inferior! Why shouldn't you, at least speculatively, concern yourself with the reduction of human language to dogs' language? Or cats', if that suits you better?!

GOODMAN: You keep trading language with speech. What angers you the most is speech, and at the same time, the speech itself is the only thing under the sun that truly interests you. You would eliminate something that anchors you as a historical being.

HITMAN: Why do you detest paradoxes?

GOODMAN: How can you proclaim an idea to be equally acceptable and unacceptable and even necessary for certain objectives, if that depends only on whether you view those objectives through a scientific, political, or counter-intelligence lens? Clearly, you seek two ways of discovery, of which one is "higher" because it reaches the essence, and other "lower" because it deals with plain language or incomplete knowledge. Well then, if there is only one, the highest knowledge, which encompasses all, lower, and lower-than-lower, obviously limited discoveries, why can't we have a breakthrough? There are many soldiers out there who are wannabe philosophers. And my only issue with that is: why, then, are they always running in circles?

HITMAN: We'll see how far you'll get with your feline philosophizing!

GOODMAN *meows*, HITMAN *leaves*.

HEADQUARTERS

LIZZY, FRANKIE

LIZZY (*on the phone*): Private property or not, this is a public institution with its own house rules. Visiting hours are clearly posted, and there are clear rules about the times and circumstances under which a patient is to be allowed to go home! Do you have an official release, signed and sealed? You don't! (*Listens.*) What matters is that you voluntarily brought your bitch here for treatment . . . (*Listens.*) Ma'am, what kind of clinic do you think this is? It's unheard of! That would be the end of this Institute! (*A moment later.*) We are in the position to decide what's best for the bitch! Good-bye. (*A moment later.*) Yes, we are right! (*Slams the receiver down.*)

FRANKIE (*meekly*): Damn, you're tough.

LIZZY: I can tell you this much: watch that mouth! I am sick of your lies and plots! I already showed the door to Leptin and that, whatever you wanna call her, of his. I told Hitman, it's either me, or the two of them! If you want to stay friends, don't cross the line. I ain't the kitchen maid from the country side no more!

SURVEILLANCE ROOM

HITMAN, LEPTIN

HITMAN: Have you ever considered ethical integrity of specialists who sell to foreigners the knowledge that generations of domestic scientists gained in domestic institutions funded by the money of our citizens? Give it some thought, it is an endlessly fascinating topic to meditate on!

LEPTIN (*broken*): Stop torturing me, please.

HITMAN: Of course, let's leave morals aside, that's an old bag of tricks. Rather, let's talk business. See, Leptin, while we are on the subject of business: your debt is of the kind that can never be fully repaid.

LEPTIN: I am aware of it. I am not a dissident, I am not a traitor, I am not two-faced, I will make an effort while being abroad, I will do everything in my power . . . I will translate, I will send. The codes are in the middle drawer.

HITMAN: Good. So—what do you say? You scratch my back and I'll scratch yours?

LEPTIN: I am a man of the word.

HITMAN: You are a knight of the digits.

LEPTIN: You scratch my back, and I'll scratch yours.

HITMAN: What's my name again?

LEPTIN: Hitman.

HITMAN: That's my pseudonym. Why?

LEPTIN (*making an effort*): It's a metaphor. You relegate men to . . .

HITMAN (*laughing*): No, Leptin! I shoot them. (*After a pause.*) Here's your release.

PATIENTS' WARD

DOT: For some time now the situation has not been good here in the animal kingdom, politically speaking. And it isn't good because we are not united and we do not have proper leadership. If we want to keep up with the times, if we want to shake off the hegemony of men, then we need to change a whole lot amongst our ranks. We must be better organized. We have to become more effective. And we can't accomplish this without a plan, without clear goals, without our own leadership, capable of making sacrifices for the benefit of the group's well-being, and making considerable effort to maintain it. In considering potential candidates for the chief of the animal kingdom, we must be highly critical. We must keep in mind the moral and intellectual qualities of such individuals, as well as their skills and characteristics. Thank you for your attention—I hereby open this discussion to the floor.

FLO: I have to say, I don't exactly understand the motivations of the working presidency. What seems to be the problem? Us animals, we have traditionally established leadership. It's well known who and why that is: lion is the king of all animals!

STELLA: Right. In the best-case scenario—the king of four-legged gangsters!

TOM: Lion is the highest leader in the kingdom of mammals!

BO: Well, that is up for discussion!

FANNIE: How can such a bloodthirsty and not particularly intelligent animal be the king?

IKA: He's the strongest, no doubt about it . . .

MARY: All right, but do you find it necessary that everyone should tremble in fear before him? Do we really have to have the government of terror?

BLACKY: How is he supposed to rule if no one is giving him the time of day? He must be an authoritative figure! Strong-arm politics is a necessity in the midst of relations characterized by idiosyncrasies, where everyone wants to have it his way and looks only at narrow personal interests!

ROCKY: It is possible to be a powerful ruler if you are greatly loved by everyone. If you are loved, you don't need to be particularly strong! It is enough to be wise and just.

DOLLY: The lion is not only strong, he is also a gentleman: charming, cavalier, and handsome!

ROCKY: We cannot use good looks as criteria for a ruler! Beauty and strength is to be displayed in athletic competitions and beauty contests. As far as I am concerned, he could even be a Mister Universe! Still, he cannot be the king, or the president—that is a political function that necessitates utterly different qualities.

TOM: Which ones, for example?

ROCKY: Foresight, stately intellect, diplomatic patience, sense of responsibility . . . and so forth!

TOM: I propose the bear!

BO: I reject the nomination!

TOM: Why?

BO: I could care less about it, I am telling you. And besides, I live in captivity.

BLACKY: A captive leader! This is the epitome of our situation, how brilliant!

BO: No, no . . . And, once again, for good: no!

MARY: If we recall the fairy tale *Puss in Boots*, Tom would appear to be the perfect candidate.

TOM: I am not a puss *in boots*, besides, I intend to devote myself mainly to family and personal interests . . .

BLACKY: To be honest, I would feel more than stupid if I were to be governed by a cat. I would probably become illegal or turn to dissidents.

DOLLY: I understand you perfectly.

LEPTIN *enters the ward, and goes directly toward* TOM. *Silence.*

LEPTIN: Goodman?

TOM: Yes?

LEPTIN: Goodman, Veronica and I are running off to Cologne.

GOODMAN: What about Alice?

LEPTIN: Don't worry, I will adopt her. Of course, she will have to stay at Grandma's at first, until we get a firmer footing.

TOM: Who will you work for in Cologne?

LEPTIN: It's a commercial gig, Goodman.

TOM: You're a thief, Leptin.

LEPTIN: The market is intended for the people, not *against* them!

TOM: Yes, just like the nuclear power.

LEPTIN: Millions of lonely, aging, neglected, deprived people have no one left in the world to talk to, to confide in, except for a dog, or cat. How many of those beings could we make happy if we offered them the ability to communicate with their pets?

GOODMAN: Men who love their animals understand them even without translation. That's the whole truth. Leave, I can't bear to look at you anymore.

LEPTIN *leaves.* ALICE *sneaks in from some corner and goes to* TOM.

ALICE: Uncle Goodman! (*After a pause.*) Uncle Goodman!

GOODMAN: Go home, Grandma is waiting for you.

ALICE: But I'd like to stay with you.

GOODMAN: There's no room left.

ALICE: I would like to get inside Mary, the white Persian kitty, if you can tell me how it's done.

GOODMAN: Grandma is waiting for you.

ALICE: But please!

GOODMAN: What would Grandma say?

ALICE: Please!

GOODMAN: Answer the question, Alice.

ALICE: Grandma forgets everything: she forgets who I am, where I am, she forgets that I even exist.

GOODMAN: Come near Mary and kneel beside her. (ALICE *does so.*) And now, look her straight in the eyes.

HEADQUARTERS / SURVEILLANCE ROOM

HITMAN *and* PROFESSOR HEGEL *converse via intercom.*

HITMAN: Set aside all the guidelines you put together and write new ones!

HEGEL: How do you mean?

HITMAN: I mean, so that names like Rocky, Mary, Dolly, and Flo, for example, appear in the Patient's Council.

HEGEL: What about our statute?

HITMAN: The statute stays the same!

PATIENTS' WARD

VITO (*after a long and painful pause*): I am embarrassed to think that some may find me shameless, but I must openly admit . . . Well, to be brief, I believe that monkey is the smartest animal.

TOM: Well, well, well, how did you figure that?

VITO: Based on observation.

GOLDIE: Not only does it sound shameless, it is also pompous.

VITO: Monkeys belong to the class of primates. According to all scientific classifications, chimps are Homo sapiens' nearest cousins. It is hardly a secret that man is only a slightly improved model of a chimpanzee. On the ladder between the typical class of animals and man, chimpanzee occupies the very top. With that in mind, I feel like I could unleash my inner reserve . . . I sense enormous potential within me, long neglected . . . I feel that I am a promising asset, and it would be a pleasure to be able to devote myself to personal growth for the benefit of all. That's all for now, thank you for your attention.

DOT (*after a pause*): We've heard Vito' pledge for candidacy . . . If the delegates could please speak up . . . offer their remarks . . . (*Silence.*) I find it charming that Vito proposed himself without a reserve . . . That speaks to the honesty and immediacy of his character—qualities that are auspicious, without a doubt . . .

FLO: Umm, yeah . . . A ruler shouldn't always put all of his cards on the table . . . He should be capable of—I beg your pardon—petulant bluffing!

GOLDIE: It is my turn to be open, unambiguous, and earnest, though I would like to explicitly emphasize that I am neither a monkey, nor a leadership candidate. (*Shortly afterward.*) It's a simple dilemma: do presently gathered delegates truly wish to elect someone similar to a human? If we are already flirting with the possibility of going for a beast similar to man, why don't we take it a step further and simply choose a man? I insist that monkeys, with chimpanzees at their helm, have all but lost their animal identity; that, at this stage of their development, they are neither here nor there; faulty animals as much as they are faulty humans . . . They are degenerates, monsters, *the junk* of both animal and human worlds. (*Applause.*) We mustn't bow down to monkeys' self-conscious, self-serving logic, which leads, or rather *would* lead our community to ruination of its authentic animal sovereignty, to decadence and breakdown, to agony and death. (*Applause.*) In conclusion, I hope that our animal world will be capable of preserving its animal nature, that it will be able to defend the heritage of animal spirit, its habits and customs, its dreams and ideals, the wisdom and values of our ancestors! With that in mind, may our leader be a *true animal*, and not an animal *who endeavors to be similar to man*! (*Applause.*) It's beautiful to be an animal. It's animal to be an animal! (*Applause.*)

IKA: That was *fat* . . . gotta give it to him.

FANNIE: What do you think, who's behind him?

STELLA: That remains to be seen . . .

VITO: With sadness and bitterness, I come to the conclusion that certain factions easily bow down to demagogical provocations aimed at creating conditions in which the hysterical hunt on intellectuals during pre-election debates squelches the strength of solid arguments and sound reasoning!

GOLDIE: Exactly! I am allergic to intellectuals! I can't stand intellectual cynicism! I reject defeatism and relativism! I raise my voice for the triumph of faith in one's own strengths, for the renewal of tried populist values, for the renaissance of provincialism, minority, and primitivism!

Dead silence.

VITO (*with irony, and resignation*): There you have it . . . the agenda for the twenty-first century.

GOLDIE: You have a better one?

DOT (*clearing his throat*): We have heard Goldie's thoughts. (*Shortly afterward,* DOT *continues in a more guarded tone.*) It is good that the debate is becoming heated . . . That's healthy . . . There are probably thoughts out there that will shed new light on this discussion . . .

LEPTIN *and* VERONICA *enter. It's a farewell. With a briefcase in hand,* LEPTIN *stops near the door in silence. With a purse in hand,* VERONICA *goes from one animal to the next, and stops next to* BO.

VERONICA (*confidentially, but not conspiratorially*): If I had a bomb, I'd hit Hitman with it. I say my good-byes. I will raise the anchor that keeps my boat at bay from the waters of nothingness. It takes courage to be nothing, and nothing but nothing, and I am parting with everything I feel inseparable from. In just one spasm, I'll vomit all my goodness, I'll rip the ties, burn memories of umbilical cords, and run away from here. (*Suddenly more intense.*) Split him in half, shred him to a million pieces, tear him apart! Be a ruthless avenger and a brutal assassin!

VERONICA *keeps going, unlocks* BO's *cage and goes from animal to animal. When she reaches the Persian cat, she recoils and starts to cry.* LEPTIN *pulls her away, almost forcefully.*

VERONICA: Bye-bye, kitty! Bye-bye, kitty!

They are gone. The meeting resumes as if nothing happened.

DOLLY: Goldie set in motion several trains of thought that merit our attention. Those trains of thought point at the dangers of thrusting our government into the hands of someone not typically animalesque! Though I ordinarily find Vito charming, what bothers me is his *lack of typical animality* . . . By that I mean that he's peculiar and, to say the least, *different* than us! In my opinion, the throne should be occupied by someone who is not different from the rest of us.

DOT: Thank you, Dolly. (*Scanning the room.*) Would anyone else like to take the floor? So then, we are seeking a typical representative from our ranks, a spokesperson whose animality we'll be able to identify with . . .

FANNIE: "Nothing human or human-like can ever, in any form or under any circumstance, represent anything animal." Is that the truth, is it really so? I, dear friends, believe that such logic hangs upon a thin thread. At this point, one needs to firmly assert that human and animal natures are *identical in origin, lineage, and matter.* From a different perspective, we can view both worlds as being *simultaneously* extremely human and animal. Which means that we are aware of the paradox we can never truly neither transcend nor abolish. Such paradox is referred to as the dialectic unity of opposites. What does that mean? It means that all of us are "human" in our own right, but also that humans are "animal" in their own right. Man is, as we well know, a multifaceted animal: he can be sly as a fox, hungry like a wolf, silly as a cow, busy as a bee, sick as a dog, hung like a horse, drunk like a fish, and so forth . . . And, in the end, man is a man after all!

GOLDIE: Enough philosophizing! Shut up!

VITO: Let her speak and finish what she has to say!

GOLDIE: No one is entitled to abuse the right of speech!

DOT: Silence! (*After a pause.*) Go on, Fannie.

FANNIE: Please understand, then, that a chimpanzee can, in principle, indeed be considered a representative of the animal world! There are no formal legal obstacles to that—assuming, of course, that the majority of representatives of other species should so decide. Personally speaking, however, I am not convinced that such decision would be reasonable. Why? I'll tell you why: this ridiculous creature could just as easily be a successful candidate for the position of a court jester, but for the fateful, serious and responsible political function, in spite of his obvious intelligence—he can't and he mustn't! And why? Because a leader without stateliness is like a soup without salt—tasteless!!

BO: Bravo! Bravo!

FANNIE: We don't need a leader who will amuse us, but one who will drive us to despair! It is true that, of late, we have observed certain tendencies that turned the original order of things upside down: comedians, humorists, satirists, and jokers are getting deadly boring and cheap, and politicians are endlessly fucking around! I am not sure where it all leads. Once upon a time, we used to fight *for* ideals, now we fight *against* them. Once upon a time, the expression "May citizens drink, the government will pay" used to apply; nowadays, the government is constantly drunk at citizens' expense. That drunkenness has lasted too long. When will the sobering up begin? (*Applause.*)

DOT: We have now heard the brilliant, though somewhat drawn-out presentation by our dear Fannie who, all in all, being the representative of the fairer sex, was able to express herself fairly well. I did notice that certain listeners, regardless of how interesting or original the speeches, occasionally nod off, some even snore in their sleep. Stella, Ika, Mary, and so forth. Let's continue, please. (*Dead silence.*) Do we have any other candidates?

GOLDIE: The options are not exactly stellar.

BO: A dinosaur would be the most stately option.

DOT: You are well aware that those colleagues are no longer amongst the living for some time now.

BO: May they rest in peace!

ALL: May they rest in peace!

FLO: Excuse me, but what about dragons? I don't see them anywhere? It's as if the earth had swallowed them!

DOT: If I am not mistaken, the last one of them perished in a bloody battle under the sword of Saint George.

FLO: Death to the saints!

ALL: Death to the saints!

STELLA: Long live the winged bull, the divine Lamasu!

ALL: Long live!

MARY: Long live the ancient foremother of all cats!

ALL: Long live!

ROCKY: Long live Pegasus!

ALL: Long live!

MARY: Long live the sphinx!

ALL: Long live!

HORNER *enters the ward, goes straight toward* TOM. *The animals go quiet.*

HORNER: Doctor Goodman, I regret the events in which I participated, and I repent for the actions I aided. And yet, if you don't mind mine saying this, I'd like to tell you that I find your behavior rather strange. I am disgusted by science that neglects God. The man who lowers himself to the level of communicating with a beast, tarnishes the Almighty, who created him in his image and word. Every science is relative and incomplete, because it is anthropomorphic. Yours couldn't even be called that. You are playing with fire, you've embarked on a dangerous journey. Your stay in a cat could hardly be considered honorable. Personally, I find the notion of transcendental finality to be the highest truth and the only certainty. It's still not too late for you to withdraw, to leave those horrors behind you, all is not lost yet. Erase the traces of your errors, even if it is with blood, don't stumble, gather your strength to get rid of shadows and illusions. Here, if your soul is heavy, share that righteous act with me.

GOODMAN: I can't bear to look at you. Get lost!

HORNER *leaves, the debate continues.*

DOT: I believe that our discussions slipped off to a dead-end track. I have nothing against mythology, on the contrary, I am a fiery believer and supporter of our glorious history which convincingly proves that we used to be creatures to be feared, respected and revered . . . yes . . . even holy creatures. But we must be aware that those times are gone and our present isn't the least bit rosy. Therefore, I propose that we descend from the intoxicating mythological heights to the firm, shit-covered, earthly ground. It is there, on that ground, that our candidate, the chimpanzee Vito, awaits us. Which brings up one last, clear and purely practical question. Lion is a born leader. Sovereignty, so to speak, runs in his veins. So, all the aspiring candidates for his throne must possess certain leadership skills! What kind of skills does our colleague Vito have?

VITO: The social life of chimpanzees is highly developed. The hierarchy is simple and strong: on one side, the leader of the herd; on the other, the followers.

TOM: You were the leader of the herd?

VITO: I was the leader of the herd.

BLACKY: What are the rights and responsibilities of the leader?

VITO: The leader is the absolute master of the herd. No female is allowed to stray with a rookie. The females who let themselves go get a beating. In such a way, the leader sours any and all flirtation with other males.

DOLLY: Oh, heavenly creatures, but that is a harem!

VITO: Sure, what did you think?

BLACKY: What happens to the females who break the rules of the harem?

VITO: Nothing good can come of it.

DOLLY: Hey, sultan, and what are the females' daily duties?

VITO: Daily duties include satisfying my horniness, petting my fur, and picking out parasites. I take care of the herd's safety, which gives me no rest. It is a huge responsibility.

BO: I am not sure how to comment . . .

ROCKY: I imagine a true leader quite differently.

VITO: For example?

GOLDIE: In the first place, he shouldn't be allowed to bang everything that crawls and jumps . . . he should let everyone else fuck to their heart's content.

VITO: The way we do things is that the one who is the strongest and the healthiest takes care of the progeny. That warrants a healthy population.

BLACKY: What about the others?

VITO: The others masturbate, or indulge in homosexual pleasures.

FANNIE: Monkey business!

STELLA: Poor creatures . . . they must be constantly exhausted.

VITO: No way. Monkeys celebrate life: they play, crack jokes, scream, screech, drum on trees, jump, and do gymnastics. As acrobats, they have no equals.

DOT: Before I pass your candidacy on to the voting pool, I have one last question: why are you here, Vito?

VITO: I am in treatment . . .

DOT: What for?

VITO: Does it matter?

DOT: Of course it does. Very much so.

VITO: I've had growths . . .

DOT: Where?

VITO: On the calluses of upper extremities, along the inner joints . . .

DOT: Weren't you in surgery for that?

VITO (*increasingly more defeated*): After the surgery, they reemerged with a vengeance . . .

DOT: I suppose the growths are not benign . . .

VITO: The test results are not in yet!

DOT: Vito, you are seriously ill.

VITO (*in despair*): I am not!

DOT (*ruthlessly*): Terminally ill.

VITO (*in tears*): Oh my God! Oh my God!

DOT: Unfortunately, an effective cure against cancer has not been discovered yet.

VITO: Jesus, Mary, and Joseph . . . help me!

DOT: My friendly advice to you would be to withdraw your candidacy.

BO: Withdraw!

VITO: God almighty, have pity on me!

BLACKY: Withdraw!

VITO: Cure my growths, kiss my calluses, heal my wretched wounds, make me healthy . . . make me healthy . . .

DOT: The Almighty punished you with a serious illness, you can't be the king of all animals.

IKA (*zealously*): His body is rotting, and he's wrestling for the scepter!

VITO: I withdraw. I withdraw! A kingdom for my health! (*Sobbing overcomes him.*)

DOT: I believe we may now reinstate the lion, our only candidate, as the king of all animals. (*A moment later.*) Any objections? (*No one speaks.*) I hereby announce that the council of delegates confirmed the appointment of our favorite sovereign, the invincible, formidable lion! (*Applause.* VITO *tears his hairs out and thrashes on the floor.*) Let's wish our chimp a speedy recovery. (*Applause.*) Let's wish for a miracle, so that the doctors may find a cure for cancer.

ALL: Let's wish for a miracle!

IKA: One, two, three, four . . .

ALL: One, two, three, four . . .

VITO: One, two, three, four . . .

BO *suddenly breaks out of his lethargy, and begins to sing at the top of his lungs.*

BO (*sings*): "Death is at our doors with her heavy sword
Coming to cut down the zoolinguistic ward

CHORUS: She watches her clients straight into the eyes
Unafraid of threats, of teeth, paws, cries

BO: A bundle of muscles, a pile of bones
While Death smiles, poor beast groans

CHORUS: Its mighty courage quickly melts and wanes
One, two, three . . . the beast no longer complains"

HITMAN *and* PROFESSOR HEGEL *enter the ward. When* BO *notices them, he flings the cage door open and heads toward* HITMAN. HITMAN *recoils, pulls out a pistol, and shoots six times.* BO *is hit, but advances nonetheless, catches up with* HITMAN, *knocks him down with the hit of a paw, and kills him. Then moves over to* PROFESSOR HEGEL, *who is completely paralyzed, throws him in the cage, locks him up, swallows the key, and dies.*

HORNER *and* FRANKIE *enter, armed up to their noses.*

HORNER: Do it so they don't suffer too much.

FRANKIE: The list, where is your list?

HORNER: Do it with the taser!

FRANKIE: I'll do the chimp in with a knife!

HORNER: The chimp is not on the list!

FRANKIE: I don't give a flying fuck!

HORNER: He's got cancer, his meat is unusable!

FRANKIE: We'll sell it with a discount!

HORNER: I sure won't!

FRANKIE: Shut it! Give me the machete.

HORNER: We got the cow, the sheep, the goat, the cat, and the horse on the list! That's the first round!

FRANKIE: Get out of my way or I'll kick your ass!

HORNER: Watch out!

ALICE *emerges from the Persian cat.* HORNER *and* FRANKIE *stop dead in their tracks.*

ALICE *heads toward* TOM.

ALICE: Uncle Goodman! Uncle Goodman! Uncle Goodman! Uncle Goodman! Uncle GOOOOOOOOOOOOOODMAAAAAAAAAAAN! Uncle Goodman!

RAT *comes out of a dark corner. It stops in front of* ALICE, *staring at her. It's as if everything was happening in a dream and in reality at the same time.*

ALICE (*to* TOM): Dad!

GOODMAN *emerges from* TOM.

GOODMAN: Put your weapons down. The experiment is not over yet.

End of Miracle.

CHICKEN HEAD

György Spiró

GYÖRGY SPIRÓ
Photo by Gabriella Györffy, www.gimagine.com

GYÖRGY SPIRÓ'S *CHICKEN HEAD*:
CRIES FROM A CONDEMNED COURTYARD

Eugene Brogyányi

As no previous play had done, *Chicken Head*, written by György Spiró in 1985 and premiered in 1986, exposed the socioeconomic and moral exhaustion of Hungary in the last decade of communist rule. In its unabashed directness, the play single-handedly challenged a tradition that had characterized the best of Hungarian drama for over two decades. In the early 1960s, the government of János Kádár, which had been installed by the Soviet tanks that crushed the Hungarian Revolution of 1956, began seeking legitimacy at home by gradually loosening its grip on artistic expression. Within constraints and respecting certain taboos—the Soviet occupation, the official assessment of 1956, the legitimacy of the government, and one-party rule—playwrights could increasingly employ metaphor and parable to depict individual and social conflicts generated by lack of freedom. Many of these writers adapted the latest European dramatic trends, such as absurdism and epic theatre, while others continued the time-honored Hungarian tradition of the polemical historical drama, all in service of a theatre-between-the-lines. As a result, a tacit and fruitful conspiracy emerged between the playwright and the public, in which audiences drew reassurance from the "coded" messages they received from the stage, and drama thrived.

The price of this relative freedom of expression was that the public intellectual became an unwilling supporter of the very system he was indirectly criticizing, and a number of plays from those Kádár-era decades dealt with the resulting moral crisis of the post-1956 intellectual. These plays were based on a basic question: Is it possible to live with integrity in a system whose ideology is belied by reality?

This question also informs a generational shift that occurred in 1979 with the appearance of three plays: *Encounter* by Péter Nádas; *Halmi, or The Prodigal Son* by Géza Bereményi; and *Hallelujah* by Mihály Kornis. Like Spiró, these authors were children during the dark days of the fifties, and grew to adulthood observing the compromises of their parents' generation. Each play has at its core a son's confrontation with a tainted paternal legacy. *Encounter* is a ritual of cleansing, replete with musical underscoring. A young man enters the room of an aged woman to learn about his deceased father who, it turns out, was once the woman's lover, then her torturer during a Stalinist interrogation, after which he killed himself in front of her. At the end of her revelations, the woman bathes the passive visitor, puts him to bed, casually takes poison, and leaves the room which may or may not be a real place. *Halmi* makes of Hamlet a contemporary anti-hero who can only rebel through the total and irrational disavowal of the world that his two fathers—one biological, who left the country in 1956, the other his uncle, who reared him—have bequeathed him. In *Hallelujah* a man is awaiting the arrival of his father in a room with his grandfather. Time and place are in flux; the stage is traversed by crowds and characters from a disintegrating society; the dialogue is built on free association. The situation is static, and when the father finally shows up, nothing is resolved. These three plays are superb works of drama of a new generation, and each takes a highly critical look at a deeply troubled society. They also continue the tradition of theatre-between-the-lines, in the form of a ritual, a grotesque Shakespeare paraphrase, and an absurdist rhapsody, respectively.

The theatre of coded messages produced brilliant plays and raised public morale, but it also stifled the inclination of drama to talk straight. *Chicken Head* was the breakthrough. Even though the play, produced in 1986 by Budapest's finest theatre company, the Katona József, featuring the grande dame of the Hungarian stage, Hilda Gobbi, ran for years, the assessment of its message had to wait until after the change of regime. In 1991 the play was identified by the esteemed critic Zsuzsa Radnóti as "the distress signal of a country inexorably heading toward the socioeconomic and moral zero point, to the exhaustion of the people's resilience, of their strength and emotional reserves."

The action of *Chicken Head* takes place in the typical inner courtyard of a run-down apartment building on the outskirts of Budapest. The four tiny apartments of the one-storey building open onto this squalid space. The residents live solitary lives but have no privacy. They and other characters who cross paths here represent various social strata, which is reflected in the way they speak. Spiró's careful calibration of sociolects underscores his play's theme: the catastrophic breakdown of even the possibility of communication among characters so destroyed by their circumstances. One of Spiró's daring innovations, shocking many audience members at the time, was the raw authenticity with which those at the bottom of the social scale speak. These characters pack their inarticulate utterances with profanity never before heard on the Hungarian stage. Their fragmentary statements express barely cohesive thoughts, and hardly ever respond to the other atomized characters, mostly expressing the chaotic inner world of the speaker. Some characters use everyday speech, while only one, a teacher of literature, speaks in a refined, educated way. Even these characters, however, do not really use language for communication. In their dialogues they often talk past each other, motivated not by the desire to understand and be understood, but to maneuver out of an undesirable situation. There is yet another linguistic level, the exalted literary language of the great poet, Endre Ady (1877–1919). The quoted poem centers on the very question at the core of the play, raised by an old woman in her moment of crisis: Is there a God? The play opens as she, the main character, discovers the hanged corpse of her beloved cat, the only being that gave meaning to her life and filled her days. She spends the play, which takes place during a single day, trying to make sense of her pain. She concludes that there must be a God who is punishing her for her sins; otherwise there is no meaning to anything. Her new purpose in life is to atone by doing good in the time remaining to her.

Ironically, the old woman is murdered at the end of the play by the very boy to whom she decides to leave her money, not realizing that it was he who hanged her cat. The first killing, then, sets in motion the events that lead to the second, though we see neither on stage, just as the true meaning of the characters' utterances is often masked rather than revealed by their words. The force that drives the events in *Chicken Head* may be referred to as a lack of communication, miscommunication, or indeed the impossibility of communication. The boy has come home to visit for the first time after two years in a State institution. He was sent there after the old woman reported his father for child neglect. The old woman sees the boy's unexpected appearance on this day of crisis as a sign from above. He was sent to replace the cat. Her reminiscences about the two are parallel: they both had thin little necks; they both liked the food she gave them. To the boy, her remarks have the effect of ripping off his mask of toughness, and of undermining his idealized memories and illusions about his father. He misinterprets the father's complaint that the old woman "stole" his money, meaning the amount he would have gotten in State support if the boy had become his ward instead of being taken away. Thus, the boy wants to acquire the money, the old woman wants to give him the money, and yet the result is a pointless tragedy as each character seeks a remedy to a desperate situation.-

In contrast to the three plays from 1979 described above, in which the father-son nexus represents the collision of past and present, in *Chicken Head* the father and son are both in the present, living at the same level of infantilism. They are the products of a system that sustained itself by keeping its citizens in a childlike condition, robbing them of the autonomy needed to become adults—don't question the Party, the State is taking care of things, just do as you're told. Of the twelve characters in *Chicken Head*, the old woman is the only one with an identifiably historical past. She refers to sins she committed during the siege of Budapest (1944–1945); the others are too young to have direct memories of the years before communism. Having a past is what makes her crisis and her sudden need for transcendence possible, though she too suffers from the inability to communicate. Even the teacher, passionate as he is about literature, uses it as a refuge from life and from true involvement with others.

Hungary was in a state of ferment in 1985. That summer, forty-five intellectuals secretly and illegally gathered at a campground in the forest of Monor, near Budapest. This was the first coming together of the democratic opposition, which a few years later would negotiate the end of communist dictatorship in Hungary. Though Spiró himself did not engage in openly political activity, *Chicken Head* was clearly part of the ferment. The play deals with a hitherto taboo topic: the existence of poverty under communism. Moreover, as part and parcel of the breakdown of communication, Spiró exposes the breakdown of the social apparatus. A policeman tells his new partner they need not go into dangerous places. A representative of the District Council assesses the building for new gas lines, even though another agency has already decided to tear the building down. The State institution where the boy lives is run by corrupt and violent employees. The literature teacher is also reduced to living in squalor, as if his role in educating the next generation has little value to society. The play even goes so far as to poke fun at an emblematic figure of cultural policy at the time, István Király, from whose book two girls quote a ridiculously convoluted literary analysis in a scene in which they prepare for a lesson with the teacher.

There is no direct answer to why *Chicken Head* was allowed to run and grow in popularity. A possible reason may lie in its most striking feature: the introduction of vulgar language to the Hungarian stage. Is it possible that the authorities figured the play's "subversive" message would be buried in the avalanche of profanity?

The play's setting, the courtyard peopled by various social types, is a metaphor for the whole country at the time, indeed, the whole Soviet Bloc. And like the condemned building itself, the bloc would also soon disappear. Spiró's critical scrutiny is evident in his subsequent plays as well. The loss of moral footing in the new capitalism is one of his subjects, satirically treated in plays like *The Latest Zrinyiade* (1991) and *Racket* (1996). His realistic *Dobardan* (1994) is about a Hungarian engineer's undoing as he attempts to adopt a Bosnian orphan. In *Quartet* (1996) a disillusioned émigré returns to Budapest after decades in the West, seeking the sense of humanity he remembers, only to find a society at least as alienating as the one he just left. Spiró also looks back at the sources of current crises. For example, *Blackout* (2001), set in 1941 after the imposition of an anti-Semitic law, shows that not even genuine love can survive the brutality of history, and *Soap Opera* (1998) is about the wounds such brutality leaves on its victims. A recent play, *Fender Bender* (2006), though a comedy, is reminiscent of *Chicken Head* in that it brings together practically every present-day social type, in this case, in a huge, paralyzing traffic jam in Budapest. Spiró has come to be regarded as the most dedicated chronicler of the current era in Hungary.

Of the playwrights discussed above, Spiró alone continues to write for the stage. He is also a prolific and widely read novelist. But *Chicken Head* remains his most influential work. It laid the cornerstone of a "school" of drama whose impact on the post-1989 generation of Hungarian playwrights is manifest to this day.

CHICKEN HEAD

György Spiró

Translated by Eugene Brogyányi

CHARACTERS

OLD WOMAN

TEACHER

WOMAN

FATHER

MOTHER

KID

BUDDY

SARGE

COP

OFFICIAL

CHICK

GIRL

Setting: The interior courtyard of a one-storey apartment building in an outlying part of Budapest. A coachway in the upstage wall leads to the street door. On the three visible sides of the courtyard are four doors, leading to the apartments of OLD WOMAN, WOMAN, FATHER, *and* TEACHER. *A small, shack-like garage is set against a corner of the courtyard, and in front is a freestanding wooden frame for beating dust from rugs.*

SCENE 1

Afternoon. A hanged cat dangles from the carpet-beating stand. OLD WOMAN *enters from depths of coachway, carrying shopping bag with blood dripping from it.*

OLD WOMAN: Kitty, kitty, here kitty! Come along now, meow, meow! (*She puts shopping bag on ground in front of door, searches for key.*) Kitty cat, kitty cat, where've you wandered off to? (*She opens door, turns back.*) Come along nicely, I brought your food! (*She takes in bag, brief pause, comes out.*) The chicken heads thawed—they weren't frozen through—but they haven't rotted, kitty cat, I smelled them, and they haven't turned green yet—now there'll be enough for at least ten days—(*Brief pause.*) If you knew what a line there was!—almost wasn't any left by the time my turn came around—but I just made it—I prayed the whole time—everybody was buying them up, taking them away in big bags—twenty kilos, even—I thought there wouldn't be any left for me—but there was. We're in luck, kitty cat, you know? Only that long trip—and meanwhile they thawed out, the blood was dripping—that long trip—even though I put them in two nylon bags—people were staring—the blood was dripping in the tram—now come on, come along, I'll give you some—nice and fresh—then I'll chop up the rest—put it in the freezer—so you can have yummy chicken heads—you've got it good, let me tell you, you've got it good—you don't even deserve it—kitty, kitty, meow, meow!

She starts walking around the yard looking for cat.

You didn't even eat this morning—where the hell have you wandered off to?—you must be good and hungry by now—I put it all in the sink—I'll give you some now—then I'll chop it up with the cleaver—because they're frozen on the inside—I'll put them in the freezer—you'll have yummy cat food—enough for two weeks—twelve days for sure—some life you've got, little furry creature—where can you be, kitty cat?

She sees the cat on the carpet-beating stand. Pause. She lets out an inarticulate scream, stands quaking, steps to it, seizes twine with her hands shaking, tugs at it, tears it off, presses the dead cat to herself, runs inside. Screams are heard from inside, then silence.

SCENE 2

KID *and* BUDDY *enter through coachway.* KID *goes to* FATHER*'s door, presses down handle, tugs at it, but door does not open.*

KID: Aw, fuck!

BUDDY: Whatsa matter? Ain't here yet?

KID: Goddammit.

BUDDY: Ain't home, huh?

KID *pounds the door. Pause.*

BUDDY: Ain't nobody here. Huh?

KID: Why the fuck ain't he here? Why don't he come home?

BUDDY: It's early.

KID: But why ain't he here? I come home, an' he ain't even here. (*He pounds and kicks the door.*)

BUDDY: Why don't you got a key?

KID: From where? Huh? Jerk.

BUDDY: Why didn't they give you one?

KID: 'Cause they didn't. Dork.

BUDDY: My old man gave me one.

KID: Okay, he fuckin' gave you one. I don't give a shit, dammit.

BUDDY: How come your old man didn't give you one?

KID: Dork. Shut your fuckin' face.

BUDDY: Okay, let's split.

KID: What the hell for?

BUDDY: You wanna fuckin' hang out here, or what?

KID: It's fuckin' botherin' you?

BUDDY: We'll come back.

KID: Dork! I pictured it all. I get home, he's here—I had the whole thing figured out back there—I come home, an' the old man's here—I seen it just like that a shitload of times, goddammit, an' it was good—so fuckin' good—I seen it all, see?—we take in a game, drink beer, everything.

BUDDY: There ain't no fuckin' game today.

KID: I fuckin' pictured it, see?

BUDDY: Ain't no game no place today.

KID: I don't give a shit, dammit. I pictured it—a shitload of times—I fuckin' remembered it all—all of it—why ain't he home?!

BUDDY: We'll come back.

KID: Sit the fuck down, dammit. Get the hell outa here.

BUDDY: What's up, man? What the fuck's up with you?

KID: Nothin' dammit. Stupid asshole.

BUDDY: Eh, he'll come home.

KID: Shut your face, jerk.

Brief pause. BUDDY *sits down.*

KID: The other guys, they were fuckin' sleepin'—an' I was picturin' comin' home, an' then I was already here—an' it was all just like I wanted it—it was this—here—this was mine—somethin' only I had—I could always see this here—this yard—they snore—you can't sleep—the duty officer comes in at night to make sure nobody's jerkin' off . . .

BUDDY *laughs.*

KID: Jerkin' off ain't allowed—but we do whatever the fuck we want—a light's always on so the duty officer can see—not everyplace—I got it good now, I'm on a lower bunk—it don't shine in my face . . .

BUDDY: I'd go for the top bunk.

KID: You can fuckin' have it.

BUDDY: It's better on the top, I think.

KID: Okay, it's fuckin' better. Like you know. Try makin' your bed—they'll kick you right off if you stand on theirs—me too—anybody stands on my bed—kick him right off—try makin' your bed in two minutes—'cause the fuckin' duty officer's comin', an' if it ain't straight, you get the shit smacked outa you. So go ahead, take the top bunk.

Brief pause.

KID: But it ain't up to you anyway, like you fuckin' get to say what you want. They let you have it across the face so fuckin' hard you shit. What the fuck you think? Your fuckin' shoelace breaks, you get one. It's lunchtime, you spill some soup, you get one. An' they knock your fuckin' elbow, you're carryin' your tray, holdin' your spoon—shit yeah—an' ain't no fuckin' good rattin' on 'em—at night in comes the goon, by mornin' you don't know where your fuckin' kidneys are.

BUDDY: Holy shit—fuckin' rough, man.

KID: They swipe your fuckin' steel file an' grease it—you don't know who—them. Then you do the fuckin greasin'—in two weeks you're greasin' like a motherfucker—an' they puke on your fuckin' clothes—then you get dead fuckin' drunk an' puke all over theirs—I'm tellin' ya, man, ain't like you think.

BUDDY: What do they grease?

KID: Fuckin' file. Whaddya think?! Your prick?!

BUDDY: Your file?

KID: Okay theirs. What a jerk. Theirs.

BUDDY: Oh.

KID: Look, fuck it. You pick out a weaker kid an' fuck with him—that's what you gotta do—then they take you in. Otherwise they fuck you over. 'Cause if you don't show 'em that's what you're like—your ass is grass—I'm fuckin' tellin' ya.

BUDDY: Still, must be good.

KID: What?

BUDDY: Well, back there.

KID: Damn fuckin' straight.

BUDDY: It's somethin'—after all—somethin'—ain't shit here. Back there, you fuckin' got somethin'.

KID: They can do any fuckin' thing they damn well please. We bust ass in the factory, black market stuff, we steal the goods for 'em, do the work, they sell it—that's how it goes, we gotta get it out, too—'cause if not, they fuck us over—the motherfuckers—an' then they feed us this line about we oughta be grateful—about bein' one big family—an' they're our whatsis—our parents, our guardians, all that—an' we oughta be grateful we got a fuckin' ass to bust.

BUDDY: Eh, they shovel that shit every place—us too—same thing.

KID: An' then this is what I got—this fuckin' yard—I seen it a shitload of times—like this, only it was bigger—I don't know—but everything was bigger, higher—I wish to hell the old man was here!

BUDDY: Why? Whaddya want from him? Did he write?

KID: Shut your fuckin' face, jerk.

BUDDY: Why? You said he never even wrote—you said so yourself.

KID: How 'bout I fix it so you gotta get your fuckin' face stitched back together.

BUDDY: Why? Whaddya want from your old man?—he don't even know where the hell you are.

KID *suddenly hits* BUDDY *in the mouth.* BUDDY *grabs his face and stares uncomprehendingly.*

BUDDY: What the hell was that for?!

KID: Just shut up.

Brief pause.

KID: Be glad that's all you got—what the fuck you mouthin' off for, jerk? Back there you'd fuckin' learn—I even warned you—they don't open their mouth back there—the guardian's a fuckin' boozer—they're stuck with him 'cause there ain't too many—an' you don't know why he smacks you—he hates every kid—he's only there for the apartment—'cause they get apartments in there—an' he's a boozer. Shit yeah.—What's that?

BUDDY: What?

KID (*points to garage*): What the hell's that?

BUDDY: A garage. Ain't it? A garage.

KID: Whaddya mean garage?

BUDDY: Garage.

KID: Wasn't no garage here! This thing wasn't here!

BUDDY: I don't know, it's here now.

KID: How come there's a garage here?! In here. How come?

Brief pause.

BUDDY: Okay, look, we gonna hang out here or what the fuck? Let's split. Let's get the hell outa here. To the square.

KID: Why? What the fuck's there? Huh? What's there?

BUDDY: Nothin'—we can sit—check it out—I sit there an' watch—in case somebody comes—they come—you came, didn't you? I look, I say holy shit, this guy's just like him, gets closer, I'm lookin', just like him. Huh? An' I was fuckin' glad, so why the hell you smackin' me? I was fuckin' glad you was comin'. Be some hell-raisin'. Somethin' at last—'cause ain't ever nothin'—I just sit there an' watch—so why the hell? I never ratted on you, never—huh?—did I?

KID: Whaddya mean?

BUDDY: I remember! I remember everythin'! They fuckin' took you away, an' me here, no buddy, didn't even know how come. So I come around askin', nobody don't know nothin', but I remember!

KID: That was fuckin' long ago. Since then—I been in eight fuckin' institutions since then—fuckin' eight—can't put shit over on me no more—I know the score—ain't nobody puts shit over on me—ain't easy to fuck me over. Not me no more. Right away I know whose ass gotta be kissed—an' they fuckin' kiss mine too, right away, I pick' em out. There been stupid fuckin' guardians who fuckin' like kids, ooh-an'-ah over you, fuckin' pretend they're concerned, then they pull out an' that's that. I don't fall for none of it—that's where it's at, man—where it's at is where it's at—all their bullshit aside—I can tell, even the tough guardians are scared, man, an' don't dare pull just any shit on anybody—me neither no more. They can't pull just any shit on me.

Brief pause.

BUDDY: Where's the cat, that fuckin' cat?

KID: What?

BUDDY: Fuckin' climbed down! (*He laughs.*) Fuckin' jumped off, huh? The cat! (*He indicates the torn twine.*)

KID: Got taken down.

BUDDY: She took it down, huh? (*He laughs.*) Musta had a shitfit, huh? Probably had a shitfit. Too bad we missed it. That fuckin' cat. The way it was kickin' the air—lashin' out at us, damn near scratched me. (*He laughs.*) Its four legs was goin' at it. Stupid cat. Too bad we missed seein' her take it down.

KID *goes to the door, pounds.*

BUDDY: What's up? Your old man get back meantime or what?

KID: Why ain't he here, goddammit? One time I come home, why ain't he here?

BUDDY: Let's get a fuckin' move on. We'll come back.

KID: Why can just any shit be pulled on me? Christ all-fuckin'-mighty! Why can just any shit be pulled on me?!

BUDDY: Look, let's get a fuckin' move on.

WOMAN *enters through coachway, bags in both hands.*

KID: Hello.

WOMAN: Hi.

WOMAN *puts down bags, searches for key, opens both locks, as* KID *and* BUDDY *watch.*

WOMAN (*turns back, notices* KID): What's this? Is it you?

Brief pause.

WOMAN: They let you come home?

KID: Yes.

WOMAN: How you've grown.

KID: Guess so.

WOMAN: Your sister didn't come?

KID: I don't know.

WOMAN: Why? Where's she?

KID: I don't know.

WOMAN: Because we haven't seen her for years either.

KID: Me neither.

Brief pause.

WOMAN: And now you're here to stay?

KID: No—this is just three days—would you know where my father is?

WOMAN: No.

WOMAN *picks up bags.*

WOMAN: How you've grown. You must have to fight the girls off, huh? Well, okay.

KID: Good-bye.

WOMAN *goes in, closes door, brief pause.*

BUDDY: Holy shit.

KID: What?

They stare at door.

BUDDY: Some tits, huh? Holy shit.

KID: Eh, that over-the-hill broad?

BUDDY: She's still okay.

KID: Eh, she ain't got it. Her?

BUDDY: She got enough. Why? You wouldn't lay her?

KID: Go ahead an' fuck her. You're even fuckin' chicken to say hello.

BUDDY: Why the fuck should I say hello to her?—I never did before—I don't even know her.

KID: You been hangin' out here for years, what the fuck you mean you don't know her?

BUDDY: Why should I say hello to her? Huh? Why should I? Fuck her.

Brief pause.

BUDDY: Let's split. Us here—ain't shit here—we'll come back—or go on in there an' fuck her—c'mon, let's get a fuckin' move on.

KID: Why ain't he here, goddammit? Why ain't nothin' the way it oughta be? Nothin'—ever. Goddammit.

BUDDY: C'mon, let's get a fuckin' move on.

Both exit.

SCENE 3

OLD WOMAN *comes out, weeps. Goes to* TEACHER'*s door, knocks.*

TEACHER (*in dressing gown and slippers, comes out, stops, looks at her*): Good day.

OLD WOMAN *sniffles.*

TEACHER: Is something the matter?

OLD WOMAN: She was still warm! She was still warm!—if I'd gotten home ten minutes sooner—if the tram had come—now how am I going to pass my days?! (*She weeps.*)

Brief pause.

TEACHER: Excuse me . . .

OLD WOMAN: I come home, sir—from the market—bringing her the chicken heads—I stood in line for a half hour—and the tram didn't come—I thought there wouldn't be any left for me—there was a long line—and I waited—and the chicken heads thawed—everybody was staring—then I get home, I call to her, she doesn't come—I thought she wandered off—though she didn't have anything to eat this morning—and then I see her—I see her . . . (*Weeping.*) Hanging there—they hanged her—on the carpet-beating stand—what's that thing doing here anyway?—around her thin little neck—around her neck—twine around her neck—sir!—around her thin little neck . . . (*Weeping.*)

TEACHER: Horrible.

Brief pause.

TEACHER: But at least she had a good life.

OLD WOMAN *sobs.*

TEACHER: You did everything you could for her, that's the important thing— yes—it's difficult to say anything at a time like this—she was a beautiful kitty, a healthy, friendly, pretty little animal—I was very fond of her.

OLD WOMAN *sobs.*

TEACHER: I was taking a nap—to rest up for my next lesson—I'm very sorry something like this could happen—I condemn it—but there really isn't anything to be done . . .

OLD WOMAN *sobs.*

TEACHER: But she had a very good life, that's the important thing. No cat could have had a better life—than she had . . .

OLD WOMAN: Murderous lowlifes—all of them . . .

TEACHER: Please excuse me, but I have to get ready for my next lesson—I had five this morning—with only an hour's break—I'm very sorry . . .

WOMAN *appears in her doorway, listens.*

OLD WOMAN: So much waiting—at the market—at the vet's—so much waiting when she was sick—I prayed for her—when they kept her there, I took her chicken heads—and if there weren't any—you can't always get them—because they grind them up—for feed—when there weren't any, I took her liver—beef liver—because pork liver's forbidden—I got her medicine from the West—when she needed it—because they didn't have any—I tended to her every need—her coat was so nice and shiny—I had her vaccinated—and then they grab her—grab that little animal—that innocent little animal—and hang her—with twine around her neck—hang her—she must have been calling for me—when—and I wasn't here—I couldn't help her—what must she have thought then?—what must she have thought?—(*Weeping.*)

TEACHER: Well, you couldn't have been here—if you were away—shopping for her . . .

OLD WOMAN: Even though in the morning—it occurred to me—there would have been enough for two days—I didn't have to go—I felt it—some voice told me there's enough for two days—not to go today—then she'd be alive now—but I didn't listen—to the voice . . .

WOMAN: Her cat died?

TEACHER: Yes.

WOMAN: What happened, they hanged it?

TEACHER: So it seems. Excuse my attire . . .

OLD WOMAN *sobs, hawking up phlegm.*

TEACHER: You'll make yourself ill.

WOMAN: Where did they hang it?

TEACHER: Somewhere—on the carpet-beating stand—excuse me, I'm not yet dressed—(*To* OLD WOMAN.) I'll bring you a sedative—do you hear me?

WOMAN: They hanged it on the carpet-beating stand?

TEACHER (*to* OLD WOMAN): Please listen to me—this is bad for you—you'll hyperventilate—this'll put a strain on your heart—you mustn't get so worked up . . .

WOMAN: It was probably the kid.

TEACHER: What kid?

WOMAN: Him—they let him home—I just met him—I was coming home—I was standing in line for half an hour at the supermarket—I come in loaded down with my bags—and there's this big hulking kid—it's him . . .

TEACHER: Please calm down a bit—with your permission, I'd like to get you a sedative . . .

WOMAN: On this carpet-beating stand? Here? Is this the one?

TEACHER (*to* OLD WOMAN): Please, listen to me . . .

OLD WOMAN: Filthy riff-raff—depraved murderers—their whole kind . . .

TEACHER: Please . . .

WOMAN: I bet it was him—I come home—I'm loaded down with my bags—all of a sudden I see them loitering around here—him and his buddy—I didn't even recognize him, but then I remembered how long it's been since I've seen him—I don't even know how long—a good long time—he got very big, but it was him—when I opened the door it occurred to me why he must be here when he's supposed to be in the institution—he probably ran away.

TEACHER: All kinds of strangers come and go around here.

WOMAN: I never see anybody loitering here.

TEACHER: All kinds of men come and go here.

WOMAN: I never see anybody.

OLD WOMAN: A defenseless little animal—a little animal—how could they?—they were born that way—they're not even human . . .

TEACHER: Please, don't speak that way, one shouldn't indulge such impulses. They're totally out of place.

OLD WOMAN: Don't you tell me what I should or shouldn't do!

TEACHER: Forgive me, perhaps I didn't . . .

OLD WOMAN: Don't you tell me, I don't care if you are an educated man, don't you tell me! You're not going to tell me how I should feel!

TEACHER: Please, it's the furthest thing from my mind to tell you—all I meant to say was that calling everybody a murderer—because of a cat—albeit a very dear animal—is not entirely proper.

OLD WOMAN: To murder a defenseless little animal—that's proper?! She was the only creature—the only . . . (*Sobbing.*)

WOMAN: Leave her alone. What are you picking on her for?!

TEACHER: I'm not picking on her. I didn't pick on the cat either. It was a very dear animal. And it's most unfortunate that—I'm very sorry, but after all . . .

OLD WOMAN *sobs.*

WOMAN: Did you see it? Was it hanging? It had been hanged?

TEACHER: No. I didn't see it.

OLD WOMAN *sobs.*

TEACHER: I'm very sorry, but it seems as though there's nothing I can do.—If she needs a sedative, please let me know—I have to get ready for my lesson.

TEACHER *goes into apartment, closes door.*

OLD WOMAN: Him too—all he can say is that I shouldn't—shouldn't what? Shouldn't! What would he be doing now if she'd been his? What would he be doing?

WOMAN: I don't even dare come home after dark—but how can I afford taxis all the time?—where can I make that much money?—I bring loads of work home, but I still can't make enough—it's terrible, the characters that hang around here . . .

OLD WOMAN: Why doesn't he mind his own business? He's always sticking in his two cents' worth. Because he's got degrees? That doesn't give him the right to stick in his two cents' worth!

WOMAN: A person can't but live in fear . . .

OLD WOMAN: What does he mean sedative?—I stand in line in the market hall—at the open-air market—all that pushing and shoving—I stand there to get her something—I get back, and find her hanging there, and then on top of it all I should take a sedative! There's no compassion in people! None!

WOMAN: It was hanged by the neck? It was hanging there?

OLD WOMAN: What?

WOMAN: The cat. The kitty. It was hanging?

OLD WOMAN *weeps.*

WOMAN: Where is it now? In there? Inside?

OLD WOMAN *points, weeps.*

WOMAN: Does it look ugly?—the eyes—are they bulging?

OLD WOMAN *sobs.*

WOMAN: You've got to bury it. As soon as possible. It's not a good idea to keep it in there—it'll start rotting—it's got to be buried.

OLD WOMAN: She was such a good kitty—a person could talk to her—when she was thirsty she climbed into the tub—she didn't even climb in, she just went toward it—toward the tub—and she already knew that I could tell what she wanted—and she always thanked me for her food—even when she was very hungry—she came to me, rubbed up against me—before eating—even when she was very, very hungry—and could she get offended!—she'd sit facing the wall—half the day sometimes—and wouldn't talk to me—and could she be grateful!—grateful—in a way nobody else could—we lived together so many years—twelve years—twelve years—and nine of them just the two of us—nine—she'd climb on the bed—at my feet—snuggle in—and sleep—and she was so—so—so trusting—yes, trusting—when she slept deeply—she'd lie on her back—and cover her eyes with her paw—just like a child—she'd lie there defenseless, because she knew she could trust me—I never hurt her—nobody ever did—little animal like that—and now—and now—(*She weeps.*)

Pause.

WOMAN: Yes—it's a good thing you had a cat—maybe a cat—is a good thing.

Pause. FATHER *enters through the coachway.*

FATHER: Hello.

He goes to door, searches for key.

WOMAN: Look what your brat did. Take a good look!

FATHER: What?

WOMAN: She's completely beside herself. Just take a look!

FATHER *looks at* OLD WOMAN, *confused.*

WOMAN: Your stupid brat! Yours! That's what I'm talking about.

FATHER: What?

WOMAN: He hanged her cat! Here on the carpet-beating stand! Strung it up! Your son did, yes, your son! Good thing it was just the cat! Good thing!

FATHER: What cat? Whaddya want? Where's my son? Huh? What's goin' on? What is it this time? What the hell is it this time?

WOMAN: Can't you see she's crying?

FATHER: Yeah. She's crying. So what?

WOMAN: Well it's no wonder. None at all. Of course your son turns out like this. A sadistic beast.

FATHER: Whaddya want from me? What the hell d'ya want for chrissake? Where's my son, huh? Well, where? He's in an institution, ain't he? Well, ain't he? Whaddya want? What the hell d'ya want? You're always lyin', the two of you. Up an' down. All the time. But whaddya want now? Didn't she have him taken away? Huh? Wasn't it her? Wasn't that enough? Ain't I workin'? Am I or ain't I? I got a job. I'm a workin' stiff. What else do you want, huh? What'd I do? To who? What cat? Will you two ever get off my case?! What am I doin'? I ain't doin' nothin'. Goddammit!

WOMAN: Your son killed her cat, you understand? He killed it.

FATHER: Good for him. Damn good. He ain't even here. Well, is he? Not since who the hell knows. Where is he? Here?

FATHER *opens apartment door wide.*

FATHER: Is he here? Is he? Take a look if he's here. Well, where is he? C'mon over. You. C'mon over here, take a look. Huh? Where is he? Let the old woman come over too. Take a look. Where is he? Huh? For chrissake!

TEACHER (*steps out in shirt and jacket, but still without tie, still in slippers*): Please, if possible, don't shout. Please.

FATHER: Why shouldn't I? They're always fuckin' with me! Always fuckin' with me! How come? Huh? You got education for chrissake, tell me, what'd I do?

TEACHER: Please, be so kind as not to shout. I can't do my work.

TEACHER *goes back, closes door.*

FATHER: 'Cause he's got education? That's why I'm always the one? What'd I do to him? He's a jerk. An asshole. All his education. He lives here too. The prick.

FATHER *goes in, slams door.*

WOMAN: If I ever get the money, I'm getting the hell out of here. What am I doing here?

OLD WOMAN *weeps quietly.*

WOMAN: Please stop. Please go inside—please bury it somewhere—all right? Please go on in. That's right. Please take care of yourself. And please bury it—as soon as possible—it's got to be buried.

OLD WOMAN *goes inside.* WOMAN *closes her door, goes to garage, examines lock, then returns and goes into apartment, closes door.*

SCENE 4

Two policemen enter through the coachway, stop, look around.

SARGE: Damn long driveway.

COP: Yeah.

SARGE: This is one of them old whaddya-call-its. When carriages used to drive in. A coachway.

COP: Yeah.

Pause.

SARGE: They can come into these kind. At night. 'Cause it's dark. So they come in.

COP: Yeah.

Brief pause.

SARGE: Nothin' goes on daytime, 'cause it's daytime. Only at night. 'Cause there ain't no lights usually. Damn dark.

COP: Yeah.

Brief pause.

SARGE: If you come in at night—come in with your back against the wall—understand?

COP: Which one?

SARGE: What?

COP: Which wall?

SARGE: Which wall?

COP: 'Cause there's a wall here—and there.

SARGE: It don't make no fuckin' difference, one of 'em. What does it matter? One of 'em, that's all. So they can't come at you from behind. Understand? That's how you go. Slow.

COP: Yeah.

SARGE: But you don't have to come in. You see it's too damn dark, so the hell with it.

COP: Yeah.

SARGE: You go to the bar—you go in—the two of you—there's always two of you—you go in—you don't do nothin'. They're fuckin scared of you anyway. You're inside, then you split. Understand? Don't take no booze—they always offer—on some excuse—they try to suck up to you—'cause they're afraid. Understand? You don't show 'em you got a fuckin' load in your pants. 'Cause they're afraid. If you're checkin' Personal I.D., check the others. Understand? Not the regulars.

COP: How do I know?

SARGE: What?

COP: Well, that they're not.

SARGE: Not what?

COP: Not regulars. How do I know?

SARGE: 'Cause you're there all the time, an' you see who's there all the time, an' who ain't.

COP: Oh yeah.

Pause.

COP: What're we doin' here?

SARGE: We're here, dammit. We don't gotta be doin' nothin'.

COP: Yeah.

SARGE: We look around, 'cause this is our beat, so we let 'em see us, then we split.

COP: Nobody sees us.

SARGE: 'Cause they ain't here. Or they're inside. We look around, an' we split.

Pause.

COP: An' what're we doin' now?

SARGE: We're here. This is our fuckin' job.

Pause.

COP: Hey, a carpet-beating stand.

SARGE: Yeah.

COP: We had one like that.

SARGE: Oh yeah?

COP: Yeah. Just like that.

SARGE: Well, it's a carpet-beating stand.

Pause.

COP: I don't even know what happened to it.

SARGE: To what?

COP: The carpet-beating stand. At our place. At my whaddya-call-it's. My stepmother's. The first one. We had one just like that. Then it wasn't there no more. I don't even know when—I didn't pay no attention—they just took it away—but when was that?

Pause. FATHER *comes out.*

FATHER: Hi guys.

SARGE: Hi.

FATHER: I'm bein' fucked with again, dammit. Always somethin'.

SARGE: Why? What's up?

FATHER: I'm comin' home—I had a shitty day at work—nothin's workin' out—I'm runnin' between two machines—my vise ain't worth shit—then I'm comin' on the bus—it's crowded as all hell—an' then I'm comin' home an' they come at me—they're yellin'—I don't know what the hell their problem is—they're always fuckin' with me—that's how it always is—goddamn them.

SARGE: Yeah.

FATHER: He ain't even here—since who the hell knows—'cause both of 'em got taken away—him an' his sister—an' then they fuckin' accuse me—I don't know which way is up no more. How 'bout a drink?

SARGE: Can't now.

FATHER: A short one, how 'bout it?

SARGE: Can't.

FATHER: Okay, but even so, how 'bout it?

SARGE: Not now.

FATHER: I'm tellin' ya, man—this can't go on—how the hell am I supposed to put up with this? Shit. I come home and then this. You really won't have a drink? Homemade.

SARGE: No thanks.

FATHER: You get this? I'm comin' home—all fucked out—an' then this. Ain't enough shit all the time—this too.

OLD WOMAN *comes out, black kerchief on head, carrying the dead cat. She stops center. They stare at her.*

OLD WOMAN: I don't know—she's got to be buried.

Pause. OLD WOMAN *stands still.*

SARGE: Cat. Dead.

COP: Yeah.

OLD WOMAN: I don't know—I didn't even—she was still warm—and now I've got to bury her—I don't know . . .

Pause. OLD WOMAN *puts cat down, stands, then goes back into apartment.*

FATHER: This is what she's pinnin' on me. Her fuckin' cat.

SARGE: What?

FATHER: That my kid—when he ain't even home—since who the hell knows. Old bitch.

OLD WOMAN *comes out with shovel.*

OLD WOMAN: Got to be buried. (*She looks around.*)

FATHER: Not here. This is a garden—we ain't gonna have carcasses rottin' here—not here.

OLD WOMAN *looks at him. Pause.*

FATHER: No way—carcasses here—then we'll have flies.

OLD WOMAN: They said she's got to be buried—where . . . ?

Pause.

SARGE: In my opinion I don't know, but it's okay.

FATHER: Let 'er—for all I care—but not here—this is my garden.

SARGE: Whaddya mean? It ain't just yours—it's a common courtyard.

FATHER: I don't care—let 'er get a permit—from the Council—what do I know?

OLD WOMAN *stands and weeps.*

SARGE: Go on, dig it for her.

COP: C'mon, Granny, gimme it, I'll do it.

OLD WOMAN: No! Get away from here! Get away from here.

COP *shrugs. Pause.* OLD WOMAN *begins digging.* WOMAN *appears in doorway, watches.* OLD WOMAN *digs, they watch.* OLD WOMAN *picks up cat, embraces it, strokes it, kisses it, places it in ditch.*

COP: No coffin? (*He laughs.*)

OLD WOMAN *glares at him, then sweeps dirt into ditch. They watch her. She kneels, smoothes dirt with hands. Pause.*

COP (*more quietly*): She prayin'?

SARGE: Shut up.

OLD WOMAN *kneels, perhaps prays, stands up, goes into apartment.*

FATHER: Nuts—huh?—completely off her rocker—mournin' a lousy cat—stupid . . .

SARGE (*to* COP): No point mouthin' off. She's fuckin mournin'. Happens.

COP: Okay, I just . . .

SARGE: Your job is dealin' with the fuckin' public, the shittiest job there is. That's how come you get more dough—so you know when you gotta keep your mouth shut.

OLD WOMAN *comes out, carrying bag dripping with blood.*

OLD WOMAN: What do I do with this? What do I do with this now?

She goes to grave, stops.

OLD WOMAN: Two weeks' worth—two weeks'—I stood in line—I carried it home—the tram wouldn't come—now what do I do with it? Her dish is inside—in the kitchen—in front of the sink—her little dish . . .

OLD WOMAN *rushes in.*

COP: What's this?

SARGE: Must be cat food or somethin'.

OLD WOMAN *comes out carrying plastic dish.*

OLD WOMAN: This was her dish—what do I do with it now?

Pause.

OLD WOMAN: I look around—in the kitchen—I see her dish—and I cry. I just can't look at it—I can't—her dish—I can't leave it there. For twelve years—she ate out of it—this was her dish. It was always there—under the sink—she'd tug the food out of it—pull it across the floor—I always had to wipe up after her—for twelve years—every day—how I scolded her!

She stands, tries to break dish, cannot, puts it on ground, then goes into apartment.

FATHER: She's out of her mind. I mean it—too much—an' then they listen to her—not me, only her—she reports me—an' then they believe her, her! This the Council don't see! Why ain't the Council here now?!

OLD WOMAN *comes out, cleaver in hand. Goes to dish, hits it with cleaver repeatedly, until it breaks to pieces. She hits bag full of chicken heads also, the others watch.*

OLD WOMAN: There—there's your cat food—there—it's yours—all yours . . .

TEACHER *appears in doorway, by now in shoes, but still without tie, watches.*

OLD WOMAN (*grinds debris into ground with feet and shovel*): There was never room for my food—in the freezer—now there'll be room—my food'll be in there—in the freezer—I dragged you to the vet's—when your paw got infected—I bought medicine—medicine from the West—never again for anybody—never again—I've had enough—(*She stamps the ground.*) There—there . . .

She pants, looks around spitefully, throws down the shovel next to the cleaver, rushes into the apartment, slams door. Pause.

FATHER: Out of her mind—oughta be locked up—huh?—completely off her rocker—an' she reports me—they come out here—nose around—say things ain't in order—I ain't feedin' him—even though they didn't give me no apartment—they gave me nothin'—an' then they come out here—'cause the old woman—this moron—says she'll take 'em in—she will—who asked her to?—what business is it of hers?—an' then they come—me with egg on my face—what do I do with 'em by myself?—I was on disability, wasn't I? You tell 'em, Teach, wasn't I?—an' then they come—nose around—at my place—for chrissake—they act important—when a person like this oughta be locked up—off her rocker . . .

TEACHER *goes in, closes door. Pause.* WOMAN *goes in, closes door. Pause.*

SARGE: Right. So we'll be movin' along—we'll be back.

FATHER: Well, ain't she off her rocker?—an' then they take away both my kids—'cause of her, goddammit—'cause what the hell did I do?

SARGE: Let's go.

COP: This carpet-beating stand—we had one like that—but what happened to it? I don't even know. Too bad I can't go back there—to find out—when . . .

SARGE: Okay, good-bye.

FATHER: See ya 'round.

COP: See ya.

SARGE *and* COP *start to leave.*

FATHER: She's off her rocker—I'm tellin' ya—buries her cat—I'm tellin' ya . . .

SARGE *and* COP *disappear through coachway.*

FATHER: See you guys around! (*Brief pause.*) Buries her cat—I'm tellin' ya—(*He goes into apartment, closes door.*)

SCENE 5

OLD WOMAN *comes out, stops, pauses, then starts toward* WOMAN'*s apartment, stops, goes to* TEACHER'*s apartment, stops, knocks.* TEACHER *opens door, still without tie, book in hand.*

TEACHER: Hello.

OLD WOMAN: Excuse me, sir—this must be—for bothering you . . .

TEACHER: Not at all, it's just that I'm preparing for a lesson.

OLD WOMAN: Excuse me, sir—but somehow now . . .

TEACHER: Yes, of course. (*He sighs.*) I was just now preparing for a lesson, but—come in, please.

OLD WOMAN: No, I don't—but the thing is that I have to—don't worry, I've calmed down—I'm not going to—I got over my—my—I'm no longer so upset—the way I was before when I—I was pretty muddled, wasn't I?

TEACHER: No, not at all . . .

OLD WOMAN: But I've—believe me, I've calmed down—really—and that's not the reason I'm now—it's just that it can be so painful—but don't you worry, sir—I won't cry—not anymore—it's just that it can be so painful . . .

TEACHER: Yes, of course.

Brief pause.

OLD WOMAN: Because I'd thought about it—I was always afraid—of what would become of me if—if—(*Her voice cracks, brief pause.*) I won't cry, sir—don't worry—because I was worried about what would become of me, and I thought that if I died first—if she outlived me—it wasn't very nice of me—I know—because then what would have become of her?—who would have fed her?—I just wanted to be spared—so I wouldn't have to mourn her—so she'd have to mourn me—it wasn't very nice of me.

TEACHER: Yes, well—we all tend to think that way—sometimes . . .

OLD WOMAN: Because I imagined—if it's to be her—then what if—if she goes first—if—and I cried, too—in advance—so that—how can I say it? you understand?—as if she'd already gone, even though she was alive—but I cried, so that—how can I say it?—to have mourned in advance—you understand—but it can't be done like that—no—all I wanted to do was cry then—and it was good to think about this really—because then I could cry—a person has to cry every once in a while—has to—but this is different now—completely different from the way it was then—I can't say just how, but it's completely different—please tell me, sir—don't be angry with me, but—because this is so wicked now—is there a God?

Brief pause.

TEACHER: Why do you ask?

Brief pause.

OLD WOMAN: Because if there isn't—I don't know, but if there isn't then I—I don't understand anything at all. Not a thing, sir. But if there is—if there is, then—you understand?—because if there is, then maybe after all, it's him, you understand?—him—who's punishing me—and then this—then this—makes sense. Because if it's him, then I deserve it—even this—I deserve. Even this, believe me.

Brief pause.

OLD WOMAN: There must be a God, sir. And I'm—I'm getting what's coming to me—because I've sinned so much. Yes. And then this—this—how can I say it?—then what's happened—has to be—then it had to happen this way—and I have to bear it—this too—because I deserve it. Yes. I never went to church, sir—except when I was very little—but not since—I didn't think about these things—only later—but not then either—not really about these things—not this way—only when I sat in the waiting room—at the vet's—there were a lot of people—with parrots, cats, dogs, hamsters—with guinea pigs, white mice—there were lowlifes there too—who caught stray dogs—and took them in—for a twenty—to be experimented on—they were wicked people—I could tell—it shows—and the dogs—poor things—didn't suspect—they're stupid—but the others were decent people—there were children—and old ladies—old gentlemen—I looked at them—and prayed: my God, don't let me become like them—even though I had only a cat—but that's what I prayed for even so—they were all decent people—and I was wondering why fate is so rough on them. That's what I was wondering. Once—when was that?—once there was a nice old woman—she must have been eighty, ninety years old—her face was all furrowy—full of furrows—she was bringing a little kitty—that was all that was left to her—a kitty—the kitty's sister had already died, not long before—and now this one was sick—the one that was left—and the old woman was very afraid—well, she was telling me that they had a mynah bird—it was a very smart bird—and when her husband died—the old woman's husband—the mynah bird knew exactly what happened—and didn't eat—and starved to death. It was a very smart bird, the lady told me. A very smart bird.

Pause.

OLD WOMAN: I was there a lot—she was sick often—and also it was good there—we talked a lot—they were constantly complaining—always them—they never listened to me—not me—but still it was good—I sat there and wondered—what makes people so unfortunate—not all—just those who don't have a family—but an awful lot of people don't have a family, sir—an awful lot of people don't—for example—not you either anymore, sir, right?—don't be angry with me for bringing it up—I wondered what the reason for that could be. And a person gets old—and is left all alone—and it's terrible—there's nothing worse—and there's nobody left to mourn you—what could the reason be? But I didn't really think about these things then—the way I should have—because I had my cat . . .

TEACHER: Yes . . .

OLD WOMAN: I don't want to hold you up, sir—but this—now—while you're young, you think there must be possibilities—in spite of everything—all the hopelessness—when my little girl died during the siege—she was still so very little—but that's how it was then—a lot of people died then—and I thought something could happen—but no—my marriage was no good, sir—still I thought there've got to be possibilities—but there weren't—and when my husband's leg went bad—you didn't live here yet, sir . . .

TEACHER: No, I didn't.

OLD WOMAN: He was diabetic, and his toes began to rot—then the rot moved on up—they amputated his leg at the knee—he walked on crutches—I took care of him for a long time—even though I didn't like him much—but I took care of him faithfully, because if I couldn't love him, at least I should take care of him—then they cut off the whole leg—and I took care of him and gave him a decent burial—I didn't think about this then either, really—because I had things to do—because I had hope, I definitely had hope in possibilities—I thought it just can't be that there aren't any. And it was a bad thing when I had to retire, very bad, but then I had my cat—and I took in work here at home—that was good—not much pay, and I got fed up—and I still didn't have to think about these things—sir, there has to be a God—who's punishing me for my sins!

TEACHER: Well, yes.

OLD WOMAN: Do you know why God is punishing me for my sins? Because I wasn't good. That's why all this has happened. I didn't love my husband. I have to say it right out, sir. I couldn't love him—I didn't give it a thought for a long time—only when he'd say I love the cat more than him—he no longer had his leg when he said that—that's when I realized that I really did love the cat more than him—and I lied and told him he's an idiot, but he wasn't—he knew it too—but I could see he was pleased I said it—that's why I did—it's true I loved my cat more, and I didn't love him. I took care of him—cooked for him—but I didn't love him. That was a sin. Don't say anything—I know. And it doesn't make up for it, my visiting his grave—I even pay extra—they still don't take proper care of it.—And I had even bigger sins—in the Nazi times—right before the siege—some people came to me to hide them—and I was afraid—and I told them to go away from here, because I was afraid—everybody was afraid—and they got caught, I found out later—and they didn't come back. I wouldn't help them—because I was afraid, everybody was afraid—my little girl was alive then—but they died because of me, sir, that's what happened—I never told this to anybody, but that's what happened, sir . . .

TEACHER: You can't be sure that was the reason . . .

OLD WOMAN: I know it was because of me, sir—I know it—though I forgot about it right away then, and I didn't think about it later, but it was definitely a great sin, sir. And if God is punishing me this much—this much—then it had to have been a great sin. And there were other great sins too—sins I committed—there were a bunch . . .

TEACHER: Look . . .

OLD WOMAN: And in forty-six I had an abortion—because I was starving— everybody in the city was starving—but why couldn't I get any food? Tell me, sir, why? I could have, even if the whole world was starving! And then I would have had a child again, and abortion was illegal then and they aborted it even so, because my husband and I decided it had to be that way—his pay was low—and I thought so too—because the world was a bad place then—but now I know that was a sin too—a great sin—because the world's always bad—it's always bad—I know—and also I didn't want a child by him . . .

TEACHER: Look, people commit many sins of this sort, everybody does, and yet God doesn't punish everybody the same way. I think that everyone has his own God, you see. Everyone has his own. Because he's inside, you see. And there are those who are never aware of this. In them there is no God. But in spite of that they're still human, only different—a little—and we mustn't look down on them, because they're human beings too. We mustn't, precisely because we have God in us. We have someone inside of us. And for this reason we are capable of suffering. Feeling and suffering deeply. And this is our wealth, our immeasurable wealth. And this is good. It is a gift from the Lord. He makes an exception of us, because we suffer. We are favored by him.

OLD WOMAN: And I don't know—but he must be watching us if he punishes us this much. And not the smallest offense escapes him—it must be like that—because if not, then—then we'd be suffering for nothing—so terribly—but this way maybe all this must be a kind of—a kind of—you know . . .

TEACHER: Moral lesson.

OLD WOMAN: That's it! Moral lesson! About the persons we've become! Don't you think so, sir? Excuse me for holding you up . . .

TEACHER: Oh no, not at all.

OLD WOMAN: I'm thinking now that—it's about time—I became good—What do you say to that, sir?

TEACHER: Well—I think you've been good all along, and that those sins you mentioned weren't such serious sins . . .

OLD WOMAN: But if they weren't serious, why is God punishing me so harshly?!

Brief pause.

TEACHER: Yes—perhaps they were sins after all—true sins—major sins . . .

OLD WOMAN: You see?—and now I have to—I have to—do penance—that's it!—because of them—that's what I have to do now—but if I'm good—I can still be good for a while—then maybe I can change something for the better—and things might even turn out better for me, too.

TEACHER: Of course. There's nothing that can't be made better.

OLD WOMAN: The way it is now, I don't know—I get up in the morning—and what do I do, sir? I wouldn't go to the market just for myself—even though it's cheaper over there—and now I don't have to buy anything for the cat either—I get up in the morning—and then what? But if I'm good now—then there can still be something—do you understand, sir? There're still possibilities.

TEACHER: Of course.

OLD WOMAN: What can I do that's good, sir?

Brief pause.

TEACHER: I can't say, suddenly like this . . .

OLD WOMAN: It should be something that lasts a long time. Something that's—somehow—difficult.

TEACHER: Yes. I understand.

OLD WOMAN: I don't know—I could clean house for you, sir—every day—for free . . .

TEACHER: Thank you very much, but I like to do my own cleaning.

OLD WOMAN: But I'd do it for free . . .

TEACHER: That's not the point, it's just that I enjoy doing it myself.

OLD WOMAN: I understand—I don't know—maybe for these people here—the wife's always going away anyway . . .

TEACHER: For them? He's always taking his wife back—instead of finally putting his foot down—he deserves what he gets. It would be wasted on them, but we'll think of something. We'll definitely figure it out. I'm here, trust me, we'll figure it out. Right now I have to get ready for a lesson, but then we'll figure it out. And please be reassured, the intention is in itself already a sign of goodness.

OLD WOMAN: What do you mean?

TEACHER: Good intentions count. And we'll figure it out. I have to go—good-bye, good-bye.

TEACHER *goes in, closes door.* OLD WOMAN *stands, then knocks at* WOMAN's *door.* WOMAN *opens it.*

OLD WOMAN: Excuse me for bothering you . . .

WOMAN: Not at all . . .

OLD WOMAN: I'd like to do your housecleaning—for free, for free—every day—I'll do your shopping—I have time—I have an awful lot of time—and that's good—shopping—on the way—and standing in line—there's always something—there're faces—a person can watch . . .

WOMAN: Thank you, but I get along just fine the way I am . . .

OLD WOMAN: But tell me, what should I do?! Tell me! Tell me!

WOMAN: Oh dear.

OLD WOMAN: To live alone like this—you're pretty—young—and you live here alone—you need a man—I'll get you one—you know what?—I'll get you one.

WOMAN: Please don't. I can handle it. I'm loaded with guys.

OLD WOMAN: Oh come now—your guys!—they leave you after a single night—you think I don't see it happening?

WOMAN: Because that's what they're like. What does it matter? This is how I like it.

OLD WOMAN: It can't be that there's no decent man for you—it just can't be . . .

WOMAN: Oh no?

OLD WOMAN: No. It can't be allowed—I should know—it already ruined me. Have a baby—by anybody—don't be taking those stupid pills—you need a family—I'll help . . .

WOMAN: Where do you intend to look?

OLD WOMAN: For what?

WOMAN: Well, the guy. I have twenty a year. Minimum. At least fifteen. Where are you going to find me this guy?

OLD WOMAN: I'll look into the matter—I have time—I will—I'll find one eventually—for instance, here's the teacher . . .

WOMAN: The teacher! He'd like to be ten years older than he is—he purposely walks stooped—when he knows he's being watched—the teacher indeed!—I don't need help—why don't you get a new cat?

OLD WOMAN: Not that!—never again—I'm not cheating on her—not even if—not even if she's—dead—no—every time I cheated on my husband—it always turned out bad—even though I didn't love him—it was bad even so . . .

WOMAN: Well sure, if there's someone to cheat on!

Brief pause.

WOMAN: Take heart. You're upset now, but it'll pass, and then everything'll turn out all right.

OLD WOMAN: Don't you understand?—you don't. It's not that—that she died—that's not it—you don't understand. Neither does the teacher—in spite of all his education—he still doesn't understand . . .

WOMAN: He doesn't understand anything—not a thing. Well fine, then please come in, I have a little cognac, I got it at work, from one of the guys, he wants to get me into bed, but I hold out until I get cognac, so come on in, it'll do you good . . .

OLD WOMAN: I don't know—isn't there a place—where a person can get along—as long as we're around—where a person can still be useful—isn't there?

WOMAN: Why, me too—I come home—I bring work, I draw, I measure, it's no fun—but if I don't bring work home—then what? Where can I go? I can go up to my girlfriend's and we get plastered. But I can't go there every day. She comes over here, we cry, and get plastered, but she can't come here every day—we couldn't stand it—I go to my mother's—every Saturday afternoon—and then the Saturday afternoon visits get to be a chore—at my class reunion—last year—they were showing their kids' photos—a bunch of them are already divorced!—I sit here at night—alone—it's better that way—because they probably stink—have athlete's foot—herpes—a bunch of strangers—I sit and put on a record—I drink—without that I probably couldn't even sleep . . .

OLD WOMAN: I don't know—this whole thing—when I'm feeling on edge—I don't know—I try keeping busy—even though they've come up with so many smart things—all sorts of things—but how you ought to live your life, especially once you're not so young any more . . .

WOMAN: Even if you're still young . . .

OLD WOMAN: If my brother hadn't been killed in the war—he probably would've had a bunch of buddies—then I would've had suitors—a bunch of them—but—listen—I have a little money—it's hidden in the wall—so I'd have it—I saved it up—back when I was taking in work—to have it—and if I borrowed from it, I always replaced it—even out of my pension—I'd eat only soup if I had to—so I've got it—because I thought, what'll happen if she has some serious problem—and it costs a lot—even though it couldn't possibly cost a lot—couldn't possibly—or if we go away on some trip—that was foolish, because she wouldn't let herself be taken—I bought one of those baskets—I buckled it closed—but it still had to be held closed, because she pushed—she was very strong—and did she cry!—in the basket—even so I thought we'd go somewhere some day—I had no idea where—now what do I do with it?

WOMAN: It'll come in handy, don't worry, the way prices are going up.

OLD WOMAN: But I don't need it—what do I need it for?—I'll give it to somebody—there must be somebody who needs it a lot . . .

WOMAN: Not me—I have money, see? I make ends meet, I even own a garage—a few years ago I wouldn't have dreamed—that I'd have an apartment, and a garage—well I do—that I have. (*She weeps.*)

OLD WOMAN: But there's no problem . . .

WOMAN: Now I should buy myself a cat? To go chasing after? And if it dies? Should I buy a dog? It's still early for that . . . (*She weeps.*)

OLD WOMAN: Oh, my dear God.

WOMAN: How can it be—that I come home—and I rush about in the room—my room—mine—I waited it out—I can't help it that the old fellow died—I took care of him—he stank—nobody would even give him the time of day.

OLD WOMAN: Why, I bought him apples . . .

WOMAN: Nobody—but me—I had to take the stench—but I can't help it if it was good for me that he died—why, did I kill him? I took care of him as if I'd been his daughter—and I even mourned for him—and then I could've had his room—but I stayed in the small one—and I wake up with a start at night—the floor creaks—even though I had it repaired—I threw out a bunch of money—my expenses weren't all covered—the floor still creaks—the wardrobe creaks too—even though I threw his out—bought a new one—but he's in there too—almost every night—as if I'd poisoned him—or else he's just taking revenge on me for still being alive—I take tranquilizers by the fistful—I bring up guys so I won't have to listen to it alone—only with sleeping pills—even though I'm too young for that—why aren't there convents any more?—so nice and cool—ah, this whole thing—please excuse me. Excuse me.

OLD WOMAN: Why—I sit in the kitchen—I heat the place with the electric stove—the kitchen isn't so large, after all—

WOMAN: Excuse me—I'm moving away anyway—I'm going to trade this in—garage and all—that way I'll get two whole rooms—in exchange for the one and a half with the garage—I'll throw in the car, too—and I'll furnish my room—and I'll furnish another one completely—so if he comes, it'll be there for him—as long as it's far away from here—that can only be an improvement, and things'll work out. Please excuse me. And believe me when I say I loved that cat. Really. So that—please believe me—whatever I can do—really.

OLD WOMAN: If you like—I can sleep here at night—at your place—and then it won't creak . . .

WOMAN: No! No! I can't stand being in a room with anybody! I can't stand anybody's smell! This is my apartment, mine!

OLD WOMAN: All right—I didn't—I didn't—or maybe you could sleep at my place—there surely isn't an old fellow there . . .

WOMAN: No chance—I furnished this apartment—every stick of furniture—and I painted it—no chance—I come home, I close the door, and everyone can go to hell—I could have had a telephone—a guy tried to make it with me by telling me he'd get me one—that's all I need—to have everybody coming here to use it—from all over the neighborhood—that's all I need . . .

OLD WOMAN: Okay, I didn't mean to . . .

WOMAN: Because they're envious—incredible how envious people are—because I succeeded—what the hell did I ever succeed in?—but I worked at it—and nobody ever gave me a hand—ever—so let them work at it too. What do they think? Nobody's gonna settle in on me—no way . . .

OLD WOMAN: Why?—is that what I want? Is it?—my dear girl, do I want to oust you? You can rot in your apartment for all I care—in your garage—drop dead in your apartment, dear girl!

She runs into apartment, slams door.

WOMAN: Everybody can go to hell! Leave me alone! I've had it!

She runs inside, slams door behind her, sound of chain latch can be heard. TEACHER appears in doorway, looks about, mutters, goes back, closes door.

SCENE 6

CHICK *and* GIRL *enter, stop in front of* TEACHER*'s door.*

CHICK: Laza's goin' with Mara now, but they're just makin' out, Loni said they're just makin' out, Loni's all upset 'cause she's still got eyes for Laza, but Laza doesn't give a damn for her, even though he's only makin' out with Mara, an' Loni says he hasn't even felt her up yet. Laza's sure got big hands, huh?

GIRL *(leafing through her notebook)*: Uh-huh.

CHICK: Cut that out now. What's the point?

GIRL: Wait, just a minute. *(She reads.)* "An authentic expression of Symbolism must be ambiguous if it is to get at the essence of things, because things are unambiguous only on the surface." *(She looks up.)* Things are unambiguous only on the surface. Things are unambiguous only on the surface. *(She reads.)* "While Symbolism rejects as simplistic and naive Positist . . . Pos-i-ti-vist causality . . ." *(She looks up.)* Positivist causality . . .

CHICK: Laza's hands are unbelievably big, huh? Just think how big his cock must be.

GIRL: Yeah. *(She reads.)* ". . . rejects as simplistic and naive Positivist causality, it does accept existence as an attribute, thereby positing a world, devoid of causes and precedents, that is enigmatic yet predetermined . . ." *(She looks up.)* Enigmatic yet predetermined, enigmatic yet predetermined . . .

CHICK: If you were Mara, would you let him lay you?

GIRL: Leave me alone now, okay? *(She leafs through notebook, reads.)* "Para . . . paradoxically it is through a motif of partic . . . particularity—the personal image of God created for the I—that antipar . . . antipartic-u-larity, the need for species identity, has found expression."

CHICK: What?

GIRL *(shrugs, reads)*: "As a sense of responsibility toward all mankind, this genically subsumed characteristic . . ." *(She looks up.)* Genically subsumed characteristic, genically subsumed characteristic . . . *(She reads.)* ". . . explains the union of the image of God with motifs so typical of species identity . . ." *(She looks up.)* What does geni . . . genitally subsumed characteristic mean?

CHICK: What?

GIRL: Genitally subsumed characteristic: what's that?

CHICK: The hell if I know. You're a woman and Laza's a man, right?

Brief pause.

GIRL (*reads*): ". . . motifs so typical of species identity as historical time." (*She looks up, pause.*)

CHICK: Mara doesn't even have tits. Does she?

GIRL: Leave me alone.

CHICK: She doesn't even have tits. D'you think they'll grow out? They're not going to, that's what I think. I'm gonna get me a guy, he'll have a car, a Mazda—or a Honda—he'll have long hair—you'll see . . .

GIRL (*reads*): " . . . motifs so typical of species identity as historical time . . . " (*Brief pause. She weeps.*)

CHICK: What's the matter now? Idiot.

GIRL (*wiping her tears, sniffling*): I don't even know why I wrote all this out . . . I wrote out a bunch of stuff . . . (*She reads.*) ". . . . All of the symbols, directly or by implication, refer to the central figure, the I. The redup . . . reduplication or amassing of substantives and verbs, moreover, demonstrates that neither by themselves nor as a group can they give full expression to the subject . . ."

CHICK: Let's see. (*She takes notebook, flips pages.*) A shitload of stuff you wrote out here. This all from the textbook?

GIRL: Not just. Another book too. A real thick one.

CHICK (*reads*): "The natural and spiritual aspects of man have become isolated from each other . . ." (*She looks up, sighs, reads.*) ". . . Man's spiritual aspect glistens in godlike splendor compared to the other aspect, which is trapped in a biological prison, in death and in sex." (*She giggles, looks up.*) You're an idiot. (*She reads.*) "Respect for mankind has become expressed in terms of the love of God, in other words, our love of ourselves: Pro-meth . . . Promethean humanism." (*She looks up, sighs, reads.*) "A deeply worldly feeling, an-thro-pological optimism, has gained expression through this love, in religious—albeit twistedly religious—terms."

Pause. CHICK *reads it over again silently, knits her brow.*

CHICK: Big deal. All it means is man exists and he's miserable, and then there's this happier being, who's only in the mind, and that's God. (*She reads on silently, giggles.*) Hey, get this. (*She reads.*) "A major feature of man as historical-social being, and as spiritual being, has attracted increasing attention: his earthly nature, his immortality as an earthly being, his communality, his species identity. The poet's attention to this aspect of man is demonstrated, in grammatical terms, by the waxing comparative." (*She stops, cries out.*) Waxing comparative! That's a good one! (*She reads on, shouting.*) ". . . the waxing comparative. In "Love of Ourselves" there are 47.8 comparatives per 100 poems. In the later poems the number jumps to 56.6. As so often in lyric poetry, such tendencies are indications of the essential thrust of the work." (*She looks up, grinning.*) You believe this?! Waxing comparative! Is that really what it says in the book?

GIRL: Yeah, sure.

CHICK: Waxing comparative! Sublime!

GIRL: Let's go in.

CHICK: What's the big rush, idiot?

GIRL: I have to, so I'll get accepted! I have to! I can't take it anymore—I have to get away—an' I'm going to—because I can get accepted outside the capital—understand?—for you there's no problem—they kiss your ass—but I can't take it—understand? My stupid rotten father—my stupid rotten mother—I can't take it!

CHICK: Don't go getting hysterical on me, stupid idiot.

Pause.

CHICK: Breaking your sweet ass won't help if you're stupid . . .

Pause.

CHICK: Waxing comparative!

With a burst of laughter, CHICK *knocks at* TEACHER's *door.*

TEACHER *comes out in suit and tie.*

CHICK *and* GIRL: Good day, sir.

TEACHER: Good day, ladies. Come in, please.

Girls go in, TEACHER *follows, closes door.*

SCENE 7

OLD WOMAN *comes out holding sheet of paper. Hesitates, then steps to* WOMAN's *door, knocks.* WOMAN *opens door to extent chain permits.*

WOMAN: Hello.

OLD WOMAN: This is—if you don't mind . . .

WOMAN: Please don't be angry—I'm sorry about before . . .

OLD WOMAN: What?

WOMAN: Don't be angry about before . . .

OLD WOMAN: Oh, that doesn't matter . . .

WOMAN: I didn't mean it—I was so upset . . .

OLD WOMAN: Read this—what do you think—is it all right this way?

WOMAN: What's this?

OLD WOMAN: Last will and testament.

WOMAN: Last will and testament?

OLD WOMAN: Take a look at it, please—is it all right?

WOMAN *undoes chain, opens door, comes out, takes paper, reads.*

OLD WOMAN: It even says so on top: Last Will and Testament.

WOMAN: Uh-huh. (*She reads.*)

OLD WOMAN: I was sitting inside—crying again—then I had to kneel down—in the kitchen—strange, it happened in the kitchen—I was kneeling—and then I prayed—and then I cried—and then all of a sudden—I don't know—as if a voice—really—I don't even understand—but it was as if—as if I was being spoken to—being told what I've got to do—and for who . . .

WOMAN: Wardrobe with mirror—couch—and the bed . . .

OLD WOMAN: Double bed—with box springs—we had it made—it's more than forty years old—it's a very sturdy double bed—hardwood frame—they don't make those any more.

WOMAN: And who're you leaving all this to? All this?

OLD WOMAN: Well, him—he's such a nice little boy—poor thing—he was so fond of me—the way he took care of his father—that stupid oaf—and he was so glad to be able to come into my place and warm up—he never came all the way inside—just stood by the door—he was all blue—but this'll be good now—because as I was kneeling there—that's when it happened—as if somebody—whispered to me—I heard it—I don't even know, it was a kind of—voice—and everything became clear—I calmed down—and I knew what I had to do. So then I sat down—wrote everything down—everything I have—I itemized it all—I didn't leave out a thing—I walked all around the apartment—nothing was left out . . .

WOMAN: Right—so what am I supposed to do?

OLD WOMAN: Well, tell me if it's all right like this, or if it needs anything else—because this really is a good thing I'm doing—it's good—so this has to be in order.

WOMAN: Well, it seems to be okay—it's just, I don't know—I think it was the kid who—who hanged the . . .

OLD WOMAN: I wrote Last Will and Testament as the title—see?—it's right there.

WOMAN: It's there. But I think—him of all people—I think . . .

OLD WOMAN: I even put the date at the end—today's—and where I wrote it up—and I signed it—I don't know, but shouldn't there be some kind of seal on it . . . ?

WOMAN: I don't know—I don't think so . . .

OLD WOMAN: And is this one copy enough . . . ?

WOMAN: Must be, since it's in your own handwriting . . .

OLD WOMAN: Well then, sign it.

WOMAN: Me?

OLD WOMAN: Because I need two witnesses—I know—I heard there have to be two witnesses—everything needs witnesses . . .

WOMAN: Okay, I could sign it, of course, and then what? Let's say he inherits everything when you die—of course, let's hope that won't happen for a long time—

OLD WOMAN: Well, a few more years maybe.

WOMAN: And then he gets it afterwards.

OLD WOMAN: Afterwards, of course. I need it till then, what I have, because I use it.

WOMAN: Right—okay, I could sign it—but how urgent is it, after all? There's plenty of time, you could have second thoughts again and again.

OLD WOMAN: Never. This is how it's going to be. I knelt there—on the kitchen floor—and all of a sudden—I knew this is how it's got to be. And that's that.

WOMAN: Right—I don't know—I never witnessed anything like this. If I sign it now, and somebody contests it—and my signature's on it . . .

OLD WOMAN: What do you mean contests it?

WOMAN: Okay, never mind, I was just wondering . . .

OLD WOMAN: Why don't you sign it already?

WOMAN: I'll sign it—but it needs two witnesses anyway . . .

OLD WOMAN: If it needs two, I'll get two.

WOMAN: Maybe the teacher could be the other. (*She knocks at* TEACHER's *door, brief pause, knocks again.*)

TEACHER (*opens door*): Yes?

WOMAN: Sir, there's a problem here.

TEACHER: I've got a lesson now. Afterwards I'm at your service.

WOMAN: Yes, but if you'd just tell us if this needs a witness.

TEACHER: Please, I'm working now. Afterwards I'll be happy to oblige you.

TEACHER *closes door.*

WOMAN: Let's not bother the teacher. In the meantime you can think it over—and if you still think so—then . . .

OLD WOMAN: I don't understand! Nothing's ever simple! Never—when it ought to be! Why is that?

WOMAN: Look, it'll keep.

OLD WOMAN: No, it won't! There were so many things I wanted to do and later nothing came of them! I don't have enough time! I don't have any time!

WOMAN: Oh dear, now why are you carrying on? . . .

OLD WOMAN: You don't understand—neither did I for a long time—as long as there's time, you can't know what it's like—not to have time . . .

WOMAN: But you're in very good health.

OLD WOMAN: Well, that's just it—there's nothing wrong with me—still I've got to pass on . . . (*She weeps.*)

WOMAN: Oh my God. Please don't. What is it now . . . ?

OLD WOMAN: Nothing ever came of anything—and a person—couldn't even understand any of it—life was long and boring—still somehow—there was a minute or two—when I dream—then I can see it—it was so much like now—I dream about it often—I'm running in the yard—long ago—my mother's there—my father—and then I think—in the dream still—that anything's still possible—only meantime I'm afraid, afraid they'll die—my mother—my father—and I watch to see if my mother's sick yet—because I know she will be—but she isn't sick yet—but I'm very scared she will be—and my father's very young—and I don't understand—he hasn't been killed in the war yet—how can I remember this—I must have been how old?—four—but I already know in advance—things a person's not supposed to know in advance—then I don't know—when I wake up—whether I ought to be happy because I saw them—or whether the whole thing's horrible . . .

OLD WOMAN *sobs.* WOMAN *fidgets.*

WOMAN: I don't know—why don't you come in?—I've got some cognac . . .

OLD WOMAN (*angrily*): Why don't you sign it?! Is that too much to ask?—to scribble your name there—even that?

WOMAN: That's not the point . . .

OLD WOMAN: A person never does anything bad—all her life—she just helps— helps others—and then this is what she gets—when she's the one who needs something!

WOMAN: But that's not how it is . . .

OLD WOMAN: Why, will it wear you out? Strain your hand?

WOMAN: You need two witnesses anyway . . .

OLD WOMAN: The teacher's an educated man—even so, if it comes to helping, he won't—not even him!

OLD WOMAN *throws herself at* TEACHER'*s door, pounds.* TEACHER *angrily opens door.*

TEACHER: Don't bother me! The nerve!

OLD WOMAN: That's right! The nerve! A person begs for some help, and then— and then . . .

WOMAN *waves to* TEACHER, *signaling problem with* OLD WOMAN.

OLD WOMAN: Because it's all the same to you if a person drops dead right beside you! Even though it would take only a single word—but nobody could care less! That's the truth!

CHICK *and* GIRL *appear in doorway, giggle.*

OLD WOMAN: I suffered through it all—fine—through all of it—fine—but this is too much! When did I ever get anything—in my life—When? Tell me! When? And then a person writes it down—late—but finally—she does it—something good—and then not even that—not even that—they won't even give you a signature—even that's too much for them—(*She weeps. The girls giggle quietly.*)

WOMAN: She wrote her will, it's got to be signed—two witnesses . . .

TEACHER: Give it here, please.

TEACHER *takes it from* OLD WOMAN, *reads it, brief pause.*

TEACHER: You're leaving all this to him? All of it to him?

OLD WOMAN *nods, sniffles, blows nose.*

TEACHER: Fine, I find nothing reproachable in this. We'll sign it nicely, and then everything will be in order. (*He searches pocket for a pen.*)

GIRL (*handing him a pen*): Here, sir.

TEACHER: Thank you. (*He signs paper, hands it to* WOMAN.)

WOMAN: I don't know—this sort of thing requires your personal-identity number, too.

TEACHER: Very well, then. (*He takes back paper, writes.*)

WOMAN: I don't know mine by heart. Just a minute. (*She goes into apartment, brief pause.*)

TEACHER: There now, you see? Everything has a solution. Everything can be brought to a felicitous conclusion. And it really isn't necessary to pound the door.

OLD WOMAN: I knelt there—on the floor—and prayed—in the kitchen—for God to help me—and you see, he did. He suggested this to me. I'm sure it was him.

TEACHER: Yes. So then everything turned out all right.

OLD WOMAN: Thank you very much, sir.

TEACHER: Not at all.

OLD WOMAN: It's good there are good people. I always knew you were a good person, sir.

TEACHER: Yes. Now please excuse me, I have a lesson.

TEACHER *ushers girls in, follows, closes door.*

OLD WOMAN: In spite of everything—it's good there are good people—(*She waits, knocks at* WOMAN's *door, brief pause.*)

WOMAN (*opens door, remains motionless*): I don't know where I put it . . .

OLD WOMAN: Doesn't matter. When it turns up, you'll add it.

Brief pause.

WOMAN: Okay.

OLD WOMAN: Here. (*She holds paper out toward her. Pause.*)

WOMAN: It might be better—if you gave it some more thought—him of all people—what good is that . . . ?

OLD WOMAN: What?

WOMAN: They'll take it away from him anyway—they'll drink it up—they're always shouting—they won't even wait—till you're—that's what they're like—and I can't take it. It'd be better if you didn't get involved with them. I've had dealings with the court—God forbid I should ever have to again—a proceeding, and all the complications—it'd be much better if you didn't. I'm telling you. Or go to the whaddya-call-it—go to the—the notary public, that's it, you could do that, go to the notary public, and get an official seal stamped on it—that's the best thing to do, and then I won't have to get mixed up in anything. Otherwise anything I can—any time—please believe me . . .

Brief pause. WOMAN *slams door. Sound of chain. Pause.*

OLD WOMAN (*tears up paper, throws it in front of* WOMAN's *door*): There, you worm—there—there—clean it up!

OLD WOMAN *runs into apartment, slams door.*

If necessary, intermission can come here.

SCENE 8

KID *and* BUDDY *enter through the coachway.*

KID: But they don't give you no dough—except in place of some dumb worker who's jerkin' off in the john meantime—once what happened was a guy gave me a fifty—there's one of them leather things—y'know—hangs around the neck—one of them leather sack things . . .

BUDDY: Change purse?

KID: Yeah. So I changed it for a bunch of singles—so it'd be full—'cause I wanted it to be full—an' then it was . . .

BUDDY: Fuckin' good move.

KID: 'Cause soon as we get somethin'—we drink it up—heavy drinkin', man—there's this fuckin' millionaire—this private-sector guy—got two fuckin' Mercedes—two—but he's okay—'cause if we want, he's open till eleven—even later—two fuckin' Mercedes—beats a rusty fuck . . .

BUDDY: Shit, man, that's a good one. (*He laughs.*) That's a good one. Beats a rusty fuck! That's a good one!

KID: It's a good place—we fuckin' go there—an' they buzz off—even though it's a tough place—an' then the Bad-ass comes on with a song—top of his lungs—an' us along with him—an' nobody gives us no fuckin' lip—'cause we're the Wolves—I even go there alone sometimes—start singin' some number—an' they don't dare say nothin'—even when I'm alone . . .

BUDDY: That's good. That's good.

KID: You can get out at night—I did it a shitload of times—I tied a bunch of sheets together—an' climbed down—from the fourth floor . . .

BUDDY: Like on TV?

KID: Shit yeah—even now I came out—up an' walked right out—fuckin' guard starin' drop-jawed—not everybody'd dare—an' then the chicks waitin' downstairs—two, three of 'em—an' then you go at it—all night—then when you're done, back up the sheets, man . . .

BUDDY: Wow . . .

KID: They blow you—then you smack 'em one—an' that's it . . .

BUDDY: Holy shit, man . . .

KID: 'Cause they like me, man. They really go for me—just me.

Pause.

KID: We got everything there—there's this secret tunnel—everybody knows about it—there's a bunch of machine guns down there—only we ain't found it yet—but we will—an' when we do—I'm tellin' ya, man . . .

SCENE 9

OLD WOMAN *comes out carrying broken crutch.*

BUDDY (*quietly*): Watch it, man—the old bitch . . .

Pause. OLD WOMAN *sticks crutch into freshly dug earth, pushes it as far as it will go.*

KID: Hello . . .

OLD WOMAN *looks at him, does not recognize him.*

KID: Hello—don't you recognize me?

OLD WOMAN: What?

KID: It's me—don't you recognize me?

OLD WOMAN: Who?

Pause.

OLD WOMAN: What?

Pause.

OLD WOMAN: You—it's you?

KID: Well, sure . . .

OLD WOMAN: God in heaven—it's not true—this can't be true . . .

Pause.

KID: Will you fuckin' say hello . . .

BUDDY: Hello.

OLD WOMAN: You're bigger than—your father—dear God . . .

KID: I'm strong too—I work out—there's this way of workin' out—you push against a wall—it don't move, but I get strong that way . . .

OLD WOMAN: To grow so much—in such a short time . . .

KID: Not so short . . .

OLD WOMAN: This is something—I thought—you had such a thin little neck—you were such a skinny little boy—with such sad, intelligent eyes—such a frightened little face . . . How can this be . . . ? How . . . ?

KID: Well, I don't know—but it's good, 'cause they can't beat me up no more—I can't be pushed around no more . . .

Brief pause.

OLD WOMAN: I don't know—do you remember?—you came into my place when they locked you out—you came in to warm up—remember?

KID: Well, yes.

OLD WOMAN: I gave you food—but you didn't want to eat, you were just cold—remember?

KID: I did eat though—it was some kinda whaddya-call-it—noodles—with somethin' . . .

OLD WOMAN: Noodles?

KID: Yeah, that was good.

OLD WOMAN: Cheese dumplings?

KID: Coulda been—some kinda noodles . . .

OLD WOMAN: What could it have been—noodles and cheese? When did I ever make noodles and cheese?

KID: It had a little—sort of—paprika in it. It was good.

OLD WOMAN: Then that was potato noodles!

KID: I don't know . . .

OLD WOMAN: Sure, that's what that was! Don't you remember?

KID: Yeah—yeah . . .

OLD WOMAN: Well, of course! And how you liked it—of course it was potato noodles!

Pause.

OLD WOMAN (*to* BUDDY): The way he ate, poor thing—the way he wolfed it down—though he said he wasn't hungry . . .

BUDDY: That's funny. (*He laughs.*)

OLD WOMAN: Because sometimes his father didn't feed him for three days—and him wasting away . . .

KID: No, it's just that—he didn't have no money then—that's why . . .

OLD WOMAN: Oh go on, he had money!

KID: No, he didn't—really—he didn't.

OLD WOMAN: He sent you to steal food, didn't he? And he just lay there—supposedly pining after his wife—who went a-whoring!

KID: No! He was sick! He was on sick leave!

OLD WOMAN: Sick! As soon as you were taken to the institution he was up and about—because there wasn't anyone to feed him! Him sick—ha!

BUDDY *laughs.*

KID: Shut your face, jerk!

Pause.

KID: That's not how it was—no matter what you say—it's not—he had fever—he was on regular sick leave—who woulda taken care of him—who?

OLD WOMAN: What are you defending him for now?—he didn't even heat the place—you were frozen—you were blue from cold—don't you remember?

KID: Well, 'cause it was cold . . .

OLD WOMAN: But he did heat the place—while you were at school—and how!—it only got cold by the afternoon—so you'd feel sorry for him—I saw it—so you'd feel sorry for him . . .

KID: No!—no! . . .

OLD WOMAN: What do you mean no? I saw it!

KID: No!

OLD WOMAN: You didn't even have a cap—I knitted one for you—I lent my pot—and then I had to beg to get it back—and they didn't even clean it—I had to scrub the filth out—even your mother, when she was here . . .

Pause.

OLD WOMAN: So now you're here—it's good—that you came back just now—but I knew it—I asked for it—and the Lord granted it—I don't know—if you're hungry, I could cook something for you now. This is like—what do they call this sort of thing—it's an act of grace—from the Lord . . .

KID: Did you happen to see my father?

OLD WOMAN: So now you're here—(*To* BUDDY.) he was such a nice, smart little boy—well then I'll go in now and write another one—so it'll all be in order for him, you know?

BUDDY: Uh-huh . . .

OLD WOMAN: I don't know—he won't fit in the bed—but I'll buy a long one—I didn't think of that—and will you be growing anymore?

KID: Will I what?

BUDDY (*laughs*): Will you be gettin' any fuckin' bigger?

KID: Shut your fuckin' face!

OLD WOMAN: What's this language? Don't use language like that!

Pause.

KID: I didn't . . .

OLD WOMAN: I'm going to tell you now—that I sensed this—and a long time ago at that—I bought everything—baby things too—and children's things—such nice things—because I saw them in the shop windows, and they appealed to me—they were so good to touch—the material—and I bought all sorts of things—and I hid them—so my husband wouldn't find out—they're down in the cellar—in mothballs—I don't know—I guess by now you've outgrown them—you were so much smaller—when I bought them—but they'll come in handy when you get married—for your child—so I'll add those too—I'm going in now to write it up again—my God—just when a person seems to be at the end of the line—then all of a sudden—(*She smiles, goes in, closes door.*)

SCENE 10

Pause.

BUDDY: She's completely nuts, the old bitch . . .

KID: It ain't true—I only went in 'cause it was cold—it ain't true I ate—the fuckin' old bitch is lyin'—what the hell could my old man do about the heat?—he didn't have nothin' to heat with—not a fuckin' thing!

BUDDY: She didn't notice the cat . . .

KID: Shut the fuck up before I break your face!

BUDDY: Now what's up?

KID: Why ain't nobody here?—goddammit . . .

BUDDY: Maybe he came back meantime . . .

KID: Shut your fuckin' face—shut it . . .

BUDDY: Okay, I didn't . . .

Pause. KID *pulls himself together, knocks, silence. Pause.* KID *knocks louder, then kicks door.* FATHER *opens it.*

FATHER (*shouting*): Goddammit! . . .

Pause.

KID: Dad . . .

Pause.

FATHER: What's up . . . ?

KID: Dad . . .

FATHER: Is it you?

Pause.

BUDDY: Hello.

Pause.

FATHER: God, you're big.

Pause.

FATHER: You run away? You run away or what?

KID: I didn't run away! I didn't run away! They let me out!

FATHER: They did?

KID: For three days!

FATHER: What? For three days?

KID: For three days! They let me out!

Pause.

FATHER: So they let you out. (*Pause.*) Well—hi.—They let you out, huh?—and is there a document?—'cause they'll come nosin' around—an' I'm the one they'll pin it on—understand?

KID: Sure I got one—why don't you believe me—why . . . ?

FATHER: Okay, I believe you—just y'know—so then they let you out?

Pause.

FATHER: For how many days—what'd you say?

KID: Three days.

FATHER: That's good, three days, that's good. What is this—vacation or what?

Brief pause.

FATHER: You coulda wrote—to let me know—you coulda wrote you're comin'. You shoulda wrote—to let me know when—next time write first—when you're comin'. Huh? Say somethin'.

KID: I didn't know.

FATHER: What?

KID: That I'd be getting' out . . .

FATHER: Why didn't you know—they didn't tell you or what?

KID: No.

Pause.

FATHER: Okay—no problem—if they didn't tell you, they didn't tell you—okay—then you couldn't know—when you'd be comin'—ya see—no problem—I'm home—good thing I'm home. (*Brief pause.*) You been here already?—when I wasn't—you been here already? Today?

KID: Yeah.

FATHER: Look here—tell me—did you touch that cat? Huh? The old woman's cat—an' don't lie to me!

KID: No.

FATHER: No?

KID: No.

BUDDY: We didn't even see no cat.

FATHER: It died on her, an' she's blamin' me—you sure?

KID: Sure.

BUDDY: Sure.

FATHER: You can tell me—the stupid old bitch—she had it comin'—huh? So tell me—nobody'll hear—did you touch it?

KID: No.

BUDDY: No.

FATHER: No? Okay then—that's good—then it's okay.

Pause.

FATHER: So then you came home—for three days—to have a good time—huh?

Pause. They stand still.

BUDDY: Okay, I'll be goin' now—I'll drop by later on.

KID: I don't know—I'll go too . . .

FATHER: Where you goin' now?! Why can't you stay put a while?! You ain't goin' no place!

BUDDY: You stay here—I'll drop by later on—see ya—goodbye.

BUDDY *runs out. Pause.*

FATHER: You can go with him—if that's all this is to you—bein' able to come home at last—after all that time—an' then you can't stand bein' with your old man—just you go ahead . . .

Pause.

FATHER: If you'da wrote—then I woulda had eats waitin' for you—somethin'—anythin'—woulda been better—next time try lettin' me know . . .

KID: But I couldn't—they didn't want me to—'cause then they need that fuckin' thing—that whaddya-call-it—from the Council—that document thing—but the Council guy—the custody supervisor—he won't issue one—if the parent don't ask for it—an' you didn't—you didn't ask for it—an' without that it's no go—but then the assistant director—he couldn't take it no more—me always botherin' him—he's a decent guy—he let me out—even without that Council document—an' he ain't even supposed to . . .

FATHER: Yeah? Well, I don't know—they didn't say nothin' to me . . .

KID: I wrote to you—long time ago—to invite me home—an' then the Council guy'll inspect . . .

FATHER: Here? Nobody's inspectin' here—I had enough of that—they can go fuck themselves—(*Brief pause.*) Whaddya mean?—you didn't write—I never got nothin'—really—whaddya mean, when?

KID: Long time ago—I don't know any more—year an' a half—I don't know—

FATHER: I didn't get it—didn't get nothin'—probably got lost—mailman don't even come here—I didn't get nothin' . . . .

Pause. They stand still.

FATHER: So then—how is it down there . . . ?

KID: It's good.

FATHER: It's good?

KID: Yeah—good.

FATHER: What'd you say? Where is it?

KID: The place I'm at now?

FATHER: Yeah.

KID: You know—where the factory is. We live next to a farm.

FATHER: But they didn't take you there first . . .

KID: No—I was here—in one of them transit detention centers—an' then all over the place—I don't know—they shuffle you from one place to another . . .

FATHER: How's the food? Shitty, huh?

KID: No, it ain't bad—it's okay.

FATHER: It's okay?

KID: It's okay. There was places it was bad—but not too many. You can have seconds an' everything.

FATHER: Cut the shit—I bet they starve you—the bastards—they steal the food right outa your mouths . . .

KID: No—really—they do steal—but not food—an' if they do, there's still enough—

Pause.

FATHER: An' what d'you guys do?

KID: I don't know. Whatever needs doin'—we hang out . . .

FATHER: And?

KID: Nothin'.

FATHER: An' what's up—you learnin' a trade?

KID: Yeah. But there ain't that much of it—we do grindin'—we hang out—like that . . .

Pause.

FATHER: That stupid sister of yours—she's probably makin' money already . . .

KID: I don't know, 'cause they don't keep brothers an' sisters together—so I don't know what's up with her . . .

FATHER: Eh, she's probably makin' money already—never wrote once—probably became a whore, huh?

KID: I don't know.

Pause.

KID: Once there was one hell of a fuss—they stuck a frog in the guardian's bed . . .

FATHER: What? A frog?

KID: Yeah—but they didn't know who . . .

FATHER: Who was it?

KID: The dimwit—we had one—a real jerk—he'd raise hell all night—they made us get up—we stood there at attention—but nobody ratted—hell of a fuss . . .

Pause.

KID: There was lotsa frogs—there's lotsa frogs over there—we made 'em smoke cigarettes—you gotta stick it in its mouth—it smokes an' smokes—gets all puffed up—an' blows up . . .

FATHER: The frog?

KID: Yeah.

Pause.

FATHER: Don't you do no smokin'—ya hear? Don't smoke . . .

KID: Eh . . .

FATHER: You smokin'?

KID: No.

Pause.

FATHER: Well there ain't nothin' around here—Frank went away . . .

KID: Frank?

FATHER: Yeah—he had that shitsure lotto system—y'know . . .

KID: Frank?

FATHER: Yeah—he went private sector—came back once—says he's makin' five times as much—probably lyin'—but he is makin' money—he was wearin' a suit— good thing he wasn't wearin' them whaddya-call-it gloves—gloves, y'know—he don't even go to the game no more—somethin', huh?

Pause.

KID: Once I dreamt—it was real bad—I dreamt you got your leg cut off—the machine did it—I don't know—an' you was runnin' at me—on one leg somehow— an' blood was pourin' outa the other one—which was missin'—an' I was runnin' away from you—an' you on one leg . . .

FATHER: My leg was cut off?

KID: An' you was runnin' . . .

FATHER: Which one was cut off?

KID: I don't know—I can't say—was there anythin'?—with your leg . . .

FATHER: Nah—my leg?

Brief pause.

KID: An' then—this happened too—I was scared slivers was gonna go in my eye—an' they'll take out my eye—an' they took it out—the whole eye—I could see outa the one they took it outa—I could see what they took out—but nothin ever goes in.

Brief pause.

KID (*pointing at garage*): What's this—this wasn't here—what's this?!

FATHER: A garage—belongs to that stupid broad—she's got a car—it's in there—'cause she don't know how to drive the fuckin' thing—flunked five fuckin' times—funny, huh? (*He laughs.*)

KID: But why a garage—how come it's in here?

FATHER: Well—it's a garage.

Brief pause.

KID: The shed used to be there . . .

FATHER: Yeah.

KID: It was like—the shed—you could always go there—the shed . . .

FATHER: It was crumblin' away—from rot—what's the big deal . . . ?

Brief pause.

FATHER: How'd you get so fuckin' big?

Brief pause.

KID (*takes paper bag from pocket, opens it*): Dad—look . . .

FATHER: What's this?

KID: I made it—outa metal plate—with a saw—they're animals—look—I didn't use no outline . . .

FATHER (*picks up one or two little figures, looks at them*): What's this?

KID: Which one? That's a cow.

FATHER: This?

KID: You got it upside down—it's a cow . . .

FATHER: Yeah, a cow.

KID: All kinds of animals—I just kinda start, and it gets to be an animal—first I used to give 'em to the chicks—'cause they liked 'em—then I got a ten-spot for each—not bad, huh?

FATHER: Pretty good.

KID: I'm a damn good grinder—get this—I didn't know I could do it—they said it's hard as hell—I can use a tiny little boring bit too—even the chief tool-maker has me doin' it—how 'bout that . . . ?

FATHER: That's good.

Brief pause.

FATHER: I was relaxin' before—I was readin' . . .

Brief pause.

KID: Dad—I'm a Wolf now.

FATHER: What are you?

KID: A Wolf—'cause while the guardian's there—or the workin' stiffs—they lay low—but then they go away—an' at night the Wolves take over—they're tough as hell—whoever don't kiss their ass, gets the living shit beat out of him . . .

FATHER: Whaddya mean Wolves?

KID: The gang—you can't sneak away—they'll beat you up—when I was little I thought I could raise hell—once I even landed in the hospital—'cause of that—my two teeth here, they knocked 'em out. (*He shows him.*)

FATHER: Motherfuckers.

KID: But now I'm a Wolf too—it don't matter if it's a new place—I know right away—how to be a Wolf—by the time I was in eighth grade—right off I pick out the gang leader—you can tell who it is—an' I tell him it's okay—I don't wanna fuck him over—even though he ain't even always the biggest guy—but you can tell . . .

FATHER: That's okay then . . .

Pause.

FATHER: Me, I'm in my prime—the best age—not even forty—huh?—any woman sixteen to forty-five suits me—but not just anybody—I got pretty picky—your fuckin' mother took away my best years—she wrung me out—like a dishrag—but never again—I learned my lesson about what I'll take an' what I won't—these little chicks come up to me—at work too—there're these little chicks—all they've got on is their smock—not even a slip—nothin'—they're makin' eyes at me, smiling' like hell—but I watch out for myself—learned my lesson—what I'll take an' what I won't . . .

Pause.

KID: And Dad—you okay?

FATHER: Me? I'm okay. Why—what else would I be?—nothin' special—I bust my ass—I work days—morning shift—but we'll figure it all out—what to do these three days—I don't know—we'll go someplace—here an' there—everything . . .

KID: And—I don't know—somebody takin' care of you?

FATHER: Me? I don't need nobody—what do I gotta be taken care of . . . ?

KID: I don't know—like me—back then . . .

FATHER: Eh—what for?—that was then . . .

Pause.

FATHER: You were a decent kid—really—when I was laid up—you were real decent—an' they took you away just then—just when I was laid up—the bastards—your stupid sister didn't even spit in my direction—only you—an' then they grabbed you an' took you away . . .

Pause.

FATHER: Okay, so then—it's a mess inside—so what, huh? Not everything's where it used to be—but we'll fix it up . . .

KID: I'll clean up.

FATHER: Eh—what for?—it'll be okay . . .

Brief pause.

FATHER: Hey—I was thinkin'—what a shit-brained thing—you learnin' some stupid trade—why don't you go to work?—make money.

KID: I don't know—everybody's doin' it this way . . .

FATHER: It's shit-brained. Take me—if I wanted—I could make more than them fuckin' senior skilled workers—if I wanted—only what the hell for?—hey—what if—let's say you got out—came back—an' went to work—a big guy like you—I don't even know what the hell you need a trade for—you could be makin' money—I could be makin' money—together, I'm talkin' real money—if they'd let you out—'cause this way whaddya get?—years you're workin' for them—they don't give you nothin'—only when you get out—an' by then—I don't know—c'mon home—we'll talk 'em into it—okay, so they'll come nosin' around again—the motherfuckers—but we'll talk 'em into it—we can shovel the shit, dammit—the two of us, huh? (*He laughs.*)

KID: Dad—I wanna stay here—Dad—(*He breaks into tears. Brief pause.*)

FATHER: Don't cry—why—what I been sayin'?—hey . . .

KID: It's so bad—so fuckin' bad . . . (*He weeps.*)

FATHER: Hey—I'm sayin' we'll take care of it . . .

KID: I don't wanna go back!

FATHER: You don't wanna, you don't wanna—okay—that's what I say too—we'll fix it—you're here now—what'd you say, for how long? How long you staying'?

KID: I don't wanna go . . .

FATHER: When you leavin'?—tomorrow?

KID: Day after.

FATHER: Okay—so it's three days—huh?—that's good—stop cryin'—before, you said it's good over there—didn't you?—the food—the Wolves—why, what'd I say?—I said you'll come home—an' we'll make a shitload of money—but for now you'll go back—'cause they'll get you for runnin' away—they'll come after me—an' lay it all on me—I know—an' then the whole deal's blown—don't you get it?

Pause.

FATHER: Okay, so this is for three days—so whaddya wanna do?—What're we gonna do?

KID (*whimpering*): I don't know.

FATHER: Whaddya mean you don't know?—am I supposed to know?—at your age I knew—I was chasin' chicks—goin' to the movies—stuff like that—we didn't have TV in them days—we played soccer—with the buddies—you guys down there—you play soccer?

KID: Ain't no field . . .

FATHER: How come?—that's how come we never win the championships—I always say—'cause there ain't no facilities—the paper says so too—even so there ain't—how come there ain't no field?

KID: I don't know—there was a ping-pong table—they took it away—a guardian—he got it . . .

FATHER: The ping-pong table? An' it ain't even his, huh?—belongs to you guys—an' he took it—huh?

KID: I never even seen it—they told me about it . . .

FATHER: You guys oughta take a stand—make him bring it back—why don't you guys take a stand?—don't let him—that's how they get everything—'cause you let 'em—so it's no fuckin' wonder they take it—tell 'em I said so . . .

Pause.

FATHER: Okay—let's say we go now—okay?—we'll go around—or you go to the movies—I don't know what's playin'—I'll give you some money—I'll give you a twenty—okay?—meantime I'll do some readin' 'cause I usually read—after work—I'll give you a twenty . . .

Pause.

FATHER: An' then meantime I'll straighten up—I didn't have no time—but now 'cause you're here—it's a good thing after all—you comin' home—I'll straighten up . . .

Pause.

SCENE 11

Female OFFICIAL *enters through coachway, carrying briefcase and shopping bags containing food and drink.*

OFFICIAL: Good day. Is this forty-four?

FATHER: It is.

OFFICIAL: I don't understand. There's no house number. I've been wandering around here for half an hour. No street sign, no house number . . .

FATHER: 'Cause it fell off—an' then I made one—put it out—it was up—'cause the old one was all—y'know—all faded—then the Council came—they said y'know—it ain't standard—they took it down—said they'll take care of it—been nothin' since then.

OFFICIAL: I don't understand, at the neighboring lot, on that wooden fence, it says twenty-eight . . . I asked around, nobody knew anything.

FATHER: The mailman too—he don't come in—'cause he says he don't gotta—if there ain't no number—an old woman lives here—she goes out there—when she's expectin' her pension—'cause the mailman don't come in—we don't even exist. (*He laughs.*)

OFFICIAL (*puts down bags, takes a plan from briefcase, opens it, studies it*): I don't understand . . . this isn't what's here.

FATHER: What're you lookin' for?

OFFICIAL: I'm from the Council.

FATHER: The Council?

OFFICIAL: Yes.

FATHER: Say, if I could just—this here's my son—they took him away an' put him in the State's custody—but it's bad for him there. Could you get him out?

OFFICIAL: That's a custody case. (*She studies drawing.*)

FATHER: They took him away—for no good reason—his sister too—why don't you come in?—everything's in order here—it's clean—I got a job—an' then they take my kids away!

OFFICIAL: I told you that's a custody case. There're officials who deal with custody cases. Go to them. (*She looks around.*) I don't understand.

FATHER: Let him out—and appoint me his y'know—make him my—my—whaddya-call-it—my y'know . . .

OFFICIAL: Your ward.

FATHER: That's it! 'Cause it can be done—I know it . . .

OFFICIAL: Custody case. (*She points at garage.*) What's that?

FATHER: A garage.

OFFICIAL: There's no such thing.

FATHER: Belongs to that woman—who lives in there . . .

OFFICIAL: It's not a dwelling?

FATHER: That? I'm tellin' ya—it's a garage—belongs to that woman . . .

KID: Used to be a shed—a shed—mine.

FATHER: I'll get her out here—don't you bother—(*He knocks at* WOMAN*'s door, silence, knocks again.*)

WOMAN (*opens door, but only a crack, as far as chain allows*): What is it?

FATHER: Come out here—the Council's here because of the garage.

WOMAN: What do you mean the Council? I got the permit, it's mine.

FATHER: The Council says it's a dwelling.

WOMAN *undoes chain, comes out, goes to* OFFICIAL.

WOMAN: Are you from the Council, comrade?

OFFICIAL: I am.

WOMAN: This is my garage. I got a permit for it—it's inside, I can bring it out. There wasn't anything here. Just a broken-down shed. I had this built.

OFFICIAL: It's not indicated on this drawing.

WOMAN: What do you mean it's not indicated? I was at the Council a year and a half ago . . .

OFFICIAL: And when did the Council inspect the premises?

WOMAN: I don't know . . . (To FATHER.) Did they inspect?

FATHER: When they took my kids away—my son—for no good reason—'cause the old woman denounced me—even though she's nuts—she just buried her cat—tell her, didn't she just bury her cat? Didn't she?

WOMAN: She did.

OFFICIAL: What is this, a garden? Because according to this, it's a garden.

FATHER: It's a garden.

OFFICIAL: Not an interior courtyard?

Brief pause.

FATHER: This a garden?

WOMAN: I don't know. Why, is there a difference?

Brief pause.

WOMAN: The teacher probably knows—and he can tell you this is a garage—

She goes to TEACHER'*s door, knocks, pause, knocks again.* TEACHER *opens.*

TEACHER: Please, will you let me work!

WOMAN: Excuse me, but this comrade's from the Council—could you tell her—is this a garden or a courtyard? And tell her that's my garage. Please tell her.

TEACHER: Please—I've asked you a hundred times not to bother me while I'm teaching . . .

WOMAN: But this comrade's from the Council!

OFFICIAL (*to* TEACHER): Is this number forty-four?

TEACHER: It is.

OFFICIAL: Nothing here corresponds to this. I'll have to check it all out because of the gas lines, but the neighboring lot's number twenty-eight, and there's no number here. This garage isn't here at all.

TEACHER: Just a moment. What gas lines?

OFFICIAL: Well, you're going to be tied in to the gas lines.

TEACHER: Now?

OFFICIAL: Within the next three months.

TEACHER: Excuse me, but the way I understood it, they're going to tear this whole thing down.

OFFICIAL: Of course.

TEACHER: If they're going to tear it down, then why tie in the gas? It might have been a good idea some time ago, but if they're going to do away with everything here, then why tie in now?

OFFICIAL: It was in the plan to have gas here, but there wasn't enough capacity. Now there is.

TEACHER: This is going to cost the Council a great deal of money.

OFFICIAL: That's right. So be grateful you're getting it.

TEACHER: If they tie us into the gas lines now, we'll use it for a few months, a half a year, a year maybe, then the bulldozer will clear everything away. The public utility lines will be moved. Tremendous expense. They'll build one of those ten-story apartment blocks of the kind that're already around here. They'll lay new pipes.

OFFICIAL: That's right.

TEACHER: Wouldn't it be simpler not to tie us in now?

OFFICIAL: That isn't your concern. It's been approved.

WOMAN: Don't make a fuss, sir. If there's gas, then they'll have to give us better apartments in exchange for these.

TEACHER: It's still a waste. The State is squandering a great deal of money.

CHICK *and* GIRL *listen with interest at* TEACHER'*s doorway.*

OFFICIAL: That's how it is. Are you sure this is forty-four?

TEACHER: This is forty-four.

OFFICIAL: Even the dimensions look wrong.

TEACHER: If you please, as long as they're determined to tie in the gas, fine, so be it. But then perhaps they needn't tear it down. This isn't in such bad shape, neither are the other buildings in the neighborhood—they've renovated many of them, not so long ago. One of those tall buildings hardly accommodates more people than all the ones they'd be tearing down to make room for it. And there are lovely gardens around here, fruit gardens, all of which will have to be destroyed. It would be a shame.

OFFICIAL: There's been a resolution. Just be glad you're getting everything for free.

TEACHER: These buildings are brick. They've got cellars; they're in good shape; they can easily take another forty, fifty years. More than a prefabricated housing development.

OFFICIAL: Please leave me alone. I'm just doing my job. You can always go to the complaints office. Extended office hours are on Mondays.

FATHER: Gimme a document that says everything's okay here, I don't drink, I got a job, he's makin' money too, look at the size of this kid.

OFFICIAL: Explain to him that that's a custody case.

FATHER: You're from the Council—an' now I'm appealing to the Council—about how it was when my wife left me—I was left here—wrung out like a dishrag—an' my son took care of me—'cause I wasn't even able to get up—that's right—an' he brought me food—everything—he cleaned the house—did the wash—'cause his sister strayed off too—except for him I'd have croaked right then an' there—he was still just a little kid—but he could take care of everything—an' then they denounced me—an' the Council took him away from me. Ain't that the truth? Tell her! Ain't it?!

WOMAN: That's how it was, because the old woman wanted to help, to take him in with her, and that's when there was an inspection, and that's when the State took note of what was going on here—but he couldn't be turned over to the old woman, because they would have been feuding all the time—so they took him away . . .

OFFICIAL (*sighs, looks at* KID): And?

FATHER: He wants to come back—'cause it's no good for him there—why can't he come back?!

KID: Let me stay here—I don't know—back there I always dreamt about coming back—an' then me an' Dad—here—even though he didn't even write—but I'd like to be back here—with him. (*He weeps.*)

OFFICIAL: You'll have to go to the Custody Division.

FATHER (*opens his apartment door*): Please come in—it's neat in here—clean—see for yourself—this is where he belongs . . .

TEACHER *goes back, ushers the girls inside, closes door.*

OFFICIAL: The official in charge of custody cases will come out, all right? (*She puts drawing back into her briefcase, picks up shopping bags.*)

WOMAN: Excuse me, I have a permit for this garage—I can show you—it's inside—with this garage—I'm entitled to a two-room apartment with full conveniences—in return—go ahead, assess it . . .

OFFICIAL: They'll be out.

OLD WOMAN *comes out of apartment wearing a clean dress, somewhat unsuited to her years, in makeup, carrying sheet of paper.*

OLD WOMAN (*shouting*): You get away from there!

OFFICIAL *jumps away in fright.*

OLD WOMAN: You're trampling the grave! The grave! Get away from there!

WOMAN: Just a minute—it's only a cat—they hanged it . . .

OFFICIAL *starts to leave,* FATHER *rushes after her, grabs her by the arm.*

FATHER: This rotten old woman—I'm denouncing her now—'cause she had my son taken away—she's the one . . .

OFFICIAL: Let go of me!

FATHER: She had no right! She had no right! She's crazy—she buries her cat here—crazy—an' she's the one the Council believes!

WOMAN (*to* OLD WOMAN): She's from the Council . . .

OLD WOMAN (*to* OFFICIAL): Please sign this for me—it's my last will and testament—because only the teacher's willing—nobody else—please sign it for me . . .

OFFICIAL: Let go of me!

OLD WOMAN: I'm leaving everything to him—to this boy here—everything—the furniture—everything—my money too—ten thousand forints—that too—I wrote it up all over again—please sign it . . .

OFFICIAL: I'm not signing anything—let me go—you're all crazy—I'm here to get you gas . . .

FATHER: She had my son taken away—'cause she wanted him for her ward—it was a trick—to get the money—if he's her ward—then she gets paid . . .

OLD WOMAN: Don't you understand, you blockhead, I'm leaving everything to your son?! Don't you understand?!

FATHER: What?

OLD WOMAN: This is a will—I'm leaving everything to him—my money—ten thousand forints—and I'm going to take him in—I'll write a petition . . .

FATHER: You got money, huh? The money you stole outa my pocket—I figured it all out—'cause the subsidy for a ward is at least four hundred a month—I know that—I'm no fool—you think I don't know? Up to now you stole 9,600 forints outa my pocket—9,600—I figured it out!

OLD WOMAN: What are you talking about? I stole—from you?

FATHER: 'Cause if I'd been the kid's whaddya-call-it—his guardian—the kid's—this one here, I ain't even figurin' in my daughter—then in that much time that's what it comes to!—It's all figured out!—That's how much you owe me!

OLD WOMAN: Well I never . . .

FATHER: You denounced me—you said I just lie around—(*To* OFFICIAL.) This one denounced me—she said I just lie around—'cause I was laid up—'cause this one here—she wanted to get the money—the support for the kid—she figured it out! But she didn't get it after all—'cause the custody official came—an' saw what the story was—but I didn't get it either—goddammit—neither did I! (*To* OLD WOMAN.) 'Cause if you hadn't been such a rotten lowlife—then I woulda got it!

WOMAN: The way that happened was that the official who came out could see that all hell would break loose if the lady—even though she meant well—she really did . . .

FATHER: Well I woulda wrung 'er neck—that's for sure . . .

WOMAN: The poor boy was such a decent kid—he took care of his father—he cut school, went to work—so there'd be money—they threw him out of school for stealing money . . .

KID: An' I didn't even steal! Only from my sister! I didn't even steal!

WOMAN: His father was just lying there—he was certified as sick—the boy even cooked for him, cleaned house, everything—it's too bad the Council had to come out just then—I know the Council meant well . . .

OFFICIAL (*frees herself*): Go to the Custody Division! (*Runs out through the coachway*.)

OLD WOMAN (*shouts after* OFFICIAL): At least sign it—I need two witnesses—sign it!

OFFICIAL *disappears*.

FATHER (*shouts after* OFFICIAL): I never even spanked him—never! Everybody beats their kid—not me, ever! (*Brief silence, to* KID.) Did I—ever?

KID: No.

FATHER: There you go! A few whacks, but beat you—never! Kids oughta be taken away from where they're beaten half to death—but no—only from me—when they're big—when they're makin' money—that's how come too—'cause if they ain't here—then I don't get a bigger apartment—that's what it comes down to—I know it! 'Cause the Council too—how come they gotta meddle in a person's life—how come?—when it's so damn hard as it is—then how come they gotta meddle—how come?!

WOMAN: They meant well—believe me they did—that was a very decent custody official.

FATHER: Then what was he doin' meddlin'—in a person's life—what was he doin' that for? (*To* OLD WOMAN.) Filthy squealer.

OLD WOMAN: We have nothing to talk about. I'm leaving everything to your son, do you understand? But you and I have nothing to talk about. (*To* WOMAN.) Neither do we—you cowardly bitch—can't even sign a thing like this—but that's all right—because the Lord doesn't want evil to rule in the world—(*To* KID.) You'll see . . .

WOMAN: Me a bitch! Here I am defending you—and then you—you—but that's just like you—always—you drove away the only one—the engineer—the oarsman . . .

OLD WOMAN: I did what? To who?

WOMAN: He was the only guy—you wouldn't leave him alone—he had to go in for coffee—you were here whenever he came—and he couldn't take it—he was the only guy—who . . .

OLD WOMAN: You've lost your mind.

WOMAN: I have? Oh yeah? What did you tell the old fellow?—about me—all the time—I know all about it—he told me—that all I was interested in was the apartment—all the time that's what you said—because I'm young and attractive—you were mean—jealous—I know all about it . . .

OLD WOMAN: What? Me? He was an old geezer!

WOMAN: He was younger than you!

OLD WOMAN: A feeble old geezer! I felt sorry for him—because you just did the bare minimum for him—and he was left to rot here by himself all day—so I asked him in—I bought him apples—and you were afraid I was after his apartment—because there's only meanness in you—nothing else . . .

WOMAN: You're always spying—whenever I talk to the teacher you come rushing out—so nothing should happen between . . .

OLD WOMAN: Well I never . . .

WOMAN: Oh yes!

FATHER (*laughs, to* KID): How 'bout this? They're at each other's throats—pretty good, huh? (*He laughs.*)

WOMAN: You shut up—all you can do is stand around gawking!

FATHER: Dumb bitch—you go to bed with anybody—you think I can't tell?—anybody—your tits are always hangin' out so I can see 'em—filthy bitch . . .

WOMAN: All of you can—can just . . .

WOMAN *runs inside, slams door behind her, sound of chain.*

OLD WOMAN: Because she wanted my cat—she wanted to lure her away from me—and that stupid animal—it even rubbed up against her . . .

FATHER: Your cat! (*He laughs.*) Your stupid cat! Your cat croaked, my dear! The kitty kicked off! "Kitty cat, kitty cat, meow, meow, here kitty!" (*He laughs, begins hopping around crutch in an Indian "war dance," tapping his mouth while emitting "war cries." He summons* KID.)

KID (*laughs*): Dad—Dad—(*He joins* FATHER *in war dance.*)

OLD WOMAN (*watches, straightens up, stands motionless*): Dear God—thanks be to you, Lord, for reminding me—reminding me once more—Lord . . .

FATHER *and* KID *continue dancing and making rhythmic, yelping sounds.*

OLD WOMAN: You know, Lord, why this is necessary—you know, my God . . .

FATHER *and* KID *stop, panting,* FATHER *throws arm around shoulder of* KID, *who is taller than he is.*

OLD WOMAN (*wipes her tears, smearing her rouge*): That's all right, Lord—it's all right even so—even so—(*She goes into apartment, closes door.*)

FATHER (*panting*): I'm tellin' ya, man—huh? (*He laughs, panting.*) I'm tellin' ya, man—shit, man . . .

KID (*laughs*): Dad—you said it, man . . .

MOTHER *enters through coachway carrying shopping bags, stops.*

FATHER (*out of breath*): Oughta get more exercise, huh? Soccer—or somethin' . . .

KID *notices* MOTHER, *steps aside, looks at her, becomes ill, sits down in front of garage, stares at her, pause.*

MOTHER: What's up?

Pause.

FATHER: Nothin' dammit—nothin'—your kid's here—can't you see?

MOTHER *looks at* KID, *says nothing.*

FATHER: Go on in—straighten up for chrissake—I can't even give him nothin' to eat—where the fuck you been—when he's here—an' straighten up, goddammit—take your bed to the kitchen—'cause he's sleepin' inside—with me—you fuckin' got that?—what're you starin' at?—get goin'—an' put your shit away . . .

MOTHER *goes into apartment, pause.*

FATHER: Your mother's here now—came back long time ago—she's here now—she came back—an' now she's here—at least she cooks, huh?—no point kickin' her out now—no big deal—at least while she's here—she cooks, huh?—What's up? What the fuck's wrong now? Why don't you say nothin' to her?—She's your mother for chrissake.

Pause.

FATHER: Ain't even nothin' between us—she could come back—what am I supposed to do?—where's she supposed to go?—she's always gettin' herself thrown out—so where's she supposed to go?—let her cook—I don't care—let her do what she wants—let her get married—if she can find some loser—but she's always comin' back—she can't get it together. (*He laughs.*) Who needs an over-the-hill-broad like her?—She's got ideas—but it ain't so simple—so I don't say nothin'—for a man this ain't old—this age—I ain't even forty—whatever I want—I'm in my prime—any broad sixteen to forty-five suits me—but I watch out for myself—I learned my lesson—what I'll take an' what I won't . . .

Pause.

FATHER: What're you sittin' there for?—your mother's cookin'—I'll go on in. (*Brief pause.*) You c'mon in too—probably hungry, huh?—see ya inside. (*He goes into apartment, closes door.*)

Pause. KID *sits in front of garage door, keeps still.*

SCENE 12

BUDDY *enters through coachway, stops.*

BUDDY: What's up?

Pause. BUDDY *sits next to* KID *in front of garage.*

BUDDY: I was sittin' out there—waitin' for somebody to come by—nobody came.

Pause.

BUDDY: What's up?

KID: Fuckin' bitch . . .

BUDDY: What's up?

KID (*gets up, seizes cleaver*): I'll smash in her head—I'll smash it in . . .

BUDDY *keeps still.*

KID: I'll smash in her head! (*He screams, attacks lock on garage door, breaks it off.*)

BUDDY: We takin' the car?

KID (*panting, throws down cleaver*): Fuckin' bitch . . .

WOMAN (*comes out*): Jesus! What are you doing?! Why?! (*Runs back inside, leaves door open a crack, latches chain, looks out in terror.*)

BUDDY *opens garage door, looks in.*

BUDDY: It's a Polski.

WOMAN: Please—don't!

BUDDY: She's scared to come out—(*He laughs.*)

WOMAN: Don't do it—please—don't!

BUDDY: We takin' it?

KID: Sit the fuck down.

BUDDY: Can't you drive?

KID: No. Sit the fuck down!

BUDDY *sits down, pause.*

WOMAN: Please, please—don't . . .

Pause.

BUDDY: The broad's havin' a shitfit . . . (*He laughs.*)

KID: Shut up.

Pause. WOMAN *stares terrified.*

SCENE 13

TEACHER *comes out with* CHICK *and* GIRL.

TEACHER: So then till next week.

CHICK: Yes, sir. (*She takes out money.*)

WOMAN: Sir!

TEACHER (*looks at her*): Yes?

WOMAN: Nothing—only—excuse me for bothering you—during your lesson . . .

TEACHER: No problem—no problem—(*Pause.*) I'd just like to add that this prayer, this brilliant, deeply human prayer is a prayer of desperation. It is perhaps the greatest Hungarian poem, not only of this century, but in general, because, as I've pointed out, like the greatest writers of the age, Dostoevsky and Nietzsche for example, the poet here grapples with experience that remains, as they say, relevant to this day, insofar as the world is in exactly the same predicament, the entire world, if you please. But that's not the main reason. Rather it is because this brilliant, desperate, deeply felt, profoundly human prayer, this self-torturing outcry, is the ultimate expression of the spirit that believes in spite of itself. And, I dare say, that in this, the poem surpasses even the greatest of them. Because in this poem it is not repentance that drives the poet to the Lord, nor even belief in the Lord's existence. This is not a weak man seeking solace here, but a mature, serious man, one who is weighing the consequences of renouncing this nevermore-to-be-resurrected God, if you please.

Meanwhile CHICK *and* BUDDY *are exchanging glances.*

TEACHER: And by coming to terms with this weakness, to which he owns up, he is no longer weak, as is clearly demonstrated when he writes:

"Let's give ourselves to him in faith,
In spite of all he is our utmost Wraith,
Since no belief can any more persist,
Let's trust a Lord who might, might not exist."

Note, if you will, that till now he's been referring to him as God, and now all of a sudden he calls him Wraith, with a capital "W" naturally. A Wraith can just as well be a sinister spirit. So what the poet is saying here is that whether or not there is a God, whether he is good or bad, in any case he must exist, even if, indeed especially if, "no belief can any more persist." This is an incomparably deep thought emanating from a solemn, desperate man. The poet is saying here that no matter what that certain spiritual entity may be, that spiritual aspect hovering above man, be it even ruinous, be it hostile toward man, it is still better that it exist, than not exist. And this is what we find in the last stanza, in the most beautiful four lines of Hungarian poetry, which I ask you to memorize:

"For he 'spite all remains our utmost Wraith,
And it cannot be, for nothing's direr than
That Life belongs to no one, or
That Life belongs to man."

GIRL *slips money into* CHICK's *hand.*

TEACHER: Note, if you will, that good or bad, Wraith is designated "our utmost Wraith" here. In other words it matters not what his nature is, so long as he exists. And the explanation is that it is horrifying and impossible first of all that life be nobody's—note, if you will the paradox wherein the adjective that is independent of the poet, "dire," commingles with the outcry that arises from the depths of the poet's desperation, "it cannot be." And only then comes the truly profound, truly great thought, which life has since confirmed, the most terrible prophecy ever uttered by a poet, the weightiest Cassandrian augury, which has come to pass:

"And it cannot be, for nothing's direr than
That Life belongs to no one, or
That Life belongs to man."

Because man is unworthy of life, because when man gains mastery over life, he wreaks havoc upon it.

Brief pause.

TEACHER: So please memorize not only the last stanza, but the last two. (*Brief pause.*) And when you realize these things for yourselves, then these eight lines will come to mind, even if you don't fully appreciate them now.

GIRL: But we do appreciate them, sir.

TEACHER: And if they come to mind, then no matter how strange it may seem, you will be comforted. You'll be comforted because you'll feel that you too are part of something grand, something horrifying in which souls as magnificent as Endre Ady have already suffered. And then you will become aware of the beauteous, great community made up of humans, of those who are capable only of wreaking havoc upon Life—but if you sense this, then that Spirit, that Wraith, about which Endre Ady writes, will make his presence felt in you—the Lord will make his presence felt in you.

TEACHER *wipes tears from his eyes, pause. The girls stand still. Pause.*

TEACHER (*clears throat*): So please memorize the last eight lines—I have to go now.

CHICK: Thank you, sir. (*She hands him money.*)

TEACHER: Yes . . . (*He takes it.*) Thank you. So then, till next week.

TEACHER *quickly goes into apartment, leaves door open.* CHICK *and* GIRL *titter.*

CHICK: Ssh!

GIRL: Ssh!

TEACHER *comes out carrying empty shopping bag.*

TEACHER: I forgot to do my shopping—when I came home after school, I didn't have my bag with me—I've got to hurry—good-bye. (*To* WOMAN.) Good-bye.

CHICK, GIRL: Good-bye, sir!

TEACHER *hurries out through coachway.*

BUDDY: Get a fuckin' loada that . . .

GIRL: Okay, c'mon.

CHICK: What's the rush?

GIRL: C'mon, will you?!

CHICK: What a cute guy.

GIRL: C'mon.

BUDDY: Get a fuckin' loada that . . .

KID: Leave me alone.

BUDDY: They're starin' at us. Huh? They're starin' at us.

GIRL (*to* WOMAN): Hello.

WOMAN (*quietly*): Hi. Hello.

GIRL: Okay, c'mon.

BUDDY *stands up, goes a little closer to girls.*

CHICK: Cute guy—the one who's sitting. Huh?

BUDDY *stops.*

CHICK: Can't get a rise outa him.

BUDDY *bursts out laughing.*

GIRL: Don't bother.

CHICK: Looks like this bull is a steer.

GIRL (*laughs, then stops*): Not worth it.

CHICK *and* GIRL *start toward coachway,* WOMAN *keeps still, watches.*

CHICK (*looks back*): He can't come.

BUDDY (*to* KID): What the fuck you waitin' for?

KID: Filthy sluts.

CHICK (*angrily*): C'mon.

CHICK *and* GIRL *exit through coachway.*

BUDDY: Now what the fuck was that for—huh?—couldn't you tell they wanted us—couldn't you fuckin' tell?!

KID: Will you shut your motherfuckin' face!

WOMAN *listens in terror.*

BUDDY (*goes back to* KID, *sits down*): What's up now—huh?

Pause.

BUDDY: Good lookin' chicks—what the fuck . . .

Pause.

BUDDY: What's up—your old man split or what?

Pause.

BUDDY: 'Cause you ain't got no fuckin' key—I told you to get one—I got one . . .

Pause.

BUDDY: Look—she's starin'—the broad—she's starin' . . .

KID: Shut your face, you stupid asshole jerk . . .

Pause.

KID: She took my old man's money—ten thousand forints—the rotten old bitch . . .

BUDDY: What?

KID: Rotten old bitch—everything's her fault . . .

BUDDY: What?—that old bitch—the one with the cat . . . ?

KID (*to* WOMAN): What're you starin' at?! What the hell you starin' at?! What?!

WOMAN: Don't—please . . .

KID: You took away the shed—it was mine—why'd you take it away?! (*He weeps, pause.*)

BUDDY: Don't—hey . . .

WOMAN: I didn't know—I'm sorry—I didn't know . . .

BUDDY: What's up now . . . ?

WOMAN: What can I give you?—if you want something—I'll gladly . . .

KID: Go to hell!—stop starin'!—I'll smash your car to smithereens if you keep starin'!

WOMAN: Don't—not that—I won't stare—but not that . . .

KID: Go to hell!

WOMAN *withdraws, but leaves door ajar.*

BUDDY: We trashin' it—her car—huh . . . ?

KID: Stupid asshole jerk . . .

BUDDY: Now what . . .

Pause. TEACHER *returns carrying bag containing bread, milk, wine, cold cuts. On hearing footsteps,* WOMAN *appears in doorway.*

WOMAN: Good day, sir.

TEACHER: I didn't take my bag this morning—forgot—so I had to go shopping now—I had five lessons, I forgot. So I had to go after teaching—right away in the afternoon—otherwise I can't get East German earplugs—and those are the best—they're in short supply. They're the best. (*To the boys.*) Hello fellows. (*To* WOMAN.) The constant sound of TV, you know—I even have to use sleeping pills.

WOMAN: Yes, you've mentioned it before.

TEACHER: But I try to limit my use of sleeping pills—Géza Csáth smoked opium—have you read him? I'll tell you about him sometime—he wrote beautiful stories—well, good-bye.

WOMAN: Good-bye, sir.

TEACHER *goes into apartment, sound of lock. Pause.*

BUDDY: Hey—she's starin'.

KID *takes cleaver, studies it.* WOMAN *closes door, sounds of chain and locks. Pause.*

KID: She ripped off my old man—took his money . . .

BUDDY: The old bitch?—at least we wasted her cat—huh?

KID *puts down cleaver, pause.*

BUDDY: No point shittin' bricks—no big deal—we go in an' she fuckin' gives it back . . .

Pause.

BUDDY: Damn straight she'll fuckin' give it back—she won't dare squawk—we go in an' she gives it back . . .

Pause.

BUDDY (*picks up cleaver*): She'll see this—shit in her fuckin' pants—then she'll fork over the money, man.

Pause.

KID: Four hundred's mine.

BUDDY: What?

KID: 'Cause she stole nine thousand six hundred—an she's got ten thousand. So four hundred's mine.

BUDDY: Why—I'm goin' too—ain't I?

KID: I didn't ask you to.

BUDDY: Like she'll give it to you alone—jerk.

Pause.

KID: Then two hundred's yours.

BUDDY: Why two hundred? Five thousand.

KID: In a pig's cunt! Nine thousand six hundred's Dad's.

Pause.

BUDDY: Aw c'mon—your fuckin' old man . . .

KID: Watch your face—I'll fuckin' let you have it again . . .

Pause.

BUDDY: I don't know—we oughta have y'know—stockings—over our heads . . .

KID: Dork. What the hell for?

BUDDY: Well that's how they do it—ain't it?

KID: Dork.

Pause.

SCENE 14

COP *and* SARGE *enter through coachway.* KID *and* BUDDY *stand up,* BUDDY *holding cleaver.*

BUDDY: Hello.

SARGE: Hi.—Who's this?

BUDDY: It's y'know, it's him.

SARGE: Personal I.D.

KID *takes out booklet, hands it over.* SARGE *looks at it.*

SARGE: Oh, is it you? I didn't recognize you. (*To* COP.) His son.

COP: Yeah.

SARGE: But you're in an institution—right?

KID: Yes.

BUDDY: He ran away! He told me! He ran away!

Pause. KID *leers at* BUDDY, *takes out a document, hands it over,* SARGE *looks at it, hands it to* COP.

SARGE: Is it a regulation leave permit?

COP *studies document.*

KID: It's regulation.

SARGE: I didn't ask you.

Brief pause.

COP: Well—it's a permit.

SARGE: Is it stamped and dated?

COP: Stamped. Dated.

SARGE: Letterhead?

COP *nods.*

SARGE (*takes it back*): This is a regulation leave permit. For how many days?

KID: Three.

SARGE: I didn't ask you.

COP *looks at document.*

COP: Three.

SARGE: This is a regulation leave permit for three days. (*He hands document back to* KID.) Nothing's allowed to be kept in the Personal I.D. book.

KID: There ain't nothin' in it.

SARGE: I didn't say there was something in it, I said nothing's allowed to be kept in it. Isn't that what I said?

Pause.

SARGE: Isn't that what I said?

KID: It is.

SARGE: The Personal I.D. always has to be kept on one's person.

KID: I had it on my person—didn't I have it on my person?

SARGE: I didn't say you didn't have it on your person. Did I say you didn't have it on your person? (*To* COP.) Is that what I said?

COP: No.

SARGE (*to* KID): Is that what I said?

KID: No.

SARGE: The Personal I.D. must not be mutilated.

Pause.

SARGE: This one is not mutilated. Its loss must immediately be reported to the appropriate police authorities.

Pause.

SARGE: There. Here ya go.

KID *takes booklet, puts it away.*

SARGE: Have you seen your father yet?

KID: Yes.

WOMAN *opens door a crack, listens.*

SARGE: Well, okay then. Carry on.

Pause.

SARGE: What's up? What've you guys been up to so far?

BUDDY: Just shootin' the breeze.

SARGE: Okay. Carry on.

WOMAN: Good day.

SARGE: Good day.

Pause. WOMAN *withdraws, sounds of chain, locks.* KID *starts toward* OLD WOMAN*'s door,* BUDDY *follows after brief hesitation.* KID *opens door, both go in. Pause.*

COP: That was a woman . . .

SARGE: Yeah.

COP: A whore, huh?—probably a whore—oughta be kicked in the ass—what's she always fuckin' for?—(*He laughs.*)

SARGE: Was that supposed to be a joke? That's just fuckin' stupid!

Brief pause.

COP: Not me—no—really—I'm on the up an' up—just, y'know—when they stare . . .

Pause.

SARGE: Okay.—Young guys like that, sometimes they forge another date on—they scratch out the old one—or they use ink remover—you gotta watch for that—an' they tell you they had it but lost it—on the train . . .

COP: Yeah.

SARGE: But this one's a decent kid—when his father was laid up—he took care of him—even though his father was laid up—this was when his wife left him second time around—she was still a good looker then—an' his sister was a tramp—she went hookin'—so this kid's a decent kid.

Pause. COP *leans against wall.*

SARGE: Beat, huh?

COP: Nah, just y'know . . .

SARGE: I never said this was easy—walkin' around all day—all over—fuckin' pain in the ass—huh?

COP: No—just in my back . . .

SARGE: Well that's how it goes—in the cold—the heat—you're breathin' dust—smoke—to keep the peace—that's how it goes.

Pause.

SARGE: You'll get used to it—an' havin' to watch out for yourself—keep your eyes open—you'll get used to it.

Pause. Suddenly screaming, collapsing are heard, then silence. COP jumps away from wall, looks around startled.

SARGE (*impatiently*): Whatsa matter—you shit in your pants?

COP: What was that?!

Pause.

SARGE: Nothin' dammit—probably the TV—some crime show . . .

Pause. They listen.

SARGE: So okay—we been here too—so now let's go . . .

KID and BUDDY *emerge from* OLD WOMAN's *apartment, pale, their hands and shirts bloody, they stop.*

BUDDY: Why'd you have to—why . . . ?

KID: Her brains—her brains . . .

Both are nauseated. SARGE and COP stare, then leap at once, throwing themselves on KID and BUDDY, prostrate them. KID and BUDDY do not resist. The boys are handcuffed together.

SARGE (*to COP, kneeling on KID and BUDDY*): Take a look—

COP *hesitantly goes in. Pause. COP comes out, ill, then slowly, breathing deeply, recovers.*

COP: Caught in the act! Caught in the act!

SARGE *and* COP *pull* KID *and* BUDDY *to their feet, take them at a running pace out through the coachway and disappear.*

SCENE 15

WOMAN *opens door, undoes chain, comes out, sniffles, goes to garage door carrying new lock, puts it on, picks up old lock, starts back, stops, goes to* TEACHER's *door, knocks, waits, then goes in own door, locks it.*

SCENE 16

Pause. FATHER *and* MOTHER *come out.*

FATHER: Where's that kid . . . ?

MOTHER: What's-his-ass came in today—the jerks—an' all day—'xcept me—all day they was runnin' around—an' me—no time to take a leak even—an' that y'know—died, huh? Sounds fishy to me—I heard it on the radio—real fishy—at ten—but I couldn't go out—the rest of 'em—for me they couldn't give a shit— Liz 'specially—I got a headache—but they're all gonna croak too—an' then I'm comin' home—by the church—in his heart, huh?—for real?—with that thing— that whaddya-call-it thing—it's wood—y'know—it's got a hook-like—at the end—metal—huh?—I don't get it—it's y'know—terrible—an' them hangin' out there—all the time—I ain't even got the time to take a leak—an' them with their big mouths . . .

FATHER: Okay—not now . . .

MOTHER: 'Cause—I've had it—they're comin'—Liz too—the dumb bitch—she comes over to me—shootin' her mouth off—an' there I am—but I told her—why not?—if the big shots can—huh?—you'll see . . .

FATHER: Shut the fuck up!

Pause. Sound of Leonard Cohen song, "Who by Fire," can be heard coming from WOMAN's *apartment.* FATHER *pricks up his ears.*

FATHER: She's got company already—hear that? Company already!

Pause, song is heard.

FATHER: Okay. The kid's here—straighten up the fuckin' place—'cause it's bad for him—if he sees we messed with the room—you'll move into the kitchen— long as he's here . . .

MOTHER: Why should I move—move where?—an' the radio said—that the—the—y'know . . .

FATHER: 'Cause you're movin' into the fuckin' kitchen—that's why—an' then he fuckin' comes home an' that how it's gonna be then too . . .

MOTHER: Whaddya mean he comes home?

FATHER: He's comin' home—an' then I'll get appointed—he'll be my whaddya-call-it—my—he'll be my—he'll be my ward—that's the word—an' that's at least four hundred a month—see—'cause I'm gonna get appointed—'cause now it's can-do—he's a strong kid—good an' strong—he'll go to work—the hell with that learnin'-a-trade bullshit— right away he'll be earnin' four big ones—five—fuckin' strong kid—get it?—how much does it cost to feed a kid like that?—let's say he eats a thousand-worth—he gets let's say one for himself—that leaves two—maybe three—see—so get the fuckin' lead out—straighten the place up . . .

MOTHER: I'll straighten it up—I'll throw out the stupid books . . .

FATHER: Just you try, bitch—just you try . . .

MOTHER: I'll throw 'em all out—tales—seventy-seven Hungarian folk tales—an old bastard like this—readin' tales . . .

FATHER: 'Cause they're fuckin' nice—an' none of your business—what I do—you be glad you ain't out on your ass—so now get the hell inside—an' it's gonna be like I say around here!

MOTHER *goes in. Pause.*

FATHER: Okay—'cause it's gonna be like I want.

He starts into apartment.

FATHER: What the hell's on TV?

He goes in, slams door.

SORROW, SORROW, FEAR, THE ROPE, AND THE PIT

Karel Steigerwald

KAREL STEIGERWALD
Photo courtesy of Karel Steigerwald

SORROW, SORROW, FEAR, THE ROPE, AND THE PIT: KAREL STEIGERWALD'S UNEASY DREAM

Štěpán S. Šimek

Karel Steigerwald was born in 1945. After graduating from the Prague Film Academy (FAMU), he worked as a screen and television writer, and began to write plays in the late 1970s. His plays during that time dealt mostly with distinct periods of Czech history, and using metaphor, allusion, and writing between the lines, Steigerwald's work entered into a silent conspiracy with Czech audiences attuned to such techniques, and he pushed the limits of what would pass by the communist censors. *Sorrow, Sorrow, Fear, the Rope, and the Pit* was his first play produced after the Velvet Revolution. It premiered at the Divadlo na zábradlí in Prague in the spring of 1991, directed by the legendary Czech director Jan Grossman.

Steigerwald dates the writing of the play between October 1989 and March 1990. His work coincides with the immediate prequel to and the unfolding and eventual triumph of the Velvet Revolution. The play is essentially a chronicle of totalitarianism in twentieth-century Europe. Not surprisingly, the plot is complicated, in part because the author adheres to a strict principle of non-linearity. In addition, a full understanding of the play requires more than a cursory knowledge of twentieth-century European history. It simultaneously takes place in Russia in the thirties, Prague in the fifties and late eighties, Berlin in the sixties, and Germany during WWII. It is populated by an assembly of starkly, expressionistically drawn archetypes taken from different periods of European totalitarianism, ranging from a typically Czech, Švejk-like "everyman" to Osip and Nadezhda Mandelstam to the Ahashver-like eternal Jewish refugee to communist apparatchiks of the fifties. Rather than a plot-driven play, Steigerwald creates an epic historical fresco, a true *theatrum mundi* in which the concrete situations and characters metamorphose through time and space becoming symbols for the universal. By repeating the basic themes of flight, betrayal, changing alliances, torture, fear, and the inability to take a stand, among others, which are carried by a cast of nine recurring archetypes in various twentieth-century historical re-incarnations, Steigerwald paints a devastating picture of Europe in general and communist Czechoslovakia in particular. In order, however, to decipher the nightmare-like scenarios in the work, it may be necessary to assign more concrete faces to the symbolic archetypes that populate the play and to lay out the basic story, explaining some of the historical events to which the text alludes.

The Characters

An expressionist technique, which will also prove quite evident in the chronological discontinuity of the plot, is at work in the portrayal of the play's characters. Most are archetypal figures representing different participants in the East European communist system; yet many are amalgams of real figures, and others are based on historical personalities.

SIMON is based on the Russian poet Osip Mandelstam, who fell victim to the Stalinist purges in the late 1930s, and died probably in transit to the Soviet Gulag in 1938.

MARIA, Simon's wife in the play, is inspired by Mandelstam's wife Nadezhda. After her husband's arrest, she continued being persecuted by the Soviet authorities, often living in hiding and frequently changing her residence. She wrote an account of her life in Stalinist Russia entitled *Hope against Hope*. Several aspects of the play are lifted directly from her book.

ANNA, Simon's "mistress," is based on perhaps the greatest Russian poet of the twentieth century, Anna Akhmatova. Akhmatova belonged to the same group of poets as Osip Mandelstam, and her love affair with Mandelstam was well known. Like Mandelstam, she was severely persecuted by the Stalinist regime, but she managed to survive.

NOVAK is a typically Steigerwald-esque figure of the spineless opportunist. Written with an accent not retained in this translation, Novák is as commom a Czech name as Johnson in English. In the play Novak is a Švejk-like Czech opportunist. He is the quintessential "Czech little man" and his various re-incarnations as informer, torturer, and an "ordinary old man—salt of the earth whose legs are shot," clearly implicate each and every Czech audience member in the crimes of the past.

RUBEN is the sum of all Jewish refugees in the course of twentieth-century Europe.

MIXA, similar to Novak, is an archetypal product of communism. He is based on several Czech communist poets, who despite their often mediocre talent successfully maneuvered the various stages of communism, falling in and out of official grace by collaborating with the regime on one hand and testing the limits of freedom on the other.

VASKA and HELGA are realizations of the ubiquitous enforcers of totalitarian regimes in general and of Czech communism in particular. They represent the countless Marxist pseudo-intellectuals who attained respectable positions within the ruling intellectual elite, but who, under the mantle of intellectualism, brutally enforced the ideological purity of the regime.

The Plot

In its very basic form, the play traces the nightmarish journey of the Russian poet Simon and one of his poems across twentieth-century totalitarian Europe. Persecuted in Russia in the 1930s and unable to publish under his own name, Simon is approached by his friend, Mixa, a poet officially tolerated by the government and a Party faithful, who offers to publish Simon's poem under his own name. Simon refuses, is arrested, and vanishes in the Gulag. However, years later, at the behest of the Party, Mixa becomes something of a literary detective, whose work consists of discovering literary works that have been published under assumed names, tracing the texts' original officially forbidden writers, and punishing both the actual and the assumed authors. During that time, in a pile of confiscated forbidden manuscripts, Mixa discovers the same poem that Simon wouldn't let him publish under an assumed name years ago. Assuming that Simon is long dead, he decides to steal the poem and claim the authorship of it, thus re-launching his career as a major poet. Throughout the play, he is haunted by the re-appearing ghost of Simon, his wife Marie, and other historical ghosts of the past. Mixa undergoes a number of metamorphoses from sensitive poet to Party apparatchik to victim of Stalinist terror to rehabilitated communist and apologist for the regime to a posthumous symbol of the nation.

Places and Times

The eight scenes of *Sorrow, Sorrow, Fear, the Rope, and the Pit* take place in six different historical periods and four different geographical areas. The play's dream format allows time and space to transform with unprecedented fluency while still locating the action in a particular chronological framework.

The play opens (and frequently returns to) the front of the West German Embassy in Prague in late September 1989. At that time, more than two thousand East Germans packed the muddy compound of the embassy, and every day more than six hundred others continued to climb the fence in full view of the Czechoslovak guards. The East German exodus is generally considered one of the final nails in the coffin of East European communism. Less than two months later, the Berlin Wall came down and the Czech Velvet Revolution was in full swing. By January 1990 the Soviet Bloc had dissolved completely. The first scene of the play quickly transports us to Moscow in the 1930s. We are at the height of the first Stalinist purges, which targeted primarily intellectuals, artists, and professionals. Osip Mandelstam was arrested and disappeared in a Gulag at that time. Steigerwald uses Nadezhda Mandelstam's memoir to paint a picture of the period and to establish the major plot line of Mixa's offer to publish Simon's poems under his name.

The first scene eventually returns to Prague in the 1970s during the so-called normalization period, the time following the Czech communist reform movement known as the Prague Spring in 1968. The increased liberalization of Czechoslovakia, the opening of the borders to the West, and the general movement away from the Soviet Union was crushed by the invasion of Czechoslovakia by the armies of the Warsaw Pact in August 1968. The Soviets installed a puppet regime that quickly re-established communist orthodoxy, systematically quieted the opposition, and placated the population into passive resignation at best and active collaboration with the regime at worst. The 1970s are often called the darkest period of modern Czech history because of the levels of widespread resignation, complacency, cynicism, and an overall sense of bleakness.

Scene 2 returns to Prague in 1989 and Moscow in the 1930s, where Simon is arrested. The uneasy dream, however, also moves the characters to Hungary during WWII, where the eternal refugee Ruben is trying to organize an escape from a Jewish internment camp, and then to Czechoslovakia in the 1960s during the Thaw when, following the death of Stalin in 1956, the countries of Eastern Europe embarked on a mild liberalization of their regimes. They still insisted on the primacy of the communist ideology, but rehabilitated many of the victims of Stalinist terror.

Steigerwald's juxtaposition of German and Soviet tyrannies in the 1930s and 1940s respectively is illuminating; the enormous leaps he takes across historical periods offers unique insight into a network of violence and irrationality. We move from witnessing the absurd behavior of the victims of Stalinist terror, whose belief in communism remained unshaken in the 1960s despite the tortures they endured, to the even more absurd spectacle of "Germans fleeing from one German country to another German country" in 1989.

Scene 3 also takes place in Prague in 1989. Against the backdrop of the West German Embassy, we hear the legend of Simon's death in a Gulag. Scene 4 paints a stark picture of Czechoslovakia in the 1950s during yet another round of Stalinist purges. The Czech purges were primarily directed against the Communist Party members whose loyalty may have been in question or whose powers within the regime had become too dangerous for Stalin's protégés within the Czechoslovak Communist Party. Mixa, not unlike many Czech and Slovak communists during that period, is tortured but continues being loyal to the communist ideal, professing his love for the Party. The scene of Mixa's torture and blind faith is juxtaposed to a scene in Russia in the 1930s, where the victims of the previous Stalinist purges and their widows are roaming the landscape with nowhere to go.

Scene 5, the last set in Prague 1989, is one of complete disillusionment. Against the absurd backdrop of fleeing Germans, the characters are confused, angry, and struggling to make sense of the past. Historically, we are at the very end of communism—the Wall will come down in less than two months, the validity of the communist ideal will be rejected, and the long suffering that accompanied the march of communist progress will appear to have been in vain. The play could end here, but Steigerwald relentlessly forges ahead with his nightmarish vision. Scenes 6 and 7 bring us back to Berlin in the late 1950s and early 1960s at the time of the building of the Berlin Wall and to Czechoslovakia in the 1960s during the period of the Thaw. The anticipated fall of the Wall at the beginning of scene five contrasts starkly with the image of the refugees colliding with it almost thirty years earlier. The disillusionment accompanying the end of history in 1989 is set against the optimism and the ongoing belief in the communist ideal during the 1960s. The absurdity of history and the grotesque clinging to discredited beliefs, which are among the major themes of the play, seem to be coming full circle in those three scenes.

As if to remove any possibility of a happy ending, however, Steigerwald returns to the 1970s—the era of normalization mentioned above. Here the play ends in an angry diatribe by the spineless opportunist Novak delivered at the very height of the admittedly darkest and most desperate period of Czech history in the twentieth century. As a stark contrast, and perhaps as an Eastern European rebuke to Francis Fukuyama, Steigerwald seems to be placing the end of history there, rather than in 1989.

Steigerwald's tragic and infinitely bleak picture of the past, however, severely clashed with the feeling of optimism and the sense of new beginning in Czechoslovakia in 1991. The Prague production was received coldly by the critics and the audiences, whose sights were set forward immediately following the Velvet Revolution. Steigerwald's uncompromisingly honest look at history and his refusal to end the play on an optimistic note struck a wrong chord at that time. However, as the crimes of the previous regime became more and more evident, and as the evidence of willing collaboration with the communist regime by an unprecedented number of Czech citizens became public, Steigerwald's ultimate imperative of "No more!" has gained renewed urgency not only in the Czech Republic, but across the globe a well.

SORROW, SORROW, FEAR, THE ROPE, AND THE PIT

Karel Steigerwald

Translated by Štěpán Šimek and Roger Downey

CHARACTERS

SIMON—A man, who perished once somehow. They say he was a poet.

ANNA—A sick girl. She claims she loved Simon once. But she couldn't have known him. She lived in a different time.

MARIE—Simon's widow. Somehow she outlived him.

NOVAK—His legs are shot. An ordinary invalid. Salt of the earth.

RUBEN—An eccentric. It's whispered that he was the poet's brother. But it's probably not possible because he lived in another country, at another time, and unlike the poet, he was a Jew.

MIXA—A well-known poet, persecuted during the Cult of Personality; later rehabilitated. He hasn't gotten bitter. He fought for peace.

VASKA—An informer and scientist. They say he was Mixa's illegitimate son. It's probably a lie. But it has no bearing on the play anyhow.

HELGA—An emancipated woman but unfortunately an informer as well. Also an editor, professor, and engineer. Nobody knows why her left shoe pinches.

MIXOVA—Mixa's widow. If he died. If he didn't, just his wife. But it's quite certain he did die. We went to his funeral. He enjoyed it.

The play uses motifs from the fate of Osip Mandelstam, as described by Nadezhda Mandelstam in her book Hope Against Hope. *It also uses paraphrases of Osip Mandelstam's verses. Even the play's title is possibly a verse by the poet. One line quotes a poem of Anna Akhmatova. Some passages resemble motifs from Ilya Ehrenburg's memoirs presented in the book* People, Years, Life . . .

It seems we dream the plot of the play. Characters who speak and interact with each other couldn't possibly speak and interact with each other. They do it regardless. Be that as it may. We must believe it. We are lying in a coma, and at random the monsters of olden days creep into our dreams and demand their due. They all are cadavers. If we only could wake up. Good night and good day.

SCENE 1

SIMON *doesn't rush onto the stage; he enters tired; looks around.* NOVAK *who's been sitting on his suitcase a long time already, observes him with interest.*

SIMON: No foreign sky gave me shelter . . . (*Pauses, notices* NOVAK, *looks at him for a long while.*)

NOVAK (*pause*): Well, so . . . they're gone. You come running up too late, they're all gone.

SIMON: Who?

NOVAK: The ones waiting to see if the other ones would let 'em across. And they did. Hauling 'em off all night like cattle to the slaughterhouse. Me, I'm against it.

SIMON: I don't know what you're talking about.

NOVAK: How's that?

SIMON: Someone invited me. He must live near here.

NOVAK (*short laugh*): It's deserted here, I'm the only one here. All I want's a cold beer and my old lady's roast pork on the table. Yessir! C'mere.

SIMON: An older man. I haven't seen him for a long time.

NOVAK: I'm the district chairman. My old lady's dead, I'm on my own.

SIMON: Would you know what he wants with me?

NOVAK: Me, I been to Munich. Recently. For a day . . . To see for myself. Look around, understand? . . . You listening to me?

SIMON: Where am I?

NOVAK: Where d'you think? Right here in Prague, front of the West German Embassy. I been hanging out here, it's been a kick! I wanted to compare how it looks—in the West—I mean, because over there they got some things better'n we do and we got others. Jesus, did they show me! Let me tell you something, what we done to ourselves here, it's enough to make you sick. I don't need to watch my mouth no more. Plug your ears if you got a problem with it.

SIMON (*examines* NOVAK): Do we know each other?

NOVAK: I doubt it. Maybe from the district committee, I was well known, 'cause I used to have functions. Today I got shit . . . (*Pause.*) You don't mind me talking dirty?

SIMON: He asked me here and hasn't come . . .

NOVAK: So since I come back from Munich I been having doubts. Pissed off all the time. So tell me, have I been a sucker my whole damn life?

SIMON: Forgive me, I don't understand you at all. I mean, individual words I understand, but the sentences make no sense to me at all.

NOVAK: Oh, I know, I'm stupid. I got no schooling.

SIMON: Individual words I grasp.

NOVAK: I was a normal decent individual; I made sacrifices. And they fucked me over. You still don't mind: my talking dirty?

SIMON: Maybe you don't want to say anything.

NOVAK: They conned me, too. Lied to me. Lied to themselves, now that's the point.

SIMON: You don't want to say anything, but you're talking.

NOVAK: Like for example, you honestly believe we knew about those . . . camps . . . Other day, on Russian TV, I seen how they were digging skulls out of a field . . . 300,000 skulls, a little hole in the back of each one. That was overdoing it some, wouldn't you say? Supposedly in Ukraine somewheres. This I didn't know about! Stacking them in pyramids like melons in a field. I mean it was a field, but it wasn't melons in it.

SIMON: But why don't you want to talk to me? You're all alone here. Is it only the sound of your own voice you want to hear?

NOVAK: You got to agree it wasn't our fault, 'cause we didn't know about it. Know what I mean? Hell of a guy, that Stalin, wiped out 50 million of 'em, what they say now. Oh, yeah, they wrote that, in a Russian paper. Thank God I didn't know then. Why you keep looking back of you? Not even the ones shooting the others in the back of the neck knew. That's how regrettable and well planned it was.

SIMON: Maybe we're speaking two different languages.

NOVAK: My conscience is clear. After all, the basic idea was all right, if they hadn't gone and spoiled it . . . Still, the TV overdid it, they're all liars. And you know how I know? Because, 300,000? That's just a few too many. They went too far; screw the dirty fuckers, screw 'em up the ass. Are you starting to mind me talking dirty.

SIMON: Why are your hands shaking?

NOVAK: Because I'm so pissed. But other than that, I'm happy, basically, I laugh, I'm an optimist, I'm used to it. You don't talk a lot, do you? (*Gets up and shuffles off.*) I'm going to look and see if some new Germans have showed up. (*Shakes head.*) Germans . . . running from one German country . . . . right back into another German country. From a German country to a German country . . . They make me a laugh.

SIMON: What Germans? Running from what? (NOVAK *leaves.* SIMON *looks around again, insecure. And he calls after* NOVAK.) You haven't even told me where I am. Maybe I should have asked what year it is. You mentioned Stalin, that I understood. But what was it I didn't understand: Stalin . . . was? (*He awaits answer; silence.*) Or will be? (*Pause.*) Or is? And is what? A man? Where am I? When is this?

Only now he notices MIXA. *It's because* MIXA's *been standing by the portal and looked like a drape.*

MIXA: Simon, you came . . . I've been waiting since morning . . . (*Steps toward* SIMON, *offers his hand.* SIMON *doesn't move.*) It's been a long time.

SIMON: A long time.

MIXA: Everything's different now, you know: show-trials, traitors, Trotskyites, and Jews. Great days. But where's it all leading?

SIMON: Are the times better or worse?

MIXA: So what have you been up to all this while? (*Pause.*) Me, now, I keep a low profile. (*Pause.*) No, actually I don't, I know my way around. I always manage to con them in the end. (*Pause.*) Me, I like things modern. They'd kick you out of the Party if they could, but you've never been a member. It's rough these days . . .

SIMON: You good Party types keep rising through the ranks. Because every day someone higher disappears and someone else moves up and takes his place. They're cutting you off from above.

MIXA: That's right. Sometimes better ones replace worse ones, true, but sometimes the cut-off ones were pretty bad already. We're all candidates for death.

SIMON: But you don't think about it, do you?

MIXA: Not in the daytime. We're like the old Greeks—the one who disappears is already forgotten. We don't like the dead. We've abolished funerals.

SIMON: You've got that real bandit charm. You started off a brown-eyed street kid.

MIXA (*laughs, he likes the bandit charm*): Neatly put. I lived through famine as a kid, you know; that's why I've always longed for stability, money enough, trust in our leaders.

SIMON: Maybe they'll finally leave us all in peace. It's time. There are enough dead already.

MIXA (*astonished*): Us yes, we'll have peace, but what about you? They wouldn't let you publish; maybe they won't let you live, either.

SIMON: Some night I'll rise from my bed, stretch out my arms and nod to Marie. Come, I'll tell her, come, it's time. And point to the open window.

MIXA (*observes him with great admiration*): Beautifully put. You're a true poet. (*Pause.*) "Sorrow, sorrow, fear, the rope, and the pit . . ." What a beautiful line . . . . (*He observes* SIMON.)

SIMON: That's a line . . . from the Bible.

MIXA: I heard it was out of one of your poems. (*Pause.*) I'll make you an offer. Let me put my name on them; they'll get published, people will read them. Royalties to you, of course.

SIMON: No. That wouldn't be possible.

MIXA: It's for your own good. You get the money, and your poems are free to fly.

SIMON: How can you know about my poems. Nobody knows them!

MIXA: If you only knew . . . (*Waves his hand.*) If I could only speak . . . You're naive. You won't change anything. And don't go off thinking we've got it so bad here. Things could be a lot worse. We've got a castle here, full of rooms, in every room a poet living with his children. Those children grow up and turn poet, too. Not so bad, huh. So can I publish your poems?

NOVAK (*returning*): Gone, of course. And who stays? Me and the other idiots. If just once my old lady don't get the pork on the table, if one dark day the beer should run dry . . . they'll be hearing from me.

SIMON (*leaving*): No.

MIXA: You're hurting yourself, it's not about you, it's about your poems, letting them fly away from the nest.

SIMON: You're a fool.

NOVAK: Pork, beer, one dark day, I say to myself. Pork I got, beer I got, the old lady died on me. Go on, plan a future!

SIMON: Better not to call me anymore. Don't invite me, don't look around for me. It could do you harm. (*Exits.*)

MIXA *waves after him, and at the same time tries to prevent* NOVAK *from seeing* SIMON. *He obstructs his view.*

NOVAK: Oh, so it was you he was looking for? Seemed a little . . . bzzz.

MIXA: Sleepwalking fool. He wasn't looking for anyone, he didn't even know where he was.

NOVAK (*bursts into laughter*): As if we wouldn't know who we are, where we are, and why we are: I got them papers that were giving us trouble, chief. (*Hands* MIXA *a bundle of papers.*) I'm looking forward to seeing how you nail the one who wrote them! Even though nobody's signed his name on 'em.

MIXA: Let's see. (*Grabs the papers.*)

NOVAK: I admire how you sniff out these poets and uncover them. They haven't got a chance . . . poor little assholes . . .

MIXA (*reading*): "Sorrow, sorrow, fear, the rope, and the pit . . . "

NOVAK: I know my way round office work 'cause I used to have functions, but I got no experience with this poetry stuff. Now you're a first-rate poet, that's why you got this job. But how do you uncover 'em, these undercover authors?

MIXA: Fear, the rope, and the pit . . . magnificent line . . .

NOVAK: No name on it, so it's none of our business. Let's toss it out. I'm always glad when there's less work to do, though I'm glad to have more work, 'cause working makes me glad. You follow me?

MIXA: I'll get rid of these myself, you can cross them off the register, and there's no call to go talking about it everywhere, either. Our work's not an appropriate subject for conversation . . . though it's nothing to be ashamed of: they told you that, didn't they?

NOVAK: Yeah, that's exactly what they told me. Then they pointed out the coat rack, my locker, my key, and how to get to the cafeteria.

MIXA: So why are you frowning? Aren't you satisfied?

NOVAK: I am, 'cause I'm used to being satisfied, but I still can't get it out of my head, how they broke the pipe to my house digging up the street outside, and I still can't get anyone to fix it. All right, I'm just a tool, I understand, the individual's not important, but I still don't have no water. And my legs are getting bad, I can't hardly walk on them. I'm not criticizing, I just don't have water. I don't want nothing special, even if I did have functions once. A guy in my building goes for my groceries, and his girl friend helps with the water, but all they are's a couple of young punks. Our own people don't help, see, but these punks do. What's that you're reading there?

MIXA: Some "poetry stuff."

NOVAK: Good stuff? Popular? Hot stuff, maybe?

MIXA: File the rest of those people with the pending cases and you can take off for home.

NOVAK: Don't read it myself. 'Less it's hot stuff. (*Pause.*)

MIXA (*reading*): Uh-huh, sure.

NOVAK: I got all them folks filed yesterday already. Little Miss drinking water, she goes round all painted up. Maybe she ain't pretty to him if she ain't painted up. I like beauty, what you call your natural beauty. I'm past all that now. You know Vobornikova, she got so drunk on a department retreat once, she went and broke her arm.

MIXA: Sorrow, sorrow, fear, the rope, and the pit.

NOVAK: How's that? (*Sees* MIXA *reading, smiles sympathetically. He's a decent Joe.*) I've had my fun . . . One night Vobornikova, she was in Administration, she wound up in some woods out toward Slivice, coming back from celebrating International Women's Day, rolled down a hill and through the roof of a pig-sty. Folks come running out with an ax, expecting a burglar, and what do they see, all covered with blood, but little Vobornikova from the Admin Department. Only it wasn't blood, see, it was only red wine. So they haul her right away back to her husband in Zbraslav, totally stoned: you think he was laughing? Dummy. (*Pause.*) I read somewheres that poets go in a lot for suicide when they're young. (*Pause.*) So, you ever think of suicide? Since you're a poet too? Though a little older now, huh . . .

MIXA: Go on home, I don't need you any more today.

NOVAK: I don't see where the fun comes in (*Pause.*) committing suicide. (*Pause.*) It's against the word of God. But then, God's on his way out too, isn't he? (*Pause.*) Can I say something? They put me in here, so I do it. Just the same. (*Pause.*) I don't see who needs this, catching people who put their names on other people's stupid books. The one you get the goods on, he's got problems, true, but otherwise it's all just a waste. That's what I wanted to say, just so it was clear. (*Pause.*) Because I'm a straightforward guy. (*Pause.*) So, I'm going now. (*Pause.*) Good night. And take it easy; you're not as young as you used to be, for a poet you're already pretty old. (*Pause.*) So, tomorrow . . . (*Leaves;* MIXA *doesn't pay attention; reads.*)

SCENE 2

ANNA *and* SIMON *burst onto the stage, exhausted.* ANNA *collapses from exhaustion.* SIMON *lifts her, they stumble on with their baggage.* NOVAK, *who's been sitting on his suitcase for a long while, observes them with interest.*

ANNA: My God, free at last . . .

NOVAK *is pleased.*

SIMON: I was afraid they were going to shoot.

NOVAK (*only now do they see him*): They won't shoot; they won't let 'em. You got yourselves a nice little hideaway here, we're protected by the wall but we can see just fine; we could be the first ones out of here, I bet. (*Looking the new arrivals over.*) As for freedom, that's still a long ways off.

ANNA: Are they sending cars for us?

NOVAK: Maybe. Trains, maybe. People pouring in from all sides. The first ones in just walked through the gate, they're in the clear now. Later on they locked it.

ANNA: Here comes another one. With a suitcase.

NOVAK: Smart guy. Walking along like a Sunday stroller, now boom! Onto the fence.

SIMON: They've got him by the legs. Pulling him back . . .

NOVAK: And our people got him by the arms. Same thing been going on since sun-up.

ANNA: What if they tear him to pieces!

NOVAK: They won't tear him to pieces; although he's not looking so hot: he's an old one. Most of 'em here are young ones. Like you.

ANNA: What if they just leave us here?

NOVAK: They can't, there's too many of us. I don't give a fart about that freedom of yours, what I want's some peace and quiet. But something in my head keeps hurting, some kind of discomfort, disturbance, I don't know. So I says to myself, go on, get away. And I took this bag and here I am. (*Pause.*) There, see, he got in, got loose from them.

SIMON: What if they do leave us here? We'll be standing in the street, in the winter, in the dark, till we die . . .

ANNA: Forsaken, like fools . . .

SIMON: For a thousand years . . .

NOVAK: You got yourselves a nice little hideaway here, here we're right on the border. Why, little while back the German ambassador drove by, seen him with my own eyes. You're looking pale, Miss. They brought tea round earlier, least if it wasn't the ambassador it was someone just like him. I'm here alone. My old lady's dead.

RUBEN (*enters, looks at* ANNA *and* SIMON *suspiciously*): Are you new here?

NOVAK: Still out of breath. Just nerves, probably, they didn't know if they were going to make it. Some don't. Grab 'em, ship 'em back to the Vaterland. It's tragic, that's what it is, I never would have believed I'd ever run away like this. I always believed in the government.

RUBEN: Not me. (*Coldly, formally.*) We should form up in groups of thirty each.

SIMON: Why? Where's there to go? Where and why? (*He hugs* ANNA, *who starts crying. He leads* ANNA *off.* NOVAK *calls after them.*)

NOVAK: There's a fountain in the square, splash some water on her face. She's crying, you're crying. The government's done for. Why? Why? Nothing but why.

RUBEN: To be organized when they start interviewing us. (*Leaving, stops, examines* NOVAK.) Don't cry, all this is normal. I've been running all my life. Just now the East German ambassador drove by . . . Not that he's the ambassador of anything. (*Leaves.*)

NOVAK (*probably observing a distant fence*): Groups . . . I'm no fool. When the busses roll up I'll be first in line. My wife didn't live to see all this. She believed in the government, like me. (*Looks out.*) That's quite a crowd there; could be they're passing out cigarettes. Tell the truth, why keep lying. I'm alone. My wife's alive, she run off on me. (*He leaves.*)

MARIE *and* SIMON *enter, tired, anciently ragged, carrying various unidentifiable bags. They aren't of our time, that's for sure.* SIMON's *gazing at the ground, he looks like a sleepwalking idiot.* MARIE *takes care of him.* ANNA *appears on the other side, contemplates them as if they were a pair of icons, stops crying, goes to* SIMON, *strokes him.*

ANNA: Are you praying the cup be allowed to pass you by?

SIMON (*doesn't respond*): I don't understand all this. Where are we?

ANNA (*strokes* SIMON *again*): How humiliating . . . to have to beg . . . for food . . .

MARIE: But it's not our fault the world's the way it is . . .

MIXA (*enters and opens his arms with joy*): Here you are, I've been looking for you, longing for you, I love you, Simon, my friend . . . (*Tries to embrace SIMON, who evades him;* MIXA *won't be put off.*) Why humiliating? That's the way they make atonement . . . we know what for. One egg, that's all, and the account's settled.

RUBEN (*enters and examines all present in a hurry*): Tell me, is there a guard here; that Hungarian guard, is he a guard here?

SIMON: Why Hungarian? Am I imagining all of you? Anna, are you a dream? Is this Russia?

He only now notices VASKA, *since in his immobility and in the dark of the corner he looks like a drape.* RUBEN *finds him for us.* VASKA *yawns and looks at his wrist watch. He emits a brief moo.* SIMON *notices* RUBEN, *extends his hands to him, but* RUBEN *doesn't see him, he is leaving.* SIMON *gets up and follows him.* MIXA *observes his departure with apprehension. But* RUBEN *and* SIMON *don't leave. They gaze at each other, into each other's eyes. They're trying to recall something.*

SIMON: I don't know where I am. What's happened to my brain?

MIXA: Where'd he go? Is he coming back soon? Good evening; I almost forgot to say hello. The times are such a person almost forgets to say hello.

ANNA: What do you want? You'd be happier at home.

SIMON (*to* RUBEN): Anna, am I dreaming you? Am I raving? I'm seeing things that can't possibly be.

MIXA: I happened to be passing. Came to sit and reminisce. Ask the poet if he maybe hasn't written something new. Someone'll give him an egg, and he'll come back, right? Where's there to go, this time of night?

ANNA *starts crying.* MARIE *embraces her.* RUBEN *turns away from* SIMON. *He probably hasn't recalled anything.*

RUBEN: So you're those two Hungarian guards . . . (*He only now sees* HELGA. *She looks like* VASKA; *blends into her background. Sleeps.*) And I'm this Hungarian

Jew. If this guard here was German I'd be finished . . . no way out.

SIMON: We're in Hungary?

ANNA: We're free!

RUBEN (*goes to* ANNA, *kneels down, whispers*): They corralled us in the gymnasium, but they don't watch the back. That's our chance.

SIMON: We're in a gymnasium? I thought we were in a street in front of an Embassy.

MIXA: It's raining, where would he go? It's dark.

ANNA: It's late. They'll arrest him.

MARIE (*raises her head*): When they're standing at the door, I'll let them in. I have no choice. They'll say, good evening. Or they'll say, "Is he home? Home with you?"

ANNA: They won't say a thing. With incredible efficiency they'll stride to the kitchen. Simon will just smile and say, "Is it me you came for?" "Your papers," they'll say.

Pause.

MIXA (*laughs briefly*): Why would they arrest him. Women—always seeing danger everywhere.

RUBEN (*enters and examines* VASKA *and* HELGA): Do you know where they'll take us? The World War's almost over and we don't even know where they'll take us after Hungary.

SIMON: I am not in Hungary, I am in Prague! The war ended long ago! (*He despairs.*)

MARIE: It hasn't started yet. I'm deep in Russia: a thousand miles deep. No foreign sky gave me shelter. No foreign land left me free. I had to watch as it unfolded. And my tormented nation watched with me.

RUBEN: Wouldn't want to let them catch me. We're everywhere, here and there, then and now. So, do you know where they'll bring us? (*Pause.*) I know.

MIXA: Some kind soul will give Simon an egg and he'll come back. You shouldn't let him wander round loose like that at night . . . God knows where . . . or did he say where he was going?

MARIE: Herzen Street, number 35. Moscow. It's midnight already and it's raining.

ANNA: Prague, Nerudova Street, it's not raining. I came by train, came on foot.

RUBEN: They say we're waiting for a train. They say they're taking us to Poland. Don't you know why? (*Pause.*) I do.

ANNA: Babel, the wise Isaac Babel, a tiny, almost undetectable hole in his head. A tiny opening. Who did that to him? (*To* MIXA.) Did they send you?

MIXA: What do you mean, send? Who? I just came around. It's dark out. A hundred below. We mustn't suspect each other this way.

MARIE: Sorrow, sorrow, fear, the rope, and the pit . . .

ANNA: Don't! Never say those words out loud!

MIXA: He mustn't go writing such things down, for God's sake!

RUBEN: Are there guards in back behind the shed? I wouldn't want to go fall right into their hands. I've been on the run before, and I'll be on the run again. One time I was running across Romania on a bootleg German passport with my picture glued into it. This century it's the only way to travel.

MIXA: Across Romania! What a crazy way to go, chief!

RUBEN: They interrogated me in their office at the Bucharest airport. They didn't like the looks of me: I couldn't speak German, but then, they couldn't either. They went at me in Romanian about who I was. Gerhard Wagner, it said on the passport. Only tucked into my shorts I had my high-school diploma, birth certificate, driver's license, all that, so's not to have no identity on the other side. Six hours they questioned me and through the six hours, I slid my papers inch by inch down my trousers and under the carpet. Finally they believed me, and I flew to Vienna, and the papers stayed under the rug.

MIXA (*laughs*): You sure took them in. Imagine their faces when someone got around to rolling up that rug.

RUBEN: I wasn't laughing, I saw nothing to laugh about.

SIMON: We're in Romania?

SIMON *slowly exits, and all the others watch his exit. Pause.*

MIXA: Sure, it was tragic but it makes a great story. Why try not to laugh if it's worth laughing at?

SIMON (*enters*): I managed to get an egg. In times like these. People are frightened and still they share the last thing they have.

MIXA: Sorrow, sorrow, fear, the rope, and the pit . . . Why do you write lines like that? They could cost you your life!

SIMON: It's possible. We can be confident, our country rates poetry higher than anything, higher than life. Poetry has unusual weight for us. They're willing to kill for it.

MARIE: And sensible people ask, "Why write such verses," and get no answer. Is there a sensible answer?

SIMON: Anna, I am not in Romania, am I?

RUBEN (*circles around* HELGA): You say there's no Germans there. I'd rather have a look for myself. (*Goes to* MIXA.) The one with the poems there, that's my brother. He's a poet. He's not a Jew, but he's still my brother. Or the other way around, he's a Jew and I'm not. That could be. He's probably Russian. My brother and I are different nationalities. I admit that doesn't quite add up, but where do things add up? You're not in Romania, you're in Prague. (*Turns to* HELGA.) I find myself in need of some identity papers, you know of any papers like that? (HELGA *shrugs, so he goes to* VASKA, *whispers in his ear.*) Now, you must have exceptionally good papers, I don't imagine they'd give a guard lousy papers. That's the kind of papers a Jew like me needs, for my dad. He's inside, in the gym. And our three uncles, cousins, aunts, brothers- and sisters-in-law, fiancés, our whole huge family. We've never all been together in our lives until now. I know you won't have papers for everybody. I imagine you only have papers for one. My brother hasn't had any papers for years, they wouldn't give him any. He's a poet. (*Leaves, comes back.*) He lives in another country . . . (*Leaves, doesn't return.*)

SIMON (*to* ANNA): I don't know any of these people. I don't understand what they're saying. I don't know where we are.

NOVAK (*returning importantly*): There are new people here already, pouring in by train, by car, on foot, it's crammed full all the way from the Embassy to the streetcar tracks. Some even flew in.

MIXA: What do you mean, flew in? Does man have wings?

NOVAK: Well, that I can't say, if man has wings or not. They flew in through the air, they sensed a crack so they came pushing through, like minnows, to freedom.

SIMON: The ambassador we saw, he was real. We saw him, didn't we? We're not in Romania. (*Shakes* ANNA.)

ANNA: Yes, he was real.

NOVAK: It's not freedom I need. What I need is to shake off this discomfort of mine.

SIMON: And this street, it does exist. Thousands of people are standing here and hoping.

ANNA: This street is a dream.

VASKA *and* HELGA *revive. They sniff out the space, pull out their pistols, and threaten the others who automatically raise their arms and automatically obey, so the two don't need to give any orders. It all happens calmly, like a dream. The two empty some bags of documents on the floor, rummage through them, and search some of the others.*

ANNA: See? They didn't say hello.

HELGA: Are you registered here?

SIMON: So you finally came, after all. (*Sits down, apathetic.*)

ANNA: They came on your heels, and you didn't hear them.

VASKA: We came quietly, on tip-toe. (*He laughs.*) Do you have papers?

SIMON *gives them to him without a word.* HELGA *peeps over* VASKA's *shoulder into the documents.*

HELGA: Isn't it weird? One of these days people will sneer at you, saying, "Why on earth did you confess to every last little thing that came into our heads?"

MIXA: I can vouch for that. That's how we end up.

VASKA: "Why did you keep on confessing," they'll ask you. (*Shakes head with surprise*.)

ANNA: The tiny opening in the wise Babel's skull.

SIMON: Is this an arrest? But who's being arrested? Who are these people? I don't know them . . .

HELGA (*notices* MIXA): You run along home.

MIXA *gets up to go*, ANNA *stops him*.

ANNA: Why didn't they check your papers? Why you exactly?

SIMON: A suspicious person would say Mixa's been keeping an eye on me, so I don't burn any papers when the doorbell rings at night. And they didn't ring, did they? But let's not suspect each other.

MIXA (*returns*): And let's not even think things like that. You want to know who I am? They let me out in December, after five years. They gave me a little piece of paper, "no objections on national security grounds." Rehabilitated. I was lucky. I went straight home. My family didn't know yet. They knew I'd been executed. We spent that Christmas with justice smiling down on us. After New Year's I took the bus into Prague to see my old boss Inneman. "Comrades, I've been rehabilitated, take me back into the Party." And they took me. They actually forgave me for doing time in prison without being guilty.

HELGA: So: "Was it fun?" inquired Inemann.

VASKA: "Tell us. Comrade Commissar enjoys hearing funny stories from there," said Inemann.

MIXA: I told how in the camp I fell in the mud. Inemann nodded and said, "Comrade Commissar will laugh at that one. Comrade Commissar will like that." So I became Rector of the university, going to peace conferences fighting for peace and the black past passed into the past. That's how I was then; no one has the right to keep on asking why we confessed to anything that came into their heads!

VASKA: Fine, Rector, fine.

HELGA: You amused us.

VASKA (*about to hit* MIXA, *who runs away*): And now it's beddy-byes!

RUBEN (*to* SIMON): Why don't you defend yourself? Why not run away? I told my father, "We have papers, off we go." He refused. "You never know," he said. "We've only got the one set of papers," he said. "Do you know where they'll send us," I said. "I know," he said and went on sitting. "It's destiny," he said. "Well, what if it's destiny for us to get away," I said. Nothing. So I went alone. In terrible pain I walk through the gate, the Hungarians didn't check, the year's 1944, and I realize my father's already dead. And my relations with him. All of them. Six million relations and they all waited for it. In Romania I had too many papers, and here I had too few. Just the one set.

SIMON: Where did you get them?

RUBEN: Bought them.

SIMON: What with?

RUBEN: What with? What with? What do you think with? With a gold watch. I didn't wait for them to load us onto wagons and haul us away.

SIMON: We're waiting for them to load us onto wagons and haul us away? From Germany to Germany? But we're not Germans, you know. We're fools.

RUBEN: Sometimes it's bad if they haul you away, and sometimes it's bad if they don't.

SIMON: Was it your father's watch?

RUBEN: I said to him, you have a watch, there's a Hungarian guard outside who'll trade it for papers and you can get away.

SIMON: It was you who got away!

RUBEN: What was I supposed to do when he didn't want to? How long do we have to talk about this situation?

ANNA: Mixa predicted that they'd give you an egg. How did he know?

HELGA (*notices the bag* MARIE *packed for* SIMON): How do you think he knew? Why did you pack so much for him?

VASKA: So many things?

HELGA: Well, why?

SIMON: Well, why do you think?

VASKA *and* HELGA *take the bags they chose and lead* SIMON *off. The rest are frozen.*

ANNA: Simon, aren't you at least going to eat the egg?

SIMON: Gumilyov told me once, "I envy you: you'll die in a attic. When they were going to hang Sacco and Vanzetti, I was organizing a campaign to rescue them. I went to the priests to get them to protest the execution. They said they were willing if I'd promise to organize a protest if something similar happened to the priests. I had to admit then I was defeated."

VASKA, HELGA, *and* SIMON *exit.*

MARIE: They took him away and I'm waiting here for a different hour to strike. Why?

ANNA: We're waiting till we can go into the street without being noticed.

MARIE: Into the street? Where to? Why? To whom?

ANNA: We must look like two drowned women.

SCENE 3

MIXA *and* MIXOVA *burst onto the stage, exhausted.* MIXOVA *collapses from exhaustion.* MIXA *lifts her, they stumble on with their baggage.* NOVAK, *who's been sitting on his suitcase for a long while, observes them with interest.*

MIXOVA: My God, where will this end? You were a member of the Central Committee, weren't you?

MIXA: Look at all those people . . . all running away.

MIXOVA: They used to drink your health and now they'd as soon shoot you down as look at you.

NOVAK (*only now noticed by the others*): They won't shoot, too many people on the run for that. (*Goes to* MIXA, *looks him in the face from close up.*) I'm not running, I'm just here to watch. I'm enjoying myself, it's a lot of fun. A little while back I saw the Ambassador, he was shitting in his pants, too. People from all over crowding into his country, that's a laugh and a half. My name's Novak, I was on the County Trade Union Council years back. I didn't get no higher 'cause once they managed to conquer space they shoved us workers out, stuck in Doctors and Professors and Instructors everywhere, and now they got people running off wholesale. Not that I give a shit, I pull up to the table with my belly growling and holler at my old lady, "Bring on the pork," flush it down with a beer. 'Scuse my dirty mouth.

RUBEN (*enters and examines* MIXA *with suspicion*): Are you new here?

NOVAK: Still out of breath from nervous exhaustion, whether they ought to hit the road or not. They're the ones who made this mess, now they're running away from the mess they made. I get a kick out of that. (*Takes a full shopping bag from* RUBEN.) And thanks for doing the shopping. I heard about your brother, what all happened to him. (*He consoles* RUBEN.) Things were awful back then. You can pick them apple off the tree by the back fence, my legs are shot, I don't pick apples no more, give 'em to the kids.

RUBEN: I don't have kids.

MIXOVA: Isn't it strange, why, my husband and I don't have children either. We don't know why.

NOVAK: I saw a murder once, young feller. (*Elbows* RUBEN, *and holds forth to him.*) Shoe salesman, got to arguing with a bus driver in the street. Killed him dead; completely pointless. Your brother was against the government, wasn't he. There was some point to him dying, not this other one. One fine day a telegram come, says your brother had a heart attack. Thanks again for the shopping, you been a big help. I can't make it to the store anymore, my legs are shot. Your brother, he's been rehabilitated.

MIXA: That's great! Congratulations. And is the judge smiling too?

MIXOVA: Why not? Everyone's happy if they're let do the right thing.

RUBEN: I went in my brother's place. In his name so to speak, him being dead. The trial was a waste of time. The judge kicked us out, trampled on the affidavits, tore them to pieces, threw them out the window into the street. He beat up the stenographer, drank the ink, broke a window, went home. Seems rehabilitation's not the thing any more. We stood outside the courthouse smiling and happy. That's how I see justice.

NOVAK: Don't I know it! Years back I used to be on the County Trade Union Council. Even after I retired I gave State Security the benefit of my experience. I haven't got bitter, I just don't give a shit. I talk dirty 'cause I'm pissed off, even though I'm optimistic.

ANNA *enters carrying a bag which* SIMON *was arrested with; she's crying.*

ANNA: They killed him!

MIXA: No they didn't. He just died.

NOVAK: Just as well; otherwise he'd've had to go on living.

MIXOVA: What a lot of nonsense. He's still alive. He's sitting in front of a cabin somewhere in the north, in the woods, cooking soup. He walks in the forest, chewing a piece of bark. (*To* NOVAK.) You're that clerk. I mean that person who was assigned to my husband!

NOVAK: My name is Novak, and I get a supplementary pension because I served past retirement.

MIXA: Finally, you're here. Can we get started now?

NOVAK: I got a copy of the telegram. It was his heart that killed him.

MIXA: He's alive, it's obvious. They saw him in the woods. They talked to him. He disappeared in the underbrush, he's shy.

MIXOVA: That's very, very interesting.

MIXA: Everything's a mess. They let a dead man out of a camp, and send comic telegrams about a live one. In this office alone there are thirty people I can't find.

NOVAK: I didn't think that telegram was funny. After all, dead's dead.

MIXA: They saw him in the forest near Stettin.

MIXOVA: Further north; Kaliningrad. In Finland, among the glaciers. Up where the legends breed.

MIXA: Those people are missing from my files and God knows where they are. Mess everywhere you look. Yesterday I went fishing, they weren't biting. (*Snaps at* NOVAK, *who's been taking notes*.) That's off the record.

NOVAK: In the forest near Stettin? Interesting. I got those people here in my bag, those thirty. I had 'em stuffed in there back under your predecessor already.

MARIE *enters carrying the bag* SIMON *was arrested with. She's crying.*

MARIE: A man named Kazan stayed with me. Three months I hid him. According to his information Simon died in a typhus epidemic, in a camp near Irkutsk. They were still short of uniforms, so he died in his own clothes. The worst freeze didn't come till after he died, Kazan said, so he didn't suffer much.

ANNA (*embraces and consoles* MARIE): That was when Bertrand Russell visited our country, but professional humanitarians aren't interested in individuals, only humanity as a whole. Russell's name didn't give us hope; nothing did. Russell praised humanitarianism in generalities. Smoke was rising from the camps but it didn't get up his nose.

MIXA: In the interest of fairness I have to admit that when Russell did come, his intervention seems to have eased conditions for lexicographers.

ANNA (*to* NOVAK, *who is frightened by the word*): Lexicographers are just people who put together dictionaries

MIXA: They weren't putting dictionaries together in the camps.

NOVAK (*agitated*): See, they were there. All thirty of 'em. (*Shakes papers out of suitcase and looks at them in wonder.* MIXA *takes one of the papers and absorbedly scrutinizes it.*)

MIXA: Sorrow, sorrow, fear, the rope, and the pit.
(*Browsing.*)

"Cruder than the songs students sing,
Far coarser than a Party cell

I teach the hangmen how to twitter
Even if they still can't spell."

Somebody must have written that.

NOVAK: Who?

MIXA: That's just what we have to find out, man. That's our assignment. Who wrote it, and who put his name to it instead.

NOVAK: But there's the name of the writer, right there.

MIXA: Don't be naive; as if anyone would sign it. And if somebody signed it, they signed it with an alias. They're foxy. Pass me those thirty people so I can file them, otherwise I'll never get clear of this mess. Dammit, you've got thirty-one of them here!

NOVAK (*studies the document and wonders*): Well, well, one too many. Should we . . . throw it away?

MIXA: We should . . . let's see . . . who knows (*Compares different documents.*) . . . he's not on this list. Some kind of physicist? Wad it up and toss it in the garbage so it doesn't make trouble for us.

MIXA *buries himself in studying the document which caught his attention.* NOVAK *waits devotedly for* MIXA *to finish reading.*

MARIE: Kazan's story was confirmed ten years later by someone called Chaim. I met him too. The typhus is right, and the story about the clothing is also correct.

ANNA: But Chaim said he was still alive when the ice broke in spring and transports to the island started.

MARIE: Kazan said he died on the boat.

ANNA: That part was wrong. He went on living. I heard they blew up the ship so they wouldn't have to feed the prisoners when the freeze came. Not true. Somebody named Marek saw him with his own eyes still on the island. Only he wasn't sure it was him. Sitting by a campfire reciting Petrarch. That sounds right. He loved Petrarch.

MARIE: Years later I heard a different story from the islands: people came into his barracks, real hard-core criminals, shouting "Poet!"

ANNA: Did they frighten him?

MARIE: Yes. But they'd come because there was a poet in their barracks too, dying. We don't know who, though. He visited this poet dying in his bunk; the poet was already delirious but he came to again and they talked all night about Petrarch. Towards morning the dying poet died. The tough ones stood all night in front of the barracks, silent, waiting. That's how it was. Unfortunately I haven't learned when and where it happened. People forgot the poets' names, and the names of the witnesses too. Petrarch is the only piece of evidence.

ANNA: I heard he escaped. They didn't want to admit a failure, so they declared him dead.

MARIE: In that case he made it to Kaliningrad. Or to Finland? Sometimes people can walk a thousand miles in the frost.

ANNA: But his clothes were left in the camp. Coat, hat, pants, and shoes. Did he run off naked? Kazan said it was 85 below then. (*Pause.*) Or he borrowed clothes from a peasant, that's how it was. He bought a whole outfit. He traded bread for a janitor's clothes. Chaim couldn't remember the janitor's name. It was in Khabarovsk.

MARIE: That's impossible. No one in the world owns two sets of clothes. The one who'd give clothes to a person without clothes would freeze to death himself.

ANNA: No! At 3:27, on a Friday, he scratched on a forest ranger's frosted-up window. He sold him the clothes that had belonged to an uncle who died in that incident with the mining engineers. Then he went off through the icy solitude in an unknown direction, brave and clothed. That's how it happened. All of us heard about the incident with the mining engineers who were taken in a hurry, without their clothes.

MIXA *carefully folds the document he was studying and puts it in his pocket.*

MIXA: Well, he certainly left behind some wonderful poems. He's immortal now, but back then some were of the opinion he was mortal. This is all changing. We don't ever mark time, we move forward. I already admired his poems, luckily they survived. I can take some credit for that, some, I don't mean to stress it.

NOVAK: After the rehabilitations, the papers said he died.

MIXA: Weak heart, advanced age.

MIXOVA: Such a strong heart yet weak at the same time, I don't understand that.

MIXA: He died young, it's the poet's lot. We were more than friends. (*He goes to* MARIE, *strokes her*.) That's why he entrusted his poems to me. I kept them safe in hiding places in the crevices of memory, in the country with a farmer.

NOVAK (*laughs*): They could have found them on you and . . . (*Makes a face and indicates a cut throat*.)

MIXA: I didn't matter, the poems did. I was able to publish some of them. Understandably, I had to use my name; logically, at the time, I couldn't use his. (*He explains to* MARIE.) But they are his poems, not mine.

NOVAK: Such strange tales, and it's us who create them. (RUBEN *attracts his attention*.) Say there, aren't you the thirty-first we have one too many of? That's right, it's him. Or maybe not? (*He roots around where he threw the wad of paper a while ago*.)

MIXA: Be quiet, Novak, what's over is over, time's not some kind of endless chain on our legs, let's not look backward. What's there to see. Just take him out of the garbage and file him the usual way.

NOVAK: What we're actually doing with these ideas of ours is providing first-hand real-life experience for writers so they'll have something to write about . . . I can't believe that.

MIXA: I think you're an idiot.

NOVAK: They should be grateful to us! Like about those camps. People like reading about them nowadays. Have a nice cry about 'em. And who invented 'em? Us! They write 'em up and get their names in the paper, and nobody knows a damn thing about us.

MIXA: Be glad they don't. Who's next?

NOVAK: Some guy called Chaim. Mental case. Liar. Goes by the name of Kazan sometimes. We got him out in the cage in the courtyard. Calling himself Marek now. Says he's a physicist.

MIXA: Let's have a look at him. (*He daydreams*.) I often went to Paris. In the time of the Thaw, right after Stalin's death. People were breathing deep, you wouldn't understand it.

NOVAK: I mourned for Stalin. He was a smart guy. Now they're calling him a murderer. Does that make sense? We committed all those murders in his name. Would we have done something like that for a murderer?

MIXA (*not listening*): I talked to Sartre. Hopes were high, peace conferences everywhere. Did you take the keys for the cage so we don't need to come back? In the streets people were smiling uneasily. "Will there be war?" Joliot-Curie looked out the window in that way he had. "Will they stand up for peace?" ordinary Belgians asked. (*Leaves, calls from off.*) The lock's all rusty, how long's this guy been squatting here?

NOVAK: He was in a camp for twenty-five years, then they rehabilitated him, all is forgiven, that's all been abolished. And he's got it in his head he was in a camp twenty-five years, so they passed him on to us. He's innocent but sick. I keep asking him all the time, "What's illness and what's guilt?" (*Leaves after* MIXA *and calls.*)   And don't yank on the lock, he's not locked in. The lock doesn't work anymore either . . . (*Exits.*)

MARIE: The camps lived on legends. No one can imagine the terrible crowding in the overfilled barracks, where a corpse with a tag on its foot lies next to the living. No one saw him dead, only he himself and the dead, no one washed his body, no one laid him in a grave. The feverish raving of the martyrs of the camps knows no time. I know one thing, he died somewhere. Before death he lay on a bunk somewhere. He was still alive when I thought him dead already. Others knew even less of the fate of their dear ones.

ANNA: My case was never closed, and it never will be . . . Those are his last verses. Nobody knows them, but the wind preserved them, the sky preserved them, the waters preserved them, and time brought them to our ears.

MARIE: We must look like two drowned women . . .

SCENE 4

NOVAK *sits laughing on the suitcase.* VASKA *and* HELGA *bring food, a kind of improvised picnic.*

NOVAK: Did you notice him, our poet?

He roots in the suitcases and bags, which remind us of those which SIMON *was arrested with, and which people used for* NOVAK's *groceries. They are always the same sloppy cases, all the cases and bags that appear in this story.*

NOVAK: How content he is, how peacefully he puts his little rhymes together . . . (*Pulls sheets of paper from one of the suitcases, reads them with pleasure.* VASKA *and* HELGA *stop eating and drinking, astonished.*) "My journey," he writes, "is a smile and a joy and a gift. It isn't a coffin, a grave, or a gallows . . . "

VASKA: Sorrow, sorrow, fear, the rope, and the pit . . .

NOVAK: Just as disgusting! Who wrote that one?

HELGA: That's unknown, we haven't figured out yet.

NOVAK: There's no better poet in the world! How smug he is!

HELGA (*again eats with appetite*): What of it? Didn't we surround him with comforts?

VASKA: Doesn't he do his writing in a castle? Didn't he get prizes?

HELGA: Why should he care about some sorrow or other?

VASKA: Well, why, do you think?

HELGA: But take away his comfort and his nice house . . . .

VASKA: Run him out of the castle and run down his poetry . . .

HELGA: Right off he'll hate you. (NOVAK *gets up, thinks, struggles with something within, reaches a decision.*)

NOVAK: OK, he's yours. Do whatever you want to him, I bet he still won't turn against us. He won't get bitter!

VASKA *and* HELGA *joyously set off. They trip over the food and beverages scattering them.* NOVAK *follows them with his eyes, laughs heartily. He finds the two greyhounds amusing. And when he turns around, he starts with surprise. Three women,* ANNA, MARIE, *and* MIXOVA, *gather the food, and greedily eat it. They are all ragged and in a wretched state.*

ANNA: This is how we live our lives. I'm unhappy, you're unhappy, too.

MARIE: Happiness means almost nothing.

MIXOVA: My husband had the phantom of power in his hands.

MARIE: Power: what is it? A friend's smile, a bowl of hot soup . . .

MIXOVA: He joyfully inhaled government air through his nose.

MARIE: . . . dry shoes . . .

MIXOVA: When they took him away they took everything else, too. Apartment, car, room in the castle, and shopping vouchers.

MARIE: A residence permit . . .

ANNA: What's a word like that supposed to mean?

MARIE: Happiness is too general a word.

NOVAK *has been watching them with amazement the whole time. Wondering, he shakes his head.*

NOVAK: Now, what kind of monsters might these be? Old witches . . . but with an ex-middle-class look about them. Tattered old owls, how did they get here? You girls got residence permits?

MARIE: Why ask? They don't issue permits for the cities.

ANNA: I read that in London they don't make problems about issuing them to anybody.

MIXOVA: That I don't believe. There has to be some sense of order, even in London.

NOVAK: So, grannies, you just pack up and get on out of here. Grubbing in the garbage like stray dogs in Italy.

ANNA: And where should we go?

NOVAK: Where you belong. Go to hell.

MARIE: We couldn't get residence permits anywhere.

NOVAK: Why's that? In this country everybody gets a permit. (*The women shrug their shoulders.*) Try militia H.Q. in Petrovka!

ANNA: We were turned down there.

NOVAK: Well, I won't let you gnaw on your leftovers here! (*Adds good-naturedly.*) If you got to . . . take it along . . . (*With his foot he pokes the food that* VASKA *and* HELGA *left behind on the floor.*) Oooh, jailbirds, eh?

MARIE: I wasn't convicted. Look . . . (*Shows* NOVAK *a dingy paper.* NOVAK *reads unwillingly.*)

ANNA: It was her husband who was convicted. (*Shows another paper.*)

NOVAK: All right. Really. But what difference does it make if it was her husband. Suppose he is her husband! If they didn't give you a permit, they didn't give it to you, what can I do about it?

MARIE: You could give us a permit.

NOVAK: Me? Go to hell, you old bags! (*He laughs.*)

ANNA: His answers don't add up . . .

MARIE: And this is how exile's passed along.

MIXOVA: It's not his fault, he's only carrying out his orders.

ANNA: He shouts because we resist him.

MARIE: We're all only carrying out our orders. The lucky ones carry out only innocent ones. Rejection of medical certification, decrease in living space.

MIXOVA (*eagerly*): No permit for foreign travel. No land allocation to build a summer cottage on. New car voucher rejected . . . (*Both women look at her, amazed.* MIXOVA *falls silent, embarrassed.*) Well, that's not nice either. Wouldn't you agree . . .

ANNA: Only born losers get orders to beat faces in, drive people into exile.

MIXOVA: But don't forget the good things. They'll accuse you of subjectivism. What about rural literacy, building up industry, peace, the theatre of Meyerhold?

ANNA: You could add that the sky is still there, and the stars, and soft rain.

MARIE: Won't we ever find out what all that's happened means?

MIXOVA: It was all explained at the time of the Thaw, Khruschev told the world about errors on the road to communism. My husband started traveling to peace conferences.

ANNA: We'll never find out. Too many people are implicated in the past . . .

MARIE: . . . Is that why it'll never be understood?

ANNA: Some gave birth to it, others were born of it, and others yet are dead.

MIXOVA: You have no self-discipline at all, that's what it is . . . They jailed my husband, too, but I didn't get bitter . . . He came home to Jičín right on Christmas Day, and we were happy. That Catholic holiday suddenly attained deep meaning for us too. Later I got my degree in philosophy. In just six months.

MARIE: Then you must be aware that the only allowed form of recollection is that which demonstrates one's record as a loyal builder of socialism, as one who can distinguish the main objective from the secondary, the historical goal from one's own crippled, trampled life.

NOVAK: That's a notion, hag. That's an notion I've never heard before!

MIXOVA: What about it? The people in the camps understood! Even my husband understood! He bore his suffering with discipline. He didn't defame the Party.

ANNA: And those who sent him there are nodding in approval. All of it was historical necessity. Even error, wrongdoing, lives trampled underfoot, execution.

MARIE: One night I woke up and saw Simon wasn't sleeping. He stood at the foot of the bed, head thrown back and arms spread wide. "Come," he said to me, "it's time. As long as we're together." And pointed to the window.

ANNA: Did you answer: "Let's wait"?

MARIE: Yes. Was I right to? How much suffering would I have spared myself and him?

MIXOVA: We spent that Christmas with justice smiling down on us.

NOVAK: I'm probably dreaming you, you old hags. You're probably some horrible dream! Clear out, or I'll kick your asses. Fuck off and join your devils in hell! (*The women flee,* NOVAK *half laughs, half shakes his head*.) I must be crazy. I'm seeing things that can't happen. And just the same they do.

Noise. VASKA *and* HELGA *throw* MIXA *on stage in a wretched state. And they continue to torture him.*

VASKA: Look here, poetry!

HELGA: Which you wrote!

NOVAK: So you arrested that one? Well, after all, why not.

VASKA: Sorrow, sorrow . . .

HELGA: . . . the rope, and the pit . . . you predicted things nicely for yourself.

VASKA: So far all we've done is beat you up.

NOVAK: The little shit stole some poems or other from a prisoner. But that's not important. I'm concerned about his loyalty. We have to look into it.

HELGA: But it's going to get worse!

VASKA: We'll move you into a smaller apartment.

HELGA: We'll take your phone away from you.

VASKA: None of your friends will talk to you anymore.

HELGA: They'll be afraid of you . . .

VASKA: You've already been forgotten.

MIXA: I haven't done anything wrong.

HELGA: We won't publish a single poem of yours ever again.

MIXA: You're making a mistake, I'm not against you. Not me. I'll never say anything bad about you.

NOVAK (*satisfied*): So, you see, boys and girls. We spit on his poems, and he's silent. You abuse him and he's grateful. This one will never badmouth us.

VASKA: We'll crush his legs, and you'll hear how he'll sing.

HELGA: He'll curse us, we're his bane. He praised us when we were his boon.

NOVAK: Not at all. He loves us, that counts more than pain. Crush his legs . . . (VASKA and HELGA *trample* MIXA's *legs.* MIXA *faints.*) . . . but keep him alive. So I can hear how he praises us. Sometime I get the feeling I'm God. I don't respect people either.

VASKA and HELGA *drag off the half-dead* MIXA. RUBEN *enters, looks amazed at* MIXA.

RUBEN: Haven't you been defeated yet?

NOVAK (*very friendly, embraces* RUBEN): Why, not at all, old friend. We'll never be defeated. We're marching at the head of history's parade . . . and thus I probe a man. Poems: imagine . . . I watched him steal them with my own eyes, and now he's ready to give his life for 'em. Isn't that idiotic?

RUBEN: Are you evil? Are you a hangman?

NOVAK: Why evil, right away? All I am is curious. What do you think he'll do now? He'll wake up in the morning and find out they trampled on his legs.

RUBEN: You accused him in vain, he's obedient as ever . . .

NOVAK: For how much longer? And how far should we go? How extreme should we get? And why? Who knows? He knows I'll have him killed. Will he ever raise his head?

RUBEN: He believes you'll forgive him.

NOVAK: There's nothing to forgive. He didn't do anything. I ruined his legs for him. Doesn't he need them?

VASKA and HELGA *pull half-dead* MIXA *back on stage.*

HELGA: My hair's falling out. Will I still be a woman?

VASKA: And your right shoe pinches you.

HELGA: The left.

VASKA: What?

HELGA: The left one. And just the same both shoes are the same size, and my feet are the same size too. I keep thinking about it, night after night.

NOVAK: How'd it go? Did he curse us?

VASKA: No. He wants to talk to you.

HELGA: He wants to explain that he's innocent.

VASKA: He believes it.

HELGA: But he can't say it.

VASKA: Guilt is always. Guilt is forever.

HELGA: And he doesn't know it, even though we told him so.

VASKA: He can't believe you'd accuse anybody for no reason.

HELGA: He thinks it's only a mistake, and it'll all be cleared up.

NOVAK: Mistake? That's only a provisional explanation. Did you beat him to death?

RUBEN: And what is the final explanation?

NOVAK (*short laugh*): I'll tell you. There were these three buddies, and the shit was coming down. Nobody knows where from or why, "sorrow, sorrow, fear, the rope, and the pit" . . . And suddenly one of them, the Secretary of Culture, comes joyfully running down the hall and yelling: "It's all right, President, you're in the clear, I'm in the clear, it's the Chairman who's in deep shit." Knowing how lucky you are they dumped your buddy in a pit, not you; that's the final explanation. Look, he's coming to.

MIXA (*croaks*): I'm guiltless.

NOVAK: Maybe so. Maybe not. But someone's got to go into the pit, you ought to be glad it's not me.

MIXOVA: Why have they done this to you! My sweet innocent baby, what's happened to your legs? Why did they smash them?

MIXA: Are you crazy? You mustn't talk about them that way. Vilify them, hate them. We loved them while they were passing out good things, and we have to accept evil from their hands, too. They are the Party.

NOVAK: Why?

MIXA: They know why. The multitude is wiser than you and me.

RUBEN: This is extremely interesting. They arrest an innocent person, and crush his legs. And he says, "Thank you, you were probably right."

NOVAK (*jumps up joyfully*): "Mr. President, I'm in the clear, you're in the clear, it's the Chairman who's in deep shit." The best luck's when bad luck hits my best friend instead of me.

MIXA: I won't get bitter.

NOVAK: That's appreciated.

VASKA: You won, as usual.

HELGA: The guy really won't get bitter, and won't hate us.

VASKA: We tested his love.

NOVAK: We've deepened that love. Let the guy go free, so he'll sing our praises everywhere, and put him in charge of the peace movement.

RUBEN: So . . . injustice exceeding common comprehension.

NOVAK: Look at him, he suffers without guilt, and loves us just the same. Tell us some of the funny things that happened in prison.

MIXA: Suffering is not punishment for committing sin.

NOVAK: We love to laugh. Laughter is liberating. Don't be surprised at that, even we experience tension and distress. What'd you expect? We've dared too much.

MIXA: I know the Party often punishes the faithful, in order to strengthen them.

NOVAK: Yeah, that's a good one. (*To* RUBEN.) My friend, you obviously think a man's responsible for his wrongdoings and that Justice punishes them. And that there's such a thing as injustice, too. You thought so, admit it.

RUBEN: And that's not the way it is?

NOVAK: No.

RUBEN: And how is it, then?

NOVAK: This is how it is. You see, if men suffered for their guilt, a question would arise that could drive you crazy: Why do the innocent suffer?

MIXA: The main thing now is that everything's explained, that truth came to light. I'll go straight home to Jičín, Christmas is just round the corner. They forgave me for being innocent. Rehabilitation came.

NOVAK: It's still not enough. Sometimes I feel like killing everybody in the world. How many people you think there are on earth. Do you know?

RUBEN: Fortunately not.

VASKA: Four billion . . .

HELGA: . . . seven hundred million . . .

VASKA: We have them all accounted for . . .

HELGA: To the last little shit.

VASKA *and* HELGA *rejoice, exit.*

NOVAK (*to* RUBEN): You think I'm evil, but really I'm good. I'm giving people what they want, not what they don't. I believe it all myself, too: you know—good beer, pork, one dark day, my old lady, alone on the suitcase, got no choice but rejoice. I wouldn't lift a finger for freedom, 'cause I don't need it. I need to get rid of this discomfort. See, an ordinary idiot, and thoughts like these. (*Loads cases into his arms, as before; about to leave. Sighs.*) It'd be nice, wouldn't it, to test people this way. Load them with a heavy load. Talk about me and testing people. The most I did was pinch their fingers in the bars. I'm just an ordinary asshole . . . And my legs are shot. (*Leaves with loot, loaded like a camel.* RUBEN *looks at* MIXA *on floor,* MIXOVA *kneeling beside him.*)

RUBEN: To Israel! To Venezuela!

INTERMISSION.

SCENE 5

SIMON *and* MARIE *burst onto the stage exhausted.* MARIE *falls down exhausted.* SIMON *picks her up, they stumble on with their suitcases.* ANNA, *who has long been resting on a suitcase, observes them with interest. On a fence hangs a worn shopping bag, under which lies* NOVAK *in a wretched state.*

MARIE: My God, and we call this living? How much longer will we be running like this?

SIMON: We shouldn't have come here. Is there anywhere we two can run to? Death is sure to catch up with us somewhere, if we're not dead already.

MARIE: Maybe we're alive, but I'm not happy.

SIMON: Well, who said you were supposed to be happy. Happiness is too general a word.

MARIE: I've been afraid that they were going to shoot at us.

ANNA (*they only now notice her*): They won't shoot. They're too dumbfounded to. (*Goes to* SIMON *and looks in his eyes.*) From the *Personals Column*: "Dearest one, sweetest one, most of all most foolish one. My sweet horse. Let me make it clear I'm not forcing anything on you. I won't come on Saturday. I'm sending you a ten-spot so that you'll love me. Love's got the face of ten smokes and two beers."

ANNA *kisses* SIMON.

SIMON: I know you, you're Anna. I've been waiting for you, out in the country.

MARIE (*yells*): She'll destroy you. She'll suck you dry and finish you off. What's in her head's the same as what's between her legs!

ANNA (*dances*): From the *Classifieds*: "Young woman, very inexperienced, quiet, decent, inconspicuous, seeking sublet in central Prague. Have trouble sleeping, as if my bed were somehow too big to doze off in."

MARIE: What does she know? No one pays the least attention to us, everyone keeps their distance . . . You're wrapped up in all humanity, but can't see your own wife next to you.

ANNA (*dances again*): From *Our Letters Column*: "May we suggest that our readers pay attention to the following, and work out a plausible explanation on their own. It makes no difference where they discover it. Our editorial board is in such dire straits that our most faithful readers are beyond its comprehension."

MARIE: Tedious babble from a stupid street girl, and you're listening to it.

SIMON: Aren't we allowed to love things that are tedious?

ANNA: "You, my beloved horse, don't let yourself be caught by some whore or other. I'm sending you a ten-spot so that you'll love me."

MARIE: "Our strongest feelings we suppress. All the rest is emptiness. Open, public sentiments are classified advertisements."

ANNA: From the *Diary of Love*: "I adore you."

RUBEN (*enters, studies others with suspicion*): Are all of you new here?

ANNA: They're still out of breath from nervous exhaustion, wondering if they ought to hit the road or not.

SIMON: And we still don't know whether we're alive.

RUBEN: We're forming up in groups of thirty so when somebody starts talking to us we'll be organized. Have our own identity. (*He leaves.*)

ANNA: Sure. We're standing in a street, there are thousands of us. They don't kill by thousands anymore.

MIXA (*enters and extends his arms with joy*): Here you are, I've been looking for you, loving you. (*To* ANNA.) Back then we kept a smile on our face, but no laughter; laughter would have aroused curiosity. "What are they laughing at? Could they be making fun of . . ." (*Notices* ANNA *taking old, worn-out shopping bag from the fence. He wonders kindly.*) You do the shopping for that old swine?

SIMON (*waves his hand*): I can't stand here waiting in the street for someone to ship me off me to some kind of freedom. (*He takes the shopping bag from* ANNA's *hand and leaves.* VASKA *and* HELGA, *unseen until now, move and follow him.*)

ANNA: Old Novak? Why call him a swine. He's just old and not very well.

MIXA: Ask anybody, he hurt them all. They were all afraid of him when he was in power.

MIXA *kicks the prone* NOVAK, *who groans with pain.*

MARIE: Now his legs are shot. Strange, the way we don't punish anyone, take revenge on anyone.

MIXA: But we haven't forgotten. (*He goes to* NOVAK, *examines him.*) He's alive, the animal. His kind lives forever.

ANNA: What is it that you haven't forgotten?

MARIE: Humanity wraps us like the filmiest of membranes, a puff of wind and it blows away.

ANNA (*to* MIXA): Someday in the main street, up to our knees in dirty snow again, a campaign could start against "cosmopolitan elements." Maybe you'll get frightened, and go hang yourself.

MARIE: I know, Herzen Street, number 35 . . .

RUBEN: He lives in our village, his legs are shot, he hangs a bag on the fence and we do his shopping with it.

MIXA: Leave the bag on the fence, the whole tortured village and all his victims are looking at you.

ANNA: The man's legs are almost gone, and I will do the shopping for him.

MIXA: You have no idea how much I suffered. You were expelled and criminalized, proscribed, you lived in solitude, but quietly. I wasn't allowed to, I suffered. I had to lie, you didn't! Who'll compensate me for it!? Leave the bag hanging on the fence, you don't want to serve the ones who caused our misfortune.

MARIE: I always knew in time that our suffering would shrivel to the grimace of a petty quarrel. As for the bag, Simon left with it long ago.

RUBEN: Everything's going well. The Ambassador just drove by. (*He sees* MIXA *is puzzled.*) Is that you? (MIXA *nods insecurely.*) I heard you took part in his interrogation then. After the arrest.

ANNA: They arrested Simon, and he's been dead a long while now.

MIXA: I was there unofficially, hidden in a closet. I was there as an author.

RUBEN: Later, in the newspapers, you said the prisoner looked pitiful. His trousers were sliding down, he answered incoherently, he squirmed and he lied.

ANNA: You wrote that his equivocations were laughable.

RUBEN: He was generally laughable. That's how you put it in the paper. The spittle ran out of his mouth, and he stank of fear. He was my brother, now he's dead. "Dogs die like dogs," you wrote, in the year 1951.

MIXA: Today I'm ashamed, but understand that, even then, public opinion was on the side of the powerful against the weak.

RUBEN: To many people he didn't seem innocent. He wrote that poem. Why did he write it? It was indefensible.

MIXA: He was a writer and he stank like an unhousebroken puppy.

MARIE: Sorrow, sorrow, fear, the rope, and the pit . . .

ANNA: Everybody wondered why he was picked up and everybody found a reason.

MARIE: He's not one of us, he's a stranger, they said.

ANNA: He wasn't reasonable, they said.

MARIE: It was only to be expected, a terrible character like that, they said.

ANNA: They said he was sulky.

MARIE: And is that enough justification for killing?

The same bag with which SIMON *has left appears in* MARIE*'s hand.* MARIE *wants to leave with it, too.*

MIXA: Just the same, I beg you, leave that bag on the fence! Back then I . . . I only wrote about those things, this one here carried them out . . . (*He kicks* NOVAK.)

MARIE: I'm already dead, but you still haven't taught me your brand of inhumanity.

MIXA: If that's the situation I can't stand by you. (*He wants to leave, but* RUBEN *stops him.*)

RUBEN (*shakes his head*): Is this by chance the man with a face for every situation? He certainly looks a whole lot like him. (MARIE *puts down the bag and listens attentively.*) I'm on the lookout for people like that. There are already ten TV crews in the street and some are letting themselves be filmed in senseless exultation. I survived the camps and I'm not rejoicing. I survived because they never got me into one.

MIXA: I'm really glad. At least somebody was lucky. (*He leaves.*)

RUBEN: It wasn't luck, it was my remarkable vitality.

MIXA (*returns fast*): Were you hiding out? The whole war? Congratulations.

RUBEN: Me, a Jew with a price on my head, crossing half war-torn Europe on black-market papers in a black-market van, selling tobacco bought on the black-market.

ANNA: You're his brother. Simon's brother.

MARIE: I always thought you didn't exist.

RUBEN: So what. So I don't exist. Everything's a dream for us. Now I'm looking for a man with a face for every situation. I made a fortune in tobacco but the fortune was worthless. They haven't managed to force me to my knees. After the war I made a run for Australia. And they caught me in Berlin. Someone's got to give us a hand someday, don't they?

ANNA: But they killed Simon. Why?

MARIE: Why? It's high time that we understood. For nothing! Nothing, that's a serious reason for killing.

HELGA *joyfully bursts in with the bag with which she had arrested* SIMON. *All automatically assume positions to be searched, as during an arrest.*

HELGA: Congratulations, he's been pardoned. He'll come back to you. It's a miracle, because they don't give out pardons.

MARIE: A miracle is only a momentary spark. What happens to magic gold gotten by night from a dodderer when day comes?

ANNA: Just mud!

VASKA: A telegram has come, rehabilitation's starting.

They all gradually relax.

HELGA: And the telegram will be valid, once we've checked it's not a fake. A miracle has happened, let's all rejoice!

MARIE: The only good life's the one that doesn't need a miracle.

HELGA: Why not grant joy? Freedom without delay?

VASKA: The way we used to drive round the country, all for the sake of collectivizing the countryside.

HELGA: And today we'll scare you. (*She pulls a mouse out of her pocket and scares both the immobile, but not scared women.*)

VASKA: We'll bake it in an electric cooker.

HELGA: Or we'll fry us up a cat. (*They both laugh and rejoice.*)

VASKA: Cat and mouse. A faithful pair!

HELGA: Two cats and two mice.

VASKA: Siamese cats!

HELGA: Siamese mice. That's us guys' idea of fun.

VASKA: Intellectuals' nerves . . .

HELGA: . . . are instantly in tatters . . .

VASKA: Collectivization . . . those nights . . . the village is quiet . . . us sweating . . .

HELGA: And a strange black cloud . . .

VASKA: Twenty truckloads of guys and ten thousand black coffees . . .

HELGA: Our day! Boots slathered in oil and smelling like a gun-belt . . .

VASKA: And a gun, my friend . . .

HELGA: Those rich peasants were dying of fear . . .

VASKA: That's all gone already . . .

HELGA: Back then there was no place for softies.

VASKA: There was no call for their kind. And today we're crowded in with them at a stupid German Embassy.

HELGA: Today we're both engineers, with doctorates.

Both leave laughing. HELGA *throws* SIMON's *bag on the floor, mice crawl on their shoulders.* MARIE *picks up the bag, examines it,* ANNA *looks at her.* NOVAK *jumps up. His legs are back, he waves a pistol around. He probably had a bad dream.*

NOVAK: He's not one of us! He's a stranger! When that thought gets in my head I just have to do the guy in! That's how we were! We knew them all, proud Polish aristocrats, vague liberals, indecisive English. The future devoured them along with the wooden paneling of their villas. We were still barely boys in those days, but we were burning!

MARIE: Boys who make history are cruel, as boys are, but they don't follow through. Otherwise there'd be nobody left.

ANNA: Why's it so easy to turn the young into killers?

MARIE: Despising life is easy when you're young. Blood flows in torrents and murder's something everyday, they even murder one another. I read how Robespierre strangled Danton, and Danton devoured Marat.

ANNA: And Marat drowned Robespierre in a tub.

MARIE: At Ekster's studio, Mayakovsky once read a poem describing how they drowned the Czarist officers. At the time, it made me laugh.

ANNA: And what did Simon say?

MARIE: He was silent. Mixa pounced on me like a maniac, how could I show so little respect for human life. He healed me of the ailment forever, but didn't value human life himself.

MIXA (*enters carrying bag* SIMON *left with*): You think my voice could stop the executions? That's my excuse. My explanation. (*He throws the bag on the ground.*)

NOVAK (*rushes up to the bag*): We wanted to create a kind of revolutionary woman. The French created one in their revolution; we didn't. A new kind of woman. The kind of woman who eats her meals in the canteen. Her children are looked after by the state. (*Goes to* RUBEN, *leans on him.*) These days my legs are shot, you're the only one who helps me. (*He drops bag from weakness.*)

RUBEN: Our people understand when we stand up for our own kind, for a friend, a sister, but they ask, "Why stand up for a stranger and get caught in the crossfire yourself?"

NOVAK: I heard about your brother, what happened to him. I'm sorry. (*He presses* RUBEN's *hand.*) They went and killed him; that hurts. I think, if war came, I'd even kill my son, shoot him down like a partridge. (*He goes to all one after another, consoles them. The pistol in his hand gets in the way.*) But that war didn't happen, I've had different jobs and official functions. Lately they broke my water pipe digging in the street, and nobody will ever fix it. I'm cursed by an awful indifference to individuals, but I deny nothing. They could shoot me any day, just like they shot the ones I turned over to be shot. Our times demanded it, great times, but hungry. I'd never turn bitter. But I'm afraid that no one understands me. (*He offers his hand to* MARIE. *She evades him, turns away.*)

MARIE: In Sochinsk they liquidated many young people "for sowing demoralization in the electro-technical industry." No, you don't deny anything.

VASKA *and* HELGA *break in pitifully.* VASKA *carries* SIMON's *bag.*

VASKA: How do you like his luck? Gets a telegram telling him he's free, I look at him closer as I'm reading it to him—he's dead?

HELGA: Could he have died of sheer joy? Did his heart burst from happiness?

VASKA: Did he die on purpose?

They throw dead SIMON *on the stage.* ANNA *and* MARIE *go to him.*

ANNA (*takes his lifeless head in her hands*): Position number four, my horse.

MARIE: What the hell was that? What position?

ANNA: Position number six. A dark premonition is settling over me, I eat too much with tears in my eyes. Stroke me, go to sleep. I stagger from a tavern where I shocked several people. I was short half a dollar for the train. Outside the tavern I beg it off this very shocked lady. I have a cigarette in my mug and talk very correctly.

MARIE: What position? (*She shakes dead* SIMON.) Say something, why aren't you talking, we'll all end up admiring this painful, tough talk from a good-looking girl.

ANNA: Position number seven. I ask for her address, to send the money to. I'm begging, but nobody gives me a thing. Night waits for me in an unknown city, hungry and with an awful cough. What could your shoe size be?

MARIE: In the end you probably wanted to be loved by two women. But you're alone.

Both women have a tug of war over SIMON. *Each would like to embrace and caress him. The dead is no help to them.*

ANNA: Position number twenty seven. Especially, don't get caught by some whore or other. Life's discoveries: the editorial board will now go grab a bite to eat, and then play volleyball. My bed is big, I'm always groping for something with my hands.

MARIE (*yells at* SIMON): Will you please go away. Go away and let me live.

ANNA: *Editorial*: "Mister poet, you write me for nothing about nothing. Come Saturday morning by bus, the ticket's twenty-five, I'll pay your way back. Two hundred and ten different positions with tears in my eyes."

They let go of SIMON, *he falls from their hands. They probably realize they won't get him to do anything anymore.*

MARIE: We probably look like two drowned women . . .

SCENE 6

RUBEN *dressed for travel and with large suitcases, leads a crowd of similar people. They all have large suitcases, they are all dressed for travel, and they are scared.*

RUBEN: So we have gotten out.

Only NOVAK *isn't traveling. He sits on his spot and howls with laughter, rubs his hands with glee. Clearly somebody's not succeeding at something.*

RUBEN: From Budapest. Through Prague and Dresden to Berlin. Hear that noise? It's the World Youth Festival in the Peace Zone. In the War Zone, only breathless silence reigns.

MIXA: I know; uneasy times. (*He takes off his glasses and thinks back.*) During that time I was under unjust arrest. I only became a soldier for peace after the Rehabilitation began. I didn't have to be rehabilitated, of course—since I'd never been sentenced. (*He embraces* RUBEN *in friendly fashion.*) Truth prevailed in my case, though I was still in jail, before the era of the Thaw.

ANNA: And why are we running away to Berlin?

RUBEN: Be quiet young lady, so they don't hear us.

MIXOVA: My husband came straight home from prison on Christmas Eve. We spent that Christmas with justice smiling down on us, and somehow it prefigured the era of the Thaw that Khrushchev gave to mankind.

MIXA: My wife and I, hand in hand . . .

MIXOVA: . . . looking at the black sky of Christmas . . .

MIXA: . . . and saw in it . . .

MIXOVA: . . . a Soviet citizen, soaring . . .

MIXA: That night we foretold the flight of the first astronaut. After the Thaw began I mentioned it to Ehrenburg. He told me: "Yes, man foretells the future, because he needs hope."

MIXOVA: Within the next six months I became professor of philosophy at the Institute. It was philosophy then . . . Change was intense, life fast, substantial, full of ecstasy . . . We were confident the Party would rectify everything.

MIXA: We didn't get bitter.

MIXOVA: And how often did you hear then, "This or that Comrade has grown embittered . . . "

VASKA: Why all this stupid babble? You could give us all away . . .

HELGA: We're not in the West yet. Soon as we get to the west zone you can babble.

MARIE: What zone? Where are we running to now?

RUBEN: I assembled squads of delegates for the World Youth Festival. With counterfeit documents. Some weren't even young, they were running to Israel or Bolivia. From the Zone of Peace to the Zone of Silence one crosses many courtyards.

ANNA: And in terrible fear that someone will catch us. For tens of years we've feared every uniform, every silent civilian.

RUBEN: Quiet please, now; we'll cross the courtyard one at a time.

MIXA: And smile, we're at a Youth Festival, after all, we're delegates.

MIXOVA: Maybe we should wave merrily at people.

RUBEN: We'll wave at them once we're on the other side.

ANNA: It's the same in all directions, there is no other side.

MARIE: But we don't know that yet. So we're running. Back and forth? Why?

RUBEN: Follow me! To freedom! Across the courtyards! To Bolivia!

They all disappear in the direction in which RUBEN *leads them. Only* VASKA *and* HELGA *stay. They strap on their pistols and stand guard. And* NOVAK *sits laughing on the suitcase.*

NOVAK: Across the courtyards! They're off by twelve years! Or they started out twenty years too early. (*He gets up, goes to* HELGA. *He looks in her eyes.*) A crime's not a crime 'cause of what you do but 'cause of when you do it.

RUBEN, *dejected, without a suitcase, handcuffed, wanders back, stops near* VASKA *and* HELGA, *looks at* NOVAK. *The others follow in handcuffs.*

RUBEN: There aren't any courtyards there anymore, but there's a brand new wall.

VASKA: And do you have any papers, or did you just come as you are?

NOVAK: Like I was saying, too soon or too late. At the moment it's a crime.

ANNA: We ran into a wall.

MARIE: But that was long ago. We only learned about it now.

ANNA: All walls, in all directions round us.

RUBEN: All my life I've had papers, documents for every situation.

HELGA: And today you don't have any!

RUBEN: Today I was sure!

NOVAK: Pretty funny, use a Youth Festival to cover an escape and be off by twelve years.

VASKA: You're not one of us, you're a foreigner. Where do we return you to?

ANNA: We don't know where we are, what place we're in. Where's Prague?

HELGA: Prague, then. We'll return you to Prague, they can lock you up there.

RUBEN (*embraces* MIXA, *laughs*): So for the first time in my life, I became a Czech citizen. I'd never been a Czech before. They put me in a Czech prison.

NOVAK: About that festival, pal; you read about it in an old newspaper, right? Didn't keep up with events. Things change fast these days. How else could you screw up so bad?

VASKA: So move it, sweethearts.

HELGA: So move it, shitheads.

They lead the dejected crowd away. A pile of suitcases is left; NOVAK *sniffs round it.*

NOVAK: Funny thing, take a trip and all at once it's a criminal offence. I could split a gut laughing. (*He checks out suitcases.*) They left all their stuff here . . . in their hurry . . . (*He is approaching some suitcases;* SIMON *appears, sadly observes* NOVAK *peeking into bags.*) It all goes to the state anyhow. Confiscated . . . Nice suitcases, some of them . . . should the state get it, or me . . . (*He gathers up all the suitcases in a very complicated manner.*) It's not really stealing from them but from the state. And from the state I can . . . It's not even stealing when the state stole it first . . .

SIMON: I thought . . . I'd get your groceries . . . groceries and water, since you can't walk . . .

NOVAK *jumps and the suitcases fall from his arms.*

NOVAK: You're a bad dream! A horrible dead shadow. How much longer are you going to haunt me?

SCENE 7

All the suitcases that have appeared in this story are lying open on the stage, mixed up, ransacked. RUBEN *sits amid them tired and helpless.* ANNA *lies at his feet and cries.*

ANNA: I sat on a suitcase once before. Four years old, in Berlin, on a train platform at night. It was a youth festival. We were running away to Argentina, and to Bolivia, and to Israel. They caught us.

RUBEN: They executed my brother then. Or he disappeared. Or he got lost. Froze to death. Nobody knows.

ANNA *goes to one of the suitcases, pulls out a doll. She holds it by the leg like a dead rabbit.*

ANNA: This is the doll I was holding in my arms then. A man in a leather coat looks at me with a smile.

VASKA: Where did you come from, little girl? Tell uncle, where from?

RUBEN: What did you say?

ANNA: I said that we were running to Argentina, to Bolivia, to Israel.

HELGA: Gave away her old man! Gave away her old lady!

ANNA: I gave them away, but you arrested them.

VASKA: And who wrote those poems, sticking out of your pocket there? Papa? Mama?

HELGA: And is it really your papa. Is it your mama?

VASKA (*reads the verses*): Sorrow, sorrow, fear, the rope, and the pit . . . Well, see?

HELGA: You guessed right, you did. You wrote forbidden poems. Your whole damn family. You wrote what would happen to you. We'll oblige you.

ANNA: When he was writing it, he didn't know that it would be forbidden.

VASKA: We banned them before he wrote them. That gentleman, that poet.

HELGA: But you, dearie, you gave the gentleman away, you did.

ANNA: Yes. That's how I became a Czech.

VASKA: And look, you're still alive. Nothing gets eaten as hot as it's cooked. You wouldn't have thought, forty years back in Berlin, that someday you'd be happy in Prague . . .

HELGA: And you, my boy, don't you cry either. Don't open old wounds. Your brother's a famous poet nowadays. We publish him, we love him. We told you we were sorry.

VASKA: Or didn't we?

HELGA: All mistakes were admitted, what the hell more do you want?

VASKA: You weren't all saints either. You, for instance, you gave away your old man. I mean that gentleman.

HELGA: Oh, well, kids.

VASKA: Good thing it's all behind us. Already just hair-splitting for historians.

HELGA: A secret no one cares about. My shoe's pinching again. The right or the left one, but both my feet are just the same.

VASKA: We all have shoes that pinch.

HELGA: Each in a different place, right? I keep thinking about it. Same shoes, same feet, and it pinches just the same. You ought to think about it, too.

VASKA: And we caught the thief who stole the poems from your brother.

HELGA: It was one hell of a job.

VASKA: But luckily his wife gave him away.

HELGA: She turned him in, she knew everything.

VASKA: Boy, was she a brave one. Going against her own husband in the interest of justice.

HELGA: She condemned him.

VASKA: We respect her.

HELGA: There was another guy involved. He saw the whole thing, how the manuscript was stolen, how parts were erased.

VASKA: An old guy with bad legs, the kind you'd think wouldn't give a damn; but not this one.

HELGA: He went and told the truth. Great guy.

VASKA: He confirmed the truth.

HELGA: We could paint you a picture how power was abused back then.

VASKA: You won't cry, will you.

HELGA: You have to be patient. Truth always wins in the end.

VASKA: We'll tell you why. We can tell you. We know.

HELGA: But that's another story altogether.

VASKA: That doesn't have anything to do with our explanation.

HELGA: So you see, you wait and wait. And then along comes Mr. Novak, whose legs are going . . .

VASKA: . . . and the villain's own wife . . .

HELGA: . . . and they tell the truth.

VASKA: Truth prevails in the end.

HELGA: It takes ages, but "truth sets in as time sets on."

VASKA: Like you on that suitcase.

HELGA: Not to get sour, kids.

VASKA: Not to get bitter.

Both exit joyfully. ANNA *again lies at* SIMON's *feet and cries.*

SCENE 8

Funereal music is fading. Enter MIXOVA *and* VASKA, *both in black.* MIXOVA *keens,* VASKA *supports her.* NOVAK *sits on a suitcase, looks around, he too has a mourning-band on his sleeve.*

MIXOVA: A whole country bidding him farewell. (VASKA *helps her sit down. Her pain is heavy,* MIXOVA *can barely move.*) They buried a poet; but I buried a husband, that's more.

VASKA: He wrote the best poems in the history of the world. But he was silent the last twenty-five years. Why?

NOVAK *gets up, adjusts his mourning-band and silently goes to console her.*

NOVAK: Nobody expected it. You have to be brave.

MIXOVA: He no longer felt like singing, our nation's nightingale. And now all Czechoslovakia is crying.

VASKA (*to* NOVAK): Pardon me, but who . . .

NOVAK: I was his colleague. We used to work together years ago in the department for investigating which licensed crooks put their names on books by which unlicensed crooks. We had it down to a system, Ma'am; almost nobody slipped through our fingers.

MIXOVA *sobs.*

VASKA: There must be some mistake. You obviously don't know who . . .

NOVAK: Of course I know. I'm telling you, I sat at a desk right across from him. He was one hell of a poet, that's why they made him boss there. He nailed 'em all. Nothing slipped through his fingers. (MIXOVA *looks at* VASKA *with pain.*)

VASKA: Mister, you're confusing us with somebody else, will you please just move along . . .

NOVAK: I'm not confusing you with anybody, I don't even know you. But I knew him pretty well. Today they're putting him under in style. He was a real guy, yes, sir. Number One. I take my hat off to him. They don't make his kind anymore.

VASKA *roughly drags him away.* MIXOVA *sobs.*

VASKA: Come on, or I'll kick your ass . . .

NOVAK: All right, I'm going . . . I'm an ordinary idiot, they've been kicking my ass right along . . . My life's been one long string of dark days, I just didn't know it before . . .

VASKA *drags him away, and returns to* MIXOVA, *who is in tears.*

MIXOVA: They are already crawling out . . . that kind . . . they'll blacken him . . . He died and that kind are still on the scene.

VASKA: That's the way it is, life's not reserved for the better sort.

MIXOVA: And I thought it was.

NOVAK (*returns willfully and shouts*): All you know is how to kick someone's ass! We caught this secret writer one time, he said there's no privilege your official writers wouldn't take advantage of. To make it seem like they were born on some happier planet. They glorified their own trade to cover up they weren't even human any more. I didn't know that before either.

VASKA: Get the hell out of here, you swine! All you do is blacken everything and cover it with mud.

MIXOVA: Nothing is holy to you.

They chase NOVAK *away.* RUBEN *and* ANNA *have appeared, silently, unseen, looking on, shy.*

RUBEN (*to* ANNA): That's why I'd like to live in a country without writers.

ANNA: That's why I often cry when I've been drinking too much. What is it that's tearing at their brains, anyway?

RUBEN: How could we know? We're probably disturbing . . . (*Looks at* MIXOVA *and* VASKA.)

ANNA: You don't know us, we're . . . I mean I am . . .

RUBEN: I didn't want to come. Anna insisted . . .

MIXOVA: Tell me; I don't know you, but I'll be happy to help. I'm powerless myself now.

ANNA: I'd like to speak to your husband . . . (MIXOVA *sobs tragically*.)

VASKA: Don't you know?

RUBEN: What?

VASKA: He passed away.

MIXOVA: His funeral was today. I'm as pale as snow with sorrow . . .

ANNA: We didn't know . . .

VASKA: The whole country . . .

RUBEN: We didn't know he'd died. We're sorry.

ANNA: We're twice as sorry, because we knew him, but we're not sincerely sorry.

RUBEN: We'll come another time, my apologies. Forgive us. We won't come again.

MARIE: I told you, not to go there, it's not dignified!

ANNA: It's not undignified.

RUBEN: Anna thought he'd give back the money he got for the poems he stole. She's got right on her side. I'm a practical person, though. Being right doesn't help her.

MIXOVA: What do these two young people want? It's a young man and a young woman. I've never seen them before.

VASKA: They probably loved his poetry and want to pay tribute.

MIXA (*enters with a furious laugh*): Pay tribute? They came to beg, talk about old times before I died, lie about me, say that I didn't write my poems, that you did!

SIMON *appears from the darkness* MIXA'*s shouting into.*

SIMON: And isn't that true, Mixa, old friend?

MIXA: Didn't you die? Didn't they kill you in the camp?

SIMON: They did. Before that Marie and I were penniless for years, people avoided us, there was nothing to eat, nowhere to sleep. You gave me food, lent me money, you weren't frightened. But why did you steal my poetry from me?

MARIE: When they arrested Simon, you were there too. They didn't ask to see your papers. Why?

MIXA: But I didn't steal the poems, I just gave my name to them. You agreed.

SIMON: I don't know. I don't think so.

MIXA: You've forgotten about it. I spoke with you then, and you said yes. You said "make them free to fly."

MARIE: You're lying. He never would have used such a vulgar expression.

MIXA: Nobody can prove it. I didn't know then that they were such good poems. I wanted to help you. If you'd come back alive, I would have said that you wrote them. But you didn't come back.

HELGA (*enters in deep thought, she scratches her head*): My hair's getting thin. Won't I be a woman anymore? And my left shoe's too small.

MIXA: Ask Helga. She was an editor then. She published your poems.

SIMON: I don't know who Helga is.

HELGA: Who should I be? One thing or another. (*To* MIXA.) One terrific collection, then, nothing, for twenty-five years. We wondered about that.

MIXA (*to* SIMON): You think it was easy carrying your fame on my back? You think I didn't go on writing poems of my own? And you know what they called them?

HELGA: The master's weak period. We won't publish this, it would hurt your reputation.

MIXA: I was famous, and they wouldn't print a single line I wrote. And they would have if yours hadn't been so damn good, if my own poems hadn't faded in the blinding glare of yours. I could have been a poet, too, maybe not as good as you were in the end, but a poet of my own poetry. Terrible times, you paid with your life, I paid with more!

HELGA: The peace movement was all that was left for you.

MIXA: Luckily I found one last poem in my office, one of those skinny manuscripts they took from you. And I saved it. And it saved me.

MARIE: You've fallen silent. And like many writers who sneer down at millions, you're sad.

MIXA: I was able to calm down only in Paris, in the company of all the progressive writers of the day. I used to sip espresso in Montparnasse, and browse through used bookstores on the Left Bank. The world is turning left, we kept telling each other. Force of habit drove me there.

MARIE: Your habit. At the same time peasants driven off the land were begging on the streets of our cities.

MIXA: And in Paris I met friends of Sartre and de Beauvoir. We got ourselves up in existential uniform, like exiled revolutionaries wearing their faded red shirts till they're completely worn out.

MARIE: Once evil people pretended they were good, today there's no shame. You were traveling to Paris in his place.

MIXA: He was there with his poetry, you have to believe that. They all respected him: Aragon, Valéry, Sartre. I mean they respected me, because they didn't know that I was really him. (To SIMON.) I was your ambassador. Your poems were my passport. Sartre worried about peace, and us with him.

NOVAK (enters amazed, looks around): How much longer will these extinct prehistoric monsters keep creeping out of pits here? We want to forget the old days as quickly as we can! (He chases MIXA, SIMON and even HELGA away.)

MIXOVA (to ANNA): I haven't understood anything you're saying. You're telling me something completely incomprehensible. What thefts?

RUBEN: I didn't want to come, Anna wanted to.

MARIE (comes back): She knows nothing, Anna. Nobody ever told her who really wrote those books. You're hurting her.

ANNA: I only want justice.

MARIE: And new pain. (To MIXOVA.) Will no one ever halt the streams of our tears?

MIXOVA (to VASKA): She suffered a lot. She walked with him through the frozen lands, they wanted to hide among the people out of fear, but the people didn't accept them. So they dug themselves into the ground, the earth. Alive. Only Shklovsky and Pasternak offered them a hand, men already on the lists themselves. Her mind broke from pain, she doesn't even know where they buried him, she doesn't know anything anymore, she's full of bitterness, we will forgive her. She wanted to blacken us and with us the memory of the deceased.

NOVAK (*waves his arms furiously*): Damn, crawl away now, stop whining, the old days are over. (*He drives away those he doesn't like.*) We don't care about the old days. Once I stuffed thirty people in my briefcase and forgot them there, and before that, why once I even stuffed eleven others in a trash can. But I didn't forget them, those I dumped from a truck near Benesov. Awful, isn't it? But nobody better blame me. Twenty years later, after rehabilitation, they were burying them in state. I went to have a look. They had it good. Old pals of those eleven, walking in front behind the ashes. One old pal was already president of the country. What was in those urns, damn, what was in those urns? (*He notices* MIXOVA.) And don't you go sobbing into a lace hanky here. (*He notices* RUBEN.) Even the president was sobbing with emotion in front of an empty tin can. And what do you want? His hag of a widow to pay you the royalties he stole? She doesn't know anything and won't give you anything. (*To* ANNA.) And what do you want? Justice? Why? (*Pause.*) You'll all get away with it one way or another; either turn coat or die, but what about me? I'm screwed, because back then I was the one opening and closing the bars, and when we had that physicist in the courtyard, I even pinched his fingers in the bars from rage, because I believed I was supposed to be a swine. And when I finally was a swine, you shoved me out. In '57 they even gave me six years in prison, and three of them I sat in the same cage in the courtyard as that physicist before. (*Pause.*) If those Germans went and kicked off from the cold I'd be glad of it, every last one of them. One kind and the other kind. And all of you can freeze, too, for all that I care.

MARIE: Can humanity ever awake in us again?

NOVAK: Go to hell, all of you!

HORSES AT THE WINDOW

Matei Vișniec

MATEI VIȘNIEC
Photo courtesy of Matei Vișniec

BUCHAREST–PARIS–BUCHAREST

Moshe Yassur

Matei Vişniec did not see the scheduled opening of his play *Horses at the Window* at the Notara Theatre in Bucharest in 1987. A day before it was due to open, he escaped to Paris. The opening was cancelled, receiving instead its premiere in France in 1992 at the Célestins Theatre of Lyon. According to Vişniec, "This play is a major part of my life. In fact, it is the play that was in rehearsal when I left Romania; however, it did not see the limelight there. It is the play that started my career in France." After the fall of communism, it was finally presented in Romania at the Small Theatre in Bucharest, directed by Nicolae Scarlat.

Political dissidents, especially those who escaped across the borders, were considered pariahs, enemies of the people, and were excluded from every form of social activity. Film makers had their films withdrawn, and writers saw their books disappear from the libraries and book stores. It was as if these artists did not exist. In Ceauşescu's Romania, a writer had two choices: to join the chorus of court writers and sing the praises of the "Conducator," the Leader, or to stay silent. Any sign of deviation from the norm was savagely repressed. Writers, in general, kept a low profile, and only those who succeeded in singing the praises of the regime, often forced to do so, were published. Matei Vişniec pursued another possibility. Following the path of the Surrealist writers before him, writers such as Gellu Naum, Marin Sorescu, and Eugene Ionesco, to name only a few, Vişniec created a language and style with meaning he intended the public to infer, leaving the authorities in the dark. In turn, he entered into a dangerous game of cat and mouse with the censors—both trying to outsmart each other.

Born in 1956 in the northern town of Radauti, Vişniec came to Bucharest to study philosophy at Bucharest University. He received some early notice from the younger generation of poets with the publication of his first collection of poetry. Later he turned to playwriting. At first, his plays were read only by a small group of friends and literary personalities and circulated in manuscript form, but before long he became known for his language and original style. In his plays, he created a series of characters identified and named according to their particular status, profession, or predicament. For example, in the play *The Door,* the characters are referred to only by number, while in *Havel's Water,* they have such names as The Suicide and The Arms Dealer. In *Horses at the Window,* the characters are simply called The Mother, The Son, The Daughter, The Father, The Husband, and The Wife, and as such, they are recognized as archetypes rather than as individuals. Regarding the emblematic significance of the horse, Vişniec explains: "The horse is the symbol of death in some cultures and freedom in other cultures. In Romanian folklore, the horse is brother to the brigand and the hero, but this did not provide the inspiration for the play."

Vişniec grew up under an oppressive regime in a political atmosphere akin to a prison camp. One play from the sixties that many consider the best depiction of the situation in Romania at that time is *Iona* (*Jonah*) by Marin Sorescu. In it, Romania is likened to a big fish in whose jaws the character Iona is caught and cannot escape except through suicide. Vişniec was about seven years old when *Iona* was published and performed. It became a symbol of Romania and an important influence on Vişniec's work.

The cataclysmic effects of Ceauşescu's dictatorship can be felt across Vişniec's oeuvre. Death is a frequent character in many of his plays. In *Clown Wanted*, a play that had its U.S. premiere in New York in 1995, three old clowns on one side of a door wait to be called for an audition, only to find Death lurking on the other side. In *Horses at the Window,* Death makes a spectacular appearance through the use of sound. Death cleaves to the soles of thousands and thousands of boots that trample over the hero/victim's body. It is a grotesque allegory about war and manipulation in the name of grand ideas. According to Vişniec himself, it is a metaphor for the absurdities of heroism and the emptiness that is often hidden behind concepts like "homeland' and "duty"; it is about the cynical manipulation of people by a social machine. A grotesque black comedy, *Horses at the Window* rejects the very possibility of redemption. The hero dies in the war by accident, not, as expected, by an act of heroism. The Messenger is a key character in the play. He pays visits to The Mother, The Daughter, and The Wife always bringing bad news. The Son dies by accident before entering into battle; The Father is rendered insane; The Husband is trampled to death by his comrades. The Messenger, however, announces that since his name is also Hans (like the eponymous hero who never appears alive), there is nothing to worry about. Wars go on, and heroes are replaceable.

In an interview with the Romanian newspaper *Romania Libera* (March 16, 2007), Vişniec recounts an argument with a leftist French intellectual about the differences between the French and Romanian communists. Vişniec raises the question: "Who is going to speak for the hundred million dead that the communists have left behind and who are still waiting for justice? I cannot utter the word 'communism' without feeling a sense of horror. Although they are very patient, they are waiting for justice. . . . We need, I say, an international tribunal, made of intellectuals, in order to ostracize the very word 'communism.'" With his work, Vişniec has assumed the role of speaker for the dead. He uses the theatre as a space to bring the horrors of communism to light; it is this sense of horror that underscores each of his plays.

As the communist regime under Ceauşescu tightened its grip on the country in the late eighties, a sense of suffocation engulfed a handful of intellectuals and the first signs of dissidence started to appear. In 1987, Vişniec accepting an invitation from a cultural foundation in Paris left Romania and asked for political asylum in France.

Soon after the 1989 revolution, Vişniec was seen as a beacon of hope for writers seeking a new mode of playwriting in Romania. His plays were appreciated because they opened up the possibility for the social criticism of existing conditions while retaining poetic depth. Performances of his plays popped up all over Romania, being included in the repertory of many theatres, as well as in festivals. The fact that he was able in his plays to respond to specific historical events in Romania, as well as to contemporary problems through the use of metaphor and poetry, encouraged the next generation of writers to develop a dramaturgy that relied on a combination of strong theatrical imagery and poetic language. Today Vişniec is a celebrated playwright with more than three volumes of plays published and performed. In Romania, there is hardly a festival or a season that doesn't have at least one of his plays in its program. Although Vişniec continues to live and work in Paris even after the fall of the Iron Curtain, his plays are a permanent presence on the Romanian stage and are translated and performed all over the world. Vişniec is not only interested in the crimes committed under communism; his concern is with the broader human predicament of existing in modern society, in a violent world whatever the dominant ideology.

Present-day Romania is experiencing a theatrical renaissance. Freedom of expression has exploded in a myriad of new theatre groups and private theatre schools that are nurturing a new generation of artists. International festivals in Romania introduce the best productions from all over the world, thus fostering a close connection with the global theatre community. Romania with its rich theatre tradition continues to combine the classical with the contemporary, giving new playwrights a prominent and open place to be heard.

As an interesting postscript: in July 2009, Matei Vişniec contributed his play *Occident Express* to a most unusual theatre venture. Conceived by the dramaturg of the Stuttgart Staatstheater, a theatre collaborative of companies from Turkey, Romania, Serbia, Croatia, Slovenia, and Germany made its way from Ankara, Turkey, to Freiburg, Germany, aboard a "theatre train." Each ensemble contributed an original play written for the project, *Orient-Express—a European Theatre Journey*. The companies played in railroad stations, making several stops in each country along the way. The train housed the actors, technical staff, sets, and costumes of all the companies. It was considered a triumph by the press. Matei Vişniec's play contains two emblematic scenes that show an old and a new Romania. One scene centers on an old blind man in a provincial village along the route of the Orient Express who has longed to go to the West all his life. A trick by his granddaughter gives him the illusion that he has finally achieved his dream. She sets up a battered train door and a fan in front of him and asks him to hold on to the door while she directs the wind into his face, thus making him think he is on his way to the legendary West. In another scene a Croat, a Serb, a Bosnian, a Hungarian, a Macedonian, an Albanian, a Bulgarian, and a Romanian are all sitting on a fence, staring into empty space. The Bulgarian comments that he doesn't know how the Ukrainian, the Hungarian, the Serb, or even his neighbor curses, though he knows how the Americans do. The Serb promptly pipes up with: "Fuck." All agree, they have much that connects them, as they put on their earphones and listen to American music. Thus Vişniec creates paradigmatic images of the old Eastern longing for the mythical West as well as the contemporary globalization of popular culture that has washed over all as they sit on the fence between East and West, between the inability to communicate and mass consumption.

HORSES AT THE WINDOW

Matei Vișniec

Translated by Alison Sinclair

CHARACTERS

THE SON

THE MOTHER

THE FATHER

THE DAUGHTER

THE HUSBAND

THE WIFE

THE MESSENGER

All of the female characters can be played by the same actress.
THE SON, THE FATHER, THE HUSBAND (*and even* THE MESSENGER)
can be played by the same actor.

THE MESSENGER *enters in a follow spot. He comes downstage and sets up a music stand. He takes several papers out of his pocket, unfolds them and puts them on the stand. He takes up his drum.*

THE MESSENGER (drums): The year sixteen hundred and ninety-nine.
(*Drums.*) The Peace of Carlowitz.
(*Drums.*) Austria takes Croatia and Silesia.
(*Drums.*) Prussia takes the Dukedom of Goldern.
(*Drums.*) Spain takes the Dukedoms of Parma and Piacenza.
(*Drums.*) France takes Alsace and Lorraine.
(*Drums.*) Russia takes Georgia, the City of Ahaltin, and the Khan's lands of Erevan and Nahicevan.
(*Drums.*) England takes the Ionian Islands.

THE MESSENGER *exits. The light increases. Out of the dimness, a room with a window appears. In the room, a ragged armchair and a ragged suitcase. A tap fixed to the wall. At long intervals, water drips from the tap.*

THE SON *stands at the window, dressed in military uniform.* THE MOTHER *brings him his jacket.* THE SON *puts on his jacket.*

THE MOTHER: Does it fit?

THE SON: Yes.

THE MOTHER: It's not too tight?

THE SON: No.

THE MOTHER: The sleeves seem rather long. Don't you think they are rather long?

THE SON: No.

THE MOTHER: Turn round! Are you sure it's not too tight? I have a feeling it's too tight.

THE SON: It's not too tight.

THE MOTHER: Anyway, do it up! It seems to me that the buttons are rather loose. Don't you think the buttons are rather loose

THE SON: Just now a horse passed by.

THE MOTHER: Buttons must not be sewn too tightly. The tighter you sew them the quicker they undo.

THE SON: It was red with black markings. Can that be?

THE MOTHER: Have you eaten?

THE SON: No.

THE MOTHER: Then you shouldn't have put your jacket on. You should eat first, then put your jacket on.

THE SON: Yes.

THE MOTHER: Come and eat. Be careful not to make crumbs. Crumbs always fall between the floorboards. In every crack between the floorboards there are hundreds of crumbs.

THE SON (*sitting at the table, chewing blankly*): I won't make crumbs.

THE MOTHER (*fetching another ragged suitcase and filling it with* THE SON's *things*): Suitcase. In the suitcase, things must be kept in strict order. Things must be piled neatly, not thrown in. First, pack the large items you won't need right away, then pack the large items you will need right away. Next, pack the small items you won't need straightaway, and finally, pack the small items you will need straightaway. Having done all this, pull the straps and click the locks . . . like so . . . (*Click! Click!*) Did you hear that? The locks of a well-packed suitcases produce a sweet, harmonious sound.

THE SON (*oblivious to* THE MOTHER's *words, following his obsession*): The horse is back. I have the feeling it's hovering round the window. Can that be?

THE MOTHER: Socks. Socks must be kept with handkerchiefs. A handkerchief for each pair of socks, and vice versa. No one can survive without handkerchiefs and socks. Promise me you'll wash out a handkerchief and a pair of socks every evening.

THE SON: The horse is mad, honestly. It keeps looking behind it as though it were waiting for a cart.

THE MOTHER: The suitcase must never be overpacked. Overpacking the suitcase may embarrass those around you.

THE SON (*agitatedly*): The horse has stopped and is looking straight at us. Should we close the window?

THE MOTHER: Have you finished? If you've finished you may drink a glass of water. There's boiled water in the fridge.

THE SON: The horse is looking straight at me. When someone looks straight at me do they actually see me?

THE MOTHER: You ate too quickly. It's not good to eat quickly. When you eat quickly you make lots of crumbs. Have you made crumbs?

THE SON: No.

THE MOTHER: I think I heard some crumbs fall. I think a real man doesn't need to make crumbs. A real man needs to eat quietly, to eat everything and to not make crumbs. Crumbs, if they fall between the floorboards, can never be gotten out. That's why most floors smell horrible.

THE SON: His master has come. Now they are together. The horse is happy.

THE MOTHER: Do you want more water? It's not good to drink too much water anyway. A real man doesn't go about with a stomach full of water.

THE SON: They are playing. I think they're crazy, the pair of them. Really, that horse is a sly one.

THE MOTHER: Boots. You must never leave your boots dirty overnight or they'll fall on your head. Dirt destroys the leather, corrodes everything, erodes everything. And don't wander around in the rain. Rain drops are in fact very dirty.

THE SON: I heard that yesterday morning the horses took over the abattoir. Can that be?

THE MOTHER: Soap must always be kept in its box, in the dark. It must never be left in the light or it'll go bad, won't it? Besides if you wash yourself with stale soap, what's the use of washing at all? Wet towels must never be folded. Nothing weighs heavier than a wet folded towel.

THE SON: There's the cart now.

THE MOTHER: Sugar. Sugar must never be kept in paper bags. Any paper bag will have a tiny hole in it through which millions of grains of sugar can trickle.

Teaspoons. Teaspoons must be wiped thoroughly after being removed from the teacup. Teaspoons rust very quickly, that's why they should be dried immediately. It's very important that your teaspoon should not rust too soon.

THE SON: It's raining. I think he'll harness the horse anyway.

THE MOTHER: Shirts. Shirts become saggy after just two days' wear. After three days the shirt sticks to the skin. When the shirt sticks to the skin it should be taken off for good. When it rains the skin sticks to the flesh. After three days the flesh will have a rancid smell. Don't forget, the smell of rancid flesh is fatal to a man. Watch your step, the air is full of smoke and the streets are full of puddles. When someone smiles at you in the street, respond with a laugh. Lend nothing, not even a little thing like a safety pin. If someone calls to you in the street don't turn your head . . . There are thousands of people with the same name as you . . .

THE SON: The cart is ready. It won't be long before dark.

THE SON *stands and goes with heavy steps to the door.*

THE MOTHER (*quickening the rhythm, speaking louder and louder, gradually entering a verbal trance*): Wait! Muffler! The muffler must be long and narrow . . . Only that way can you wrap it adequately around your neck . . . The collar must be soft and warm . . . Never speak with the wind in your face . . . Don't point with your finger, don't hit the table with your fist . . . Don't drop playing cards and don't crumple banknotes! Don't walk barefoot on stone floors . . . Don't fall asleep with your mouth open . . . When you dream of frogs do all you can to wake up. (*She clings more and more desperately to* THE SON.) Write me a postcard every day, take care of your elbows and knees, don't think of the red horse with the black markings . . . Don't go near the horses, don't hold out your hand to touch them . . . The horses have already taken over the abattoir yard . . . Wait! Take this money but don't keep it all in one pocket . . .

THE SON: Mother, my pockets are sewn up . . .

THE SON *exits dragging the suitcase.* THE SON *exits but has forgotten to put his boots on.*

THE MOTHER *grabs them and throws herself at the window.*

THE MOTHER: Wait! Wait!

THE MOTHER *throws* THE SON *the boots, one after the other. At the same time someone knocks loudly at the door.* THE MOTHER *goes wearily to the door and opens it.*

Enter THE MESSENGER *with a bunch of carnations in his hand; around his neck he wears the boots that* THE MOTHER *has just thrown out of the window.*

THE MESSENGER (*cheerfully*): Good day, Madam, may I offer you these flowers?

THE MOTHER: What flowers are they?

THE MESSENGER: Carnations, Madam. I picked them with my own hand from the regimental lawn.

THE MOTHER: Thank you, Sir. Put them as far away from me as possible. The smell of carnations makes me sick.

THE MESSENGER: May I put them under the table?

THE MOTHER: I'd rather you put them in that suitcase.

THE MESSENGER *opens the suitcase which is already filled with carnations. He stuffs his flowers on top of the others, closes the suitcase—click! clack!—and sits on it.*

THE MOTHER: You may sit on the suitcase if you like.

THE MESSENGER: Thank you, Madam. I think I will sit for a while.

THE MOTHER: Tell me, please, are you the man with the horse?

THE MESSENGER (*playing from time to time with the suitcase locks: click! clack!*): Yes, Madam, I'm the man with the horse.

THE MOTHER: So it was you just now hovering around the windows!

THE MESSENGER: It was us, Madam.

THE MOTHER: And do you consider it right to keep your horse out in the rain? I think one should never keep animals out in the rain, except for fishes, of course.

THE MESSENGER: I'm glad you think that. You see, I'm from the regiment, I often pass by your window. Our opinion is that windows represent a reliable opportunity to establish contact with reality.

THE MOTHER: Sir, you are about to give me some bad news.

THE MESSENGER (*click! clack!*): Yes, Madam . . . But I don't know how to begin.

THE MOTHER: Has anything happened to my son?

THE MESSENGER: Yes, Madam. That's the very reason I was sent here, in order to prepare you spiritually. It's not an easy task to prepare someone spiritually. Put yourself in my position . . . Other people bring bad news quite bluntly . . . But not me, Madam, I have always proceeded with tact and delicacy. And I've always managed to break the most terrible news in the subtlest way possible. (*Click! Clack!*) I have never yet failed this moment. Thanks to my aforesaid subtle manner, many people have been grateful to me . . . I have spared them, if I may say so, thousands of tears . . . Sometimes I have even managed to turn such circumstances into an opportunity for hope, and, even good humor . . . I'm sure that, had I only known how to begin, we'd have been having a nice and pleasant chat by now . . . I have often brought a beam of light into people's homes due to my pleasant manner . . . I have won many friends and returned to many homes with pleasure.

THE MOTHER: Cut it out! My son is dead, isn't he?

THE MESSENGER: Yes, Madam. You see, I know the human soul. I know exactly when to choose the right moment, that unique and singular moment when I permit myself, for a split second, to touch the wound. (*Click! Clack!*) Please believe me, there is no one can touch the wound more delicately than I, in a lighter and more sensitive way than I . . . Sometimes I accomplish real feats of skill, my touch is so discreet and tender that the wound almost heals.

THE MOTHER (*desperate, wandering about the room*): Oh I knew it . . . I knew that it would come to this.

THE MESSENGER: In fact, I'm going to tell you everything. Yes, I want to tell you everything . . . Because my great secret lies in the way I know how to share another's sorrow . . . Because I, Madam, have an immense capacity to experience sorrow . . . That's why whenever I bring terrible news, the sorrow on my face has such a profound affect that those who are hit with the real misfortune are the first to feel compelled to comfort me . . . Look at me, Madam, take a good look at me, barefoot with my boots soaking wet . . . For I, Madam, would never leave my boots dirty overnight . . .

THE MOTHER (*crying*): Oh, shut up! Shut up! Shut up! Is this any way to break such news?

THE MESSENGER: Isn't it? Leaving one's boots dirty overnight is a crime. Dirt destroys everything, erodes and corrodes everything. (*Short reflective pause.*) Did I make a mistake? Did I miss something? I'm terribly sorry . . . I may have mixed up a few phrases. But normally, everything that I've said so far should have comforted you enormously . . . Yes, we should have been talking about something completely different by now . . . Did you know that I had a very hard and unhappy childhood?

THE MOTHER (*desperately*): But how could this have happened? How? What if you mixed up the lists. Maybe you did mix up the lists. Are you positive you didn't mix up the lists? Could you perhaps show me the lists?

THE MESSENGER (*offended, but checking his lists*): No, Madam, I never mix things up. I am always correct and efficient. My profession demands great precision.

THE MOTHER: I want to know everything! Did you know him personally? Did you know him at all? Did he die in battle?

THE MESSENGER (*confused*): Well no . . . Not exactly in battle . . . But anyway, he was in uniform . . . Even though, if I remember correctly, he had rolled up his sleeves . . . and the army regulations . . .

THE MOTHER (*nostalgically*): That how he was . . . He couldn't stand long sleeves . . . Even as a little boy he used to roll up his shirt sleeves.

THE MESSENGER: I knew there would be an explanation, there's always an explanation!

THE MOTHER: More! More! Tell me more! Did his cap suit him? Was he brave? Did he fight like a lion?

THE MESSENGER: He didn't have a chance to fight at all. He'd only just had his hair cut.

THE MOTHER: What do you mean he didn't have chance? How's that? Perhaps he wasn't given a gun.

THE MESSENGER: He was given a gun, Madam, but to tell you the truth, he didn't really know how to handle it. As a matter of fact he didn't really know much at all . . .

THE MOTHER: Nothing, nothing at all?

THE MESSENGER: Well, not quite nothing . . . He knew how to stand at attention. He was very good at that, and my feeling is that while standing to attention he could quite easily nod off.

THE MOTHER: How awful. Would you mind turning on the tap? It soothes me when I hear the water run . . .

THE MESSENGER: Why of course. (*A gush of black water.*) What kind of water is that?

THE MOTHER: Plain water. What kind of water did you think it was?

THE MESSENGER: It's black. How can you drink black water?

THE MOTHER: I don't drink it, I listen to it. My son also liked to listen to the water . . . Sometimes we would both listen to how the water ran and that made us feel very close to each other. Especially on Saturday afternoons and Sundays we would listen to how the water ran. My son knew how to turn on the tap, to let flow the exact amount of water to fit our mood . . . If we were tired, he would allow only tiny drops to drip out of the tap . . . The more tired we were, the longer the intervals between drops . . . My son was amazingly skilful with the tap . . . He knew how to tighten it so that there would be only one drop every hour . . . . Yes, he was a strange and exemplary child . . . From the moment of his birth I realized how fragile his encounter with this world would be . . . He never cried, not even in his sleep . . . He never whined, never screamed . . . . When he was a baby he would lie in his cradle and wait . . . Not a wink, not a cough, not a pee, not a poo, not a hiccup . . . Never . . . (*During this monologue, old photographs may eventually be burned.*) He was never ill . . . He would stay awake in the day and sleep like a log at night. When he got older I used to send him to buy milk and every time he would come back with a bottle of milk. I was so proud of him . . . And if I sent him to buy bread he would come back with bread, if I sent him to buy soap he would come back with soap. He always walked close to the walls and only crossed the streets at corners . . . In his youth he liked to catch flies and to fish. He was a good child, a wonderful son, quiet as a virgin . . . Did he at least say anything before he died?

THE MESSENGER: He said "Ouch!"

THE MOTHER: He said "Ouch!"?

THE MESSENGER: Yes, he said "Ouch!"

THE MOTHER: That means that it hurt.

THE MESSENGER: Perhaps it did hurt. But only a little.

THE MOTHER: Was he blown apart by a stray shell?

THE MESSENGER: Oh no. It was peacetime.

THE MOTHER: Peacetime? Then how did it happen? Who could have killed him in peacetime?

THE MESSENGER (*meekly*): The horse, Madam . . .

THE MOTHER: The red horse? Oh no! And I told him never to go near the horse.

THE MESSENGER: And yet he did go near. Just as I was coming back with the bread cart, your son got up and came over to the horse . . . He said, "Good horse!" and the horse looked him straight in the eye and simply kicked him swiftly with its hoof. That was all. It happened on a sunny Sunday morning. Your son was to be given a new pair of boots the next day.

THE MOTHER: How unlucky . . . He didn't even have the chance to wear them . . .

THE MESSENGER: That was all, Madam. I've brought you his things.

THE MOTHER (*deeply moved*): His things, did you say? What . . . ? Oh, God, I must be dreaming! So he did leave something behind?

THE MESSENGER: He left . . . he left five packets of biscuits.

THE MOTHER: That's all?

THE MESSENGER: That's all.

THE MOTHER: Give them to me, quick!

She snatches them, tears one open and starts to eat. They're good.

THE MESSENGER: Army biscuits. The regiment makes the best possible biscuits.

THE MOTHER (*munching*): May I have the recipe?

THE MESSENGER: The recipe was written on the wrapper. You shouldn't have torn the wrapper.

THE MOTHER (*munching, sighing*): I don't know what's wrong with me. For a while now every time I see a piece of paper I can't help crumpling it.

THE MESSENGER: So . . . goodbye, Madam.

THE MOTHER: Wait! And the grave? How do I get to the grave?

THE MESSENGER: He has no grave.

THE MOTHER: I mean . . . the body . . .

THE MESSENGER: He has no body.

THE MOTHER: He has no body?

THE MESSENGER: He has no body.

THE MOTHER: I don't understand. He died and he left nothing in his place?

THE MESSENGER: Exactly.

THE MOTHER: That's not possible. That's not like him.

THE MESSENGER: It is rather odd, I agree . . . I don't know how to say this to you . . . your son was as gentle as the breeze . . . He simply vanished from the universe . . . He doubled over with the pain, curling up more and more until he became merely a spot, then the spot itself disappeared . . . As far as that's concerned, he acted, if I may say so, as an exemplary soldier . . . Just think how clean the battlefields would be if soldiers left no bodies behind after their deaths.

THE MOTHER: And the packets of biscuits? Are you sure that they're his?

THE MESSENGER: They were found under his pillow in the dormitory.

THE MOTHER: Unless someone else put them there . . .

THE MESSENGER: That's possible . . . Madam, would you allow me to turn off the water?

THE MOTHER: It doesn't matter any more.

THE MESSENGER (*having turned off the water*): There we are. That's much better. I'd like to leave you in silence.

THE MOTHER: Stay a little longer. Would you like some herbal tea perhaps?

HE MESSENGER: It would be a pleasure, really, but unfortunately my horse is waiting for me. When it rains it's a real torture for him. He gets so saturated that I can hardly move him. Nevertheless, I hope you'll allow me to pay you a visit from time to time.

THE MOTHER: Good-bye, sir . . . And take care not to slam the front door when you leave . . .

THE MESSENGER *comes downstage. He sets up his music stand. He takes up his drum. He searches in his pockets and finally takes out some crumpled pieces of paper. Spotlight on* THE MESSENGER.

THE MESSENGER (*drums*): Seventeen hundred and forty-five.
(*Drums.*) The Peace of Breslau.
(*Drums.*) Turkey takes Tripolitania.
(*Drums.*) Prussia takes Silesia from Austria.
(*Drums.*) Austria takes Milan, Naples, and Sardinia.
(*Drums.*) Spain takes Sicily.
(*Drums.*) Russia takes Mingrelia and Imertia.
(*Drums.*) France loses Alsace, Lorraine, and Marienburg.

THE MESSENGER *exits. The light grows stronger. The female character becomes* THE DAUGHTER. THE SON *becomes* THE FATHER. THE FATHER *rushes into the room driving his wheelchair feverishly.*

THE FATHER: Who was here? I want to know who was here!

THE DAUGHTER: There was no one here.

THE FATHER: Someone slammed the front door. I heard them slam the front door.

THE DAUGHTER: No one slammed the door.

THE FATHER: Yes, I heard it!

THE DAUGHTER: You are wearing that *eau de Cologne* again.

THE FATHER (*rushing at the window*): So, you won't tell me who it was! You know, you are driving me absolutely crazy! Why don't you ever call me when someone comes?

THE DAUGHTER: You'll poison yourself with that smell.

THE FATHER: Oh, shut up! Why didn't you tell them not to slam the front door when leaving? You should have told them not to slam it. Why do they all slam the front door? And why do they slam it only when they leave? Why don't they slam it when they come in? Why do they tiptoe in? Why do they all tiptoe in and slam the door when they leave?

THE DAUGHTER: Where did you leave your nightcap? Why don't you put your nightcap on?

THE FATHER (*flabbergasted*): Did they smoke? (*He sniffs.*) They smoked! They did smoke, didn't they? Where did you hide the butts? I want to see the butts!

THE DAUGHTER: No one smoked.

THE FATHER (*pulling at the window; finally managing to open it*): You locked the window! Why did you lock the window? I want to let the smoke out. I can't stand smoke. You know I can't stand smoke! There you are, look how the smoke goes out!

THE DAUGHTER: It's the smoke from the trash. The trash is being burned. Close the window or else all the smoke from the trash will get in here.

THE FATHER (*eager*): Let me see! Where's the fire? I want to see the fire!

THE DAUGHTER: There's no fire. The trash burns without a flame. It's only smouldering.

THE FATHER: I'm frightened you know. What if we collapse on top of it? What if we do fall on top of it?

THE DAUGHTER: Go to sleep. If you feel frightened, go to sleep. Whenever you are frightened you should go to sleep.

THE FATHER: No. I can't sleep. When I sleep my skin turns flabby. I'd rather stay awake, believe me. And also, if I stay awake, I don't lose time. Believe me it's easier for me to stay awake. You understand, if I stay awake I gain time, time . . .

THE DAUGHTER: If you stay awake you doze.

THE FATHER: So what if I doze? I don't want to doze . . . Why do you think I doze? I doze because I feel very lonely. You understand, Isabel, that's what happens to me; in fact, whenever I feel very lonely I doze. (*Intent, grave.*) Swear to me that if I doze again you'll wake me up.

THE DAUGHTER: I swear!

THE FATHER: Say it again!

THE DAUGHTER: I swear!

THE FATHER: Every time when I'm asleep, I know that I am asleep and the worst thing is that although I know it, I can't wake myself up. This is what frightens me most, that I can't wake myself up. I never dream of anything, and yet I cannot wake up. And I feel that my skin stretches with sleeping. Are you listening to me, Isabel?

THE DAUGHTER: That's because you don't know how to sleep. You should sleep lying on your back and breathe only through your nose.

THE FATHER: And if it rains? When it rains, what do you do when it rains, if you can't breathe through your nose? You know I can't breathe through my nose, you know . . . (*Sweetly.*) Isabel . . . let's go out for a little walk.

THE DAUGHTER: It's raining. I can't take you out when it rains.

THE FATHER: So what if it's raining? I want you to take me out in the rain.

THE DAUGHTER: The wheelchair will rust.

THE FATHER: Oh, you're so mean, so mean! I'm ashamed to be your father! I'll tell Mrs. Hilda all about it, all. Everyone will hear about this, you know . . . (*Whimpering.*) I want us to pay a visit to Mrs. Hilda tomorrow.

THE DAUGHTER (*quietly*): Mrs. Hilda has moved . . .

THE FATHER (*listening*): I can hear footsteps in the street! I hear footsteps! Don't you hear footsteps? When you hear footsteps it means the rain has stopped.

THE DAUGHTER: Come and lie down. Won't you lie down? Come and lie down.

THE FATHER: No . . . No . . . I'll stay with you a little longer . . . I wanted to tell you something, something very important . . . This morning I noticed something . . . I tell you, there's something wrong, because of the clock. I think that the minute hand, every time it passes over the little hand, furiously devours a little bit of the small hand.

THE DAUGHTER: That can't be right.

THE FATHER: Oh, but it is, Isabel, it is . . . For ten days I've kept my eye on the clock, I tell you . . . I've counted thousands of times . . . I have all the measurements . . . (*He takes some small pieces of string out of his pocket.*) I've measured the minute hand as well as the hour hand after each passage . . . There's nothing wrong with the minute hand . . . But the hour hand gets smaller every time . . . See for yourself . . . thinner and thinner . . . Do you realize what's going to happen, do you realize? Isabel . . . Let me stay with you a little longer.

THE DAUGHTER: Alright. But don't go on about it.

THE FATHER: For several nights now I keep dreaming about stewed fruit jars. Is that alright?

THE DAUGHTER: Alright then, tell me the story.

THE FATHER: I won't tell unless you ask me.

THE DAUGHTER: Go on, tell me about how you met Mother.

THE FATHER (*petulantly*): I won't tell! What do you know? I don't want you to know anything!

THE DAUGHTER: Oh, come on, tell me about how you met Mother.

THE FATHER: Very simple. I was at the grocer's and she had just bought some jars of stewed fruit.

THE DAUGHTER: How many?

THE FATHER: Fifteen.

THE DAUGHTER: What did she do with so many jars of stewed fruit?

THE FATHER: That's exactly what I asked her. I went after her and I asked her, "Miss, what are you doing with so many jars of stewed fruit?"

THE DAUGHTER: What did she say?

THE FATHER: She called me a rat, a cockroach, and a madman.

THE DAUGHTER: And you?

THE FATHER: I was a sergeant.

THE DAUGHTER: And her?

THE FATHER: She took the tram. I followed her onto the tram. Six weeks later we were married. In another six weeks the war started. It was a great war.

THE DAUGHTER: That's enough.

THE FATHER: No, no, no! Ask me more!

THE DAUGHTER: And? Did you win?

THE FATHER: Like Hell we did! The bastards beat us at the last minute. But that doesn't matter. Anyway, there were more of us and better drilled than they were. Nowadays the drill is not what it used to be. Nowadays it's nothing but crap! Everybody grumbles. Even the trash man grumbles . . . How can you expect to win when all this lot do is grumble? They're all mad anyway . . . The lack of the drill . . .

THE DAUGHTER: Let me put you to bed. Come on, it's better for the wheelchair too. The springs will release a little.

THE FATHER (*in a trance*): Did I ever show you the two-cornered cross? Do you have any idea how hard it was to get the two-cornered cross in those days? Nowadays everybody gets the two-cornered cross.

THE DAUGHTER: Don't you want me to turn off the lamp? The light shines right in your eyes. And when you lie down for a rest your eyes mustn't be tired.

THE FATHER: Did I ever show you the three-cornered cross? Do you have any idea how hard it was to get the three-cornered cross in those days? Nowadays everybody gets the three-cornered cross.

THE DAUGHTER: Don't you want me to take your boots off? It's not good to sleep with your boots on. Boots are heavy and they drag you down to the bottom.

THE FATHER: Did I ever show you the four-cornered cross? Do you have any idea how hard it was to get the four-cornered cross in those days. At Trebizond only ten men escaped and only one of them got the four-cornered cross. Nowadays everybody gets the four-cornered cross. And what for? (*Choking with indignation.*) What for? What for? What for?

THE DAUGHTER: Come on, give them to me. I'll put them in the wardrobe.

THE FATHER: I'm not giving you anything! Stop nagging! I want to sleep with them on.

THE DAUGHTER: You'll catch a cold. If you keep them on your chest all day long, you'll catch a cold.

THE FATHER: You are mean. I'll tell Mrs. Hilda . . . Tomorrow I want us to pay a visit to Mrs. Hilda.

THE DAUGHTER: All your clothes have come undone because of them.

THE FATHER: But you know how I managed to escape at Trebizond, don't you? You know? How do you know? You don't know . . .

THE DAUGHTER: I know.

THE FATHER: No! No! No! Ask!

THE DAUGHTER: How?

THE FATHER: I swam, hee-hee!

THE DAUGHTER: You swam, hee-hee!

THE FATHER: Yes, yes, yes! By God! I swam all night long among swollen corpses . . . Today I took a look at the river, out of curiosity . . . It seemed to me that there was still something floating . . .

THE DAUGHTER: Don't you want me to turn on the water? It will calm you if I turn on the water.

THE FATHER: Yes, turn it on! I was just thinking of teaching you to swim. And that's just the way to start, you have to learn to get used to water. Nowadays things are so frail, much more frail and they sink much more quickly . . . That's because they don't have any joints, you understand? That's why you have to learn how to keep afloat right away. You could learn this in an evening if you wanted to. Even this evening, you understand?   It is very important to keep afloat, no matter how shallow the water is. Do you have any water?

THE DAUGHTER (*filling a glass*): I have a glassful.

THE FATHER: Is it deep?

THE DAUGHTER (*contemplating the glass*): It's black.

THE FATHER: Are you afraid of it?

THE DAUGHTER: No.

THE FATHER: That's good. Being afraid of deep water is the worst thing for a swimmer.

THE DAUGHTER: I'm not afraid of water, I'm afraid of air. Father, is there air in the water?

THE FATHER: One never knows how much. You have to drink the whole glass. It's the only way to determine the amount of air in the water.

THE DAUGHTER: All of it?

THE FATHER: You have to drink all the water that you will swim in. It's the only way to become a good swimmer.

THE DAUGHTER (*suddenly tired*): It's late. Don't you think we should draw the curtains? The cockroaches will get in.

THE DAUGHTER *begins to push the wheelchair towards the door. The light dims.*

THE FATHER: Have you drunk it? Now wait . . . The best thing you can do now is wait . . .

The voice of THE FATHER *drifts away down the corridor.*

THE FATHER: He who knows how to wait is a saved man . . . If you know how to wait, the brain is able to rest by itself . . . He who manages to rest is able to wait more easily . . . the more rested one is while waiting, the less important things appear to him . . . But it is better to wait alone . . . Mrs. Hilda didn't wait alone and that's what finished her . . . He who does not wait alone does not deserve to wait at all . . . The best way to wait is in the dark . . . He who has black curtains is a saved man . . . Because he can have darkness in his room at anytime . . . Anytime . . . Anytime . . .

The sound of the front door being opened. Steps coming up. THE DAUGHTER, *lighting the way with a lamp, ushers in* THE MESSENGER. *The latter carries a wheelchair that seems to have been flattened by a bulldozer. He carries the eternal bunch of carnations.*

THE MESSENGER: Only if I'm not disturbing you . . .

THE DAUGHTER: No, not at all. It's just that I don't know what it is all about . . .

THE MESSENGER: What? Is it possible that you don't remember anything?

THE DAUGHTER: No . . . but maybe it's because of the afternoon . . . Every afternoon I feel somehow troubled . . . But I think it's because of the light . . . Every afternoon the light has a slight flicker to it . . . But that must be because of the dark . . . The dark comes so slowly that I can almost feel my own skin caving in on me . . .

THE MESSENGER: It's quite possible . . .

THE DAUGHTER: Anyway, come in . . . You may sit on that suitcase.

THE MESSENGER: Thank you, Miss. (*He stuffs the bunch of flowers into the suitcase.*) It's quite comfortable here.

THE DAUGHTER: Are you sure you haven't come to the wrong house?

THE MESSENGER: Oh no . . . I never mix things up. You yourself permitted me to pay you a visit now and then.

THE DAUGHTER: Really? In fact, if I remember correctly, I seem to know your laugh.

THE MESSENGER: Now, you see? You realize, I would never have come of my own accord.

THE DAUGHTER: And this thing, why does it look so funny, and why do you carry it along?

THE MESSENGER: That, Miss, is a long story.

THE DAUGHTER: Strange. Even the way you talk to me seems somehow familiar.

THE MESSENGER: Do you like the way I talk?

THE DAUGHTER: I like it very much . . . It makes me feel safe when I hear your voice.

THE MESSENGER: That's because I'm a man who inspires confidence. I have always managed to get close to people quickly. By the way, maybe we should call other by our first names. Have you ever called anyone by their first name before?

THE DAUGHTER: I don't know . . . maybe, a long time ago, as a child . . . .

THE MESSENGER: Let's not dig up childhood . . . it's better to talk about the present . . . You know, I'm a messenger from the regiment.

THE DAUGHTER: I know. Every evening my father tells me about the battle of Trebizond. Were you at Trebizond?

THE MESSENGER: Let's not talk about Trebizond, that's exactly where I've come from.

THE DAUGHTER (*excitedly*): From Trebizond?

THE MESSENGER: Look at these mud stains a moment. These stains are still fresh. Look me in the eyes a moment. I may still look like a man . . . But I'm no longer a man . . . I've seen horrible things . . . My eyes are already wounded forever . . . I bear all the dead in my mind . . .

THE DAUGHTER: And my father? What do you know of my father?

THE MESSENGER: Your father escaped.

THE DAUGHTER: He escaped? Oh, thank God!

THE MESSENGER: Yes, Miss, he escaped. It's a great joy for me to bring you this news. Your father is a real hero, and this is simply due to the fact that he managed to escape.

THE DAUGHTER: Sir, can I offer you a cup of apricot pits?

THE MESSENGER (*in a low voice*): Unfortunately, a terrible thing happened to him on the road . . .

THE DAUGHTER: What do you mean? What road? What road are you talking about?

THE MESSENGER: The road back, of course. The solitude made him lose his mind.

THE DAUGHTER: What do you mean, lose his mind?

THE MESSENGER: I mean that he's gone mad.

THE DAUGHTER: But why did he come back alone?

THE MESSENGER: Because he was the only one who escaped.

THE DAUGHTER: I don't understand.

THE MESSENGER: And then there's the horse.

THE DAUGHTER: I don't understand anything. You know, I think it's because of the air . . . In the afternoon the air collapses from such a great height . . .

THE MESSENGER: Now calm yourself, Miss. If you want to we can talk about something else.

THE DAUGHTER: No, it's better if you try to turn on the tap.

THE MESSENGER (*turning on the tap*): Nothing's coming out.

THE DAUGHTER: Turn it on full.

THE MESSENGER: I turned it on full, but nothing's coming out.

THE DAUGHTER: Leave it. It's better anyway. Now I'm listening.

THE MESSENGER: You know, the longer the road, the lonelier one feels . . . And the road back, Miss, is always devilishly long . . . You see, for your father the war itself was nothing, a mere trifle . . . But the solitude on the way back was more than he could bear . . . And on top of that he was followed by the horse . . .

THE DAUGHTER: The horse? His own horse?

THE MESSENGER: It's still not known whose horse it was. It's not known whose it was and how it escaped from there. But what is certain is that it followed your father every step of the way. The horse followed him with a vengeance day after day, night after night . . . Surely it must have been a nightmare . . . Can you imagine how terrible it must be to have someone breathing down your neck the whole way back?

THE DAUGHTER: How awful! Sir, you have given me some very distressing news. I won't have a moment's peace this afternoon.

THE MESSENGER: That was all. I can also tell you, quite confidentially, that the horse is no better. I think the horse, in its way was somehow shaken, considering that . . . you know . . . animals . . . Anyhow . . . that's that. Nevertheless, the regiment offers you this excellent wheelchair which needs only minor repairs . . . It certainly is a soft, comfortable, and warm wheelchair . . . Your father will be able to spend the rest of his days resting in it . . .

THE DAUGHTER: Thank you, Sir. I'll take care of everything.

THE MESSENGER: It's quite a rare piece. Nowadays they don't make such beautiful and relaxing things. All you have to do is dust it, especially under the armrests. Dirt gathers mainly under the armrests.

THE DAUGHTER: I know that, Sir, I've spent years trying to remove the crumbs that gather between floorboards, without success.

THE MESSENGER: Patience is all, Miss. The old man's madness is gentle and calm. His presence in a corner of the room will be like a beam of light.

THE DAUGHTER: In fact, that's how he's always been. Gentle and calm, incredibly calm.

THE MESSENGER: You see? Perhaps deep inside he hasn't changed at all.

THE DAUGHTER: He was such a kind man that I can hardly remember anything about him. He never shouted at me, he never looked me in the eyes, and I don't know that he ever said anything to me . . . When I was a child he used to buy me toys, but he didn't dare give them to me . . . He'd pile them all into a wardrobe, one on top of the other, until the shelves of the wardrobe gave way under the weight of the toys. The wardrobe is still in its place today, but I have never had the courage to open it and look inside . . . Only sometimes, on cold nights, the sprocket wheels and the small springs start gently cracking . . .

THE MESSENGER: I love the way things twist and crack at night. My boots simply sag because of the dark.

THE DAUGHTER: Later, when he started growing old, he hid from me even more. He would go from one room to another easier than a shadow. He would sit at the table and eat shyly, in silence. The plate he ate from was so clean by the end that I was quite simply frightened by it. Some old people belch after eating. He would remain still for hours, his jaws clenched. When it rained, he usually sat at the window and stared blankly into space. Sometimes he would walk in the rain and his clothes wouldn't even get wet. All the doors opened silently before him, and all his gestures melted into air . . . He was so alone that it's a miracle he had children of his own. Are you asleep?

THE MESSENGER: No, Miss, I was just thinking with my eyes closed.

Suddenly a spurt of black water bursts out of the tap. Outside, cheering and military band music can be heard.

THE DAUGHTER: What's that? Have they all gone mad?

THE MESSENGER (*turning off the tap*): No, Miss, it's the parade. The liberating soldiers are coming home.

THE DAUGHTER (*running to the window*): How handsome they are! Is that all of them?

THE MESSENGER: The Devil knows. Sometimes more return than left. But it's hard to tell because of the crowds . . . Because of the crowds and because of the dark.

THE DAUGHTER: Father used to say that the liberated soldiers often parade with the liberating ones. Can that be?

THE MESSENGER: Miss, I think you should close the window.

THE DAUGHTER: I'd like to at least blow them a kiss . . .

THE MESSENGER: There's little point in that, believe me. The soldiers are blind. They are blind and deaf. The trumpets are playing for the people.

THE DAUGHTER: But I want to see the horses. The horses are innocent. I so much like to see the horses.

THE MESSENGER: Miss, avoid looking at the horses. They are no longer the horses they were. They have become vengeful and covetous. They lurk everywhere, lying in wait behind doors and at windows.

THE DAUGHTER: How sad! Do you think that even at this moment, someone is lying in wait for us?

THE MESSENGER: I don't know, Miss. Maybe, maybe not . . . Goodbye and be sure to keep those armrests clean!

THE DAUGHTER: Are you leaving already?

THE MESSENGER: It's late, and I have a few more calls to make.

THE DAUGHTER: Please take care not to slam the front door. My father is such a light sleeper that sometimes I'm even afraid to open a book . . .

THE MESSENGER: Why, of course. You can rely on me.

THE MESSENGER *comes downstage. He puts on his drum. He searches in his pockets and takes out some crumpled papers. Spotlight on* THE MESSENGER.

THE MESSENGER (*drums*): Eighteen hundred and fifteen.
(*Drums.*) Prussia takes Swedish Pomerania, Poznań, Danzig, and part of Westphalia.
(*Drums.*) Austria takes Venice.
(*Drums.*) Russia takes the Dukedom of Warsaw and Finland.
(*Drums.*) Norway is taken from Denmark and given to Sweden.

Exit THE MESSENGER. *The light increases. From now on the feminine character becomes* THE WIFE. THE FATHER *becomes* THE HUSBAND.

We hear the shower running in the bathroom. THE WIFE *is laying the table.*

THE HUSBAND (*sticking his head out of the bathroom*): And the bowls!

THE WIFE: Which ones?

THE HUSBAND (*from the bathroom*): The large ones . . . for soup.

THE WIFE: Which ones?

THE HUSBAND: The large ones! Large! Large!

THE WIFE (*realizing*): Oh!

THE HUSBAND: How long has this bloody pipe been leaking?

THE WIFE: Which pipe?

Pause. THE WIFE *continues to lay the table.* THE HUSBAND *turns off the water in the bathroom.*

THE WIFE: Shall I get you a towel?

THE HUSBAND: I've got one.

Pause. The table has an increasingly festive air about it.

THE HUSBAND (*coming out of the bathroom, bare-chested, drying himself with an army towel*): Here! See this towel? That's what I call a towel! Look at my skin . . . (*He shows her the rough towel and his reddened skin.*) Even the colonel says . . . The skin must be scrubbed . . . Scrubbed and scrubbed . . . . Oh I feel wonderful!

THE WIFE (*taking a step back and contemplating the table*): Ready!

THE HUSBAND: Glasses! Bring more glasses!

THE WIFE: How many?

THE HUSBAND: All the glasses! And bring the tray! Here . . . Another one here . . . That's enough! Have I ever told you about the colonel?

THE WIFE: No. (*Going to him tenderly but hesitating to hug him.*) Do you want the shirt with the purple stripes?

THE HUSBAND: No! No! I want my shirt!

The front door is being vigorously slammed. They both listen for a second.

THE WIFE: Hans, you're at home now . . .

THE HUSBAND: No, no! At home or in the street . . . I want my shirt! Even the colonel says . . . "At home or in the street, soldiers are soldiers!" A soldier should always be dressed correctly and thinking of victory! One cannot think of victory unless one is correctly dressed . . . With one's own clothes . . . And he who does not think of victory is a snake and a scabby toad and the homeland will crush him in the end! Do you understand?

The front door is slammed.

THE WIFE: Hans, don't get angry!

THE HUSBAND: Do you see these drops on the floor?

THE WIFE: No.

THEE HUSBAND: Well, they're from me. All morning my ear has been bleeding because of that door.

THE WIFE: With the slamming?

THE HUSBAND: And the scraping. All morning you've been scraping those damn teaspoons.

THE WIFE: I've been polishing them. You asked me to. The silverware has to be polished.

THE HUSBAND: Let me see them!

THE WIFE: All of them?

THE HUSBAND: All of them! Bring all the silverware!

THE WIFE: And the salad bowl?

THE HUSBAND: And the salad bowl!

THE WIFE: And the ice bucket?

THE HUSBAND: You can put the ice bucket against the wall for the moment. I'll see what to do with the ice bucket.

THE HUSBAND *puts on his army shirt, combs his hair. She runs to and fro fetching the silverware.*

THE WIFE (*stopping for a moment, her arms full, watching him admiringly*): Anyway, you do look fine!

THE HUSBAND: I look fine because I'm cheerful. Even the colonel says a soldier must be cheerful. A soldier must be cheerful, his brow unfurrowed; he must look straight ahead and have a look of serenity about him. Because a soldier's life is serene. Because the Cause is serene! The Cause! Above all the Cause! He who is not happy to fight for the Cause is nothing but a snake . . .

THE WIFE (*tenderly*): And a toad . . .

THE HUSBAND: And the Homeland will crush him . . . . Napkins!

THE WIFE: Yes!

THE HUSBAND: Bring them! (*Furious, he holds out a plate.*) And this, wash it! Wash it! Can't you see how dirty it is?

THE WIFE: Where do you see that it's dirty?

THE HUSBAND: It's filthy!

THE WIFE: It's not filthy. It's because of the pancakes.

THE HUSBAND: Oh, forget it! Forget it! Forget it! Everything smells of pancakes! The smell of pancakes permeates everything! Whenever you make pancakes everything smells of pancakes. My pajamas smell of pancakes. Even the sugar smells of pancakes!

THE WIFE (*a little frightened*): Hans, but what is it?

THE HUSBAND: It is! It is! Because everything must be in perfect order! It's impossible like this! The battle must be carried out in order! And the battle is everywhere, everywhere! That's why even the Colonel says the battle is fought on all fronts! The battle is long! And it's going to be even longer if there's no order! Because victory depends on it! On us! On us all! The more perfect the order, the nearer the victory! The surer the victory . . . the . . . you understand? The Colonel knows what he's talking about!

THE WIFE (*slightly rebuked, handing him the washed plate*): There you are!

THE HUSBAND: You must understand . . .

THE WIFE: I do understand.

THE HUSBAND: You mustn't take it personally. You must understand. War is not a game.

THE WIFE: I have saucers for the jam, too.

THE HUSBAND: War purifies the people. It purifies the soul! The blood! It separates the wheat from the chaff. The good wheat . . . The wheat that has the right to remain . . . to be . . . Have I told you about the Colonel?

The front door is slammed again.

THE WIFE (*desperately covering her ears*): Noooo! . . .

THE HUSBAND: I don't know what we'd do without the Colonel . . . (*Taking a satisfied look at the rather overloaded table.*) The roasting tray! The fruit bowl! The sugar tongs!

THE WIFE: I heard that Mrs. Hilda's son was killed.

THE HUSBAND (*placing the aforesaid items* THE WIFE *has just brought him on the table*): You see . . . That's what I'm talking about . . . That pipe is leaking . . . Why is it leaking . . . Who knows how long it's been leaking . . . ? The windowpanes are dirty . . .

THE WIFE: Only on the outside!

THE HUSBAND: That doesn't matter! What I'm trying to say is that things can't go on like this. What I'm trying to say is that we must be clean and responsible. All of us. Outside and in. Because Victory is knocking at the door! Victory is coming, it's there, in sight . . . It's here! Maybe it's already here! And as for us? How do we face Victory? With dirty plates, with that door that you have to slam shut? Our house must be as pure as a lily! (*Looking at the table.*) There's something missing here!

THE WIFE: The candlesticks! Maybe I should bring the candlesticks!

THE HUSBAND (*hugging her enthusiastically*): Yes! Yes!

THE WIFE (*trying to prolong the hug*): Hans! Oh my God, I've waited so long . . . What thoughts, what . . .

THE HUSBAND (*detaching himself coldly*): Come, come! Candlesticks!

THE WIFE *exits and returns sadly with the candlesticks.*

THE WIFE: Have you heard that Mrs. Hilda's son is dead?

THE HUSBAND (*placing, contemplating, moving the candlesticks in search of the best position*): Everything that lies ahead of us, the colonel says, is ours . . . Something huge, overwhelming, immense . . . Something that resembles us . . . the very image . . . our very image . . . the image of the best . . . Because war never kills! (*Lighting the candles.*) War creates! It creates real men, yes . . . yes, yes! Good men, true men . . . can only ever come to life through death . . . Through death and death alone! Death alone strengthens us! Because it is like an eye . . . watching us . . . always . . . From here, from there, from up there, from down here . . . It understands us . . . it arbitrates over us. Because beyond it lies Victory!

THE WIFE: Hans, did you hear what I said?

THE HUSBAND: Bottles! Bottles! Bottles!

THE WIFE: Empty ones?

THE HUSBAND: Empty! Empty! Empty!

THE WIFE: And he was her eldest son . . . It was so sad. Everything was covered in black . . . Their windows stayed closed for almost a month . . . And I prayed for you. Did you hear me, darling?

THE HUSBAND (*fascinated by the sight of the objects spread all over the table*): These things happen . . . Anything is possible . . . Nobody says they don't . . . There are losses . . . There are always losses . . . When the Cause is a Great Cause . . . When the future shines like the sun above . . . There are also losses . . . Blood is shed . . . But this blood . . . What is it? What? Yes, it flows . . . But it returns in another form. Because this blood will be the binder! The binding agent that will link us together! Later . . . The mortar . . . that will keep us bound to one another . . . in the name of the edifice . . . Ha! (*Short meditative pause.*) Well, there it is!

THE WIFE: Yes, there it is . . . it's true . . . Only I was so sad. The more I pray the sadder I am . . . And the more frightened. Sometimes we pray together, me, Mrs. Hilda and the little girls . . . We stay like that for hours . . . The door keeps on slamming. People run in the street. And we . . . We think . . . I think of you, I see you . . . When I pray a lot I get numb . . . And all of a sudden I start to see you . . . Mrs. Hilda has become so thin . . .

THE HUSBAND: That's no good. No, I want you plump and pretty. Turn on the lamps. All of them. (*A strong light on the table.*) My cap! (*He puts on his cap.*) The chairs . . . all of them . . . in a row . . . here . . . Where's the trash? I want the trash, too . . . The trash, the trash . . . (*He empties out the trash along an imaginary strategic line.*) And the dirty linen basket! Bring the linen too! All of it! (*He lays the linen out around the table.*) Step aside! (*Standing on a chair.*) Oh, exactly how it was! That's just how it was! Give me the jug! But fill it with water first!

THE WIFE (*filling it*): And I'm really afraid that Mrs. Hilda will simply go blind . . .

THE HUSBAND *pours water onto the table tracing a thin river between the two camps of objects.*

THE HUSBAND: Yes, yes! That's how it was . . . Look! (*He frantically places objects, moves them, knocks them over, etc.*) We . . . we were here! These ones! I . . . Maybe I'm this one! Maybe this one! (*Straightening a glass.*) We were all waiting . . . Close to each other . . . Shoulder to shoulder. Like a giant heart . . . Like a heart that has rolled over all of a sudden . . . Frightening . . . like a rounded mountain . . . No one can stand, no one can stand before the heart . . . that rolls . . . when it rolls it was like a dream, like a cosmos . . . Breaches, bang! Forests, bang! Flattened! Oops! There goes the platter . . . ! And the heart goes thud! Thud! Thud! To here! Now to the right . . . Gunpowder! Fire! Fire! Fire! What can you see? There's nothing here anymore . . . It's all been reduced to the size of a pebble, an atom . . . So that after, only from these . . . small . . . small . . . It would be easier to rebuild. (*Gradually the room becomes the scale model of a battlefield.*) Because we will rebuild! We will reconstruct . . . But . . . in our own likeness . . . Because that's what the colonel says . . . The world must have one likeness . . . And that must be our likeness . . . The likeness of the best of us . . . Now look at that! Where do you think he was hiding? Him! The loathsome, the flabby, venomous, awestruck enemy! Where do you think he hid, the enemy, almost out of his mind with terror . . . and flabby, and . . . and . . . and . . . Where?

THE WIFE: Here . . .

THE HUSBAND: No! That's us!

THE WIFE: Where then?

THE HUSBAND: Can't you think for yourself, for God's sake? Think a little.

THE WIFE (*timidly*): In the tureen?

THE HUSBAND: Like Hell in the tureen! Think, damn it, think!

THE WIFE (*crying*): I don't know . . . In the corner?

THE HUSBAND: Yes! There! Like a rat! By all the devils in Hell! There! (*Kissing her exuberantly.*) Oh my dearest!

THE WIFE: My darling!

THE HUSBAND: And now . . . imagine . . . A little more, just a little more . . . and we surround him . . . (*He uses almost all the objects in the room for this operation.*) Closer, closer . . . More, a little more . . . And maybe tomorrow, who knows, we will crush him once and for all . . . Mortally . . . (*Playing the final attack.*) Forward! Follow me! Follow me! In the name of Truth! In the name of all the devils in Hell! Forward, we'll finish them!

THE WIFE: I want! I want to finish it once and for all! Mrs. Hilda always . . .

THE HUSBAND: We will hit them . . . with our truth, with our likeness which is indivisible . . .

THE WIFE: And I'll mend the pipe, I'll clean everything . . .

THE HUSBAND: Unique . . . Eternal! We will win because our truth is eternal!

THE WIFE: I'll open the windows, I'll wash them . . . I'll call someone to mend the door . . .

THE HUSBAND: Because we are eternal! Because our God is the one eternal God!

THE WIFE: Hans, I'm so glad you do pray once in a while!

THE HUSBAND: One more move! One single last move . . . Bang! Bang! Bang! . . . To here! And now to the right! Bang! (*It is obvious that the enemy has reached the corner of the table. Giving the enemy a disgusted look.*) You worm! Do something if you dare!

THE WIFE (*looking over his shoulder*): Yes, you . . . I was always asking myself . . . Where does he sleep? What does he eat? Is he soaked through? Does his back ache?

THE HUSBAND (*still occupied with the enemy*): Better surrender. Just look at them, how this table squeaks!

THE WIFE: It's all over dear! You're all sweaty.

THE HUSBAND: Give me the towel from the suitcase.

THE WIFE: Take our towel from the bathroom. Don't you want our towel from the bathroom?

THE HUSBAND: No, no! Give me my towel from the suitcase . . . (*Wipes the sweat from his brow.*) The most amazing thing is that the Colonel is also called Hans. What do you think of that? Hans, just like me.

THE WIFE: How nice . . .

THE HUSBAND: Isn't it? When I first met him he told me we're both called Hans . . .

THE WIFE (*trying to caress him*): My fair-haired, my wonderful . . .

THE HUSBAND: We really are lucky to have the colonel . . . That's just what he told us too when he first saw us: "You're lucky to have me, boys!" (*Someone slams the front door again.*) Again! Again! Again! (*He hurries downstairs, mad with fury.*) I'll kill them! I'll kill them! I'll kill them all!

Pause. THE WIFE *waits a few long seconds, then, puzzled, goes to the door leading to the stairs. Suddenly a hand holding a bunch of carnations appears from the half opened door.*

THE MESSENGER *follows. In the other hand he is holding the end of a rope.*

THE MESSENGER: Am I disturbing you? (*He inspects the room.*) May I sit down for a moment?

THE WIFE: Please do . . . I apologize for the mess . . .

THE MESSENGER: Oh no, it is I who must apologize . . . I see you were eating . . .

THE WIFE: Are you the man who brings the flowers?

THE MESSENGER: Your guess is correct, Madam.

THE WIFE: Then I presume you want to tell me something, don't you?

THE MESSENGER: Yes, Madam.

THE WIFE: Then say what you have to say and go.

THE MESSENGER: Yes, Madam.

THE WIFE: My husband should be back any minute now . . . Didn't you meet on the stairs?

THE MESSENGER: Indeed we did, Madam . . .

THE WIFE: He went out to see who slammed the front door. It wasn't you I take it . . .

THE MESSENGER: No, Madam, I never slam anything.

THE WIFE: Has anything bad happened?

THE MESSENGER: Yes, Madam.

THE WIFE: For a while now I keep expecting something bad to happen.

THE MESSENGER: May I sit on the suitcase for a moment?

THE MESSENGER *seats himself on the suitcase and stuffs the flowers into it: Click! Clack!*

From time to time he discreetly tugs at the rope.

THE WIFE: He's dead! Poor Hans is dead, isn't he?

THE MESSENGER: Yes, Madam.

THE WIFE: And he didn't die like a hero, did he?

THE MESSENGER: Well, Madam . . .

THE WIFE: It was the horse, wasn't it?

THE MESSENGER: No, not the horse, Madam.

THE WIFE: What do you mean "No?"

THE MESSENGER: No, Madam. This time it has nothing to do with the horse.

THE WIFE: Was it wartime or peacetime?

THE MESSENGER: It was actually the final attack, Madam. The very last attack. The attack which led to victory. And he fell right under the terrified and bulging eyes of the enemy.

THE WIFE: He was shot full of lead, is that it?

THE MESSENGER (*tugging at the rope*): No, Madam.

THE WIFE: He was blown apart, is that it?

THE MESSENGER: No, Madam.

THE WIFE: Oh, come on!

THE MESSENGER: No, Madam. He stumbled and fell. The attack had just begun. He was in the first wave . . . He was rushing headlong . . . Onward. and   onward . . . (*He keeps tugging on the rope.*) Like a real hero . . . He kept on shouting . . . with all his might . . . And he was running and running . . . running . . . And the whole regiment were following him . . . They were all running with all their might and shouting . . . The Devil himself couldn't have stopped them, and the enemy watched in awe . . . And your husband at the head carrying a huge flag . . . The flag billowed in the air and . . . Maybe it was because of the air that your husband stumbled and fell . . . He fell, Madam, with the flag heavy with the air on top of him and he couldn't get up again . . . Because of the air which kept on collapsing over him . . .

THE WIFE: And? He stayed pinned down where he fell?

THE MESSENGER: Yes . . . yes . . . (*Barely stifling a guffaw.*) Yes . . .

THE WIFE: And his comrades?

THE MESSENGER: His comrades trampled him underfoot.

THE WIFE: What? His comrades trampled him underfoot?

THE MESSENGER: Yes, Madam. No one could have stopped them. They crushed him against their will. Those behind them pushed them forward.

THE WIFE (*barely stifling a guffaw*): But that's terrible! How can you trample on a living person?

THE MESSENGER: That's how it was. What could we have done? There was such a crush. No one realized what we were walking on.

THE WIFE: And did you pick him up afterwards?

THE MESSENGER: There was nothing to pick up, Madam. But I brought you the boots.

THE MESSENGER *tugs at the rope again and odd boots start to appear, tied here and there like some bizarre knots.*

THE WIFE: His boots?

THE MESSENGER: No, Madam. The boots of those who trampled him.

THE WIFE: Clearly I don't understand a thing.

THE MESSENGER: Madam, I had no other option. All that's left of him is on the soles of the boots of those who trampled him. That's why I brought them to you.

THE WIFE: And what do you want me to do with these boots?

THE MESSENGER: There are 10,000 boots . . . His last resting place is there, on the soles of these boots. I've brought them to you. Those were my orders. Do whatever you see fit with them.

THE WIFE (*overcome, choking*): Could you open the window? It's rather dark in here.

THE MESSENGER: I'll open it. But you know, outside it's just as dark as it is in here.

THE WIFE: It can't be darker than in here.

THE MESSENGER: As you wish, Madam. It's all the same to me.

THE WIFE: If you don't mind, I'd like to ask you a personal question.

THE MESSENGER: Please do.

THE WIFE: Do you think it smells of pancakes in here?

THE MESSENGER: No, Madam. How can you think such a thing? (*Sitting on top of the pile of boots.*) It's absolutely unbelievable how soft they are. Come and sit next to me, Madam. I have some further orders for you.

THE WIFE (*falling onto the pile of boots as though it were a real grave*): Hans! Hans!

THE MESSENGER: Right, the boots: the boots must be washed, Madam. They must be washed, washed thoroughly and then left to dry slowly. And after that they must be greased . . . And then polished immediately . . . This is obligatory. Whatever happens, our duty is to bury the dead properly.

THE WIFE *rummages in the pile of boots as if searching for the body. From the flies, a heavy mass of hanging boots starts to slowly descend. The light gradually fades.*

THE WIFE (*embracing the pile of boots*): Oh, Hans, how could they have trampled over your body? Over my little Hans . . .

THE MESSENGER (*consolingly, soothingly*): Come now, Madam . . . Honestly, what's the use? It pains me to see you like this.

THE WIFE: And me? What about me? What happens to me now?

THE MESSENGER (*caressing her as a certain mutual intimacy grows between them*): Leave it to me, Madam, leave it to me. I'm here. I'm always here . . . And my name is Hans too . . .

The ceiling of boots slowly engulfs them.

Selected Bibliography

Brandesky, Joseph. *Czech Theatre Design in the Twentieth Century: Metaphor & Irony Revisited.* Iowa City, IA: University of Iowa Press, 2007.

Braun, Kazimierz. *A History of Polish Theater, 1939–1989: Spheres of Captivity and Freedom.* Westport, CT: Greenwood Press, 1996.

Brogyányi, Eugene, ed. *DramaContemporary: Hungary.* New York: PAJ Publications, 1991.

Burian, Jarka. *Leading Creators of Twentieth-Century Czech Theatre.* New York: Routledge, 2002.

———. *Modern Czech Theatre: Reflector and Conscience of a Nation.* Iowa City: University of Iowa Press, 2000.

Csáki, Judit, ed. *Tradition and Innovation in Modern Hungarian Theatre.* Budapest: ITI Hungarian Center, 1999.

Gerould, Daniel, ed. *The Mrożek Reader.* New York: Grove, 2004.

Goetz-Stankiewicz, Marketa, ed. *DramaContemporary: Czechoslovakia.* New York: PAJ Publications, 1985.

———. *The Silenced Theatre: Czech Playwrights Without a Stage.* Toronto: University of Toronto Press, 1979.

Goldstein, Imre. "A History of Hungarian Drama Between 1945 and 1970." PhD diss. City University of New York, 1975.

Havel, Václav. *Letters to Olga: June 1979–September 1982.* New York: Knopf, 1988.

Kott, Jan. *The Theater of Essence and Other Essays.* Evanston, IL: Northwestern University Press, 1984.

Lamb, Ruth S. *The World of Romanian Theatre.* Claremont, CA: Ocelot Press, 1976.

Müller, Péter P. and Anna Lakos, eds. *Collision, Essays on Contemporary Hungarian Drama.* Budapest: The Hungarian Theatre Museum and Institute, 2004.

Popescu, Marian. *The Stage & the Carnival: Romanian Theatre after Censorship.* Bucharest: Editura Paralela 45, 2000.p

Pourchot, Eric. "Contemporary Romanian Theatre: Artistry, Honesty, and Adaptation in the Plays of Iosif Naghiu, Dumitru Radu Popescu, and Marin Sorescu." PhD diss. City University of New York, 1999.

Rocamora, Carol. *Acts of Courage: Václav Havel's Life in the Theater.* Hanover, NH: Smith and Kraus, 2005.

Stephan, Halina. *Transcending the Absurd: Drama and Prose of Sławomir Mrożek.* Amsterdam: Rodopi B.V., 1997.

Toporišič, Tomaž, Barbara Skubic, Tina Malič, and Mateja Dermelj. *Has the Future Already Arrived? Fifty Years of Slovenska Mladinsko Gledališče.* Ljubljana: Slovenska Mladinsko Gledališče, 2007.

Trensky, Paul. *Czech Drama Since World War II.* White Plains, NY: M.E. Sharpe, 1978.

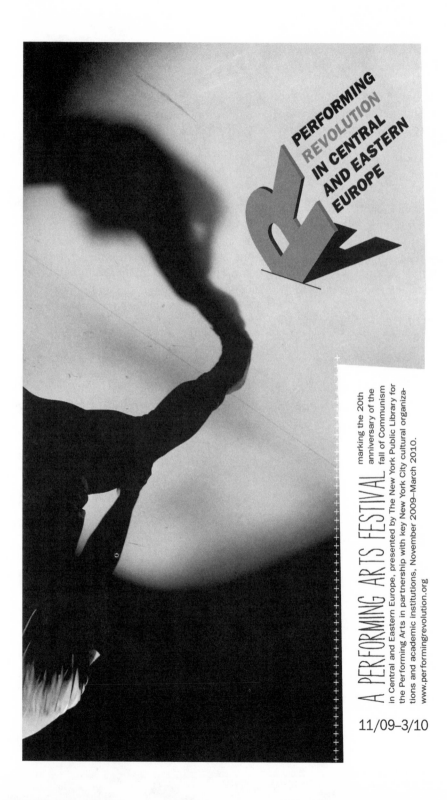

PERFORMING
REVOLUTION
IN CENTRAL
AND EASTERN
EUROPE

A PERFORMING ARTS FESTIVAL marking the 20th anniversary of the fall of Communism in Central and Eastern Europe, presented by The New York Public Library for the Performing Arts in partnership with key New York City cultural organizations and academic institutions, November 2009–March 2010.
www.performingrevolution.org

11/09–3/10

We invite you to take part in the *Performing Revolution in Central and Eastern Europe* festival.

Performing Revolution in Central and Eastern Europe explores how the performing arts contributed to the 1989 revolutions and the resulting fall of Communism in Central and Eastern Europe. Presented by The New York Public Library for the Performing Arts in association with leading cultural organizations and academic institutions, the five-month festival features more than 25 events, including theater, music, and dance performances, exhibitions, film screenings, readings, and symposia.

With a focus on the performing arts in the Czech Republic, Germany, Hungary, Poland, Romania, Slovakia, and Slovenia, the festival considers "revolution" not only within the framework of the era's profound social and political changes, but also in terms of ongoing experiments within a particular genre. From revivals of significant works from the period to new projects that reflect upon the 20th anniversary of the fall of the Iron Curtain and beyond, *Performing Revolution* is a celebration of the transformative power of the arts and its potential to reshape political and cultural systems.

Over two years in the making, *Performing Revolution* represents the collaborative efforts of a number of individuals and organizations. We look forward to seeing you at festival events.

Sincerely,

Jacqueline Davis

Jacqueline Z. Davis
The Barbara G. and Lawrence A. Fleischman Executive Director
The New York Public Library for the Performing Arts
Dorothy and Lewis B. Cullman Center

/////////////////////

www.performingrevolution.org

Major support has been provided by

The Gladys Krieble Delmas Foundation and
Trust for Mutual Understanding

Media sponsor

THE
GLADYS KRIEBLE DELMAS
FOUNDATION

TRUST FOR MUTUAL UNDERSTANDING

MAKE LIFE CREATIVE.

Festival Partners

92nd Street Y Harkness
    Dance Festival
Abrons Arts Center
Agentura Dell'Arte
Austrian Cultural Forum
Consulate General of Slovakia
Consulate General of Slovenia
Czech Center New York
Dance New Amsterdam
Erste Bank Group
The Film Society of Lincoln Center
Goethe-Institut New York
GOH Productions
The Harriman Institute at
    Columbia University
HERE Arts Center
Hungarian Cultural Center
Janeil Engelstad
The Joyce Theater
La MaMa E.T.C.
(le) Poisson Rouge
Martin E. Segal Theatre Center/
    The Graduate Center CUNY
Polish Cultural Institute in New York
Romanian Cultural Institute in
    New York
The Tank
Theater for the New City
Theatre Department at Barnard
    College, Columbia University
Untitled Theater Company #61
WaxFactory

**The New York Public Library
for the Performing Arts**
DOROTHY AND LEWIS B. CULLMAN CENTER

92Y

austrian cultural forum[nyc]

ABRONS**ARTS**CENTER
HENRY**STREET**SETTLEMENT

AGENTURA
DELL'ARTE

The Consulate General of Slovakia in New York

CONSULATE GENERAL OF SLOVENIA

CZECH CENTER
ČESKÉ CENTRUM

DNA DANCE NEW AMSTERDAM

the film
society
of lincoln
center

GOETHE-INSTITUT
NEW YORK

The Harriman Institute
Russian, Eurasian, and Eastern European Studies at Columbia

hERE

XTR M LY
H NGARY

La MaMa etc.

(le) poisson rouge
Serving Arts & Alcohol

MARTIN E. SEGAL
THEATRE CENTER

POLISH
CULTURAL
INSTITUTE
www.PolishCulture-NYC.org

ROMANIAN
CULTURAL
INSTITUTE
NEW YORK

 THE TANK

BARNARD
LIBERAL ARTS COLLEGE
FOR WOMEN
IN NEW YORK CITY

//\ <– \(⁻) \/ WAXFACTORY

PERFORMING
REVOLUTION
IN CENTRAL
AND EASTERN
EUROPE

PROGRAMS

++++++++++++++++++++++

Sneak Peek:
Festival Symposium

November 5, 2009
Thursday: 6:00–8:00 p.m.

Presented by The Harriman Institute at
Columbia University in association with
the Polish Cultural Institute in New York,
Romanian Cultural Institute in New York,
and Austrian Cultural Forum

A gathering of intellectuals and artists
about presenting the performing arts in
the context of political change. This is
a special pre-festival event and a preview
of a larger symposium scheduled for
February 2010.

THE HARRIMAN INSTITUTE,
COLUMBIA UNIVERSITY
President's Room 1, Faculty House
64 Morningside Drive (at 116th Street)
FREE
Reservations: rsvp@harrimaninstitute.org
www.harrimaninstitute.org

www.performingrevolution.org

+++++++++++++++++++++

Rebel Waltz:
Underground Music
from Behind the
Iron Curtain

November 6–8, 2009
Friday–Sunday at various times

Presented by the Hungarian Cultural
Center in collaboration with the Czech
Center New York, Polish Cultural Institute
in New York, Romanian Cultural Institute
in New York, Consulate General of Slovakia, and Consulate General of Slovenia

Rebel Waltz gives New York audiences a rare
opportunity to experience the suppressed
voices of a triumphant generation, including
Dezerter (Poland), Kontroll Csoport (Hungary), Psi Vojaci (Czech Republic), Timpuri
Noi (Romania), Bez Ladu A Skladu (Slovakia),
and Pankrti (Slovenia). The music of these
bands served as a form of political rebellion
in the 1980s; 20 years later, it is a celebration of a successful movement for change.

Rebel Waltz *is part of Extremely Hungary,
a yearlong festival celebrating contemporary
Hungarian culture throughout 2009 in New
York City and Washington, D.C.*

(LE) POISSON ROUGE
158 Bleecker Street
(between Thompson and Sullivan Streets)
www.lepoissonrouge.com
Information: www.extremelyhungary.org

+++++++++++++++++++++

Taylor Mac
The Lily's Revenge

November 6–22, 2009
Thursday–Sunday at 6:30 p.m.

Presented by HERE Arts Center

Taylor Mac's epic extravaganza *The Lily's
Revenge* tells the tale of a flower that goes
on a quest to become a man and finds
itself at the center of a revolution of flowers intent on destroying their oppressor:
The God of Nostalgia. Part Noh play, part
verse play, part vaudevillian theatrics, part
installation, part puppet theater, and part
dance, *The Lily's Revenge* continues Mac's
radical experiments in genre-squishing and
explores themes of alternative community
and homogeneity in culture.

*Supported by MAP Fund; Creative Capital;
Franklin Furnace; J. B. Harter Charitable
Trust; Lower Manhattan Cultural Council;
New Dramatists' Creativity Fund and
Working Sessions; New York Foundation
for the Arts.*

HERE ARTS CENTER
145 Sixth Avenue (between Spring and
Broome Streets; enter on Dominick Street)
$35
Tickets/Information: 212-352-3101
www.here.org

++++++++++++++++++++

Nejla Yatkin
Dancing with the Berlin Wall
November 9, 2009
Monday at 6:00 p.m.

Presented by the Goethe-Institut New York

Dancing with the Berlin Wall is a site-specific
project by choreographer Nejla Yatkin. A Berlin
native with Turkish roots, Yatkin grew up with the
Wall. While for most of the world it was a striking
symbol, for her it was a daily reality. With this
project, Yatkin reflects on her own experiences,
and also on larger issues of boundaries and open-
ness, constriction and freedom. The performance,
which incorporates dance and film, will begin at
Ludlow 38 and make several stops as it moves
to the Goethe-Institut Wyoming Building.

LUDLOW 38
38 Ludlow Street
(between Hester and Grand Streets)

GOETHE-INSTITUT NEW YORK WYOMING BUILDING
5 East 3rd Street
(between Second Avenue and Bowery)
FREE
Information: 212-439-8700
www.goethe.de/ins/us/ney/enindex.htm

www.performingrevolution.org

++++++++++++++++++++

The Wall in My Head: Words and Images from the Fall of the Iron Curtain

November 10, 2009
Tuesday at 7:00 p.m.

Presented by Words without Borders and Open Letter Books in collaboration with the Polish Cultural Institute in New York and Romanian Cultural Institute in New York

A book launch and reading for *The Wall in My Head*, an anthology of texts and images that combines work from writers and artists who witnessed the fall of the Iron Curtain firsthand, with impressions and reflections by those who grew up in its wake. Work by Mircea Cărtărescu, Zbigniew Herbert, Milan Kundera, Vladimir Sorokin, Uwe Tellekamp, and Dubravka Ugrešić is included. Authors Masha Gessen, Dorota Masłowska, and Dan Sociu will read at the book launch.

IDLEWILD BOOKS
12 West 19th Street
(between Fifth and Sixth Avenues)
FREE
Information: 212-414-8888
www.idlewildbooks.com
www.polishculture-nyc.org
www.icrny.org

++++++++++++++++++++

Theatre of the Eighth Day Wormwood

November 11–15, 2009
Wednesday–Saturday at 8:00 p.m.,
Sunday at 3:00 p.m. (post-performance talk on November 12)

Presented by the Polish Cultural Institute in New York and Abrons Arts Center

A rare revival of the Theatre of the Eighth Day's landmark 1985 production of *Wormwood*, performed by the original cast. Theatre of the Eighth Day, founded in 1964, inaugurated an underground movement of political theater in Poland. *Wormwood*, the group's last production in Communist Poland, openly described life under martial law and ultimately led to the denouncement of Theatre of the Eighth Day by Polish authorities.

Supported by Trust for Mutual Under-standing, the Marshall of the Wielkopolska Region, and the President of the City of Poznań.

ABRONS ARTS CENTER,
HENRY STREET SETTLEMENT
466 Grand Street (at Pitt Street)
$15
Tickets/Information: 212-352-3101
www.abronsartcenter.org
www.PolishCulture-NYC.org

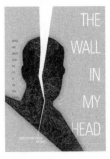

Playwrights Before the Fall: Eastern European Drama in Times of Revolution

November 16, 2009
Monday at 6:30 p.m.

Presented by the
Martin E. Segal Theatre Center

A book launch for the first multi-author international anthology of Eastern European plays to appear in English. Edited by Daniel Gerould, the anthology includes Sławomir Mrożek, *Portrait (Portret)*; Karel Steigerwald, *Sorrow, Sorrow, Fear, the Rope, and the Pit (Hoře, hoře, strach, oprátka a jáma)*; György Spiró, *Chicken Head (Csirkefej)*; Matei Vişniec, *Horses at the Window (Caii la fereastră)*; and Dušan Jovanović, *Military Secret (Vojna tajna)*. The presentation includes staged readings of excerpts from the five plays and a panel with authors and translators on the playwrights' role in the theatrical revolution of the 1980s.

The publication is supported by the Czech Center New York, the Hungarian Cultural Center, the Polish Cultural Institute in New York, the Romanian Cultural Institute in New York, and Consulate General of Slovenia.

MARTIN E. SEGAL THEATRE CENTER,
THE GRADUATE CENTER CUNY
365 Fifth Avenue (at 34th Street)
FREE
Information: mestc@gc.cuny.edu
www.TheSegalCenter.org

Deborah Brevoort
The Velvet Weapon

November 18, 2009
Wednesday at 7:30 p.m.

Presented by La MaMa E.T.C.

A concert reading of *The Velvet Weapon*, an original backstage farce written by Deborah Brevoort and directed by George Ferencz. Inspired by interviews Brevoort and her colleague Pavel Dobruský conducted in the Czech Republic and Slovakia with 43 ringleaders of the Velvet Revolution, *The Velvet Weapon* is a humorous examination of democracy told through a battle between high-brow and low-brow art.

Part of La MaMa EXPERIMENTS, a concert reading series of experimental plays curated by George Ferencz.

THE ANNEX THEATER AT LA MAMA E.T.C.
66 East 4th Street
(between Second Avenue and Bowery)
FREE
Information: 212-475-7710
www.lamama.org

++++++++++++++++++++++

Revolutionary Voices: Performing Arts in Central & Eastern Europe in the 1980s

November 18, 2009–March 20, 2010
Gallery Hours: Monday and Thursday noon–8:00 p.m.; Tuesday, Wednesday, Friday
11:00 a.m.–6:00 p.m.; Saturday 10:00 a.m.–6:00 p.m.

Presented by The New York Public Library for the Performing Arts

This exhibition examines how performances attempted to break boundaries set by the
Communist state's politicians and censors, focusing on theater, music, and dance events
that contested the prevailing totalitarian regime and anticipated the forthcoming political
and social changes. As the revolutions in most Soviet bloc countries were not the result
of a violent overthrow of power, art was one of the main arenas where "the revolutionary"
started to happen. Curated by Karen Burke, Assistant Chief, Music Division, The New York
Public Library for the Performing Arts, and Aniko Szucs, Ph.D. candidate in Performance
Studies at New York University.

*The New York Public Library for the Performing Arts gratefully acknowledges the leader-
ship support of Dorothy and Lewis B. Cullman. Additional support for exhibitions has
been provided by Judy R. and Alfred A. Rosenberg and the Miriam and Harold Steinberg
Foundation. Support for this exhibition has been provided by The Gladys Krieble Delmas
Foundation, Trust for Mutual Understanding, and the Polish Cultural Institute in New York.*

VINCENT ASTOR GALLERY, THE NEW YORK PUBLIC LIBRARY FOR THE PERFORMING ARTS
Dorothy and Lewis B. Cullman Center, 111 Amsterdam Avenue (at 65th Street)
FREE
Information: 212-870-1630
www.nypl.org/research/lpa/lpa.html

Dissident Acts: 3 Plays

Directed by Gary Cherniakhovsky

November 19–21, 2009
Thursday–Saturday at 8:00 p.m.
(post-performance talk on November 19)

Presented by the Theatre Department
at Barnard College, Columbia University

An evening of short plays by Samuel
Beckett, a member of the WWII resistance, and his political counterparts and
dramatic inheritors, the Polish and Czech
playwrights Sławomir Mrożek and Václav
Havel. Beckett's miniature 1982 *Catastro-
phe* interrogates the public role of art in
a taut homage to Havel, at the time impris-
oned for subversion of the state. Mrożek's
1958 *The Police* unveils the deep absurdity of totalitarianism, and Havel's 1975
Unveiling transforms this absurdity into
the hypocrisy of its elite. Performed by
students of Barnard College and Columbia
University, with Hana Worthen (dramaturg),
Simon Pastukh (scenic design), and Galina
Solovyeva (costume design).

*Supported in part by The Harriman
Institute, Columbia University.*

MINOR LATHAM PLAYHOUSE,
118 MILBANK HALL, BARNARD COLLEGE
3009 Broadway (at 118th Street)
$10 general admission/$5 with CU ID
Tickets: www.tic.columbia.edu
Information: www.barnard.edu/theatre/
current_season.html

Untitled Theater Company #61
The Velvet Oratorio

November 19, 2009
Thursday at 6:00 p.m.

November 30, 2009
Monday at 7:00 p.m.

Untitled Theater Company #61 premieres
The Velvet Oratorio, a retelling of the Velvet
Revolution through text, choral music, and
scenes based on Václav Havel's Vanek
plays. The text for the oratorio draws upon
U.S. State Department documents and
corresponding Czechoslovakian/Soviet
documents and interviews with journalists,
diplomats, and ordinary people who were
in the streets of Prague in November 1989.
The Velvet Oratorio is a collaborative project between Edward Einhorn (playwright),
Henry Akona (composer), and Karen Ott
(dramaturg), the same creative team that
was behind the Havel Festival.

*Supported by the Czech Center New York
and The Alma & Morris Shapiro Fund.*

BRUNO WALTER AUDITORIUM,
THE NEW YORK PUBLIC LIBRARY FOR
THE PERFORMING ARTS (NOVEMBER 19)
Dorothy and Lewis B. Cullman Center
111 Amsterdam Avenue (at 65th Street)
FREE
www.nypl.org/research/lpa/lpa.html

BOHEMIAN NATIONAL HALL (NOVEMBER 30)
321–325 East 73rd Street
(between First and Second Avenues)
FREE
Reservations: 646-422-3399
www.czechcenter.com

Information: www.untitledtheater.com

++++++++++++++++++++++

Saviana Stanescu
NY Thru an Immigrant I
or (r)evolution
(Flagstories and other
personal histories)

November 23, 2009
Monday at 6:00 p.m.

Presented by the Romanian Cultural
Institute in New York

Playwright Saviana Stanescu participated
in the Romanian revolution as a college
student in 1989. In this autobiographical
performative lecture, she explores both
her youth in Romania and immigrant experience in New York through the lens of a personal dichotomy between East and West
and an ongoing negotiation between the
old and new set of values.

BRUNO WALTER AUDITORIUM, THE NEW YORK
PUBLIC LIBRARY FOR THE PERFORMING ARTS
Dorothy and Lewis B. Cullman Center
111 Amsterdam Avenue (at 65th Street)
FREE
Information: 212-870-1630
www.nypl.org/research/lpa/lpa.html

++++++++++++++++++++++

Voices From the Center
www.VoicesFromtheCenter.net
Launch date: November 2009

Produced by Janeil Engelstad

This web-based project by Janeil Engelstad
documents life during and after Communism through interviews with performing
and visual artists, villagers, academics,
and former dissidents from Slovakia, Hungary, Poland, and the Czech Republic. For
many participants, including young adults
who were children when the Berlin Wall
came down, this is their first opportunity
to publicly speak about their lives before
and after the fall of the Wall. Additionally,
Engelstad will use interviews housed on
the website as the basis for exhibitions
and discussions at art centers throughout
Central Europe and the United States.

*Produced with generous support from
the U.S. Embassy, Bratislava, The Central
European Foundation, Trust for Mutual
Understanding, Stanica, Artreach, and
individual donors.*

Fourth Annual Romanian Film Festival

December 4–6, 2009
Friday–Sunday at various times

Presented by the Romanian Cultural Institute in New York in collaboration with Transilvania International Film Festival and Tribeca Film Festival

The Fourth Annual Romanian Film Festival features, along with new releases from 2009, a special program dedicated to the 20th anniversary of the '89 Romanian Revolution and the fall of Communism, including *The Oak* (dir. Lucian Pintilie, 1992) and *State of Things* (dir. Stere Gulea, 1996).

TRIBECA CINEMAS
54 Varick Street (at Laight Street)
$10 adults; $7 students/seniors
Tickets: www.tribecacinemas.com
www.icrny.org

A View from the East: Documentaries of Eastern Europe

January 19 and 26;
February 2, 9, 16, and 23, 2010
Tuesday at 2:30 p.m.

Presented by the Reserve Film and Video Collection at The New York Public Library for the Performing Arts

Over the past 20 years, some of the most daring and innovative documentaries have come out of Eastern Europe. This film series spotlights post-1989 documentaries made in the Performing Revolution festival's represented countries, including *The*  *Man Who Overestimated the Czech Soul: The Escapes of Josef Bryks* (dir. Jan Novak, 2007); *Diamonds in the Dark* (dir. Olivia Carrescia, 1999); *Cold Waves* (dir. Alexandru Solomon, 2007); *The Old and the New* (dir. Neven Korda and Zemira Alajbegovic, 1997); *The Orange Alternative* (dir. Mirosław Dembicki, 1989); *Dwarves Go to the Ukraine* (dir. Mirosław Dembicki, 2005); and *Do Communists Have Better Sex?* (dir. Andre Meier, 2006). In addition to the screenings at the Library for the Performing Arts, programs will be arranged at neighborhood branch libraries in The New York Public Library system.

BRUNO WALTER AUDITORIUM, THE NEW YORK PUBLIC LIBRARY FOR THE PERFORMING ARTS
Dorothy and Lewis B. Cullman Center
111 Amsterdam Avenue (at 65th Street)
FREE
Information: 212-870-1700
www.nypl.org/research/lpa/lpa.html

++++++++++++++++++++++

Györ National Ballet from Hungary

January 26–31, 2010
Tuesday–Wednesday at 7:30 p.m.,
Thursday–Friday at 8:00 p.m.,
Saturday at 2:00 and 8:00 p.m.,
Sunday at 2:00 and 7:30 p.m.

Presented by The Joyce Theater

Györ National Ballet, one of Europe's most respected contemporary ballet compan-ies, returns to The Joyce with the U.S. pre-mieres of *Rite of Spring* (choreographed by Atilla Kun) and *Petrushka* (choreographed by Dmitrij Simkin). The all-Stravinsky program commemorates the fall of the Communist regime in Eastern Europe; both ballets explore the sacrifices of personal freedom and individual expression that occur under a totalitarian government.

THE JOYCE THEATER
175 Eighth Avenue (at 19th Street)
$49; $35; $19; $10
(ticket prices subject to change)
Tickets/Information: 212-242-0800
www.joyce.org

++++++++++++++++++++

Polish Dance in the 1980s: Silence or Revolution?

January 2010
Panel Dates and Times TBA

Presented by Dance New Amsterdam

Dance New Amsterdam presents three panels intended to provoke discourse about Poland's revolution in dance during the late 20th century. The first panel will focus solely on Poland, while the others will be in a roundtable format with representatives from other Performing Revolution festival countries. With Roman Pawlowski (chief theater and dance critic for *Gazeta Wyborcza*), Roman Arndt (dance historian), Dr. Agnieszka Jelewska (Adam Mickiewicz University in Poznań), and Dr. Jacek Łuminski (Founder/Executive Director of Silesian Dance Theatre and Dean of the Dance-Theater Department, State Drama School in Krakow), George Jackson (critic and dance historian), Prof. Anna Peterson Royce (Indiana University at Bloomington), and Prof. Alan Kucharski (Swarthmore College). The panels will be simulcast online with a live blog for offsite audience interaction.

Developed in conjunction with the 2009 Understanding Dance conference in Poland, and supported by Trust for Mutual Understanding, American Express, Polish Cultural Institute in New York, and Silesian Dance Theatre.

DANCE NEW AMSTERDAM
280 Broadway, 2nd Floor
(enter on Chambers Street)
FREE
Information: 212-625-8369
www.dnadance.org

Poland in the 1980s: Searching for Revolution in Dance

January–February 2010
Gallery Hours: Daily, 9:00 a.m.–9:00 p.m.

Presented by Dance New Amsterdam

This multimedia exhibition features Polish dance documented through historical video, film, and photography. Curated by Dr. Jacek Łuminski, Founder/Executive Director of Silesian Dance Theatre, and Dr. Agnieszka Jelewska, professor at Adam Mickiewicz University in Poznań, Poland, with advisors Roman Arndt (Poland) and George Jackson (United States).

Developed in conjunction with the 2009 Understanding Dance conference in Poland, and supported by Trust for Mutual Understanding, American Express, Polish Cultural Institute in New York, and Silesian Dance Theatre.

DANCE NEW AMSTERDAM
280 Broadway, 2nd Floor
(enter on Chambers Street)
FREE
Information: 212-625-8369
www.dnadance.org

++++++++++++++++++++++

Storm Cloud Warnings: Resistance and Reflection in Polish Cinema, 1977–1989

February 3–11, 2010

**W SAMO POŁUDNIE
4 CZERWCA 1989**

Presented by the Film Society of Lincoln Center and the Polish Cultural Institute in New York, in association with the Polish National Film Archive

Polish filmmakers working from the late 1970s to the fall of Communism faced enormous challenges and censorship from the totalitarian regime, yet produced extraordinarily rich films. Titles to be screened include classics from the Cinema of Moral Anxiety and a number of films that were banned: Krzysztof Zanussi's *Camouflage*, Andrzej Wajda's *Rough Treatment*, Feliks Falk's *Top Dog*, Krzysztof Kieślowski's *Camera Buff*, Kazimierz Kutz's *Beads of One Rosary*, Stanisław Bareja's *Teddy Bear*, Barbara Sass's *Without Love*, Marcel Łoziński's *How Are We to Live?*, Agnieszka Holland's *A Woman Alone*, and Ryszard Bugajski's *Interrogation*.

Made possible through a grant for new copies from the Polish Film Institute in Warsaw and additional support from Polish Television.

WALTER READE THEATER
70 Lincoln Center Plaza
$11 adults/$8 seniors/$7 Film Society members, students, children
Tickets/Information: 212-875-5601
www.filmlinc.org

++++++++++++++++++++

Performative Aspects in Art from Eastern Europe

Works from Kontakt: The Art Collection of Erste Bank Group

February 5–28, 2010
(opening reception on February 5)
Gallery Hours: Thursday–Sunday, 1:00–6:00 p.m.

Presented by Erste Bank Group and LaMaMa La Galleria

This exhibition focuses on the historically important decade of the 1970s in Eastern Europe, demonstrating how artists articulate performative gestures on a visual level, in opposition to the dominant, politically conservative and restrictive reality. The presented artistic statements create performative environments that reflect on given societal processes and their models of inclusion and exclusion. Curated by Walter Seidl, the Art Collection of Erste Bank Group.

LA MAMA LA GALLERIA
6 East 1st Street
(between Second Avenue and Bowery)
FREE
Information: 212-505-2476
www.lamama.org

www.performingrevolution.org

+++++++++++++++++++++

WaxFactory
QUARTET v4.0

Text by Heiner Müller,
translated by Douglas Langworthy

February 24–28, 2010
Wednesday–Saturday at 8:00 p.m.,
Sunday at 5:00 p.m.

WaxFactory's sci-fi *QUARTET v4.0*
stages East German playwright Heiner
Müller's controversial text in a sterile,
post-apocalyptic world that serves as the
arena for the vicious endgames of its pro-
tagonists. In WaxFactory's production,
the actors' live performance is simultaneously broadcast with video images—captured from multiple angles by surveillance
cameras—that are edited, processed,
and projected in real time. Conceived and
directed by Ivan Talijancic, the production
features performers Erika Latta and Todd
Thomas Peters, surround sound design by
Random Logic, video by Antonio Giacomin,
costumes by Haans Nicholas Mott, and a
visual installation created in collaboration
with architect Pavel Getov.

Supported by Trust for Mutual Understand-
ing, Greenwall Foundation, New York State
Council on the Arts, NYC Department of
Cultural Affairs, and others.

ABRONS ARTS CENTER,
HENRY STREET SETTLEMENT
466 Grand Street (at Pitt Street)
$15
Tickets/Information: 212-352-3101
www.abronsartcenter.org
www.waxfactory.org

+++++++++++++++++++++

After Communism: Achievement and Disillusionment Since 1989

February 26–27, 2010
Panel schedule: Friday at 1:30 p.m.,
3:30 p.m., 7:00 p.m.; Saturday at
9:30 a.m., 1:30 p.m., 3:30 p.m.

Presented by The Harriman Institute at
Columbia University in association with
the Polish Cultural Institute in New York,
Romanian Cultural Institute in New York,
and Austrian Cultural Forum

This multi-day symposium brings together
public intellectuals, policymakers, cultural
figures, and academics from both sides
of the Atlantic to assess the global meaning of the 1989 revolutions in East-Central
Europe and their aftermaths. Speakers
will discuss the changes in our understanding of the Communist system and the
sources of its collapse, and the age of
"post-Communism," a condition whose
contours and duration remain unclear.

THE HARRIMAN INSTITUTE,
COLUMBIA UNIVERSITY
President's Room 1, Faculty House
64 Morningside Drive (at 116th Street)
FREE
Reservations: rsvp@harrimaninstitute.org
www.harrimaninstitute.org

Walter Steinacher
Yugostalgia

March 3–May 1, 2010
(opening reception on March 3)
Gallery Hours: Monday–Friday
noon–8:00 p.m., Saturday–Sunday
2:00–8:00 p.m.

Presented by HERE Arts Center and
WaxFactory

This exhibition of paintings by Austrian
artist Walter Steinacher captures the post-
Communist nostalgia Steinacher observed
during his long-term residency in Slovenia.
Most of the paintings on view are part of
a series that humorously addresses the
image of (Josip Broz) Tito, the Yugoslav
president whose death in the mid-1980s
triggered the domino effect that led to the
dissolution of Yugoslavia and the end of
socialism in the Balkan region. Curated
by Ivan Talijancic (WaxFactory).

HERE ARTS CENTER
145 Sixth Avenue (between Spring and
Broome Streets; enter on Dominick Street)
FREE
Information: 212-352-3101
www.here.org

Revolution!

March 4–21, 2010
Thursday–Saturday at 8:00 p.m.,
Sunday at 3:00 p.m.

Presented by Theater for the New City

In this new creative work, which bridges
puppetry, object theater, and circus arts,
Czech and Czech-American theater artists
join together to offer their perspectives on
the 1989 Velvet Revolution and an overview
of the idea of revolution through the ages.
Revolution! is performed in the tradition of
Central European medieval street and traveling circus shows, using stilts and strings
as a metaphor for an unstable revolution.
Created and directed by Pavel Dobruský and
Vít Hořejš with The Czechoslovak-American
Marionette Theatre and guest artists from
the Czech Republic: Facka/The Slap Theater,
Pavel Strouhal, and Hana Kalouskova.

Made possible in part with public funds
from the National Endowment for the Arts,
New York State Council on the Arts, and
NYC Department of Cultural Affairs. Addi-
tional support from Trust for Mutual Under-
standing, Ministry of Foreign Affairs of the
Czech Republic, Puppeteers of America,
Materials for the Arts, Agentura Dell'Arte,
GOH Productions, and private donors.

THEATER FOR THE NEW CITY
155 First Avenue
(between 9th and 10th Streets)
$10
Tickets/Information: 212-254-1109
www.theaterforthenewcity.net

+++++++++++++++++++++++

Yoshiko Chuma & The School of Hard Knocks
Hold the Clock

March 19–21, 2010
Friday–Saturday at 8:00 p.m.,
Sunday at 3:00 p.m.

Presented by the 92nd Street Y Harkness Dance Center and GOH Productions

Yoshiko Chuma was the first Western artist invited to work with dancers in Budapest in 1986. Since that landmark project, she has spearheaded residencies and toured extensively throughout the region. Using a combination of text, movement, and media in a live installation, Chuma challenges her collaborators—including choreographers Ursula Eagly and Jon Kinzel, and lighting designer Rie Ono—to co-create this world premiere that questions the "revolutions" in East Central Europe via the personal histories of The School of Hard Knocks.

Commissioned in part by the 92nd Street Y Harkness Dance Festival for its 75th Anniversary Season: Past-Future-Now. Funded in part by the Harkness Foundation for Dance, Jody and John Arnhold, Mertz Gilmore Foundation, New York State Council on the Arts, among others.

BUTTENWIESER HALL, 92ND STREET Y
1395 Lexington Avenue
(at 92nd Street)
$15
Tickets/Information:
212-415-5500
www.92Y.org/Harkness

+++++++++++++++++++++++

SAMETOVÁ–VELVETY
Directed by Pavel Dobruský

March 25–28, 2010
Thursday–Sunday at 7:30 p.m.

Presented by Agentura Dell'Arte and The Tank

Set in the Communist Ministry of Culture, a lonely young janitor daydreams while cleaning up the excrement of the regime. In her fantasy, the Velvet Revolution happens and she is selected to be the new minister. Using classic Czech cynicism and humor, this dance theater work utilizes an interactive set of panels that chronicle the events of the Velvet Revolution, and draws on influences from Hasek, Kafka, Kundera, and others. Performed by Hana Kalouskova, with an installation by Milan David, and documentary materials and projection by Pavel Stingl.

THE TANK
354 West 45th Street
(between Eighth and Ninth Avenues)
$15
Tickets/Information:
www.brownpapertickets.com
www.thetanknyc.org

VENUE ADDRESSES AND TICKETING INFORMATION

92nd Street Y,
Buttenwieser Hall
1395 Lexington Avenue (at 92nd Street)
Tickets/Information: 212-415-5500
www.92Y.org/Harkness

Abrons Arts Center,
Henry Street Settlement
466 Grand Street (at Pitt Street)
Tickets/Information: 212-352-3101
www.abronsartcenter.org

Bohemian National Hall
321–325 East 73rd Street
(between First and Second Avenues)
Information: 646-422-3399 or
info@czechcenter.com
www.czechcenter.com

Dance New Amsterdam
280 Broadway, 2nd Floor
(enter on Chambers Street)
Information: 212-625-8369
www.dnadance.org

Goethe-Institut New York
Wyoming Building
5 East 3rd Street
(between Second Avenue and Bowery)
Information: 212-439-8700
www.goethe.de/ins/us/ney/enindex.htm

The Harriman Institute,
Columbia University
President's Room 1, Faculty House
64 Morningside Drive (at 116th Street)
Reservations: rsvp@harrimaninstitute.org
www.harrimaninstitute.org

HERE Arts Center
145 Sixth Avenue (between Spring and
Broome Streets; enter on Dominick Street)
Tickets/Information: 212-352-3101
www.here.org

Idlewild Books
12 West 19th Street
(between Fifth and Sixth Avenues)
Information: 212-414-8888
www.idlewildbooks.com

The Joyce Theater
175 Eighth Avenue (at 19th Street)
Tickets/Information: 212-242-0800
www.joyce.org

La MaMa E.T.C.
The Annex Theater
66 East 4th Street
(between Second Avenue and Bowery)
Information: 212-475-7710
www.lamama.org

La MaMa La Galleria
6 East 1st Street
(between Second Avenue and Bowery)
Information: 212-505-2476
www.lamama.org

(le) Poisson Rouge
158 Bleecker Street
(between Thompson and Sullivan Streets)
www.lepoissonrouge.com

Ludlow 38
38 Ludlow Street
(between Hester and Grand Streets)
Information: 212-439-8700
www.goethe.de/ins/us/ney/enindex.htm

Martin E. Segal Theatre Center,
The Graduate Center CUNY
365 Fifth Avenue (at 34th Street)
Information: mestc@gc.cuny.edu
www.TheSegalCenter.org

Minor Latham Playhouse,
118 Milbank Hall, Barnard College
3009 Broadway (at 118th Street)
Tickets: www.tic.columbia.edu
www.barnard.edu/theatre/
current_season.html

The New York Public Library
for the Performing Arts
Bruno Walter Auditorium and
Vincent Astor Gallery
Dorothy and Lewis B. Cullman Center
111 Amsterdam Avenue (at 65th Street)
Information: 212-870-1630
www.nypl.org/research/lpa/lpa.html

The Tank
354 West 45th Street
(between Eighth and Ninth Avenues)
Tickets: www.brownpapertickets.com
www.thetanknyc.org

Theater for the New City
155 First Avenue
(between 9th and 10th Streets)
Tickets: 212-254-1109
www.theaterforthenewcity.net

Tribeca Cinemas
54 Varick Street (at Laight Street)
Tickets: www.tribecacinemas.com
www.icrny.org

Walter Reade Theater
70 Lincoln Center Plaza
Tickets/Information: 212-875-5601
www.filmlinc.org

FESTIVAL CALENDAR

KEY
D Dance
E Exhibition
F Film
L Literature
M Music
S Symposium
T Theater
W Website

NOVEMBER

November 5 / *Sneak Peek: Festival Symposium* / The Harriman Institute, Columbia University / S

November 6–8 / *Rebel Waltz: Underground Music from Behind the Iron Curtain* / (le) Poisson Rouge / M

November 6–22 / Taylor Mac / *The Lily's Revenge* / HERE Arts Center / T

November 9 / Nejla Yatkin / *Dancing with the Berlin Wall* / Ludlow 38 + Goethe-Institut New York Wyoming Building / D

November 10 / *The Wall in My Head: Words and Images from the Fall of the Iron Curtain* / Idlewild Books / L

November 11–15 / Theatre of the Eighth Day / *Wormwood* / Abrons Arts Center / T

November 16 / *Playwrights Before the Fall: Eastern European Drama in Times of Revolution* / Martin E. Segal Theatre Center/The Graduate Center CUNY / L / T

November 18 / Deborah Brevoort / *The Velvet Weapon* / La MaMa E.T.C. / T

November 18–March 20, 2010 / *Revolutionary Voices: Performing Arts in Central & Eastern Europe in the 1980s* / The New York Public Library for the Performing Arts / E

November 19–21 / *Dissident Acts: 3 Plays* / Barnard College / T

November 19 / Untitled Theater Company #61 / *The Velvet Oratorio* / The New York Public Library for the Performing Arts / M / T

November 23 / Saviana Stanescu / *NY Thru an Immigrant I or (r)evolution (Flagstories and other personal histories)* / The New York Public Library for the Performing Arts / T

November 30 / Untitled Theater Company #61 / *The Velvet Oratorio* / Bohemian National Hall / M / T

Ongoing / *Voices From the Center* / www.VoicesFromtheCenter.net / W

DECEMBER

December 4–6 / *Fourth Annual Romanian Film Festival* / Tribeca Cinemas / F

Ongoing–March 20, 2010 / *Revolutionary Voices: Performing Arts in Central & Eastern Europe in the 1980s* / The New York Public Library for the Performing Arts / E

Ongoing / *Voices From the Center* / www.VoicesFromtheCenter.net / W

JANUARY

January (Dates TBA) / *Polish Dance in the 1980s: Silence or Revolution?* / Dance New Amsterdam / **S**

January–February / *Poland in the 1980s: Searching for Revolution in Dance* / Dance New Amsterdam / **E**

January 19, 26 / *A View from the East: Documentaries of Eastern Europe* / The New York Public Library for the Performing Arts / **F**

January 26–31 / *Györ National Ballet from Hungary* / The Joyce Theater / **D**

Ongoing–March 20 / *Revolutionary Voices: Performing Arts in Central & Eastern Europe in the 1980s* / The New York Public Library for the Performing Arts / **E**

Ongoing / *Voices From the Center* / www.VoicesFromtheCenter.net / **W**

FEBRUARY

February 2, 9, 16, 23 / *A View from the East: Documentaries of Eastern Europe* / The New York Public Library for the Performing Arts / **F**

February 3–11 / *Storm Cloud Warnings: Resistance and Reflection in Polish Cinema, 1977–1989* / Walter Reade Theater / **F**

February 5–28 / *Works from Kontakt: The Art Collection of Erste Bank Group* / *Performative Aspects in Art from Eastern Europe* / La MaMa La Galleria / **E**

February 24–28 / *WaxFactory* / *QUARTET v4.0* / Abrons Arts Center / **T**

February 26–27 / *After Communism: Achievement and Disillusionment Since 1989* / The Harriman Institute, Columbia University / **S**

Ongoing–February / *Poland in the 1980s: Searching for Revolution in Dance* / Dance New Amsterdam / **E**

Ongoing–March 20 / *Revolutionary Voices: Performing Arts in Central & Eastern Europe in the 1980s* / The New York Public Library for the Performing Arts / **E**

Ongoing / *Voices From the Center* / www.VoicesFromtheCenter.net / **W**

MARCH

March 3–May 1 / *Walter Steinacher* / *Yugostalgia* / HERE Arts Center / **E**

March 4–21 / *Revolution!* / Theater for the New City / **T**

March 19–21 / *Yoshiko Chuma & The School of Hard Knocks* / *Hold the Clock* / 92nd Street Y / **D**

March 25–28 / *SAMETOVÁ–VELVETY* / The Tank / **D** / **T**

Ongoing–March 20 / *Revolutionary Voices: Performing Arts in Central & Eastern Europe in the 1980s* / The New York Public Library for the Performing Arts / **E**

Ongoing / *Voices From the Center* / www.VoicesFromtheCenter.net / **W**

IMAGE CREDITS | **Cover** > *Dancing with the Berlin Wall* | Photo: NY2Dance | **Inside Cover** > Taylor Mac's *The Lily's Revenge* | Photo: Lucien Samaha | **3** > Rasa Todosijevic, *Was ist Kunst? (What Is Art?)*, video, 1976 /// *Rite of Spring* | Photo: Béla Szabó /// Saviana Stanescu | Photo: Rares Avram /// *Wormwood* | Photo: courtesy Theatre of the Eighth Day | **4** > Rasa Todosijevic, *Was ist Kunst? (What Is Art?)*, video, 1976 | **5** > Dezerter | Photo: Robert Ochnio /// Taylor Mac's *The Lily's Revenge* | Photo: Lucien Samaha | **6** > The Berlin Wall | Photo: courtesy NY2Dance | **7** > *The Wall in My Head* /// *Wormwood* | Photo: courtesy Theatre of the Eighth Day | **9** > Poster for November 1987 Orange Alternative happening, "The Eve of the Great Revolution." | Courtesy Orange Alternative Archives. Jacek Jankowski, artist | **11** > Saviana Stanescu | Photo: Rares Avram /// Gabriel Gládek, Historian, Slovakia | Photo: Janeil Engelstad /// Pavla Jonssonova | Photo: Janeil Engelstad | **12** > *Police Adjective* /// *Do Communists Have Better Sex?* | **13** > *Petrushka* | Photo: Béla Szabó /// *Rite of Spring* | Photo: Béla Szabó | **14** > Rasa Todosijevic, Theatre, *Ad Matrem–Psalm* | Photo: Robert Frackowiak | **15** > *High Noon, June 4, 1989* | Design: Tomasz Sarnecki | **16** > Rasa Todosijevic, *Was ist Kunst? (What Is Art?)*, video, 1976 | **17** > WaxFactory's *QUARTET v4.0* | Photo: Yi Zhao /// Czechoslovak-American Marionette Theatre | Photo: Pavel Dobruský | **19** > Yoshiko Chuma & The School of Hard Knocks | Photo: Tasja Keetman /// Poster for November 1987 Orange Alternative happening, *Mama Tito #1* /// WaxFactory's *QUARTET v4.0* | Photo: Tasja **24** > Polish Dance Theatre, *Panna i Smierc (The Maiden and Death)* | Photo: Robert Frackowiak /// "The Eve of the Great Revolution." | Courtesy Orange Alternative Archives. Jacek Jankowski, artist | **Inside cover** > Dezerter | Photo: Robert Ochnio /// Yoshiko Chuma & The School of Hard Knocks | Photo: Yi Zhao |

DESIGN | Marc Blaustein, The New York Public Library

ACKNOWLEDGMENTS

The Martin E. Segal Theatre Center wishes to thank The New York Public Library for the Performing Arts for the opportunity to work collaboratively as part of the *Performing Revolution in Central and Eastern Europe* festival and to express appreciation for the help and encouragement of Jacqueline Z. Davis, Director; Janet Stapleton, PR/Marketing and Management for the Performing Revolution Festival; Karen Burke, Assistant Chief Music Division and Special Curator for the Performing Revolution Festival; and Marc Blaustein, Art Director, The New York Public Library, Graphic Design Office.

The Center also wishes to express its gratitude to the following leaders of the international cultural institutes and centers who have supported our work on this project: Marcel Sauer, Director, Czech Center, New York; Laszlo Jakob Orsos, Director, Hungarian Cultural Center, New York; Corina Şuteu, Director, and Oana Radu, Deputy Director, Romanian Cultural Institute, New York; Monika Fabijanska, Director, Visual Arts and Literature Programming, Agata Grenda, Deputy Director, Theatre and Dance Programming, and William Martin, Literature Programming Polish Cultural Institute; and Clara Drew, Consulate General of Slovenia. The Segal Center wishes to acknowledge the expertise and support of George Bixby, cover design, and of Dan Breitkreutz & Sandy Wolford, The Maple-Vail Book Manufacturing Group.

Special thanks to Christopher Silsby as well as Laura Hydak, and Jake Hooker, Ph.D. Program in Theatre, The Graduate Center, CUNY, for their help in preparing the manuscript, and to Beate Hein for her assistance in editing *Horses at the Window* and Pamela Billig for her help in editing *Chicken Head*.

Ivan Talijančić, who translated *Military Secret* by Dušan Jovanović especially for this volume, wishes to express his gratitude to the following people who enabled him to embark on this adventure: the author for being such a responsive advisor and collaborator every step of the way; Simona Semenič, cherished collaborator, brilliant playwright and dramaturg, and the resident Slovenian expert on this project; Alenka Suhadolnik, the former Consul General at the Consulate General of Slovenia in New York, and her associate Clara Drew for being ever helpful; WaxFactory's associates and guest artists who participated in the private reading of the translation and whose input helped shape its final version: Melody Bates, Gillian Chadsey, Nathan Guisinger, Tiffany Hodges, Sarena Kennedy, Alexander Lane, Erika Latta, Alanna Medlock, and Andrew Schulman; and Margaret Araneo for her research and contribution to the introduction.

Also thanks to Tomaž Toporišič for sharing his knowledge of Slovenian drama.

An earlier version of the translation of *Sorrow, Sorrow, Fear, the Pit, and the Rope* was published in 1993 by the Rain City Projects in Seattle, WA. The English-language premiere took place at the Glenn Hughes Penthause Theatre of the University of Washington in Seattle on November 18, 1992, directed by Štěpán S. Šimek

An earlier version of the translation of *Chicken Head* appeared in *ContemporaryDrama: Hungary*, ed. Eugene Brognyanyi. New York: PAJ Publications, 1991.

MARTIN E. SEGAL
THEATRE CENTER

The **Martin E. Segal Theatre Center (MESTC)**, is a non-profit center for theatre, dance and film affiliated with CUNY's Ph.D. Program in Theatre. The Center's mission is to bridge the gap between academia and the professional performing arts communities both within the United States and internationally. By providing an open environment for the development of educational, community-driven, and professional projects in the performing arts, MESTC is a home to theatre scholars, students, playwrights, actors, dancers, directors, dramaturgs, and performing arts managers from the local and international theatre communities.

Through diverse programming—staged readings, theatre events, panel discussions, lectures, conferences, film screenings, dance—and a number of publications, MESTC enables artists, academics, visiting scholars and performing arts professionals to participate actively in the advancement and appreciation of the entire range of theatrical experience. The Center presents staged readings to further the development of new and classic plays, lecture series, televised seminars featuring professional and academic luminaries, and arts in education programs, and maintains its long-standing visiting scholars-from-abroad program. In addition, the Center publishes a series of highly-regarded academic journals, as well as books, including plays in translation, written, translated and edited by leading scholars.

Please visit: **http://theSegalCenter.org**

Ph.D. Program in Theatre, The Graduate Center, CUNY, is one of the leading doctoral theatre programs in the United States. Faculty includes distinguished professors, holders of endowed chairs, and internationally recognized scholars. The program trains future scholars and teachers in all the disciplines of theatre research. Faculty members edit MESTC publications, working closely with the doctoral students in theatre who perform a variety of editorial functions and learn the skills involved in the creation of books and journals.   Please visit: **http://web.gc.cuny.edu/theatre**

The **MESTC Publication Wing** produces both journals and individual volumes. Journals include *Slavic and Eastern European Performance* (SEEP), *The Journal of American Drama and Theatre* (JADT), and *Western European Stages* (WES). Books include *Four Melodramas by Pixérécourt* (edited by Daniel Gerould and Marvin Carlson—both Distinguished Professors of Theatre at the CUNY Graduate Center), *Contemporary Theatre in Egypt*, *The Heirs of Molière* (edited and translated by Marvin Carlson), *Seven Plays by Stanisław Ignacy Witkiewicz* (edited and translated by Daniel Gerould), *The Arab Oedipus: Four Plays* (edited by Marvin Carlson), *Theatre Research Resources in New York City* (edited by Jessica Brater, Senior Editor Marvin Carlson), and *Comedy: A Bibliography of Critical Studies in English on the Theory and Practice of Comedy in Drama, Theatre and Performance* (edited by Meghan Duffy, Senior Editor Daniel Gerould).

New publications include: *BAiT-Buenos Aires in Translation: Four Plays* (edited and translated by Jean Graham-Jones), *roMANIA AFTER 2000: Five New Romanian Plays* (edited by Saviana Stanescu and Daniel Gerould), *Four Plays from North Africa* (edited by Marvin Carlson), *Barcelona Plays: A Collection of New Plays by Catalan Playwrights* (edited and translated by Marion Peter Holt and Sharon G. Feldman), *Josep M. Benet i Jornet: Two Plays* (translated by Marion Peter Holt), *I Am a Mistake: Seven Works for the Theatre by Jan Fabre* (edited and foreword by Frank Hentschker), *Czech Plays: Seven New Works* (edited by Marcy Arlin, Gwynn MacDonald and Daniel Gerould).

Please visit: **http://web.gc.cuny.edu/mestc/subscribe.htm**